REAL LAW@VIRTUAL SPACE
COMMUNICATION REGULATION IN CYBERSPACE

The Hampton Press Communication Series
Communication and Law
Susan J. Drucker, *Supervisory Editor*

Real Law@Virtual Space: Communication Regulation in Cyberspace
   Susan J. Drucker and Gary Gumpert (eds.)

Outsiders Looking In: A Communication Perspective on the
   Hill/Thomas Hearings
   Paul Siegel (ed.)

forthcoming

Emerging Law on the Electronic Frontier
   Anne Wells Branscomb (ed.)

REAL LAW@VIRTUAL SPACE

COMMUNICATION REGULATION IN CYBERSPACE

EDITED BY

SUSAN J. DRUCKER
GARY GUMPERT

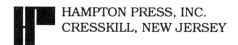
HAMPTON PRESS, INC.
CRESSKILL, NEW JERSEY

Library of Congress Cataloging-in-Publication Data

Real law [at] virtual space : communication regulation in cyberspace /
    edited by Susan J. Drucker, Gary Gumpert.
        p.   cm. -- (The Hampton Press communication series.
    Communication and law)
        On t.p.: "[at]" appears as a symbol.
        Includes bibliographical references and indexes.
        ISBN 1-57273-124-9. -- ISBN 1-57273-125-7
        1. Information superhighway--Law and legislation. 2. Computer
    networks--Law and legislation. 3. Internet (Computer network)
    I. Drucker, Susan J.   II. Gumpert, Gary.   III. Series.
    K564.C6R43   1999
    343.09'944--dc21   99-19762
                                                            CIP

Hampton Press, Inc.
23 Broadway
Cresskill, NJ 07626

CONTENTS

PREFACE

One scenario suggests that the technology of the internet was developed in order to keep legislators, judges, and lawyers busy for the next several decades. The impact of a new communication technology provides the opportunity for old regulations to be reshaped and revitalized in their impact upon the future. There is something about the process of communication that attracts administrative and regulatory zealots. Make no mistake about it, communication is the compelling factor and pressure which magnifies the efforts to regulate, restrain, and shape the accelerating technology of the Internet. The problems and social and ethical concerns of any new technology can be immense, but those of the Internet are almost incomprehensive—because of the uniquely converging and pervasive nature of the medium. Within the medium you will discover one medium enclosed within another enclosed within another. We listen to the radio, read the newspaper, order books, wine, and groceries, shop for homes, administer our bank accounts, pay our bills, watch television and films, send e-mail, manuscripts, and pictures to one another, and we globally connect and send musical greeting cards to those we love.

But how does one write and publish *Real Law@Virtual Space* quickly enough to avoid the calamity of publishing a tome that could be outmoded, out-of-touch, out-of-date the moment it appears in print? The cases, attempts at regulation, and philosophical debates about such control and oversight or the denial of restraint and restrictions, erupt with daily certainty. The *New York Times* on June 28, 1998 proclaimed that the "Internet is New Pet Issue of Congress." More than 300 bills were being considered by the 105th Congress in 1998.

> The Internet with its influence on everything from commerce and national security to privacy and crime, has become an issue as politically alluring to many lawmakers as cutting taxes, educating children and locking up criminals. It seems that not a week goes by on Capital Hill without a hearing, a meeting or a gathering about one of a bevy of Internet-related issues confronting Congress. (Alvarez, 1998)

In the short time between the completion of this volume and putting finishing touches to the galley proofs, the Internet Tax Freedom Act and the Digital Millennium Copyright Act were signed into law as was the Child On Line Protection Act. We confess to having the television on in the background while writing this preface and as we wrote, CNN reported that the Federal Communications had just announced that it was considering a regulation which would alter the rate that could be charged for online access to the Internet, allowing telephone companies to charge more than for local calls. The reporter warns—stay tuned.

The topics and subject proliferate: online marketing practices, privacy gambling on the Internet, encryption, pornography, Fair Trade, Pedophilia, junk-E-Mail, anti-trust action, violation of civil rights, copyright infringement, media mergers, filtering software—the list is endless. And the complexity is compounded by global attempts to regulate the Internet. Thus the development and impact of the European Union is grossly underestimated by most Americans. The imposition by the European Union of a new basically laissez-Faire privacy law contrasts sharply with the approach taken by the U.S. administration.

We have inherited a judicial heritage rooted in the quest for equality, justice, and constitutionality. It is a bequest that is not to be taken lightly or ever to be taken for granted. Therefore, the editors wish to thank not only our immediate family members, collaborators, mentors, and our publisher, but also a system of justice that we have inherited and to which we hope *Real Law@Virtual Space* contributes in some small degree to that tradition.

SJD   GG
Great Neck, New York
June, 1999

REFERENCES

Alvarez. L. (1998, June 28). Internet is new pet issue in Congress. *New York Times* web site: archives.nytimes.comarchives/search/fastweb?search.

1

LEGAL GEOGRAPHY:
THE BORDERS OF CYBERLAW
INTRODUCTION

SUSAN J. DRUCKER AND GARY GUMPERT

> It cannot be helped, it is as it should be, that the law is behind the times.
> —Oliver Wendell Holmes

Is virtual rape online is actionable?[1] Is cybersex or hot chat adultery? Can one be stalked in cyberspace?[2] These are just some of the challenging questions courts face as ever-increasing numbers of individuals surf, browse, cruise, wander, and roam through the placeless realm of cyberspace. The one constant discovered when exploring the evolution of media law is that technologies develop more rapidly than the concomitant legal framework. So governments around the world are faced with challenges to existing laws and, for some, perceived threats from new electronic sources and the need to "protect children, thwart terrorists and silence racists and hate mongers" ("Silencing the Net," 1996, p. 1). Communication technology challenges developments in applicable laws governing rights of privacy, free expression, and liability. In this formative period there is a widening gap between new technologies and old laws. More specifically, libel, hate speech, copyright, intellectual property, obscenity, pornography as well as sexual harassment and jurisdictional issues are topics transformed in part by the new converging technology. This volume addresses issues that will require legislative and judicial attention as the law develops and focuses on communicative rights and liabilities in the mediated realm of cyberspace.

There is little precedent, except for earlier media cases, on which to predict and judge current legal and ethical problems of the Internet. Few "cyberlawyers" have hung out shingles, so to date those seeking to evaluate what technological advances mean in relation to legal rules are generally forced "to fall back on first principles and then to rely heavily on analogies" to previous modalities (Johnson & Marks, 1993). The extension and/or creation of legal rules to new modes of distribution and channels raises questions:

- If the uses (the informational and social substance) of communication has not changed, are *new* legal *rules* and *procedures* called for by the transmission of such substance by convergent technologies of communication?
- Do technological advances require rethinking *legal principles* that have existed for previous modalities?
- What is the relationship of self-regulation and the new regulatory schema that may at times transcend traditional jurisdictions?
- Does the global nature of the Internet form a separate legal jurisdiction?

This volume addresses public and private regulations and restrictions of computer-mediated communication in the realm of online communication and the Internet. For purposes of this volume we use the popular term *cyberspace* to encompass a variety of forms of computer-mediated communication ranging from mass communication to interpersonal interaction. The term is attributed to science fiction author William Gibson, who coined the term in the 1980s. Cyberspace was described in Gibson's (1984) *Neuromancer,* "where it names a 21st century virtual dimension, entered into via a neuro-electronic interface, in which the world's data networks unfold before the user as a sensually vivid geography" (p. 5). As traditional media distinctions crumble, converging technologies challenge established laws and policies. "The digitization of information enables online transmission of services that can substitute for newspapers, books, magazines, catalogs, records, film, audio and videotape, radio, television and telephone" (Stuckey, 1996, p. ix), as well as written memoranda and personal notes. Lance Rose (March 6, 1996, personal communication), an attorney specializing in high-tech and information law notes, "there is no one coherent thing known as 'cyberspace.' It's a whole bunch of different shared communication realms, each with its own sense of space and its own structure. The term 'cyberspace,' ultimately, is no more than a convenient way of saying 'everything on the other side of the screen of a net-connected electronic device.'"

Each form of communication often raises troubling and unresolved legal and ethical dilemmas. Among the forms of communication encompassed in various conceptualizations of cyberspace are the following:

- *Internet:* Called the "network of networks" (Stuckey, 1996, p. xvi), the Internet is often erroneously used as a synonym for the term *cyberspace.* The Internet began in 1969 as a United States Defense Department network called ARPAnet (The Advanced Research Project Agency). It was opened to academic use at the same time as commercial services were introduced sometime between 1979-1981 (Stuckey, 1996). Slowly, corporations, universities, and information providers phased and dovetailed their networks into the system, agreeing on compatible connecting software or a set of standard network protocols called TCP/IP, which led to the expansion of the Internet. The standard programming language HTML, or "hypertext markup language," arrived in 1994, laying the foundation for the Internet application known as the "World Wide Web."
- *The Web:* The Web refers to the thousands of host computers and servers interconnected through the Internet featuring graphical sites called "home pages," which feature graphics, hypertext markup or highlighted text, and "hot links" that interlock sites globally, allowing one to browse or "surf" many sites. Web browsers operating on a "point and click" basis have fueled the enormous growth of the Internet. The Web allows for the display of text, images, sound, and video. Commercial online services such as America Online (AOL), CompuServe, and Prodigy provide content and organization and now incorporate Web browsers. The number of Internet users is growing at rates difficult to keep current. According to Netree Internet Statistics (1997), an online statistics generator, there were 99,264,180 people on the Internet as of January 1997. There are more than 160 countries reported to have links to the Internet, over 100 nations with full access and some through e-mail ("Silencing the Net," 1996).
- *Usenets:* Usenets are accessible from yet distinct from the Internet. Usenet comprises more than 9,000 'newsgroups' discussions or picture databases on various topics,

including those political and sexually explicit. Groups are arranged under subject headings such as "soc" for social groups, or "rec" for hobbies and games, or the often most controversial "alt" for alternative.[3]

- *E-Mail:* The most popular form of computer-mediated communication, often linked to Internet service, is electronic mail. E-mail allows for one-to-one or one-to-many communication via a nearly instantaneous means of delivering written messages and documents.
- *CD-ROM:* The CD-ROM as a closed, compete entity would appear to fall outside the scope of a study into cyberspace yet a hybrid CD-ROM that extends CD-ROM content through links to related files within online services or Web sites brings this technology into the realm of the so-called "new media" of cyberspace (see Cohen, chap. 5, this volume).

Stuckey (1996) makes the following distinction between open and closed systems:

> When introduced in 1979 online services were completely "closed"—consisting of consumer timesharing using applications users could access managed by a single provider. Then "gateways" were established that provided access to information and applications residing on third-party system. Then the shift to "open" online services using the "Internet" emerged and grew. (p. xv).

One of the distinctive characteristics common to cyberspace is the interactive nature of communication. "Interactivity" and "nonlinearity" mean that the end-user may determine the sequence, timing, and repetitions of the work and may include the option to "talk back" or submit information or comments. Access to data and interaction come on an "on-demand" basis and "enables a customized experience for users that is interactive. Users can control what information they see, and direct their communications to specific individuals or groups of any size. In this way, this technology is characterized as offering 'mass customization' or a 'de-massifying' media and potentially, the economy in general" (Stuckey, 1996, p. x). It has been said to be a truly "mass medium" more threatening than earlier media given that a personal computer and modem offer fairly inexpensive, accessible means of reaching enormous international audiences. Online technology provides opportunities for the disenfranchised to voice their political arguments, for example, as no medium ever before. Yet, one-to-one global interpersonal communication opportunities are also available. In some situations even real-time interaction is possible.

SOURCES OF CYBERLAW

Whether at the forefront of cyberspace connection or faced with establishing initial e-mail connection, governments around the globe are faced with considering appropriate policies and applying or drafting laws and regulations addressing fundamental economic, political, social, and religio-moral issues.

Sources of law range from the formal to informal, from action taken between individuals and private concerns to regulatory actions taken by state authorities, from action taken by local governments, to legislative action taken by nation-states, to international accords, to the creation of a separate and distinct cyberspace jurisdiction. In a special issue of the *Journal of Computer Mediated Communication*, Juliet Oberding and Terje Norderhaug (1996) argued that one way in which cyberspace will be regulated is through the creation and enforcement of community norms. Oberding and Norderhaug note that bulletin board operators often oversee postings and may disconnect or unsubscribe "troublemakers" (p. 12). They find self-regulation emerging from the cybercommunities forming online:

> Online communities clearly maintain community norms and have the ability to create and enforce rights and responsibilities. Offenders are censored if they breach commonly accepted rules. The Internet contains a high number of communities which make and enforce individual rules and obligation. (1996, np)

Norms and rules of conduct in the cybercommunity simply reflect the fact that laws embody the norms of a society and make enforceable the principles of morality on which a community organizes. Through the law, values become the final, authoritative, and enforceable disposition of conflict (Katsh, 1988).[4]

Contracts between parties provide another source of enforceable behavioral norms, restrictions, and restraints. For example, Information Service Providers, those providing access to the Internet, Intranet, or e-mail access, often provide explicit service agreements to be entered into or, in the employment or university setting, may distribute guidelines for use of systems seen as a revocable opportunity for access. Private service providers including Prodigy, CompuServe, and America Online, under the contract with customers to deliver service, make specific reference to appropriate behaviors and delineate rights of providers and users. For instance, Codes of Conduct included in the America Online Terms of Service Agreement states:

Some common violations of the Terms of Service. This list is not exhaustive. AOL Inc. reserves the right, but does not assume the responsibility, to restrict communication which AOL Inc. deems in its discretion to be harmful to individual Members, damaging to the communities which make up the AOL Service, or in violation of AOL Inc.'s or any third-party rights. Please be aware, however, that communication over the AOL Service often occurs in real-time, or is posted on one of the AOL Service's thousands of message boards or libraries, and AOL Inc. cannot, and does not intend to, screen communication in advance.

If you witness chat in a public chat room that violates AOL's Terms of Service, you may contact an AOL Service Guide by using the keyword "Guide Pager." You may also contact AOL's Terms of Service Staff about any violation by using the "Write to the Terms of Service Staff" icon located in the Terms of Service area of the Member's Online Support department.

C. Online Conduct.

(a) Any conduct by you that in AOL Inc.'s discretion restricts or inhibits any other Member from using or enjoying AOL will not be permitted and may result in termination of Membership. You agree to use AOL only for lawful purposes. You may not post or use AOL to:

(1) harass, threaten, embarrass or cause distress, unwanted attention or discomfort upon another Member or user of AOL or other person or entity; (2) post or transmit sexually explicit images or other content which is deemed by AOL Inc. to be offensive; (3) transmit any unlawful, harmful, threatening, abusive, harassing, defamatory, vulgar, obscene, hateful, racially, ethnically or otherwise objectionable Content; (4) cause the screen to "scroll" faster than other Members or users are able to type to it or any action to a similar disruptive effect; (5) impersonate any person, including but not limited to, an AOL Inc. official or an information provider, forum leader, guide or host, or communicate under a false name or a name that you are not entitled or authorized to use; (6) disrupt the normal flow of dialogue in a chat room or otherwise act in a manner that negatively affects other Members, users, individuals or entities; (7) post or transmit chain letters or pyramid schemes; (8) post or transmit any unsolicited advertising, promotional materials, or other forms of solicitation to other Members, individuals or entities, except in those areas (e.g., the classified areas) that are designated for such a purpose; (9) violate any operating rule, policy or guideline of any other interactive service, including but not limited to the operating policies of the International Areas; or (10) intentionally or unintentionally violate any applicable local, state, national or international law, including but not limited to any regulations having the force of law.[5]

Under such a contract, the service provider may claim the right to monitor, not only publicly posted bulletin board messages, but person-to-person messages (America Online Service Membership Subscriber Agreement, 1995).[6,7]

Monitoring assumes not only potential loss of privacy but presumably some sanctions for inappropriate behavior. CompuServe has expelled a number of users. "Users tend to feel quite territorial about the CompuServe forums . . . so our members are very much self-policing" (Wald, 1995, p. 4). At one time Prodigy screened every message that members wanted to post on its bulletin boards, causing long delays in posting, so they began using a program called "The George Carlin Scanner," and the service has only "bounced a handful over the years" (Wald, 1995). Most services have warnings, and some send warning copies directly to parents if children are found to violate appropriate behavior. America Online reserves the right to terminate service in its "Terms of Service," leading to discontinuation for violation of these terms. Thus, a father reports having his service cut off when his child reportedly typed in inappropriate words on a made-for-children chat room, an act noted and reported by a watchful America Online monitor.

The validity and enforcablity for such so-called "shrinkwrap/point-and-click agreements" is being considered by legal experts and courts alike. Such agreements are generally standardized written agreements used to create and structure relationships between companies and customers, with standard terms and conditions promulgated appearing online in the customer's initial session. These predetermined contract terms and conditions that are not negotiated by parties are sometimes marketed as "self-executing" when there is no direct contact between contracting parties and the vendor or service provider attempts to impose standard terms on the product.[8]

A distinction must be made between regulation via community standards, express or implied contract terms, and the standards imposed by governmental entities. Regulatory action has been taken or explored by states and nations and internationally negotiated accords. Most attempts to define new rules for the development of cyberspace ultimately rely on weakening or disintegrating concepts of territory, while ignoring the new network and technological borders that transcend state and national boundaries The global information infrastructure potentially undermines substantive legal sovereignty.

JURISDICTIONAL QUESTIONS AND SOURCES OF LAW

One of the fundamental and troubling questions impacting on individual rights is simply which laws govern behavior in an aspatial world of connection rather than a environment characterized by propinquity? Jurisdiction, the power and authority of a court to hear and adjudicate a given case, is a fundamental concept of law, which has historically been based on geographic area (*Black's Law Dictionary*, 1979, p. 766). Consider the following examination question that could be posed to a law school class today:

> Maurice is French. He has access to the Internet via the Microsoft Network from his laptop. Microsoft Corporation is located in Seattle, Washington, USA. Maurice is a photojournalist who travels extensively abroad. After a disappointing trip to Euro-Disneyland Maurice created a web site called the I Hate Mickey Mouse Page. (Zakalik, 1996)

If the Disney organization objects, does existing law suffice? What courts should have jurisdiction? Would this be a defamatory statement? If the image of Mickey Mouse was incorporated into the Web site, does U.S. trademark law come into play? If Maurice chose to create a hot link to an official Disney Web site, are there any legal limitations on this association with a corporate presence on the Net?

In an age when signals are beamed and borders crossed via keyboard strokes, geography becomes irrelevant. Global association may become more easily (or safely) accessed than local contact. Psychological maps are reconfigured to reflect a sense of connection not bound by the limitations of space and territory, yet many fundamental concepts of law are geographically determined. "Most attempts to define new rules for the development of the Global Information Infrastructure ignore the new networks and technological borders that transcend national boundaries" (Reidenberg, 1996, p. 45). In the *Emory Law Journal* article "Governing Networks and Cyberspace Rule-making," Joel Reidenberg (1996) explores the challenges of redefining jurisdiction in a borderless, aspatial realm:

> With the Global Information Infrastructure, . . . territorial borders and substantive borders as key paradigms for regulatory governance disintegrate. . . . International law grants legitimacy to a governing authority if it exercises sovereignty over a physical territory and its people. Constitutional governance predicates sovereignty on the existence of geographically distinct political and social units. Regulatory power has always been defined in terms of national borders. Key rights establishing the structure of an information society such as intellectual property protections, fair information practice standards and competition rules are all territorially based. The adjudication of disputes also typically depends on territorially empowered courts. Similarly, police powers to enforce regulatory

policies and decisions through property seizures or incarceration are territorially restricted. Transnational information flows on the GII [Global Information Infrastructure] undermine these foundational borders and erode state sovereignty over regulatory policy and enforcement. Geographic limits have diminishing value. Physical borders become transparent and foreign legal systems have local relevance. Network activities may make participants subject to legal rules of distant jurisdictions. Political and economic communities based predominantly on geographic proximity and physical contact have less relevance in "cyberspace" because network communities can replace physically proximate communities. Political discourse can ignore national borders while affinities and affiliations transcend distances and human contact. (p. 45)

Yet despite these fundamental jurisdictional questions that appear at the threshold of virtually every effort to recognize rights or to impose standards and restrictions on communication in open cyberspace systems, many nations are beginning to address the challenges to "border-based jurisdiction in a borderless environment." We offer a brief sample of such current activity.

Germany tried to censor racist and pornographic messages on the Internet. In January 1996, Deutsche Telekom, the national telephone company, blocked users of its T-Online computer network from accessing Internet sites used for anti-Semitic propaganda—a crime in Germany. The Justice Minister announced the government planned on introducing Internet censorship legislation in the near future.

Germany was involved with one of the most publicized international skirmishes when government officials formed a task force under the Bavarian Minister of the Interior to investigate online child pornography. This task force obtained a search warrant to investigate the Munich office of CompuServe. The offices were searched in March 1995, and shortly thereafter CompuServe's German managers stated they would support the German authorities' fight against cyberporn. Subsequently a list of over 200 suggested newsgroups were given to CompuServe by government officials suggesting it was CompuServe's responsibility to take steps to avoid possible liability. CompuServe decided to take all the groups off its servers in order to comply with German law that creates an obligation not to supply illegal material to German citizens. Shortly thereafter all but five of these newsgroups were provided access when it was found that some of these banned newsgroups were mistargeted as in the case of a news service discussion group for homosexuals ("Silencing the Net," 1996).

In April 1997, the CompuServe Deutschland manager, Felix Somm, was indicted on 13 counts of distributing pornography involving children and animals. This resulted in an outcry among free speech advocates. Subsequently, legislation was approved which greatly reduces legal responsibility of providers for material beyond their control. Under this new regulation the indictment of the CompuServe manager would probably not have been possible. In light of the new law, both the defense and prosecution in Munich argued in favor of his acquittal. Ultimately in May, 1998, a Bavarian judge imposed a sentence of two years in jail, but suspended the sentence (Cowell, 1998).

France requested members of the European Union to draft new legislation dealing with Internet issues after the March 1996 Internet posting of *Le Grand Secret* banned in France, written by late President Mitterand's physician Claude Gubler. The French service provider was subpoenaed for alleged "complicity" in making available propaganda that denies the Holocaust, an act defined as illegal in France ("Silencing the Net," 1996). In 1997, a Parisian court held a hearing examining a possible violation of the French law passed in 1994 aimed at protecting and promoting the French language. The issue before the court relates to whether the French court has jurisdiction to examine a possible violation via an English-language posting out of Georgia Tech University in the United States ("Francophones sues," 1997).[9]

Italian officials announced in April 1996 the intention to act on Internet regulations, whereas the approach taken in the United Kingdom has been to rely on existing laws such as those banning obscenity. In February 1996, an online defamation bill was introduced that included a revised defense that would clarify what a SYSOP can be expected to do in terms of editorial control (http://ntserv1.mc.maricopa.edu/dept/endlish/Moore/Writ_Law.ht m, 1997). The European Union is considering adopting some Internet-related controls, and EU culture and telecommunication ministers met in Bologna, Italy in April 1996 to discuss such action ("Silencing the Net," 1996).

In Asia there has been some regulatory activity. In March 1996, the government of Singapore announced its plan to regulate the Internet. Governmental regulators will scrutinize Internet sites about politics or religion and can block users in Singapore from connecting with foreign sites deemed inappropriate. Singapore treats the Internet as a broadcast medium regulated under the Singapore Broadcasting Authority Act of 1995. This allows only three service providers to operate: Singnet, part of Singapore Telecom; Pacific Internet; and Cyberway. The government claims it does not censor e-mail, but it did disclose that it searched individual accounts to identify those who downloaded sexually explicit material in 1994 ("Silencing the Net," 1996). Authorities state they are concerned with sex-related material and "misinformation." Singapore Infomap is a

Web site provided to "'correct" information and rebut in accurate information ("Silencing the Net," 1996). Under the new regulations schools, libraries, and even cybercafes that offer Internet access would be required to supervise use. SingNet, one of the country's three access providers, will keep out unwanted foreign material by blocking access to sites identified by the government ("Singapore bans sex," 1996). The plan ostensibly aimed at the exclusion of pornography and hate literature establishes a government licensing program for any site run by a Singapore political party (McDonald, 1996).[10] Singapore is not alone in its efforts to grapple with the challenges of technologies that lack respect for territory. In February 1996, China ordered Internet users to register with the government ("Singapore bans sex," 1996).

In June 1995, China's telecommunication minister stated that "as a sovereign state, China, will exercise control on the information" entering China from the Internet ("Silencing the Net," 1996). ChinaNet, based in Beijing and Shanghai, became available in May 1995, providing commercial Internet access; however, control of these access accounts is tight. Opening such an account requires one to register at the Postal Ministry. On January 1, 1996, the government called for a crackdown on the Internet to rid the country of unwanted pornography and "detrimental information" ("China cracks down," 1996). The government announced that it had summoned the Chinese suppliers of Internet connections to a meeting, where they announced a "moratorium" on new subscribers ("Economic news," 1996):

> The cabinet reiterated its provisional approval for global computer links but declared it "imperative" to formulate rules to govern China's use of the new technology. . . . On February 4 . . . [it was announced] that the new Internet regulations required existing computer networks to "liquidate" and "re-register," and to use only international channels provided by the Ministry of Posts and Telecommunication, the Ministry of Electronics Industry, the State Education Commission and the Chinese Academy of Sciences. ("Silencing the Net," 1996)

It was then ordered that all those using the Internet and other international computer networks register within 30 days (Lewis, 1996).

In India only the state-owned phone company has been permitted to provide international Internet services so as to maintain government monopoly on long-distance phone services (Spaeth, 1995). Guidelines being utilized to deal with cyberspace issues are based on the Indian Telegraph Act of 1885 and issued by the Department of Telecommunications. As of January 1996, commercial access is permitted, but all companies must route service via the state-owned telephone company, and service providers must ensure that nothing objectionable or obscene is carried on the network. Enforcement procedures remain unclear ("Silencing the Net," 1996). A spokesperson at the Pakistan state-owned National Institute of Electronics noted that the government in Pakistan plans to regulate Internet availability and by intervention of service providers who could stop undesirable discussion groups and electronic messages (Ajoy, 1995). In Thailand service providers are required to police their own sites for sexually explicit material, and subscribers and operators must agree not to show anything indecent. Violations of this agreement results in criminal penalties (Armstron & Daily, 1996).[11]

The government of Iran has not yet taken action with regard to Internet access, however:

> The government is trying to centralize all access through the Ministry of Posts and Telecommunications. Having screened thousands of sites on the World Wide Web and at least started blocking those deemed unhealthy. Government officials said the number of banned sites was not available, but they include those with information distributed by opposition groups like Mujahedeen Khalq, based in Iran, or by faiths that Iran abhors like the Bahai, as well as pornography and any information seen as Western propaganda. (MacFarquhar, 1996, p. A4)

With mixed feelings, Iran tiptoes into the 21st century.[12] The monthly newspaper of the puritanical clergy has called for an approach to Internet in the same way the government regulates satellite television—by a direct ban on them (MacFarquhar, 1996). In Jordan GlobeNet, a U.S. firm contracted to provide Internet service, was asked by governmental authorities to install a similar screening facility to control sexually explicit material, and in Abu Dhabi Internet clubs agreed to ban sex, religion, and politics on the Internet as a means of respecting local laws ("Silencing the Net," 1996).

Australian legislators have been working on cyberspace related issues since 1993. A Department of Communications and Arts report was released in 1994 calling for regulations of computer bulletin board systems, and a year later another version of this report entitled "Consultation Paper on the Regulation of On-line Information Services" identified goals proposing a system of self-regulation reinforced by legislative sanctions:

> Objectionable material was defined in the consultation paper as material that depicts, expresses, or otherwise deals with matters of sex, drug misuse or addiction, crime, cruelty, violence or revolting or

abhorrent phenomena in such a way that it offends against the standards of morality, decency, and proprietary generally accepted by reasonable adults to the extent that the material should be refused classification. ("Consultation Paper on the Regulation of On-line Information Services," 1996)

Some state governments including New South Wales, Queensland, Victoria, Western Australia, Northern Territory, and Tasmania have passed online censorship legislation or plan to (Micharp, 1996)[13] A Western Australia law with an effective date of January 1, 1996 focuses on transmitting objectionable material to minors.[14] All state laws are subject to change based on the adoption of a federal law. In New Zealand, under current law computer disks are treated as publications and may be censored under the Films, Videos and Publications Classification Act of 1993, and a restrictive Internet legislation was proposed that would cut off any site that transmitted an objectionable piece of material to a single user with penalties of heavy fines and the possibility of even losing the use of a telephone for up to five years. It is reported this proposed legislation is perceived as "more or less dead" ("Silencing the Net," 1996).

No laws have been proposed that specifically regulate cyberspace, but Canadian officials exploring possible regulations have focused on the fact that it is currently illegal to spread "hate propaganda" and "obscenity" in Canada, although sexually explicit material is legal as long as it is not obscene.[15]

Within the United States, despite the patchwork of regulations that often lead to overlapping and conflicting approaches to "cyberlaw," there is the "overarching First Amendment principles [that] guide resolution of legal inconsistences (Stuckey, 1996, p. xxii).

The Attorney General of Minnesota, for example, has asserted Internet jurisdiction over "persons outside of Minnesota who transmit information via the Internet knowing that information will be disseminated in Minnesota" ("Landmark Minnesota decision," 1996). The question of what constitutes "knowing" that information posted on a home page will be accessed in a jurisdiction has not been addressed.[16] The first challenge to this law arose in a case involving gambling. "Wagernet" was advertised as "a legal way to be on sporting events anywhere in the world" (Leibowitz, 1996, p. 1). The Minnesota attorney general's office filed a consumer protection suit in July 1996, asserting that the site provided service illegal in Minnesota (despite the fact that the site was not yet operational and no links could therefore be traced to Minnesota). The law was challenged in October 1996, with Judge John Connoly in St. Paul hearing the case. On December 13, the court ruled that Minnesota may enforce its law, and Minnesota is now seeking an injunction and civil penalties of at least $25,000 against those running the site. Additionally, the Sixth U.S. Circuit Court of Appeals and four federal district court decisions involving Web sites have found that mere electronic contacts may be sufficient to confer personal jurisdiction (Kuster & Kramer, 1996).[17]

A popular area of state legislation involves sexually explicit material available to minors. A score of sites have either enacted or are considering legislation to regulate speech on the Internet (Mendels, 1997). Among states to propose or enact legislation addressing indecent materials transmitted via computer are Georgia (H.B. 1630, enacted May 1996), Virginia (H.B. 7 enacted March 1996; S.B. 1067, enacted May 1995), Illinois (S.B. 838, enacted July 1995), Kansas (H.B. 2223, enacted May 1995), Montana (H.B. 0161, enacted March 1995), Oklahoma (H.B. 1048, enacted April 1995), and Maryland (H.B. 305/S.B. 133, enacted May 1996). In New York an amendment to the Penal Law, effective November 1, 1996, forbids the use of computers to transmit to those under 17 years of age material that "depicts actual or simulated nudity, sexual conduct or sado-masochistic abuse and which is harmful to minors" (McKinney's Annotated Laws of New York § 235).

The law also outlaws the use of computers to lure young people into sexual activities. The so-called pedophile law resulted from a case in which a youngster met an adult online and subsequently that adult traveled to New York and met the child face to face. This law has been challenged by in a suit filed by the American Civil Liberties Union and 14 other groups, including the American Library Association, the American Booksellers Foundation for Free Expression, the Interactive Digital Software Association, and the Magazine Publishers of America Inc. The suit filed in Federal court does not challenge the section of the law dealing with online solicitation of children, but rather challenges the portions of the law dealing with dissemination of communication that functions as what is argued to be a "chilling effect." The jurisdictional questions are raised in a number of arguments. One of the arguments in the New York suit is that the new state law violates the commerce clause of the U.S. Constitution because it would regulate communications that originate outside of the state and could place an "unreasonable and undue burden on interstate and foreign commerce" (Mendels, 1997). Another area that notes jurisdictional assumptions found to be problematic relates to the fact that Internet users both in New York and elsewhere would either have to face prosecution and up to four years in prison or refrain from positing arguably indecent material altogether (Complaint for Declaratory and Injunctive Relief, 1997).

On the federal level the United States, although not directly addressing jurisdiction, has attempted to retain some degree of authority through provisions of the newly enacted Telecommunications Act of 1996. One provision of this law, the Decency Act, makes it a felony to transmit indecent material over the Internet or online computer services if the material may be seen by children (Lewis, 1996). This part of the law declared unconstitutional by the Philadelphia District Court was argued before the U.S. Supreme Court in December 1996.

On an international level the trend has been toward recognizing that cyberspace laws established as technical obstacles are easily circumvented. To date there are no wide-ranging International accords or agreements directly related to Internet-specific issues. The area of copyright law has been most advanced in efforts to coordinate international efforts. In December 1996, 160 countries reached an agreement in Geneva on "the most sweeping extension of international copyright law in 25 years" (Schisel, 1996, p. 1). Negotiators met under the auspices of the World Intellectual Property Organization of the United Nations and agreed on two treaties. It has been argued that documents such as the Universal Declaration on Human Rights, particularly Article 19 and the International Covenant on Civil and Political Rights, will be extended. When considering a truly global information infrastructure such as that offered in cyberspace, different sources of international communication rights emerge as significant. It has been argued that the Universal Declaration of Human Rights should be expanded to encompass the notion of a right to communicate, recognizing that the means of communication have always been determined by political and social structures, and that the group controlling communications effectively controls society (Fisher & Harms, 1983). The Universal Declaration of Human Rights (Part III of the Covenant on Civil and Political Rights) presently contains a number of provisions recognizing communication rights (norms that must be complied with without qualifications or deviations and over which others have no power to deny). Viewed as a right, communication cannot be interfered with, and there is a positive obligation to provide the environment for its exercise. Article 19 states everyone has the right to freedom of opinion and expression and to seek, receive, and impart information and ideas through any media regardless of frontier. Article 21 provides for the right of assembly, Article 22 for freedom of association. Beyond these already recognized rights that have often focused on a free flow of information and have been seen as the right to be informed, a further distinct right has been advocated (Cocca, 1979). To date, groups promoting this right have presented a document to the UN Special Commissioner for Human Rights that further defines the specific communication rights.[18]

A SEPARATE CYBERJURISDICTION?

The jurisdiction is complex when the meaning of border is blurred, when the victim may be located in different countries or states and the threshold question of personal jurisdiction, whether the person would anticipate being brought into the specific court for a lawsuit, is difficult to answer. Some leading thinkers advocate that cyberspace be considered a "place," rather than a medium, with its own constitution on which to base a developing body of applicable law and self-regulatory systems (Stuckey, 1996, p. xxiii). In fact, one reaction to efforts to regulate cyberspace came in the form of a Declaration of Independence "from a political body holding no jurisdiction or authority over transactions occurring throughout Cyberspace" (Cyberspace Declaration of Independence, 1996). The Cyberspace Declaration of Independence declares cyberspace to be an autonomous zone and begins:

> We have no elected government, nor are we likely to have one, so I address you with no greater authority than that with which liberty itself always speaks. I declare the global social space we are building to be naturally independent of the tyrannies you seek to impose on us. You have no moral right to rule us nor do you possess any methods of enforcement we have true reason to fear. Governments derive their just powers from the consent of the governed. You have neither solicited nor received ours. We did not invite you. You do not know us, nor do you know our world. Cyberspace does not lie within your borders. Do not think that you can build it, as though it were a public construction project. You cannot. It is an act of nature and it grows itself through our collective actions.

The chapters to follow have been gathered to offer historical perspective, current law, and the yardsticks that will shape future laws and judicial interpretations in the development of a body of "cyberlaw." Some of the authors suggest the lessons of history and existing regulatory approaches that lend themselves to application in computer-mediated communication contexts (see Jassem, chap. 2; Ross, chap. 3; Docter, chap. 9), whereas other authors suggest the need for developing new rules (Drucker & Gumpert, chaps. 1 and 4; Tuman, chap. 7; Freedman, chap. 8, Monberg, chap. 13). Others evaluate the present situation in which existing laws are being applied as resulting in a somewhat imperfect fit (see Fraleigh, chap. 6; Fishman, chap. 10; Drucker & Gumpert, chap. 11, Donnelly, chap. 14). The scope of this volume encompasses both governmental and nongovernmental, commercial and personal, public and private sources of rights and limitations on those rights. The chapters will approach this subject of emerging concern from multiple perspectives, including legal, economic, social, and ethical approaches.

The first section provides an overview outlining the existing regulatory approaches currently being applied to the increasingly complex and frequent issues raised by the host of newly emerging computer-mediated options and activities. In Chapter 2, Jassem provides the historical context for the extension and/or creation of legal rules to new modes of distribution and interaction. He notes that although the media can be counted on to change and challenge existing laws, the issues remain fairly constant. He explores how the United States' regulatory/legal treatment has been to divide issues by carrier technology rather than by principle and provides an overview of the historical rationale for giving different communication technologies different legal frameworks and a cost/benefit analysis of such an approach.

Susan Mallon Ross (chap. 3) examines the lessons of the past significance to drafting a regulatory scheme for cyberspace. By utilizing Frederick Jackson Turner's work on the significance of the frontier in U.S. history, she examines the cultural similarities between the physical frontier and the so-called electronic/aspatial "frontier" of cyberspace with regard to enacting and interpreting of laws governing that frontier.

In Chapter 4, Drucker and Gumpert examine the dilemmas raised by the transition to postmodern media and the growing role of cyberspace in civic life. This chapter examines the application of the use of metaphors in the regulation of free speech laws and judicial decision. It examines the spatial terminology being applied to the aspatial realm of cyberspace and implications of those place-based metaphors emphasizing the need to reevaluate appropriate metaphors given the fact that, in part, cyberspace has become a locale for interaction vital to a democratic society and an alternative public forum. Rounding out the first section, Howard Cohen provides an economic overview of various computer-mediated activities, particularly Internet-based options, and in so doing, offers a grounding for understanding and predicting various matters leading to regulatory activities. The author offers a brief yet comprehensive tour of the history and infrastructure of the Internet, noting that no effective traffic management systems can exist akin to those used by telephone providers, and argues that ultimately with new technologies enabling voice and full-motion video transmission, new competition exists for the telcos, compelling them to seek legislative relief and promoting a rush to own more of the infrastructure. He examines how the Internet can and will function to facilitate global commerce and the legal implications of this new avenue of trade.

The second section is devoted to an analysis of the regulation of indecency in cyberspace. History reveals that inevitably new technologies raise concern over their use in the transmission of "indecent" materials, particularly to minors. From the printing press to photography, from musical recordings to movies, from telephone services to video games, sexually explicit content in diverse technological innovations have been the target of censorship and regulation. So it comes as no surprise that such material available via computer systems is a natural target. Attempts to regulate have therefore commonly sparked argument, debate, and deliberation of the legal issues and policy dimensions inherent in limiting sexually oriented materials. This section focuses on the efforts to legislate a policy in the United States on a federal level embodied in the Communications Decency Act signed into law by President Clinton in February 1996. The Communications Decency Act (47 U.S.C. Section 151 et seq.), or CDA, provides that posting of "indecent" material to the Net would be subject to a $250,000 fine and a two-year prison term. Online activists and media organizations formed a coalition that led to the ACLU and 18 other groups filing suit in Philadelphia, seeking to have the new indecency provisions declared unconstitutional. In June 1996, the three-judge panel of the Federal District Court in Philadelphia found the act to be unconstitutional on its face and an abridgement of rights protected under the First and Fifth Amendments. This decision was taken up by the Supreme Court in oral arguments heard in December 1996.

The four chapters in this section examine the act and the District court decision, offering insights into the issues raised by this legislative and judicial activity. The Communication Decency Act is examined not only for what it reveals about the regulation of sexually oriented material, but for the larger lessons to be learned from this early and direct attempt to regulate Internet communication. In Chapter 6, Douglas Fraleigh examines different standards by which restrictions on the content of expression in cyberspace could be judged. These standards range from protections for expression for the most favored channels of communication (the strict scrutiny test) to judicial standards applied in evaluating the constitutionality of low value speech such as obscenity (the rational basis test) and how these are applied in a broadcasting context. He then applies these tests to contexts in cyberspace.

This discussion is followed by Joseph Tuman's (chap. 7) examination of how judges educated in law rather than technology manage to deal with decisions about free speech issues raised by the use of a new technology that they may not know, understand, or use and may in fact be disinclined to learn. In Chapter 8, Eric Freedman's argument against the "inside-outside" or "protected-unprotected" approach to diverse categories of speech is provided and then applied to the context of the Communications Decency Act. Freedman's analysis of the general approach to communication freedoms within U.S. constitutional analysis places the CDA into an important conceptual framework applied even in times when the technologies of communication may be outrunning the legal mechanisms of control. This section is rounded out by Sharon Docter's (chap. 9) critique of the rationale for regulating indecent speech across various media. She examines policy alternatives concerning the regulation of indecent speech communicated via electronic communications by comparing computer-mediated communication to various preexisting models of communication, including the broadcasting, cable television, and common carrier models.

The third section deals with the property interests inherent in computer-mediated communication. When approaching electronic reproduction the legal implication that emerges most prominently is that of intellectual property. Donald Fishman (chap. 10) examines the implications of digitalization of images for copyright holders. Although much in this realm is undecided, the principle that copyrights apply to cyberspace (i.e., electronic digitalized media) has been established, but troubling issues remain with regard to display rights and what constitutes copying. Fishman addresses questions such as: Does saving or using a file constitute copying? Does downloading a file result in a copy under copyright law? When is a work "fixed" in a tangible medium of expression meeting a U.S. standard for creative works eligible for copyright protections? This discussion is followed by Drucker and Gumpert's (chap. 11) examination of these issues within the particular context of the digital reproduction of art. In examining online and CD-ROM museum collections, the authors consider the virtual museum and its relationship to the early development of the museum concept and later the impact of technology on the nature of art. The technologies of duplication including printing, the casting of molds, etching, lithography, photography, and now digitalized multimedia transmission transform the artistic experience and the laws governing artistic creations that were once based on the economics of scarcity.

In Chapter 12, Mark Lemley explores the interrelated rights of attribution, integrity of identity, and anonymity as they apply to electronic communications, a realm in which authors traditionally looked to copyright and trademark law to prevent misattribution. He asks if Net users can protect their rights to attribution and the integrity of their electronic personalities only at the expense of a loss of anonymity. John Monberg (chap. 13) examines the commodification of personal information, knowledge, and marketing data flows, and information about connections that are easily traced and collected and pose threats to privacy. By utilizing a cultural studies approach grounded in a close investigation of the use of technologies, he argues for a redefinition of data that would provide individuals with a property interest in such personal data.

This section on property interests is rounded out by David Donnelly's contribution in Chapter 14, which explores the commercialization of the Internet, particularly with regard to advertising on the Net. The relationship of unique media contexts and legal concerns and regulations regarding advertising are considered as the author suggests a set of safeguards for advertising within the context of the Internet.

Personal liberties and interests are the subject of concern in the five chapters comprising the fourth section. The right to one's good name is the subject of Dale Herbeck's contribution (chap. 15). Herbeck provides an analysis of the popularity of computer bulletin board systems and the controversies surrounding prescreening and censorship of bulletin board postings. The level of free speech protection offered controversial postings and liability of service providers for the defamatory content posted on bulletin boards is also focused on. Chapter 16 (Drucker and Gumpert) considers the personal right most associated with the conception of the protecting the individual—the right of privacy. Privacy is often conceptualized as "the right of the individual" to decide for him or herself how much one wishes to share with others in terms of thoughts, feelings, and facts of personal life. This chapter considers issues ranging from expectations of privacy in e-mail to anonymity in electronic communication, from associational privacy to encryption and electronic signatures. Chapter 17 (Roy Leeper and Phillip Heeler) takes up e-mail privacy from the perspective of having the freedom from unwanted e-mail. They examine unsolicited commercial e-mail sent to Internet users and argue that unsolicited commercial e-mail should be treated like commercial fax and should, in the United States, fall within section of the 1991 Telephone Consumer Protection Act.

In Chapter 18, e-mail is once again the focus of attention. Shapiro and Schulman explore the therapeutic uses of e-mail and the ethical as well as legal issues raised by this form of computer-mediated communication. The unsettled nature of expectations of privacy and confidentiality in e-mail contexts raise significant issues for e-mail clinicians. Finally, Sue Barnes (chap. 19) provides a glimpse into the nexus of legal and ethical issues raised by computer-mediated communication. By focusing on the significance of false identities and anonymity made possible in cyberspace, she considers concepts of self, community, and how changing conceptualizations of individual responsibilities and rights are found in the communication contexts of cyberspace.

CYBERSPACE: LAWS AND ETHICS

This volume addresses public and private regulations and restrictions, government regulations, industry self-regulation, and individual ethical and social standards that will result because the changes brought about by computer-mediated communication are far greater than the traditional concept of governmental regulation. The chapters approach this subject of emerging concern from multiple perspectives, including legal, economic, social, and ethical approaches. The rights and restrictions governing computer-mediated communication, particularly the realm of online communication, the Internet, or what is commonly referred to as cyberspace, are at a formative period. Although few definitive principles have been carved out and scant case law exists, we hope that *Real Law@Virtual Space: Communication Regulation in Cyberspace* will contribute to the debate, understanding, and evolution of this new and exciting field of communication law.

ENDNOTES

1. One such virtual rape case occurred in Lambda MOO in which a participant on the MOO (Oberding & Norderhaug, 1996), a University of Michigan student, Jake Baker, was held on charges of interstate transmission of a threat to injure, a federal offense, carrying a maximum penalty of five years in prison. The offense stemmed from stories sent via the Internet in which he and another man sent stories and discussed how they would kidnap a woman in one of his classes at gunpoint, rape her, and force her to strip and torture her with a clamp. Baker's lawyer argues the story was not a threat but a fantasy never even communicated to the woman in question herself ("Student held," 1995.

2. A woman in Michigan had a man arrested accusing him of stalking her using his computer. The two had met twice, talked on the phone, and courted on the Internet via e-mail. When she decided it was over, he continued sending her e-mail to try to win her back (Castine, 1994).

3. It was a Usenet newsgroup that was involved with the controversy over censorship involving CompuServe in 1995. CompuServe removed from all its computers more than 200 Usenet computer discussion groups and picture databases that provoked criticism by a federal prosecutor in Munich ("Silencing the Net," 1996).

4. Laws provide the standards by which society may judge right and wrong and resolve disputes in a final and enforceable manner. According to legal philosopher Karl Llewellyn (1960), the prevention and settlement of conflict and dispute both appeal to law and make up the business of law.

5.   The following extended information appears in the service provider's agreement posted online:

(i) Offensive Communication. AOL is a community-oriented service composed of many different communities of people. Our goal is to provide an interesting, stimulating and fun place for all Members. Using vulgar, abusive or hateful language undermines this goal and is not allowed. Please use your best judgment and be respectful of other Members. Remember, there may be children online. If you use vulgar, or abusive language online, even if masked by symbols or other characters, you may either receive an "on-screen-warning" by a Guide or Room Host, or in some cases be terminated immediately. A warning indicates that your language is not in compliance with the TOS [terms of service] or ROR [Rules of the Road]. Should you receive such a warning, take the time to read the AOL Rules again, comprising the TOS and these ROR which you will find posted in the Members Services area.

(ii) Harassment. When a Member targets another individual or entity to cause distress, embarrassment, unwanted attention, or other discomfort, this is harassment. AOL Inc. does not condone harassment in any form and may suspend or terminate the accounts of any Member who harasses others. You may have a disagreement with someone's point of view—we encourage lively discussion in our chat rooms and message boards—but personal attacks, or attacks based on a person's race, national origin, ethnicity, religion, gender, sexual orientation, disablement or other such affiliation, are prohibited. If you have a disagreement with someone's point of view, address the subject, not the person.

(iii) Graphic Files. AOL Inc. prohibits the transfer or posting on AOL of sexually explicit images or other content deemed offensive by AOL Inc.

(iv) Scrolling. "Scrolling" means repeatedly causing the screen to roll faster than Members are able to type to it. It is caused by a user entering a set of random characters or by repeatedly entering a carriage return or any such action to a similar disruptive effect. Scrolling is an expressly prohibited form of disruption.

(v) Impersonation. This can involve the portrayal of another person or entity, such as the impersonation of AOL Inc. staff or an information provider, authorized Guide or Host, or communication under a false name or a name that you are not authorized to use. Members must avoid the portrayal of AOL Inc. personnel or others persons in all forms of online communication, including, but not limited to, screen names, member profiles, chat dialogue and message postings.

(vi) Room Disruption. This includes purposefully interfering with the normal flow of dialogue in a chat room. Room disruption may occur by repeatedly interrupting conversation between Members, or by acting in such a way as to antagonize, harass or create hostility in a chat room. . . .

(viii) Advertising and Solicitation. You may not use AOL to send unsolicited advertising, promotional material, or other forms of solicitation to other Members except in those specified areas that are designated for such a purpose (e.g., the classified area).

If you witness chat in a public chat room that violates the AOL Rules, you may contact an AOL Service Guide by using the keyword "Guide Pager." You may also contact AOL Inc.'s Terms of Service Staff about any violation by using the "Write to Terms of Service Staff" icon located in the TOS area of the Members Services area.

6.   The realm of electronic communication raises issues with regard to some of the most fundamental acts and within legal systems such as contracts. Many service agreements are made online, thus raising issues of validity due to questions such as lack of traditional signatures to indicate intent to be bound, authentication of signatures, rules regarding offer and acceptance, authority to bind, legal capacity, and the Statute of Frauds that indicates which contracts must be set out in writing. For a full discussion of these issues, see Stuckey (1996).

7.   The AOL service agreement (Section 4.1) goes on to reserve the right to remove "any content that it deems in its sole discretion to be unacceptable, undesirable or in violation of the Roles of the Road. AOL Inc. may terminate immediately any Member who misuses or fails to abide by the applicable AOL rules. AOL Inc. may terminate with notice Member's access to and use of the AOL Service and American Online Software upon a breach of the AOL rules, including without limitation, misuse of the software libraries, discussion boards, E-mail, or public conference areas (AOL Service Agreement, 1995).

8.   In a related case the United States Court of Appeals for the Third Circuit considered several issues related to shrinkwrap agreements in *Step-Saver Data Systems v. Wyse Technology, 939 F.2d 91* (3d Cir. 1991).

9.   The case the Paris court heard relates to a challenge by two private French groups, Defense of the French Language and Future of the French Language against an Internet site set up by the French campus of the Georgia Institute of Technology, written in English. The school argues the site is in English because its courses are taught in English and its students must be fluent in English ("Francophones sue," 1997).

10.   Singapore has chosen to treat the Internet as a broadcast service. It is to be regulated under the recently passed Singapore Broadcasting Authority (SBA) Act, which defines broadcasting broadly—in terms of program transmission to all or part of the public, regardless of the means used. The Act could require computer networks to be licensed by designating them as "licensable broadcasting services." The plan to regulate affects 100,000 users with Internet accounts (McDonald, 1996).

11.   The Philippines introduced legislation aimed at censorship of the Internet, focusing on sexually oriented material (Cacho-Olivares, 1996). In March 1996, members of the ASEAN (Association of Southeast Asian Nations) reported that they planned to organize a regulatory body to deal with new information technologies, particularly with regard to pornography and disinformation (Hussein, 1996).

12.   The Islamic Republic, although seeing the benefit of electronic
       linkage to the outside world, is concerned that access will lead to
       messages from supporters of the deposed Shah as well as western
       pornography. Price limits online access for most Iranians with high
       fees charged such as three or four hours billed at between $50 to
       $130. Iranian university has a system dependent on a trunk line
       established by an institution in Austria (MacFarquhar, 1996, p. A4).

13.   In Fall 1995, 18 people were questioned and 15 computers seized in
       Queensland for alleged involvement with child pornography. This was
       possible by implementing the state's Classification of Computer
       Games and Images Act of 1995.

14.   The Western Australia law defines "restricted material" to be that
       which a reasonable adult, by reason of the nature of the article, or
       the nature or extent of references in the article, to matters of sex,
       drug misuse or addiction, crime, cruelty, violence, or revolting or
       abhorrent phenomena, would regard as unsuitable for a minor to
       see, read or hear. Service providers are liable only if they knowingly
       permit objectionable material to be transmitted. A bill before the
       parliament of New South Wales will hold individuals and service
       providers responsible for objectionable material that includes not
       only sexually explicit messages but drug- and crime-related material
       ("Silencing the Net," 1996).

15.   Obscenity in Canada is characterized by "undue exploitation of sex,"
       which is viewed as sex plus violence or degrading sex.

16.   In 1994, Zimmerman, a nationally known cryptographer, was
       informed that he was the subject of a grand jury investigation being
       conducted by the U.S. Customs Office in San Jose, CA, looking into
       the international distribution of an encryption program called Pretty
       Good Privacy (PGP). Zimmerman drafted the PGP program, making it
       available free of charge to computer users in the United States.
       Sometime in mid-1991, someone else posted the program on the
       Internet, making it available throughout the world and brining
       Zimmerman himself under criminal investigation. In January 1996,
       the investigation was dropped, but questions remain as to the degree
       of "knowing participation" required for culpability in the realm of
       cyberspace (*Netsurfer Digest*, 1995).

17.   In each case courts applied principles of personal jurisdiction
       established in the *International Shoe Co. v. Washington* "minimum
       contacts" test to assess whether due process was satisfied in granting
       jurisdiction. For purposes of minimum contacts analysis, e-mail and
       other electronic communications will likely be treated as phone calls
       or surface mail that alone have not been found to provide sufficient
       contacts to support jurisdiction (Kuster & Kramer, 1996).

18.   A Non-Governmental Organization in Consultative Status with the
       Economic and Social Council within the International Association of
       Mass Communication Researchers, continues to work on a separate
       additional "Right to Communicate" for the Universal Declaration.
       Last year we were part of a group of communication scholars and
       journalists that met to draft a declaration and report to the World
       Conference on Human Rights in Vienna.

REFERENCES

Ajoy S. (1995, June 13). Some Asian nations give Internet mixed reception. *Reuters.*

Armstron, N., &.Daily, I.T. (1996, February 26). Thai group on porn trail. *Newsbyte News Network.*

America Online Service Membership Subscriber Agreement (1995).

Black's Law Dictionary (5th ed.). (1979). St. Paul, MN: West Publishing.

Cacho-Olivares, N. (1996, March 18) My cup of tea pornography on the Net. *Business World* (Manila).

Castine, J. (1994, May 29). Cyberlove says she was virtually stalked. *The New York Daily News*, p. 30.

China cracks down on Internet. (1996, January 1) . *Deutsche Presse-Agentur.*

Cocca, A. A. (1979). The right to communication: Some reflections on its legal foundation. *Document of the International Commission for the Study of Communication Problems, No. 38.* Paris: Unesco.

Complaint for Declaratory and Injunctive Relief. (1997, January 15). Index No._____. American Library Association et. al v. Pataki and Vacco, http://www.aclu.org/court/nycdacomplaint.html.

Consultation Paper on the Regulation of On-line Information Services. (1996, July 7). Australian Dept. Of Communications and the Arts. http://www.dca.gov.au/paper_ 2.html.

Cowell, A. (1998, May 29). Ex-Compuserve head sentenced in Germany. *The New York Times on the Web.* http://search.nytimes.com/search/daily/bin/fastweb?, July 3, 1998.

Cyberspace Declaration of Independence. (1996, February 8). http://www.eff.org/~barlow.

Defamation in cyberspace. (1997, January 18).http://ntserv1.mc.maricopa.edu/dept/endlish/Moore/Writ_Law.htm.

Economic news as blackout. (1996, January 20). *The Economist.*

Fisher, D., & Harms, L.S. (1983). *The right to communicate: A new human right.* Dublin: Boole Press.

Francophones sues Net site. (1997, January 6). *The New York Times,* p. D5.

Gibson, W. (1984). *Neuromancer.* New York: Ace Books.

Hussein, R. (1996, March 9). Singapore deputy premier defends curbs on Internet. *Reuters.*

International Shoe Co. v Washington, 326 U.S. 310 (1945).

Johnson, D.R., & Marks, P. A. (1993). Mapping electronic data communications onto existing legal metaphors. Should we let our conscience and our contracts be our guide? *Villanova Law Review, 81*(2), 487-516.

Katsh, M. E. (1988). *The electronic media and the transformation of law.* New York: Oxford University Press.

Kuster, J.R., & Kramer, M.C. (1996, October 28). Coalition challenges state law guarding Net IP. *The National Law Journal*, p. C22.

Landmark Minnesota decision declares that states can address lawbreaking on Internet. (1996, December 12). http://www. ag.state.mn.us/consumer/news/OnlineScams/ggpress.html.

Leibowitz, W. (1996, September 23). Geography isn't destiny: High tech is reshaping legal basics. *The National Law Journal*, pp. 1, 16.

Lewis, P. (1996, February 16). Judge blocks law intended to regulate on-line smut. *The New York Times*, p. D1.

Llewellyn, K. (1960). *The common law tradition: Deciding appeals.* New York: Little, Brown.

MacFarquhar, N. (1996, October 8). With mixed feelings, Iran tiptoes to the Internet. *The New York Times*, p. A4.

McDonald, J. (1996, March 12). Singapore Internet users unhappy with loss of refuge in land of rules. *The New York Times Cybertimes.* http://www.nytimes.com...eek/0312singapore.html.

McKinney's Annotated Laws of New York State, Penal Law § 235.2.

Mendels, P. (1997, January 15). Coalition files suit to block New York online decency law. *New York Times, CyberTimes.* http://www.nytimes.com/library/cyber/week/011597empire.ht ml.

Micharp, M. (1996, April 13). Internet porn peddlers face jail. *Sydney Morning Herald.*

Netsurfer Digest focus on cryptography and privacy. (1995, August 21). Vol. 1, No. 3.

Netree Internet Statistics. (1997, January 3). http://www.netree. com/netbin/internetstats.

New York State Internet legislation becomes law. (1997, January 13). http://www.brownraysman.com/docket/docket6.html.

Oberding, J., & Norderhaug, T. (1996). A separate jurisdiction for cyberspace? *Journal of Computer-Mediated Communication, 2*(1).

Reidenberg, J.R. (1996). Governing networks and cyberspace rule-making. *Emory Law Journal*, p. 45 .

Schisel, S. (1996, December 21). Global agreement reached to widen copyright law. *The New York Times*, p. 1.

Silencing the Net—The threat to freedom of expression on-line. (1996, May 10). *Human Rights Watch.* gopher://gopher. igc.apc.org:5000/00/ int/hrw/expression/7.

Singapore bans sex, religion, and politics on the Internet. (1996, March 6) *The New York Times Cybertimes.* http://www.nytimes. com...eek/0306singapore.html.

Spaeth, A. (1995, October 16). National Security. The Vietnamese government wants to control Internet access. *Time.*

Step-Saver Data Systems v. Wyse Technology, 939 F.2d 91 (3d Cir. 1991).

Stuckey, K. (1996). *Internet and online law.* New York: Law Journal Seminars-Press.

Student Held on cyber "rape." (1995, February 11). *New York Post,* p. 9.

Wald, M.L. (1995, February 26). A child's Internet sins visited on the parent. *The New York Times,* p. S4.

Zakalik, J. (1996). International jurisdiction and conflict of laws. Zakalik@gale.com.

PART 1

OVERVIEW

2

DIFFERENT STROKES FOR DIFFERENT FOLKS: THE INTERSECTION OF REGULATORY PRINCIPLES AND TECHNOLOGY

HARVEY JASSEM

In this chapter Harvey Jassem traces the historical approach taken in regulating technology. He argues that much media law has been technology driven with notions such as responsibility, fairness, and access defined by the technological context in which it is applied. He examines the placement of communication laws and principles in the context of "cyberspace," focusing on the ways in which new media challenge the existing laws governing such areas of communicative rights as privacy, expression, intellectual property, fairness, and access. In providing an historical overview for giving different communication technologies and different legal frameworks, he positions converging technologies and cyberspace with regard to this historical context.

The world of telecommunication policy is coming to an end. Or is it just beginning? The policymakers find themselves struggling to do the right thing in an atmosphere of rapidly shifting sands. Originally established to promote the efficient use and growth of broadcasting and common carrier communication, the FCC and its precursor the FRC, spent much of its 60-plus years making incremental changes to a framework in which rules, roles, and players were identifiable. During those 60-plus years, there were tumultuous moments, and the media policymaking apparatus responded to and shaped some rather significant changes. It is during those phases that the very foundations of communication policy are challenged and explicated. As we move into the next century, we find ourselves in a stage of enormous telecommunication change. The telecommunication industries are all redefining themselves in terms of their functions, distribution channels, competition, suppliers, revenue sources, reach, and partners. The regulatory/policy apparatus is hurriedly adjusting to these changes and attempting to shape others. But by what principles? This chapter looks at some of the changes in telecommunication, with an eye toward the ways in which those changes affect relevant policy, and suggests the appropriate regulatory values for the coming years.

THE OLD PROBLEM OF NEW MEDIA

The regulation of electronic media has always been something of a torturous affair. When the radio telegraph was young, it wasn't clear who, if anybody, should regulate it and to what ends such regulation might be focused. There are many accounts of the U.S government's hesitant approach to the involvement with and regulation of the radio telegraph/telephone. Certainly there were military and industrial uses for this new technology, and the military and ultimately the Secretary of Commerce asserted limited jurisdiction. But it was not until after World War I, when radio manufacturers realized there was enormous potential for a new consumer product, and that the potential could only be met if competitors were kept at bay, that the industry succeed in its lobbying for government regulation of radio.

From the beginning, the scope and purpose of radio regulation was strained by ever-emerging technology. The Radio Act of 1912 made radio telegraph communication subject to revocable license from the Secretary of Commerce and labor. The purpose of the attendant regulations was the minimization of radio telegraph interference and the facilitation of radio services. In 1926, the Commerce Secretary's power to deny and control licenses was stripped by the courts, which noted that broadcasting was not covered by the 1912 Act (US v. Zenith, 1926). Later that year, Acting U.S. Attorney General William J. Donovan issued an opinion in which he opined that "while the Act of 1912 was originally drafted to apply primarily to wireless telegraphy, its language is broad enough to cover wireless telephony as well" (35 Ops. Att'y Gen 126, 1926). Nevertheless, the opinion went on to suggest that because the Commerce Secretary had no right to deny a license, licenses were essentially worthless, and hence new legislation would be needed if radio were to be regulated.

In the resultant Radio Act of 1927, the first comprehensive federal regulation of modern electronic communication, Congress charged its new Federal Radio Commission (FRC) with regulating "all forms of interstate and foreign radio transmissions and communications within the United States." Radio transmission facilities owned and operated by the federal government were largely exempt. The FRC was mostly assigned the task of overseeing the distribution of licenses, setting technical rules and standards, and creating regulations that would promote the public interest and convenience. Although the FRC could not censor radio, it was charged with enforcement of some content-related regulations (such as Section 18's equal opportunities for political candidates requirements). It was also assigned the task of distributing radio licenses in a way that would "give fair, efficient, and equitable radio service" to all parts of the country (Sec. 9). The law was amended the following year in an unsuccessful and political attempt to require that every region of the country have an equal amount of radio transmission and reception.

Significantly, this put the federal government's radio telecommunication regulatory agency in the business of regulating and promoting/protecting the business of radio telecommunication. The operative assumption was that radio service was of value to society. It must at once be shaped and protected. This *protectionist* stance became one of the fundamental principles of media regulatory policy.

In discussing this Radio Act of 1927, broadcast historian Frank Kahn (1978) noted that "communications law, while generally paralleling technological development, has never been able to keep pace with entrepreneurial innovation in the broadcast field. This was certainly true of the Radio Act of 1927. . . . [It] was curiously vague about radio networks and advertising, the two dominant elements of the unfolding broadcasting industry" (p. 32). Also missing from the 1927 Act was any regulatory authority over the telephone industry.

Regulation of the telephone industry had been reserved for the Interstate Commerce Commission, until the Communications Act of 1934, which superseded the 1927 Act and which replaced the FRC with the Federal Communications Commission (FCC). Right at the outset of this new guiding law, Title 1, Section 1 of the Communications Act of 1934, made clear the broader mandate of this new commission:

For the purpose of regulating interstate and foreign commerce in communication by wire and radio so as to make available, so far as possible, to all the people of the United States a rapid, efficient, Nation-wide, and world-wide wire and radio communication service with adequate facilities at reasonable charges, for the purpose of the national defense, for the purpose of promoting safety of life and property through the use of wire and radio communication, and for the purpose of securing a more effective execution of this policy by centralizing authority heretofore granted by law to several agencies and by granting additional authority with respect to interstate and foreign commerce in wire and radio communication, there is hereby created a commission to be known as the "Federal Communications Commission."

The framers of the 1934 Act supplied a comprehensive set of definitions that were broadly inclusive. For example, Section 3(b) defines *radio communication* as transmission by radio of writing, signs, signals, pictures, and sounds of all kinds, including all instrumentalities, facilities, apparatus, and services . . . incidental to such communication." Definitions of *common carriers, radio station,* and *broadcasting* were similarly cast. Guiding principles were those of overseeing the efficient growth of broadcasting to minimizing interference with broadcast signals, regulating broadcast station operation and content in the public interest, limiting the terms of licenses, and avoiding antitrust violations of concentration of ownership/power. These principles applied only to the aforementioned media.

Section 201 of the Act required common carriers that "engaged in interstate or foreign communication by wire or radio to furnish such communication upon reasonable request . . . [and at] just and reasonable rates." Most of the common carrier actions taken by the FCC have involved rates (tariffs) and grants of permission to build and operate telephone systems.

As broad as the Commission's mandates were, they clearly did not include all aspects of telecommunication or media-related enterprises. They did not regulate program producers, they did not regulate broadcast networks (although the FCC found a way to regulate those networks indirectly through affiliated stations), and they presumed that broadcasting (directing communication to a wide undifferentiated audience) was inexorably linked to over-the-air radio signals. Nevertheless, the framework was broad enough and the players (FCC, courts, industries, Congress, etc.) resourceful enough that the Act lasted (through various amendments, through court-reviewed FCC expansive interpretations, and through court-imposed interpretations) for more than 60 years. The endurance of this regulatory framework is a nod to the dynamic nature of the process.

It may also be a reminder that powerful interests are good at holding on to their power.

THE REGULATORY PROCESS

The telecommunication media policy apparatus in the United States is most easily found at the national level. Krasnow and Longley (1973) and Krasnow, Longley and Terry (1982) gave us the widely relied-on model of broadcast regulation, which essentially suggests that broadcast policy is the result of stakeholders and government agencies pressuring for changes that are in their best interests. Although the model has occasionally been criticized (Kim, 1992), and although it is an imprecise model, it points to the major players involved. Those players include Congress and its various communication-related committees, the Executive Branch, the courts, the FCC, the affected industries, and, to a lesser extent, citizen groups. Add to that list of players the prevailing political/economic climate (both domestic and international), and one has a good handle on relevant policy motivators.

The system is a rational one. Entities tend to favor protecting their own interests, be those interests financial, power, or political. Many of those involved in the process develop symbiotic relationships, relying on each other for their information and protection. Such a system is biased toward inertia. Those with the power are the most influential. They will tend to use their influence to maintain their power. Contributing to this inertia is what Braybrooke and Lindblom (1963) call "incremental politics," or "the strategy of disjointed incrementalism." The notion here is that policymakers are not experts in everything, that policy making is complex, and that the safest way to make policy is slowly, without being bound to (often unformulated) grand policy objectives. Policy making does not start in a vacuum; it starts with widely shared notions of the present situation. At best, this notion holds, policymakers consider how the present situation could be improved, believing all the while that whatever unintended negative consequences may emerge from their policy tweaks may be rectified by the next round of policy modifications. At worst, "bad" policy tweaks do not have to undergo much scrutiny since they appear to be marginal rather than grand shifts in policy directions. Finally, the rationality of the system yields to its form. That is, the structures are established to make policy act in ways that are consistent with their structure. Those charged with exercising *broadcast* policy see the world through lenses focused on *broadcasting*. Experts do what they are experts at. This, too, then contributes to the conservative bias of the policy-making process.

The structure of the FCC is like that of any expert agency. It was designed to represent discrete areas of expertise and authority. Although that makes sense, it also serves to shape the ways in which issues and possibilities are seen. Scrambled over-the-air subscription television, phonevision, cable television, teletext, and nonstandard uses of spectrum all faced serious confining considerations and policies by the FCC. In discussing the adventures of regulating new communication media, the cable television saga presents the richest examples.

THE CABLE SAGA

Initially, the Commission denied its own authority to regulate cable television, noting that cable was neither broadcasting nor common carriage, and hence outside the scope of the Communications Act. Furthermore, FCC officials noted that even if cable TV were deemed to be a common carrier, it would be unlikely that the FCC could stop cable TV from carrying the content (competing television signals) that those who sought regulation were objecting to (Committee on Interstate and Foreign Commerce, 1958). Common carriers (such as telephone companies) were regulated for issues of rates and service availability, not content. In 1959, the FCC decided it would not regulate cable television as broadcasting either, and it would not prohibit cable TV from retransmitting broadcast television stations or require the stations' consent (FCC, 1959). Then, when it finally stepped into the cable regulatory arena, it did so tangentially (by regulating the microwave [common carrier] portion of a cable system) and only as a way to protect broadcasting (or, more accurately, the service to the public afforded by broadcasting; Carter Mountain, 1962).

Recall that the FCC had been charged with promoting the efficient use and growth of broadcasting, and note that the relevant division of the FCC was its Broadcast Bureau. Through the 1940s and 1950s, the FCC made clear that it would not deny the granting of new broadcast licenses simply on the basis that such grants would hurt the profitability of existing stations (*Federal Communication Commission v. Sanders Brothers, Radio Station*, 1940). But when it came to competition from nonbroadcasters, the FCC was not quite such a free-market advocate. Hence, when cable television appeared to pose serious competition to broadcasting, the FCC acted against it. Yielding to political pressure, the Commission backed into cable television regulation as it denied a microwave relay license to a CATV firm that planned to bring out-of-town broadcast signals into a small community that already had local TV service (see Jassem, 1972, 1973; LeDuc, 1973). The Commission's rationale was based on the competition this

CATV presence would give the local television station. And the burden of proof necessary to halt this competition was clearly lower than the burden would have been had the competition come from another broadcaster. The unknown competitor, the threat that seemed to fall under nobody's jurisdiction, was more feared than the known threat of potential new broadcasters. This new threat also lacked powerful advocates within and around the regulatory system. The FCC's Broadcast Bureau moved to keep at bay the competing technology that it knew little about, which posed a confusing threat to its jurisdiction, and which had no powerful allies.

In the mid-1960s, the FCC finally asserted its authority to directly regulate cable television. In justifying its decision to regulate and *restrict* cable television, the FCC noted

> we have decided that a serious question is presented whether CATV operations in the major markets may be of such a nature or significance as to have an adverse economic impact upon the establishment or maintenance of UHF stations or to require these stations to face substantial competition of a patently unfair nature. (FCC, 1966, par. 139)

Through its 1965 and 1966 rulings, and various other proposed and "interim" rules through the remainder of the 1960s, the FCC very much restricted cable television's ability to develop, all in the name of protecting the broadcast system that was of such value to the viewing public. This anti-cable regulatory attitude changed in the early 1970s as a result of a coalescence of new political forces (the new Nixon administration), more effective and powerful lobbying by the growing cable television industry, stronger and more positive public discussion of the communication revolution that cable television would afford the public, and the resultant public/political pressure to let cable grow (Jassem, 1972). During this modern period of cable television, the FCC was restructured to include a Cable Services Bureau that "develops, recommends and administers policies and programs with respect to the regulation of services, facilities, rates, and practices of cable television systems and with respect to the creation of competition to cable systems" (47 Code of Federal Regulations § 0.101).

IS IT A NEWSPAPER OR A BROADCASTER?
ASKING LIMITING QUESTIONS

Ironically, although there have been a host of cable television laws and regulations codified in the 1970s, 1980s, and 1990s, the regulatory status of cable television is still not entirely clear. Many regulations have been voided by the courts because these courts applied a *newspaper* model of First Amendment Rights to cable. Other courts have applied a *broadcast* First Amendment analysis to cable. The result has been a confusing backward-focused judicial and regulatory history for cable. As Wirth and Cobb-Reiley (1987) pointed out, "A major problem with both models . . . is the automatic conclusion that newspaper or broadcast standards apply to cable without recognizing ways cable is different from both of those media" (p. 399). That is the problem and limitation of these sort of models and structures, whether those models and structures are organizing the institutions or individual's thoughts. They shape one's thinking to fit the past. They also suggest a higher degree of orderliness than is necessarily the case.

Language itself may be one of the most important modeling systems. Old established words carry with them old baggage. The *newspaper* model and the *broadcast* model are good examples. They suggest what they are by their history. They are functional because of the stability of the meanings associated with them. Certainly they must be flexible to incorporate incremental change. After all, the newspaper of today is significantly different than the newspaper of a few hundred years ago, and the television broadcast station today operates differently than its predecessor of 40 years ago. Those differences, despite reliance on computers, digital storage, stereo sound, color, and so on are not paradigm breaking. Newspapers continue to print recent news and other information and primarily distribute that information on paper, financed primarily by advertisers. Broadcasters continue to send their signals out via the electromagnetic spectrum (even though most U.S. citizens may actually receive them through cable television) and offer advertiser-supported fare. In regulatory terms, the state clings to the rules that have been "settled" with respect to these concepts. Every now and then, with seemingly increasing frequency, changes are introduced, and the question arises whether this is a significant sea-change, paradigm shift, unaccounted for category, or whether this is simply some incremental change in the old. Cable television, as is often the case, provides some really good examples. If one has a powerful and high television antenna and brings in distant television stations through it that were not intended for reception in that area, it is nothing more than that. If that same antenna is shared with several apartments in the same building, there is no change in the status either. Share it with the next door neighbor and that too generally would not constitute news. But share it with the neighbor across the street, and suddenly this is part of the new medium, "cable television." And the "cable television" designation suddenly means a host of different regulatory obligations and frameworks will apply. Similarly, what happens to the regulatory framework that applies to newspapers when those publications "publish" by making their stories available to readers who call them up using computer networks? What rules and principles apply to broadcasters who make their programming available to those on the Internet?

Not all media developments are revolutionary, but some promise to be. Tom Streeter (1987) makes the case that cable television was given special regulatory treatment precisely because the talk surrounding it maintained that this was a major new medium that was going to have monumental impact on society. Streeter notes that when the words changed from *CATV* to *cable*, the concept changed "from a description of the activity in question as a service to a description of the same activity as a technology" (p. 172). He further notes that the *technological revolution in communication* was a discussion that caught on, that with it came the notion of massive imminent utopian changes. The grand categorization of the new cable television made treating it as something new, autonomous, and not subject to existing paradigms seem both appropriate and legitimate:

> The talk treated cable as an autonomous technology and consequently obscured political and economic conditions while exaggerating cable's uniqueness; these characteristics encouraged the re-conceptualization of cable in the policy arena in a way that . . . led to the re-regulation of cable and its subsequent growth. . . . The discourse's general theme of technological revolution, of major change caused by technology, contained within it several interrelated sub-themes. (pp. 174, 178)

These subthemes included the notion that cable was a new and autonomous technology, that it was an independent economic and social force, that it could solve society's problems and could revitalize democracy. New corporate interests, combined with political forces who were not thrilled with broadcasters and political progressives who envisioned electronic democracy, joined forces to push for a new definition (and hence regulatory status) of cable. These revolutionary concepts found support in the ensuing regulations. The FCC's 1972 cable rules required cable operations to have a multitude of channels, access channels, two-way communication capabilities, local franchise review, and so on. These requirements reflected a new philosophy for media regulation. This new medium was being shaped by the regulators to be more democratic than broadcasting had been. Regardless of whether this was a political compromise designed to get the requisite political support for modern cable television emergence, the result was a new direction in media regulation. The government would push toward the television of abundance. Micro localism in program sources, content, and even operation and oversight would be fomented. Small communities would be served and would have more outlets through which they could themselves be heard. Much oversight would move from the federal government, or simply the economic marketplace, to local government franchisers. This was a bold step away from the previous model of CATV regulation, and from the then-existent models of broadcast, common carrier, or newspaper regulation.

Bold steps can be tripped up, and that is precisely what happened to most of these cable television regulations. One after another they were rescinded by the courts and or abandoned by the ever-changing FCC. They did not, after all, fit the broader models of media regulation. The resultant cable regulations reinforce the stability of all the affected media as well as the private ownership notion of media. They effectively reduce local ownership/ programming/oversight, while giving voice to the concept that program diversity is a public good that will be achieved by the marketplace, particularly now that regulatory hurdles to nontraditional television have been lowered. To date, the emerging significant competition is shaping up to be competition and participation of vertically and horizontally giant conglomerates. Program producers and cable channels are increasingly co-owned. The major threat of competition to cable operators seems to be from the giant telephone companies, not from local organizations. This is a consequence of the economics of the industry and the judicial system's insistence on the application of newspaper-like models of regulatory philosophy to cable. That model, of course, would permit few regulatory restrictions.

THE TELEPHONE HANG-UP

In the ongoing battle to simultaneously deregulate and structure what used to be known as the telephone industry, the courts, regulators, and Congress have constantly changed the rules. When he was Policy Advisor to the Assistant Secretary of the Commerce Department's National Telecommunications and Information Administration, Kenneth Robinson (1982) wrote that "experience in the telecommunications field generally demonstrates that neat regulatory or judicial boundaries are quite hard to sustain over time, given the field's technological and commercial dynamics" (p. 105). The focus of his discussion was on the attempts to regulate AT&T out of the information business. Such motivations led to strange Solomon-like rulings. It may be quite legal, for example, for the phone company to provide subscribers with phone books and voice-based directory assistance. Yet that very same phone company might be summarily prohibited from delivering that very same information over the very same phone connection if it is delivered as computer text instead of voice. In later years, as the "telephone industry" could carry more information over its facilities, and as its ownership structure changed, the regulators had an increasingly difficult time differentiating this industry from the "cable television" industry. As phone companies begin to deliver television programs to homes, and as cable companies begin to provide telephone service, the distinctions are less clear for the public and other constituents as well.

Reasonably, one might ask why drawing the line or making the distinction between the cable television industry and the telephone industry is an issue. It is an issue because what was once clear is no longer. These once-distinct media with different regulatory guidelines and philosophies are losing their distinctions. Cable and telephone have been regulated completely differently, so what happens when it is not clear whether an entity is more like one than the other? What happens to the justifications for different regulatory models when what is being regulated looks so similar? This trend toward convergence of channels and functions is forecasted to accelerate. Information, education, entertainment, communication are increasingly processed and stored in similar digital formats and are transported intermingled with each other over the same media. Furthermore, firms that were once safely ensconced in one distinct arm of the business are now integrated. Finally, the very nature of each form of mediated communication is taking on expanded attributes, including attributes that formally described other forms of communication. The computer serves as a television set, an answering machine, a point-to-point audio/video/text communication "telephone" via phone lines, cable lines, and either through the telephone switching system, cable television systems, private networks, the Internet, and so on. It is not like the "old days" when audio point-to-point telecommunications meant using the telephone system because that was the only technological option. Not only are the old distinctions blurred, but with that blurring is the blurring of appropriate regulatory models.

THE REGULATORY SYSTEM'S VALUES

The regulatory system's response to this convergence is indicative of its response to new media. Clearly, there has been pressure to reign in change. That, of course, is part of the very nature of regulation in the first place. Yet, it must be said that there have been times when the regulatory system has encouraged (and attempted to direct) this change and convergence. Armstrong invents FM radio, and the FCC largely stifles it and then permits its emergence in such a way as to hobble it for many years. Stereo broadcasting is developed and the FCC permits FM to operate in stereo but keeps the technology from AM radio (by fiat and by noninvolvement) more or less even today. High-definition television systems are developed and the FCC evaluates their goodness, in large part, in how well they can be backward-compatible, wishing to ensure that existing broadcasters will keep their dominant position and that consumers will be able to keep their existing television sets. The guiding principles of the regulatory response may be summarized as follows.

The old media must be protected, and their protection should shape the discussion of new media. New media are regulated ancillary to the old media. The existing media framework is protected by the regulatory process. New media, although not excluded, are regulated in such ways as to have minimal disruptive impact on existing media. The question is not simply "how best might this new medium develop?" Rather, it is more "how might this new medium fit alongside existing media?" The assumptions of private ownership, existing structure, primacy of the powerful are not challenged by the regulators, and when they are challenged by emerging media, those challenges are muted.

It would be wildly unfair to suggest that the regulators take a simple protectionist position. One look at the market shares lost by the major television and radio networks, by broadcast television generally, or by AT&T, makes it clear that the regulatory system has not simply protected the big and powerful incumbents. And the very communication landscape that looks so different than the landscape of 30 years ago suggests too that the regulators have not forbidden change. But the regulators have had the effect of slowing and shaping change, and they have tried hard, with substantial success, to see that the change has been in a context that permitted the continuation of the old alongside the new. That meant shaping the new so as to protect the old. UHF television was opened in such a way as to protect the primacy of VHF television. Color, stereo radio and TV, high-definition television, and just about every other telecommunication innovation were required to be backward-compatible. Americans could have had better color television, better radio fidelity, better high-definition television if these technologies did not have to be developed in such ways as to be seemlessly compatible with much older and dominant media technologies.

When it is not clear how to integrate the new with the old, establish barriers to entry, in the name of protecting the services the public gets from existing services. FM radio and high-definition television were stalled for a generation as the FCC considered the correct form for their introduction. Competition in the telephone industries had been slowed for decades. The Commission's forays into cable television regulation in the 1960s was simply a move to stop that industry's development. The power of inertia is related to the amount of mass an object has. The powerful media, and the vast regulatory systems, are indeed massive. Inertia is a powerful force, with primarily the weak newcomers exerting pressure to change it. They face difficult odds.

The regulatory system believes that the First Amendment should be applied differently to different technologically defined media. The courts, legislative branches, and FCC continue to hold different standards for broadcasting and for other forms of communication. This distinction harkens back to the very beginning of broadcast regulation, was most significantly upheld in 1969 by the U.S. Supreme Court in its *Red Lion* decision (*Red Lion Broadcasting v. FCC*, 1969), and continues today, even through calls for a different approach (see Wirth & Cobb-Reiley, 1987). The tenets of the distinction, that broadcasters rely on a limited public resource, the electromagnetic spectrum, have been repeatedly challenged, but the distinction continues to stand, even if in somewhat modified form.

Regulation is good for the regulated. For all the complaining done by the regulated industries, many of them would clamor for regulation if it did not exist, just as did the early radio station owners. Imagine how the existing broadcasters, cable operators, and phone companies would react if there were suddenly real deregulated open entry into their markets. There would be chaos in the affected industries. Investors would be rightly skittish about getting involved in telecommunication. The value of licenses and franchises would diminish rapidly. Pricing and service availability would be significantly affected.

The issues on the regulatory table are the old ones. When telecommunication regulation began, it was important that media be regulated in such a way as to encourage telecommunication's development nationwide. Concerns relating to the rights of information providers/program producers, consumer privacy, hidden charges, and so on were not at the forefront of the regulatory agenda. Now that telephone and broadcast services are universal, and cable television availability is approaching universality, there may well be new concerns on the minds of people who are affected by media. The regulatory system is less well designed to consider them than it is to consider the old issues on which there are precedents.

The regulatory system serves primarily as arbiter of the powerful. Important policies are forged when there is agreement among the major players. The operative assumption is generally that when the major players agree, the system need do little more than ratify that agreement. This, of course, is another instance in which the powerful are in better positions to determine policy than the emerging or non-well placed.

Basing regulation on the channel of communication is appropriate. This is the traditional approach and is supported by a lengthy history of legal precedent. Its value is also subject to serious question. How important is it to the consumer, indeed to the good of society, that a picture and voice arrives at its destination via a cable operated by what was once known as a cable company rather than via a cable operated by what was once known as a phone company or via the airwaves on one type of frequency rather than another? On its face, the reliance on delivery channels for regulatory philosophy and support does not make much sense.

Yet, it could offer some measure of hope for those who wish to increase operational and regulatory options. Distribution of a "television" signal via broadcasting is not really the functional equivalent of distributing that same signal via cable. If it were, there would not be so high a premium on the value of broadcast spectrum and licenses. And because there is, and because neither the regulators nor the economic marketplace can perfectly ensure power and rights in all the new media forums, it may well be useful to have some old models applied to parallel options. Clearly, the economic marketplace does not protect all social values. The marketplace would not ensure universal service, nor would it necessarily channel some media content to various dayparts. There is a long tradition in nonmedia regulation to regulate by tradeoffs. Builders wanting variances from zoning controls give towns more public space or road improvements in exchange for permission to build as they wish. With the near universality of media options, it should not be an onerous infringement to have different channels "zoned" or regulated differently.

"Regulation" has been a necessary evil and "Deregulation" a goal. The promise of new communication technologies and new media is for an end to scarcity and with that an end to regulation of the message producers and carriers. Some have argued that this faith in emerging media and in deregulation is not warranted, but it appears to offer a powerful organizing scheme.

Notions of the "social good" are not to be directly represented by the current scheme of regulation. Policy debates in media focus on technologically narrow issues. Issues tend to be narrowly cast. The incremental nature of the regulatory system has policymakers focused on particular challenges, crises, or incremental opportunities. Rowland (1984) aptly characterizes communication policy as a "'closed system' in which many of the most crucial issues are out of bounds" (Rowland, 1984, p. 429). Patricia Aufderheide (1987) argues that reliance on such narrowly focused tools as the antitrust laws fails "to comprehend the social objectives of telecommunications policy" (1987, p. 82).

It may be that there are no grand and broadly agreed-on social goals of telecommunications policy, that grand policy options cannot be expected to emerge from bureaucracies that are founded on discrete agendas, or that given the requirements of the First Amendment and the private ownership model of telecommunication, there is little legal room for social agendas in telecommunications policy. Perhaps it is simply that social objectives are not effectively pushed by the most powerful players or that the greater regulatory environment in which communication policy is made believes that the marketplace is the proper determinant of social good.

Structural regulation is the way to content regulation. Clearly such concerns as "fairness," "localism," "diversity of voices," "addressing issues of public concern" have taken a back seat to structural concerns. There is heavy reliance on the "marketplace" for resolution of concerns that were once debated in the regulatory system. In truth, the regulatory system was handcuffed in those deliberations by prevailing constructs of the First Amendment. These old issues may still be addressed by the regulators, but their discussion and the resultant action by regulators is going to be a consequence of the structural category to which they are applied. Essentially, the closer to the broadcast model, the greater is the content review and regulation that might be permitted.

FINAL THOUGHTS

Electronic media and telecommunication media are regulated in unremarkable fashion in the United States. For the reasons described here, changes in media development tend to be regulated in a slow, cautionary, and reactionary way. If media can develop without notice from the regulators, which means without challenging any of the regulated industries (for surely the regulated industries can be counted on to complain about new challenges), they may develop unfettered by regulation. If they require the protection of regulatory oversight, and many media rely on technological standards or access to spectrum or other utilities that only the government seems in a position to provide, then they will be regulated. And if they pose serious threats to the existing media systems, and if a case could be made that permits the system to touch them with regulation, they will be regulated. To the extent that challengers will be regulated, the system is designed to shape their development in ways that will be least disruptive of the existing regulated media system. New entrants that are commingled with existing players are in the best position to demonstrate that their success will not dramatically damage the existing system. They are also likely to design their new entry in ways that would protect the system they are already a part of anyway, regardless of regulatory response.

As we look to the future, it is worth noting that the investment we have in the existing media system is vast and widely shared. This investment comes from all sectors of the media system: equipment manufacturers, content providers, customers/ advertisers, and consumers. Even disregarding the spectrum issue, it is clear that from just a financial perspective, investment (ownership?) in the current U.S. media system is diffuse and potentially quite democratic. Ironically, by protecting the status quo, by imposing some order and some delay, by being biased against radical change, the regulatory/policy system may have been providing precisely the stability the media need in order to grow.

As we look to the future, a stable or even growing media presence should not be looked on as the ultimate goal and standard against which policy initiatives should be evaluated. Such protective growth (protective of preexisting media interests and structures) seems to have become the operating regulatory philosophy. It needs to change.

The future should bring a system, including a regulatory one, that is loyal not to technological legacies, which are obsolete, but to philosophical ones, which are not. The notion of a privately owned media system that has some broad public interest requirement is right because it is good. Such a framework had traditionally been limited to broadcast media (or media that were tangential to the broadcast media), with government involvement justified by the spectrum scarcity/government allocation rationale. As new media were introduced with the promise of providing abundance and making spectrum scarcity less of an issue, the "public interest" notion that was so closely tied to spectrum scarcity eroded. That the public interest philosophy was so closely tied to technology was and is a mistake. It is time to consider breaking from that old mold.

As we consider the best system of new media, it is important to recall that although the spectrum scarcity notion served as a justification for a philosophy of government oversight and regulation, it was never the cause for a "public interest" philosophy of regulation. Media operating in the public interest and with social responsibility are values that are more closely associated with a belief in democracy and informed electorates than they are with technologically based limitations. Conceivably, the government could have kept out of media regulation entirely or regulated it by auctioning off the right to use spectrum, without ever having tried to protect the public interest.

The U.S. Supreme Court was right in *Red Lion* when it recognized that the First Amendment protects the audience as well as the message producers, and that protection of the audience must be its primary focus. Significantly, that protection is not protection from strong language, but the opposite. It is protection from bland, unthinking, nonrobust, one-sided communication. It makes no sense to give the press and media special legal status unless they are serving a good that is more important than their own private interests.

The new media environment should look to the successes and strengths of the existing system and encourage development in ways that build on those strengths while being loyal to democratic ideals. The strengths of the existing system include very broadly distributed communication equipment. Nearly every household in the United States is connected to the telephone system, has radio and television receivers, and is within reach of free broadcast signals. Most households already receive cable television, and it (like direct broadcast satellite television) is available to nearly all U.S. households. Similarly, there exists a huge amount of information processing equipment and skilled technicians throughout the nation. From the huge entertainment/information conglomerates (such as Time Warner) to the local broadcast stations and newspapers, to the individuals with personal computers and video cameras, the means of message reception and production are widely distributed. Nearly all of this was accomplished with private financing. It makes sense, then, that these existing investments (both financial and resource) be protected and honored. But they must not be honored in and of themselves. Their value is in their relevance to a democracy made strong by its members' ability to produce and share in a robust dialogue and world of information. The best fundamental shift that can happen in media regulation is the ascendance of the democratic public interest standard to the level of concern that has been traditionally afforded to issues of technological interference. Critics may worry that such a broad paradigm will bring government interference with the marketplace of ideas. Correctly applied, it will enhance, rather than constrain, the marketplace available to consumers, and it will enable more, rather than fewer, voices in the marketplace.

This, then, is no more than a call for a return to a core principle of media regulation: Enhance democracy by fostering a widely available media system of many voices and regulate in such ways necessary to best protect the public interest.

REFERENCES

Aufderheide, P. (1987). Universal service: Telephone policy in the public interest. *Journal of Communication, 37*(1), 81.

Braybrooke, D., & Lindblom, C. E. (1963). *A strategy of decision: Policy evaluation as a social process.* New York: The Free Press.

Carter Mountain Transmission Corp., 32 FCC 459 (1962).

Committee on Interstate and Foreign Commerce. (1958). *Review of allocations problems of TV service to small communities, Hearings pursuant to S. Res. 224 and S. 376, Part 6.* U.S. Congress, Senate, 85th Congress, 2nd sess.

Communications Act. (1934). PL 416, 73d. Cong.

Federal Communications Commission (FCC). (1959). First Report and Order, 26 FCC 428.

Federal Communications Commission (FCC). (1965). First Report and Order, Docket Nos. 14895, 15233, 38 FCC 683.

Federal Communications Commission (FCC). (1966). Second Report and Order, Docket No. 14895, 2 FCC 2d 750.

Federal Communications Commission v. Sanders Brothers Radio Station, 309 U.S. 470, 84 L.Ed. 896 (1940).

47 Code of Federal Regulations. 101.

Jassem, H.C. (1972). *The selling of the compromise—1971—or—cable television goes to the city.* Unpublished Master's thesis, Ohio State University, Columbus, OH.

Jassem, H.C. (1973). The selling of the cable TV compromise. *Journal of Broadcasting, 17*(4), 427.

Kahn, F. J. (Ed.). (1978). *Documents of American broadcasting* (3rd ed.). Englewood Cliffs, NJ: Prentice-Hall.

Kim, H. (1992, Spring). Theorizing deregulation: An exploration of the utility of the "broadcast policy-making system" model. *Journal of Broadcasting and Electronic Media,* p. 153.

Krasnow, E. G., & Longley, L.D. (1973). *The politics of broadcast regulation.* New York: St. Martin's Press.

Krasnow, E. G., Longley, L.D., & Terry, H. A. (1982). *The politics of broadcast regulation* (3rd ed.). New York: St. Martin's Press.

LeDuc, D. R. (1973). *Cable television and the FCC.* Philadelphia: Temple University Press.

Radio Act. (1912). PL 264, 62d Cong.

Radio Act. (1927). PL 632, 69th Cong.

Red Lion Broadcasting Co., Inc. et al. v. Federal Communications Commission et al. 395 U.S. 367 (1969).

Robinson, K. (1982). Public information and "electronic publishing" services. *Journal of Communication, 32*(4), 103-113.

Rowland, W. D., Jr. (1984). Deconstructing American communications policy literature. *Critical Studies in Mass Communication, 1*(4), 423.

Streeter, T. (1987). The cable fable revisited: Discourse, policy, and the making of cable television. *Critical Studies in Mass Communication, 4*, 174-200.

35 Ops. Att'y Gen 126 (1926, July 8). In F. J. Kahn (Ed.). (1978). *Documents of American broadcasting* (3rd ed.). Englewood Cliffs, NJ: Prentice-Hall.

US v. Zenith Radio Corporation et al., 12 F.2d 614 (ND III). (1926).

Wirth, M. O., & Cobb-Reiley, L. (1987). A first amendment critique of the 1984 Cable Act. *Journal of Broadcasting and Electronic Media, 31*(4), 391.

3

FRONTIERS AND LEGAL LANDSCAPES: AS SAFETY VALVES OPEN AND CLOSE

SUSAN MALLON ROSS

Susan Mallon Ross explores the metaphor of the "frontier" being applied to the uncharted realm of cyberspace. By exploring the lessons of history taken from the exploration of the frontier in U.S. history, she provides a basis for comparison between the physical frontier and the electronic "frontier" of cyberspace. The lessons available from legislative and judicial action taken during the formative period of U.S. territorial expansion are suggested as meaningful to present times in charting new territories in cyberspace.

> Those who cannot remember the past are condemned to repeat it.
> —George Santayana, *Life of Reason* (1905/1952, p. 267)

This statement is often quoted, paraphrased, or misquoted. I first heard the quote used in a secondary school history class as an argument in favor of studying history. By understanding history ("the past"), our teacher argued, we could learn both from the mistakes and achievements of others. In the case of mistakes, we could avoid making the same ones ourselves, and in the case of achievements, we could avoid "reinventing the wheel." I remember that, at the time, it all seemed pretty negative to me. However, only now am I actively working to put a positive spin on it.

For those who do recollect ("remember") the past and its lessons, conscious participation in shaping the future is possible. Those of us who would welcome such an opportunity should not expect to avoid challenges, however, just because we are aware that others faced similar challenges before we came along. At best, we have the advantage of foresight. We who recollect the past, reviewing and making sense out of the experiences of those who have preceded us, may choose to build on those experiences or seek radically different ones for ourselves. Our forethought empowers conscious choice rather than passive condemnation. We may still err or be inefficient in our endeavors, but—if we have used our memories well—we can consciously choose a position on a continuum anchored, on one pole, by acceptance of discipline and on the other by insistence on autonomy. We can proceed with guidance—and accept with it dependence—or we can assume full responsibility (and risk)—and insist on self-determination.

In the morning of the "Cyberspace Age," we have witnessed several moments of choice concerning how free from legislative constraint will be the distribution of information through telecomputing networks in the 21st century. As we approach such moments of choice, recollection of the past can be one useful tool. In search of a template and aware of the persistent use of a frontier metaphor in attempts to explain the nascent age, I recalled Frederick Jackson Turner's (1893/1963) work *The Significance of the Frontier in American History* (commonly known as the "Turner Thesis" or the "Frontier Thesis" and cited as the *Thesis* occasionally in this chapter). Review of Turner's thesis led me to draw connections between some of Turner's ideas concerning the Western frontier that closed a century ago and ideas that others (e.g., Mitchell Kapor, Bruce Sterling, and Michael Benedikt) have been expressing about the so-called electronic (or cyberspace) frontier.

Consequently, using the "Turner Thesis" as a template, this chapter: (a) compares selected cultural phenomena Turner discerned along the western frontier with analogous aspects of the so-called cyberspace frontier, and (b) compares aspects of our times with the years that surrounded Turner's pronouncement of his thesis, the turbulent economic period from 1892-1894. In these explorations, I take a metahistorical as well as a historical perspective, analyzing how others are using history to create a vision of our future and looking closely at historical data available to them (whether they've used it or not) to help us decide whether to accept and build on their work or to resist and envision alternatives.

CYBERSPACE: ORIGIN AND DEFINITIONS

The term *cyberspace* is believed to have been coined by science fiction writer William Gibson in his 1984 novel, *Neuromancer*. In recent years, the term has been defined in a variety of ways (for a diverse and intriguing array of definitions, see Benedikt, 1992, pp. 1-3). One of the best known definitions of *cyberspace* is one used by Harvard Law Professor Laurence Tribe in the keynote address of The First Conference on Computers, Freedom, and Privacy in 1991:

> A place without physical walls or even physical dimensions—where ordinary telephone conversations "happen," where voice mail and e-mail messages are stored and sent back and forth, and where computer-generated graphics are transmitted and transformed, all in the form of interactions, some real-time and some delayed, among countless users, and between users and the computer itself . . . encompass[ing] the full array of audio and/or video interactions that are already widely dispersed in modern society from . . . the ordinary telephone . . . to computer bulletin boards and networks.

The date of the coining of the term and both the date and content Tribe's definition suggest that cyberspace is a "new" phenomenon. However, another explanation is offered in the book, *Hacker Crackdown: Law and Disorder on the Electronic Frontier* (Sterling, 1992):

> Cyberspace is the "place" where a telephone conversation appears to occur. Not inside your actual phone . . . not inside the other person's phone, in some other city. *The place between* the phones. The indefinite place *out there*, where the two of you, two human beings, actually meet and communicate. (p. xii; emphasis in original)

According to Sterling's definition, cyberspace was opened on March 10, 1876, when speech teacher-inventor Alexander Graham Bell called his assistant, Mr. Watson, for help and was heard—over Bell's experimental audio-telegraph" (Sterling, 1992, p. 5). From this perspective, "people have worked on this 'frontier' for generations" (p. xii).

Why, then, do those of us who use the term often associate it more with computers than telephones? Sterling elucidates vividly:

> In the past twenty years, this electrical "space" which was once thin and dark and one dimensional . . . has flung itself open. . . .. Light has flooded upon it, the eerie light of the glowing computer screen. This dark netherworld has become a vast flowering electronic

landscape. Since the 1960s, the world of the telephone has crossbred itself with computers and television, and though there is still no substance to cyberspace—nothing you can handle—it has a strange kind of physicality now. (p. xii)

But is this utilization of cyberspace for communication as significant, say, as the utilization of iron for tools? Does it promise to define an age in history? I believe so. I concur with the following assessment by Ithiel de Sola Pool (1991):

The future of communications will be radically different from its past. . . . If media become "demassified" to serve individual wants, it will not be by throwing upon lazy readers the arduous task of searching vast information bases, but by programming computers heuristically to give particular readers more of what they chose last time. Computer-aided instructional programs similarly assess students' past performance before providing the instruction they need. The lines between publication and conversation vanish in the sort of system. Socrates' concern that writing would warp the flow of intelligence can finally be put to rest. Writing can become dialogue. (p. 337)

This vision is supported by Frederick Williams's (1992) argument that not only has communication "become the lifeblood of organizations—of government, education . . . as well as . . . business" (p. 18), it has also increasingly become "the product or service" (p. 89) that organizations produce and market. If the defining process and product of the culture is communication, and this communication centerness is enabled by cyberspace technology, it seems appropriate to label the epoch, so-defined, the Cyberspace Age.

TURNER'S "FRONTIER THESIS" AND THE CYBERSPACE FRONTIER

Frontier is defined as: (a) border between two countries; (b) part of a settled, civilized country that lies next to an unexplored or undeveloped region; (c) any new field of learning, thought, and so on (*Webster's New World Dictionary*, 1980). *Pioneer* is defined as: (a) originally, a member of a military engineering unit trained to construct or demolish bridges, roads, trenches, and so on; (b) a person who goes before, preparing the way for others, as an early settler or scientist (*Webster's New World Dictionary*, 1980). (Such a person is not merely a settler at the frontier, but a member of the *avant-garde* there.)

Although the frontier metaphor is used frequently (e.g., in the very name of the Electronic Frontier Foundation and in the subtitle of Sterling's book), in discussing "the opening of cyberspace" (Kapor, 1992) this imagery has yet to be explored in conjunction with the landmark work of frontier historiography, Turner's *The Significance of the Frontier in American History* (1893/1963). The thesis, itself, is succinct: "The existence of an area of free land, its continuous recession and the advance of American settlement westward, explain American development" (p. 27).

Clearly, a literal interpretation is not applicable; we are exploring a metaphor. However, the persistence of the frontier metaphor in the rhetoric that attempts to explain the significance of cyberspace argues for a close reading of the text and, perhaps, reapplication of (at least some of) the ideas in Turner's essay.

At the close of his essay, first presented at the 1893 Chicago World's Fair (Columbian Exposition), Turner wrote:

> What the Mediterranean Sea was to the Greeks, breaking the bond of custom, offering new experiences, calling out new institutions and activities, that and more, the ever retreating frontier has been to the United States. . . . And now, four centuries from the discovery of America, at the end of a hundred years of life under the constitution, the frontier is gone and with its closing has closed the first period of American History. (p. 58)

As Turner states it, settlement of free western land explained an age. When the free land was gone, an age ended. When Turner made that pronouncement 100 years ago the seeds of another great U.S. age, the Cyberspace Age, had already been planted by another pioneer, Alexander Graham Bell, with his invention of the telephone.

FRONTIER AS SAFETY VALVE

Turner states, "So long as free land exists, the opportunity for a competency exists, and economic power secures political power" (p. 223). Taken in conjunction with his comparison of the frontier to the Mediterranean Sea as a catalyst for innovation in civilization, the statement quoted above articulates Turner's "safety valve" (Simonson, 1963, p. 12) concept. The Western frontier served as a safety valve because oppressed persons could go west and start over where there was both elbow room and few or no established institutional constraints. As Simonson wrote: "The availability of free land to the west supposedly allowed them to break away . . . [and] at the frontier, all men had an equal chance" (p. 12).

The problem was getting to the frontier to claim and work the free land available there. Getting outfitted for the journey west required resources; the journey itself became challenging due to encounters with, for example, extremes of weather, virulent disease, and threatened "Indians."

The "safety valve" concept invites comparison between the Western frontier and the electronic frontier. In both cases, the person considered likely to "migrate" in order to escape oppression would be a young male (Benedikt, 1992). Having used his resourcefulness to reach the frontier, that resourcefulness could be challenged and further developed because of the free land and autonomy to work the frontier offered. As the frontiersman had free access to land, having developed the necessary skills to "get there," the "hacker," as Sterling (1992) has shown in his "Chronology of the Hacker Crackdown" (pp. vii-ix), has "free" access to Cyberspace. The term *hacker* was originally a self-descriptor used by pioneers in early entry points to cyberspace such as MIT and Stanford. Such hackers were and are generally self-taught and "independent-minded but law abiding" (Sterling, 1992, p. 45).The hacker's links to the pioneer homesteader is supported etymologically. One meaning of *hack* as a verb is "to clear or make by or as if cutting away vegetation" (*Merriam-Webster's Collegiate Dictionary*, 1994, p. 521). The trail-breaking computer hacker, expert at programming and solving problems with computers and/or expert at penetrating computer system security, seems aptly portrayed by the simile. However, as Sterling also notes, using those skills not uncommonly makes hackers "by strict definition criminals" (p. 193). Indeed, in recent common usage, criminality (consistent with "strict definitions") is often presumed.[1]

Although some states, like New York, have officially "decriminalized" the term and have vowed to use descriptive language such as "thieves using computers and modems" in their communications with the press, the usage persists—and seems not actively discouraged by (at least some) flamboyant, posturing young computer users comfortable with the "cyberpunk" label and with anarchistic handles.

Looking only at the image and not the substance, Billy the Kid and the "console cowboy" (Gibson, 1984) represent a similar phenomenon. As Benedikt (1992) wrote:

> Ancient mythological themes continue to be [vital] in our advanced technological cultures. They inform not only our arts of fantasy but, in a very real way, the way we understand each other, test ourselves, and shape our lives. Myths both reflect the "human condition" and create it. . . . The segment of our population more susceptible to myths and most productive in this regard are those who are "coming of age.". . . And it is no surprise that young males with their . . . mission to master new technology are today's

computer hackers and so populate the on-line communities and newsgroups. (pp. 5-6)

This dramatic self-definition has not been without backlash. Self-styled "cyberpunks" have been compared in courts to "street punks" by lawyers and convicted by judges and juries convinced of the analogy.[2]

PERSONAL CHARACTERISTICS OF PIONEERS

As Timothy Dwight, President of Yale, saw pioneers, so probably do some members of contemporary U.S. society see the youthful members of cyberculture: "too idle, too talkative, too passionate, too prodigal, and too shiftless to acquire either property or character" (Dwight, *Travels in New-England and New-York* [1821-1822], cited in Simonson, 1963, p. 2).

Turner (1893/1963), however, saw the pioneers quite differently. Contemplating his characterization in juxtaposition with Dwight's gives us an opportunity to consider if either characterization better fit the western pioneers and if either is meaningful when applied to the cyberspace pioneers. Both characterizations "fit" some, although not all, denizens of each frontier. In Turner's view:

> The frontier is productive of individualism. Complex society is precipitated by the wilderness into a kind of primitive organization based on the family. The tendency is anti-social. It produces antipathy to control, and particularly to any direct control. The tax-gatherer is viewed as a representative of oppression. (p. 51)

Turner's list of pioneer characteristics also includes these "intellectual traits:"

> coarseness and strength . . . acuteness and inquisitiveness . . . [a] practical inventive turn of mind, quick to find expedients . . . [and] masterful grasp of material things, lacking in the artistic but powerful to affect great ends . . . dominant individualism, working for good and for evil, and . . . buoyancy and exuberance which comes with freedom. (p. 57)

In sum, Turner concluded: "frontier individualism has . . . promoted democracy" (p. 51). Are these traits also discernable among the pioneers "at" the electronic frontier—be they legitimate entrepreneurs involved in "cutting edge work with electronics" (Sterling, 1992, p. 55) or hackers involved in unauthorized computer use? Many of them seem to be. In particular, the following traits seem characteristic of at least some denizens of the electronic, cyberspace frontier: individualism, antisocial (or antibureaucratic) tendencies, experienced freedom, and "the determination to make access to computers as free and open as possible" (Sterling, 1992, p. 53).

Is the impetus toward democracy, "rule by the ruled" (*Webster's New World Dictionary*, 1980, p. 375); anarchy, "absence of government" (*Webster's New World Dictionary*, 1980, p. 50); or something else—perhaps noted contemporary media ecologist Neil Postman's (1992) "technopoly"? "Technopoly" is envisioned as an authoritarian state in which "human life must find its meaning in machinery and techniques" (p. 52).

Back in the 1890s, Turner (1893/1963) considered the idea that it might be "absence of all elected government" (p. 222) rather than "democracy" that the frontier promoted. He observed: "the democracy born of free land, strong in selfishness and individualism, intolerant of administrative experience and education, and pressing individual liberty beyond its proper bounds, has its dangers as well as its benefits" (p. 223).

The dangers Turner referred to include "laxity in regard to government affairs . . . from the lack of a highly developed civic spirit . . . [and] lax business honor" (pp. 52-53). These themes resonate in contemporary descriptions of cyberculture, as exemplified by the following passages from *Hacker Crackdown* (Sterling, 1992):

> Hackers of all kinds are absolutely soaked through with heroic antibureaucratic sentiment. Hackers long for recognition as a praiseworthy cultural archetype, the postmodern equivalent to the cowboy and mountain man. (p. 54)

> The outlaw, the rebel, the rugged individual, the pioneer, the sturdy Jeffersonian Yeoman, the private citizen resisting interference in . . . pursuit of happiness—these are figures that all Americans recognize and that many will strongly applaud and defend. (p. 55)

> Hackers vary in their degree of hatred for authority and the violence of their rhetoric. But, at the bottom line, they are scofflaws. (p. 62)

These descriptions suggest a safety valve again is needed. And the safely valve motif, indeed, emerges as Benedikt (1992) offers this "manifesto":

> It is proposed that the creation of Cyberspace is not only a good but necessary and even inevitable step (1) toward providing the maximum number of individuals with the means of creativity, productivity, and control over the shape of their lives within the new

information and media environment and (2) toward isolating and clarifying, by sheer contrast, the value of unmediated realities—such as the natural and built environment, and such as the human body—as the source of older truths, silence of a sort, and perhaps sanity. (pp. 121-122)

This safety valve, then, allows both productivity for the computer-oriented in the virtual realm of cyberspace and continued valuing of the preexisting natural and human-built aspects of earthly civilization. This contrasts with Postman's dystopian vision of "technopoly," which, Postman says, eliminates alternatives to itself by making them invisible, "it does so by redefining what we mean by religion, by arts, by family, by politics, by history, by truth, by privacy, by intelligence, so that our definitions fit its new requirements" (p. 48). At the time of this writing, it remains to be seen which vision seems the more accurately prophetic with respect to the developments of legal systems to meet cyberspace challenges. However, once again, it seems useful to consider the early development of cyberlaw in juxtaposition to history lessons left for us by Frederick Jackson Turner.

LOOSE CONSTRUCTION AND THE FRONTIER

Turner (1893/1963) argues: "Loose construction increased as the nation marched westward" (p. 46). Loose (or liberal) construction is an approach associated with Alexander Hamilton—who wrote to George Washington in support of the Bank Act of 1791 that the words of the Constitution "ought to be construed liberally in advancement of the public good" (Hamilton, 1904, p. 455).

Historian Clinton Rossiter (1964) said that Hamilton saw the Constitution more "as a grant of powers than a catalogue of limitations" (p. 189), the words of which needed to be "interpreted broadly, loosely, liberally" (p. 190) to convert "the Constitution . . . into a source of energy" (p. 190) to empower the nation's government to advance the public good in "unimagined circumstances" (p. 192), or what Hamilton, himself, referred to as "national exigencies" (Hamilton, 1904, p. 455).

As Hamilton (1961) wrote in *The Federalist:* "Constitutions of civil government are not to be framed upon a calculation of existing exigencies. . . . There ought to be a CAPACITY to provide for future exigencies as they may happen; and as these are illimitable in their nature, it is impossible safely to limit that capacity" (p. 207).

In the foregoing, it is important to emphasize the word *national* when interpreting Hamilton's constitutional theory, for

Hamilton was a nationalist, and it is Hamilton's expansive nationalism that intersects with Turner's assertion concerning loose construction at the frontier. Turner (1893/1963) wrote: "The legislation which most developed the powers of the National Government . . . was conditioned at the frontier" (p. 45).

Much of the allegedly nationalizing legislation was related to land and internal improvements—developments provoked by the western frontier of the 19th century that could be discussed metaphorically to elucidate developments along the electronic frontier on the cusp between the 20th and 21st centuries.

Legislation such as the Preemption Act (1841) and the Homestead Act (1862) can be seen as nationalizing, as under each of those laws, the national government, not some state or territorial government, enabled settlers to gain clear title to the land they lived on and improved. The Preemption Act, passed by the U.S. Congress in 1841, allowed western settlers (so-called "squatters") to preempt speculators' claims to public lands on which the squatters had settled. Before the Preemption act was passed, squatters who generally had cleared and made improvements to the land they had settled, were often forced to forfeit it to others who bought the land at public auction. The Act gave squatters exclusive rights to purchase 160 acres for as little as $1.25 per acre.

The Homestead Act was passed by the U.S. Congress in 1862 and, for the most part, superseded the Preemption Act. The Homestead Act granted 160 acres of public land in the west as a homestead to "any person who is the head of a family, or who has arrived at the age of twenty-one years, and is a citizen of the United States, or who shall have filed his declaration of intention to become such." To receive clear title, the homesteader had to pay a small filing fee, live on the land for 5 years, and make certain improvements.

The Preemption Act was supposed to mark an end to the policy of land auctions that gave speculators advantage over squatter homesteaders in competition for land—to privilege sweat equity over ready cash. However, preemptioners had to pay a fee to the government for their land prior to the still-existent land auctions, and even that relatively low amount (as low as $1.25 per acre) was beyond the means of many. Speculators, however, had the financial resources to pay at auction for the best lands—lands identified for them by paid agents (Stephenson, 1917/1964, p. 98). Notably, the Preemption Act was repealed by Congress in 1891—just two years before Turner presented his paper for the 1893 meeting in Chicago.

The Homestead Act, too, provided for settlers to gain clear title to land, up to 160 acres of land they improved and lived on for five years. However, that law was criticized because it allegedly contained no safeguards against speculation and because its benefit could be undermined by federal land grant policies (under, e.g., the Morrill Act of 1862; Julian, 1883).

Railroads also received land grants during this time—often supported by settlers who, having obtained title to land, saw railroads as avenues to better markets and increased land values (Stephenson, 1917/1967). And as the perceived need for rail transportation and the profitability of railroads grew, the agrarian vision was no longer the only American Dream, the industrial vision was also coming into focus.

Focusing on such legislation as the Preemption Act and the Homestead Act, we reflect on nationalizing tendencies when the frontier was still there and on Turner's thesis as a treatise on the existence of an ever-receding western frontier. Another way to look at Turner's thesis, however, is to look at conditions in the year Turner delivered his thesis and the years just before and after that year to reflect on legal issues that arose as soon as the frontier was gone. If, as Turner (1893/1963) wrote, "with its going has closed the first period of American history," with its going the second period of American history opened—the Industrial Age.

Turner delivered his paper in 1893 before the American Historical Association, which had convened its meeting in Chicago during the World Columbian Exposition. The exposition marking the 400th anniversary of Columbus's journey was held in Chicago according to at least one report (Trager, 1992) so that Chicago could show the world how far it had come since the 1871 Chicago Fire. It should be also noted, however, that Haymarket Square in Chicago had been the site of riots and bombing less than 10 years before the exposition. But 1893 is not notable only for the exposition with its white columnar architecture that became the only acceptable public style in the United States for 40 years thereafter (van Zanten, 1992), but also for a financial panic that had, arguably, been foreshadowed by events such as the repeal of the Preemption Act in 1891 and the bloody Homestead strike of 1892. The panic continued for the next two years and was marked, in 1894, by events such as the march of Coxey's army in protest of the unemployment that was resulting from the panic and by the Pullman Palace Car Company strike and boycott that occurred when the company reduced wages but not the rents charged to employees who lived in the company town of Pullman, IL.

These were times in which the nation needed a safety valve, as Turner claimed the frontier had been, or a safety net, such as New Deal policies provided some 40 years later. But it had neither. What the nation had was unforeseen "national exigencies" affecting the "public good" that Hamilton as the Federalist had predicted would occur—exigencies that he thought would need a strong national government willing liberally to construe the constitution.

Frontier conditions, in Turner's phrase, "called out" legal developments such as "internal improvement and railroad legislation" as well as "the disposition of the public lands" (Turner, 1893/1963, p. 46). But acts such as the Sherman Anti-Trust Act, purportedly drafted to protect the public against monopolies, soon began to be used to protect capitalist industry from the labor movement. Conditions that emerged as the frontier was declared closed called out the use of the Sherman Anti-Trust Act, Interstate Commerce Act, conspiracy charges, and even vagrancy and trespass laws to justify the Pullman boycott injunction and legal sanctions against figures such as leaders of the Homestead Strike, General Jacob S. Coxey, and Eugene V. Debs.[3] Whatever else these legal sanctions may have represented, they all represented what Turner had called "loose construction" of the Constitution—more specifically, for example, Article 1 Section 8 that empowers the federal government to regulate interstate commerce and First Amendment free speech rights. Of course, Hamilton himself opposed the addition of a Bill of Rights to the Constitution. However, only a few years after the ratification of the first 10 amendments, Hamilton's party, the Federalists, liberally construed the First Amendment and enacted Alien and Sedition Laws, which they thought necessary for a nation facing an almost inevitable war with France. As limitations on freedom of speech came out of that perceived crisis, suppression of speech also resulted from the crises of the 1890s that were perceived to be serious threats to economic and even governmental stability—in the wake of bloody incidents such as the Haymarket Square riots and bombing in 1886.

Without a safety valve (e.g., free or cheap land) and without a safety net (e.g., social security), this was a time of crisis for our nation in the early years of its Industrial Age—a time of transition that provides a useful template with which to compare our own times in the early years of the Cyberspace Age. Among the historical lessons of that era is this: Freedom makes fortunes until greed makes need.

As the 1980s drew to a close, the frontier years seemed history for cyberspace. Companies in Silicon Valley "downsized." There was concentration of capital in large software companies, putting smaller entrepreneurial ventures out of business. There was frustration among a new generation of hackers—creative and skilled but apparently without rewarding outlets for their creativity. As groups of discontents such as Coxey's army had been demonized as anarchists, socialists, criminals (McMurray, 1929/1968) and spreaders of disease, or dismissed as vagrants or tramps (or hobos), these hackers, especially when they were associated under labels such as "the legion of doom," were demonized as pirates and terrorists (see also cases documented in Ross, 1994, and in archived back issues of Computer Underground Digest). Although some of those in each collective may to some extent have deserved some of those labels, in both instances people outside the collectives, fearing what they did not understand, made "interpretations to which they were predisposed" (McMurray, 1929/1968, p. 263; referring to characterizations of Coxey's Army). Meanwhile, technology had been developed to breathe new life into the computer industry, but the widespread production of those advanced computer chips and multimedia hardware and software awaited a "killer application"[3] that would make their mass production worthwhile.

As industry waited, a series of young hackers got into legal trouble in a time when those who were making, interpreting, administering, and enforcing the law tended to lack the telecomputing literacy fully to understand the actions (or motives) of the hackers. Thus, the so-called "Hacker Crackdown" (Sterling, 1992) occurred in 1990, and a legal case "called out" by that crackdown, the Steve Jackson Games case, brought to the attention of cyberculture both the extent of governmental mistrust of hackers and the degree of computer illiteracy among those acting in our government's name. The Steve Jackson games case involved a raid by the Secret Service on a small game company in Texas in which agents seized computers and software storing e-mail, company records, and the incomplete manuscripts of several books. Pursuant to the raid, Steve Jackson and others filed and won a federal lawsuit. Specifically, the judge hearing the case ruled that the raid had violated both the Privacy Protection Act and the Electronic Communication Privacy Act. During the trial the judge rebuked the Secret Service for its "poor investigation and abusive computer seizure policies" (Abernathy, 1993) and in his decision called for "better education [of agents], investigation, and strict compliance of the statutes as written" (Sparks, 1993) unless or until Congress amended or rewrote the statutes. Sparks' voice was a voice for strict, not liberal, construction.

Other cases arose after the crackdown of 1990. For example, a BBS operator got in trouble placing bomb-making information also available in books available for downloading over the Internet (see Ross, 1994), and a student at a renowned technological university was charged with conspiracy to commit wire fraud for allegedly allowing the "the pirating of business and entertainment software" (The Tech, p. 1).

Then came the advent of the World-Wide Web, arguably the "killer application" for which industry had been waiting. And for a brief time of exhilaration it appeared that there was again a frontier with opportunities for the technologically elite or the merely computer literate that followed them into cyberspace, and, consequently, a safety valve for society. The claims staked to virtual space via the Web are even called home pages, perpetuating agrarian imagery.

Even as we spoke of democracy (see Kapor, 1993) and community (see Doheny-Farina, 1996), however, some of the dynamics surrounding industrial crises of the 1890s again began to become salient in society, among them mistrust of global movements by conservative, U.S. interests and defensive action by financially successful cyberspace pioneers who seemed to fear that a new wave of entrepreneurs would encroach on the expansive claims they had staked in cyberspace.

In this milieu developed the landmark Telecommunications Act. As characterized by a *New York Times* editorial in 1996 ("Fixing communications law," 1996)—soon after President Clinton signed it into law: "The main thrust of the law is to eliminate barriers that have prevented regional phone companies, long-distance carriers and cable and utility companies from competing with one another" (p. A28). The act also contains another provision, however, the Communications Decency Act (CDA). The CDA makes it a crime to transmit over public computer networks material "that, in context, depicts or describes in terms patently offensive as measured by contemporary community standards, sexual or excretory activities or organs" or to send "indecent material" to a minor (p. A28).

After long debate and many versions, the Communications Decency Act was passed by both houses of Congress by wide margins—415-16 in the House; 91-5 in the Senate—just one year to date after Senator Exon of Nebraska originally introduced the proposal. To supporters, the CDA is necessary to enable parents to prevent material contemporary community standards deemed inappropriate for children from being "piped right through to the house" (Coppolino, 1996, quoted in Mangan, 1996). To opponents, the CDA is a dangerously vague and overly broad infringement on the First Amendment.[4]

It often takes a dramatic current controversy such as this to provoke us to look for instructive templates in our past. In the context of U.S. history, the passage of the CDA appears comparable to other xenophobic reactions such as the Salem witch hunts and McCarthyism and saliently like the suppression of the collective action of unions and industrial armies in the period surrounding the announced closing of the western frontier. In each case, fear of the stranger has drawn legal systems into suppressive activities. Lacking a safety valve—somewhere else for the feared stranger to go, live, and let live—we construct a safety net either beneath the stranger or between the established community and the feared stranger. Sometimes the net takes the form of laws, other times prison bars. Some of these laws are intended to benefit the stranger (such as social security legislation); others, however, such as the CDA, simply limit the feared stranger's expressive freedom.

In his opinion on the constitutionality of the CDA in *ACLU v. Reno*, Judge Ronald L. Buckwalder emphasized that imprecise definitions in the CDA were especially problematic in light of the newness of the Internet. The "enforcer of statutes," he wrote, "must be guided by clear and precise standards. In statutes that break into relatively new areas, such as this one, the need for definition of terms is greater because even commonly stood terms may have different connotations or parameters in this newer context" (quoted in DeLoughry & Young, 1996, p. 19).

The words "break into relatively new areas" return us to the frontier theme of this chapter and lead us to consider an essential paradox challenging our legal system today. In the cyberspace age, are terms such as *strict* and *loose construction*, developed in the agrarian 18th century, applicable to the postindustrial 21st century? It seems, for example, that both a Supreme Court decision that the CDA is constitutional and one declaring the CDA unconstitutional would represent liberal construal (loose construction) to address the public interest in national crisis, as Hamilton intended that the court should be empowered. Were the court to uphold the constitutionality of the law, the trend toward loose construction that allowed broadcast media to be controlled "in the public interest" would be continued. However, declaring the CDA unconstitutional would also be loose construction—of a very non-Hamiltonian sort—extending the protections of the First Amendment (protection of speech and of the press; and, perhaps, protection against establishment of a state religion) to content posted to the Internet, a virtual entity, a metamedium for communicating, unanticipatable by visionaries such as Jefferson, Madison, Hamilton, and Frederick Jackson Turner.

As media are converging and traditional boundaries being deconstructed through global access to these media, what are our real constitutional options? I suggest there are at least the following:

1. Strictest construction, in which "speech," "press," and "no" mean the same today as they did when the Bill of Rights was ratified. This would allow legislation to be considered and passed, without constitutional issues coming into play for other media of communication, until or unless a constitutional amendment, such as that which Laurence Tribe suggested in 1991, were passed.

Tribe's model language for such an Amendment read like this: "This constitution's protections for the freedoms of speech, press, petition, and assembly, and its protections against unreasonable searches and seizures and the deprivation of life, liberty, or property without due process of law, shall be construed as fully applicable without regard to the technological method or medium through which information content is generated, stored, altered, transmitted or controlled."

2. Loose construction so that the provisions of the First Amendment to the Constitution of the United States of America is applied as if it read like section 2b of the Canadian Charter of Rights and Freedoms, which guarantees "freedom of thought, belief, opinion and expression, including freedom of the press and other media of communication."[5]

In the end, where would either of those options leave us in the seamless (i.e., frontier-free) World-Wide Web of global telecommunications? Specifically, where in cyberspace would the Constitution of the United States of America apply?

An anonymous Internet correspondent was quoted asking in a Canadian newspaper article in 1994: "In a borderless frontier, who sets the rules? When cultures collide via computer, who picks up the pieces?" (Cobb, 1994, p. B2).

Is "borderless frontier" necessarily an oxymoron? The second meaning of *frontier* offered earlier in this chapter (i.e., "part of a settled, civilized country which lies next to an unexplored or undeveloped region") suggests otherwise but also calls attention to legal challenges that confront the Cyberspace Age. Humanity does not have to find cyberspace; we are creating it. However, as we hypothesize about the potential value of its contribution to human civilization and develop—in random, piecemeal fashion—its architecture, we see that not one "settled, civilized country" with a single code of laws but a global village with a plethora of often conflicting legal traditions abuts cyberspace. We glimpse in nascent form a Tower of Babel that will challenge—and could undermine—the potential of the Cyberspace Age. For example, as Judge Stewart Dalzell warned in his opinion in *ACLU v. Reno*: "Any content-based regulation of the Internet, no matter how benign the purpose, could burn the global village to roast the pig" (quoted in DeLoughry & Young, 1996, p. A19).

If the safety valve provided by frontiers is really gone forever this time, will cyberlaw provide a safety net? And if it does, will that safety net look more like the restrictive CDA rather than the more expansive Tribe Amendment, or like section 2b of Canada's *Charter*? Whom or what interests will the safety net protect? The Supreme Court deliberations over the CDA, scheduled to begin in March 1997, should provide us with a glimpse of the future in that regard.

As we are in a position to interpret the outcome of those deliberations, I suggest this as a lesson of history to be gleaned from comparing and contrasting the time that gave mythic significance to the western frontier and our own, in which would-be mythmakers attempting to co-opt the frontier myth in pursuit of self-interest have begun to feel a backlash. In economic cycles of expansion and contraction, as safety values open and close, freedom makes fortunes until greed makes need.

Typically, those who are winning laud competition as an essential value until they meet competitors whose abilities threaten to undermine their already established game plan. Then, with the political power their economic power has established, they attempt hegemonic suppression of the strangers whose competition and potential influence they fear—whether the economic basis of the culture is land, capital, or information.

ENDNOTES

1. See Sterling (1992, pp. 43-152) for a more complete discussion than can be included here.
2. Detailed discussion of all these laws and legal maneuvers is beyond the scope of this chapter. In this note, however, are basic information and suggestions for further research. All sources mentioned here are included in the chapter's "References."

   The Interstate Commerce Act (1887) was a law through which the federal government exercised its constitutional right to regulate interstate commerce (Article 1 Section 8). The federal governments' right to regulate interstate commerce was used to justify actions against labor unions and their officials. The Sherman Anti-Trust Act (1890) was designed to address problems related to monopolies but was rendered ineffective by a series of Supreme Court rulings that followed its passage. Still, its provision allowing injunctions was frequently used against unions. In 1893, the United States experienced a financial panic surrounded by several years of economic depression. General Jacob Coxey lead "Coxey's Army" of the unemployed on a march on Washington in 1894 and was arrested during a protest there for walking on the lawn of the Capitol. For further information about the Pullman boycott and Debs, see Warne (1955); about the Homestead strike (and lockout), see Wolff (1965); and about Coxey's army, see McMurry (1929/1968). Another useful recent source of information about suppression of labor movements is Sachs (1996).

3. This phrase was used at a multimedia trade show in Ottawa, Ontario, Canada, in the autumn of 1991.
4. The same *New York Times* editorial ("Fixing communications law," 1996) cited earlier also argues that the law is essentially redundant because obscene materials and solicitation for sex aimed at children are already illegal.
5. In the Canadian constitution enacted in 1982, unlike the First Amendment to the U.S. constitution, which mentions only "speech" and "the press" explicitly, the expressive freedom clause of the *Charter* (section 2b) includes "other media of communication." The *Charter*, however, also includes a section (1) that allows parliament to place on fundamental freedoms granted by the charter "reasonable limits prescribed by law [that] can be demonstrably justified in a free and democratic society."

REFERENCES

Abernathy, J. (1993, January 30). Steve Jackson games/secret service trial wrap-up. *Houston Chronicle*. Reposted from *Telecom Digest, 13*(51), CuD 5.10.

Benedikt, M. (1992). *Cyberspace: First steps*. Cambridge, MA: MIT Press.

Cobb, C. (1994, March 6). Policing Internet freedom of speech and censorship collide on the information highway. *Ottawa Citizen*, p. B2.

Computer Underground Digest (*CuD*). Available by subscription by sending a one-line message: sub cu-digest to cu-digest-request@webwe.ucsd.edu.

de Sola Pool, I.(1991). Excerpted in *Taking sides: Clashing views on controversial issues in mass media in society* (J. Hansen & A. Alexander, Eds.). Guilford, CT: Dushkin.

DeLoughry, T. J., & Young, J. R. (1996, June 2). Internet restrictions ruled unconstitutional. *Chronicle of Higher Education*, pp. A17, A19-A20.

Doheny-Farina, S. (1996). *The wired neighborhood*. New Haven, CT: Yale University Press.

Fixing communications law. (1996, February 9). *New York Times*, p. A28.

Gibson, W. (1984). *Neuromancer*. New York: Ace Books.

Hamilton, A. (1904). *The works of Alexander Hamilton* (H.C. Lodge, Ed.). Constitutional Edition (12 vols.)

Hamilton, A. (1961). *In Federalist Papers* (C. Rossiter, Ed.). New York: New American Library.

Julian, G.W. (1883). Railway influence in the law office. *North American Review, CXXXVI*, 237-256.

Kapor, M. (1992). Book jacket note. *Hacker crackdown: Law and disorder on the electronic frontier* by B. Sterling. New York: Bantam.

Kapor, M. (1993, July/August). Where is the digital highway really heading? The case for a Jeffersonian information policy. *Wired*, pp. 53-59, 94.

McMurry, D. L. (1968). *Coxey's Army*. Seattle: University of Washington Press. (Original work published in 1929)

Mangan, M. (1996). *ACLU v. Reno. Final Arguments*. Posted to ifreedom@snoopy.ucis.dal.ca.

Merriam-Webster's Collegiate Dictionary. (1994). Springfield, MA: Merriam-Webster.

Postman, N. (1992). *Technopoly: The surrender of culture to technology*. New York: Knopf.

Ross, S. (1994). Electronic mail: Ethical and legal concerns in the United States and Canada. *IEEE Transactions on Professional Communication, 37*, 218-225.

Rossiter, C. (1964). *Alexander Hamilton and the Constitution*. New York: Harcourt, Brace & World.

Sachs, A. (1996). Silencing the labor movements. In C.R. Smith (Ed.), *Silencing the opposition* (pp. 123-150). Albany: State University of New York Press.

Santayana, G. (1932). From *Life of Reason*. In *Pocket Book of Quotations* (H, Davidoff, Ed.). New York: Pocket Books. (Original work published 1904)

Simonson, H. P. (1963). Introduction. In F.J. Turner (Ed.), *The significance of the frontier in American history* (pp. 1-22). New York: Frederick Ungar.

Sparks, S. (1993, March 27). Steve Jackson Games Incorporated vs. United States Secret Service, No. A91CA346SS (1993), Decision by Judge Sam Sparks (W.D. Texas. March 12). *CuD, 5.22*.

Sterling, B. (1992). *Hacker crackdown: Law and disorder on the electronic frontier*. New York: Bantam.

Stephenson, G. M. (1967). *The political history of the public lands from 1840-1862*. New York: Russell & Russell. (Original work published 1917)

The Tech. (1994, April 8). pp. 1, 13.

Trager, J. (1992). *The people's chronology*. New York: Henry Holt and Company.

Tribe, L. (1991). *The Constitution in cyberspace*. Keynote Address at the First Conference on Computers, Freedom and Privacy, San Francisco.

Turner, F. J. (1963). *The significance of the frontier in American history*. New York: Frederick Ungar. (Original work published 1893)

Van Zanten, A. (1992). World's Columbian exposition of 1893. In *Software toolworks multimedia encyclopedia*. Novato, CA: Software Toolworks Grolier.

Warne, C. E. (1955). *The Pullman Boycott of 1894. The problem of federal intervention.* Boston: D. C. Heath.

Webster's New World Dictionary (D. B. Guralnik, Ed.). (1980). New York: Prentice-Hall.

Williams, F. (1992). *The new communications.* Belmont, CA: Wadsworth.

Wolff, L. (1965). *Lockout. The story of the homestead strike of 1892.* New York: Harper & Row.

4

FREEDOM AND LIABILITY IN CYBERSPACE: MEDIA, METAPHORS, AND PATHS OF REGULATION*

SUSAN J. DRUCKER AND GARY GUMPERT

Each new medium challenges the existing regulatory structure that attempts to keep pace with technological growth. Developments in "cyberspace" result in legal issues that have been handled through the application of preexisting legal doctrines, the application of which has been justified through metaphors. The authors examine the existing metaphors being used and focus on the free speech and privacy implications of developing a distinct area of "cyberlaw." The legal metaphors, which can emerge from the spatial (i.e., real property) terms being used to describe computer-mediated communication, are explored.

We have walked or keyboarded ourselves into a critical and formative period for the new communication frontier of cyberspace, a period of growth in both the phenomenon and the regulatory schema

*Reprinted with permission from the *Free Speech Yearbook*. Copyright 1996 by The Speech Communication Association.

governing it. The one constant discovered when exploring the evolution of the media law is that technologies develop more rapidly than can new legal approaches. This fact is being faced by courts attempting to grapple with the liability and free expression implications of the technological developments that are producing the emerging principles of "cyberlaw" (Stuckey, 1994).

The relationship of outside to inside, public to private, has been transformed by our mediated capability. Relationships are neither delineated by the circumstances of place or the conditions of time. The circumstance of communication requires description if one is to understand the context of relationship and interaction. Thus communication is a functional phenomenon requiring qualitative description and assessment. Currently, communication may or may not be interactional, one way, face to face, oral, written, permanent, impermanent, electronic, nonelectronic, human, nonhuman, monosensory or multisensory, public, private, semi-public, functioning in real or delayed time.

Communication laws are found in a web of regulatory, statutory, and judicial statements aimed at human interaction and information dissemination that have been face to face or facilitated via telecommunication or mass media technologies. Yet laws designed primarily to regulate noncommunicative activities may function to promote or limit communication. The law of property and land use is one such area of regulation. Land use regulations are also particularly interesting with regard to not only physical space but to the electronic realm as well as the nomenclature of space, urban planning, and architecture have been transformed into metaphors of cyberspace. Thus, users are linked to bulletin boards, malls, rooms through ports, highways, exits, gateways, bridges, routers. The vocabulary surrounding new technologies, new uses for old technologies, and the joiner of multiple media is significant as it not only allows us to talk about a phenomenon but shapes the perception of the reality being named. In fact the words created and metaphors employed function persuasively. Kenneth Burke (1965) has argued that "naming" is an interpretive act" that functions as a guide to action toward that which is named. Thus "the command that one act one way rather than another is 'implicit' in the name" (Blankenship, 1980, p. 321).

The language of the law has been a topic of study (Bosmajian, 1982; Strauber, 1987), particularly the ways in which metaphors have functioned. For example, recently in *Metaphor and Reason in Judicial Opinions,* Haig Bosmajian (1982) focused on the role of tropes, particularly metaphors in judicial opinions in free speech cases. He argued that metaphor shaped the substance of laws having become institutionalized and relied on as principles and standards in arriving at legal judgments. The significance of metaphors such as the "marketplace of ideas" and the "chilling effect" was cited in support of this argument.

The metaphors of free expression are being expanded to encompass the ever-changing landscape of cyberspace. The adoption of spatial terminology may appear a ready and useful mechanism for making the revolutionary changes of the information age less strange, intimidating, and boundless. At the same time the technology of communications challenges developments in applicable laws governing rights of privacy, free expression, liability in such areas as libel,[1] hate speech,[2] and obscenity,[3] as well as sexual harassment[4] and jurisdictional issues.

In attempting to keep pace with technological growth, developments in "cyberlaw" have been handled through the application of preexisting legal doctrines. Media are explored through descriptive terms leading to a comparison between an existing medium and a newly emerging medium. Descriptive terms are ways of depicting or representing the characteristics of a medium of communication or form of dissemination. The descriptive terms chosen have been selected to mirror those characterizations relevant in prior unrelated free speech cases and doctrines. This is evidenced by legal doctrines that have emerged from the notion of publication (that is, newspapers, books, magazines), which may be applied to electronic publication and transmission. For example, in the realm of defamation law, the standards and concepts of libel rather than slander have been applied to broadcasting as the descriptive terms of libel have been viewed as most similar to the dissemination of broadcast information.[5] Therefore, the descriptive terms of libel (focusing on some permanence in written or printed form) have been stretched to apply to the once ephemeral signals of radio and television also characterized by large audiences.

The *Restatement of Torts* (Second) (1976) contends broadcasting should be treated as libel rather than slander as broadcasts may reach more homes than printed publications and may damage reputation just as easily as print. Similarly, broadcasting (such as radio and television) descriptive terms have been applied to the cable industry, and established principles of intellectual property rights and copyright in the realm of print have been stretched to apply to motion pictures and visual or multimedia works. A metaphor is then created comparing a body of regulatory approaches, legal principles, doctrines, and case law developed with regard to the older medium. In this way the regulatory schema of cyberspace today reflects a patchwork of regulations inherited by the application of mixed metaphors. To date the laws of cyberspace have not developed beyond the inherited regulatory metaphor stage.

The descriptive terms applied to a medium have been linked to the regulatory approaches taken to create applicable law. The descriptive terms and regulatory approaches taken from other media will be explored in this chapter as will the descriptive terms (spatial in nature) used with regard to electronic networking. The authors focus on the free speech and privacy implications of developing a distinct area of "cyberlaw" emerging from the descriptive spatial (real property) terms unique to that medium.

PHASES OF MEDIA DEVELOPMENT AND THEIR REGULATORY APPROACHES

Communication occurs in a flexible, malleable, nonrestricted environment—one which co-exists with, influences, and is shaped by the environment of the built form. It is absolutely essential to grasp the symbiotic link between the environments of place and nonplace. Although some form of mediation, and some form of social control, has always been a part of humankind, we can perhaps divide the question into several developmental periods:

1. Nonmediated period—that time in which public communication was essentially restricted to one time and place without aid of a medium to preserve or disseminate the social event. The regulatory approach was based on political or religious security as well as concerns for orderly and peaceful conduct.
2. Media period—consisting of several major periods in which social interaction is extended in time and beyond place.
    a. Thus the initial period has as its chief characteristic "chirographic distancing"—the reliance on handwriting as the primary means of communication between two or more individuals not located in the same time and place essentially altering the nature of public talk by disrupting and elongating interaction once occurring in the same time and place, now occurring at different times.
    b. The "Mass Media" period is introduced with Gutenberg's invention of print in the 15th century, thereby allowing for relatively efficient and quick preservation and replication of interaction, but also interrupted in time.
    c. The addition of electronics allows for the almost instant replication of data, but with a separation of place. Electronic communication is further divided into two

variations: (i) "media" that are/were essentially considered telecommunication "common carriers," thus defined as quasi-monopoly point-to-point public utilities such as the telephone companies; and; (ii) "mass media" that although licensed by the government transfer content to a large simultaneously attending audience generally without immediate feedback.
The regulatory approach of this period is marked by a shift to concerns not only of the communicative message but of the messenger as an institution. The "media" as synonymous with press as an entity or medium as carrier of messages created external to the utility carrying the message formed the backbone of the body of law commonly known as Media Law.

3. Postmodern media period—the time of the electronic network characterized by the introduction of cable and computer communication and in which the distinction between mass media and telecommunications become ambiguous. "Unlike the traditional media, [mass media] which generally disseminate their own message, or mail and telephone services, which typically act as common carriers for messages of others, information service providers both serve as a conduit for information created by others and may deliver information of their own devising—they are both medium and messenger" (Stuckey, 1994, p. 413). Postmodern media thus challenge the existing body of communication law based on media distinctions.

There are numerous variations of online services including electronic mail (immediate delivery of written messages), electronic bulletin boards and newsgroups (in which messages are posted for system users), file transferring systems, libraries and databases (with information often created by third parties), electronic publication, conferencing (of two or more users in real-time interaction), and listservs (which allow topics to be "broadcast" via e-mail messages). Many of these options are available through the Internet, "an ad hoc 'network of networks' that spans the globe" (Stuckey, 1994, p. 415). The Internet is a dense global matrix of 46,000 computer networks, 3.2 million host computers, woven together by telephone lines, undersea cables, microwave links, and gigabit fiber-optic pipes. Touching down in 146 countries, linking 25 to 30 million people, and growing by a million users each month, doubling in size each year (Internet Society, 1994; P. Lewis, 1994a); it is a super data highway that carries the freight of the information age—electronic mail, digital video and sound, computer viruses and more (Markoff, 1993).[6]

The evolution and development of media technology is simply a change in the way information is moved from one space to another. Walter J. Ong (1977) has said that "each of the so-called 'media' . . . makes possible thought processes inconceivable before" (p. 46). Similarly, the very nature of public interaction and the way it is regulated and governed is fundamentally altered by the technology. The developing models being applied to the protection and regulation of freedom of expression and privacy in the postmodern media period dominated by communication in cyberspace is the subject of the following discussion.

STRETCHING REGULATORY SCHEMA

> Technological advances must continually be evaluated and their relation to legal rules determined so that antiquated rules are not misapplied in modern settings. . . . Yet, if the substance of a transaction has not changed, new technology does not require a new legal rule merely because of its novelty. (*Daniel v. Dow Jones & Co.,* 1987)

Each new medium challenges the existing regulatory structure, a truism clearly evidenced by postmodern media. In an effort to provide a solid foundation to clarify overriding First Amendment rights with regard to postmodern media such as computer networks, Laurence Tribe proposed a constitutional amendment protecting information and expression without regard for the medium through which they are transmitted or stored (quoted in Resnick, 1991). Tribe's proposal states:

> This Constitution's protections for the freedoms of speech, press, petition and assembly, and its protections against unreasonable searches and seizures and the deprivation of life, liberty or property without due process of law, shall be construed as fully applicable without regard to the technological method or medium through which information content is generated, stored altered, transmitted or controlled. (pp. 1, 19)

In the event this is not accepted as a constitutional amendment, Tribe recommends this proposal be accepted gradually as a principle of interpretation.

Yet another regulatory approach taken in the past and presently being applied with regard to postmodern media has been that of "mapping electronic data communications onto existing legal metaphors." In a 1993 *Villanova Law Review* article by that title, David Johnson and Kevin Marks (1993) explore this approach noting "existing metaphors can serve as shorthand 'signals' of the types of relationships and ground rules the parties intend to adopt" (p. 488). They note: "There is substantial utility in asking ourselves how particular online environments are similar to or different from other environments where the rights and duties of participants have been analyzed more fully in the past" (p. 488).

A wide variety of legal metaphors have been brought from the nonmediated period and media period to grapple with the postmodern media period. Selection of appropriate legal metaphors "presuppose[s] that there is some 'best fit,' some metaphor that will accurately characterize all the activities involved in these systems" (Johnson & Marks, 1993, p. 487). Of these, many from the media period have been explored.

Publishing

From the mass media period the metaphor of publishing has been brought to the postmodern media. The term *publisher* as defined in the *Restatement of Torts (Second)*, (1976) includes all those who communicate statements to third persons. A publisher is presumed to have control over content and has thus been held liable for any harmful results, including the torts of defamation, false light invasion of privacy public disclosure of private facts, and intentional infliction of emotional harm (Becker, 1989). The standard of liability for publication torts has depended on the degree of editorial control and sponsorship assumed in the publication that formed the basis for a claim. A publisher once strictly liable for publication of false or obscene material under common law (a doctrine now abolished (*Restatement of Torts (Second)*, 1976) can escape liability under some circumstances, including those times not considered the primary creator of a publication. The "wire service" privilege for defamation thus absolves the publisher from liability for the mere reiteration of an actually false but apparently authentic news dispatch received by a recognized reliable source of news from reputable news service agencies (*Layne v. Tribune Co.*, 1993).

Prodigy, one of several information service providers, chose to embrace this publisher metaphor when it canceled accounts of subscribers based on the content of messages in October 1990. Prodigy announced it had decided to curtail public postings about such topics as suicide, crime, sex, or pregnancy. Critics argued this policy was part of a larger effort to suppress a consumer protest by subscribers that began when Prodigy announced an increase in the cost of electronic mail service. Subscribers posted public messages on the Prodigy bulletin board, which led the company to announce it would no longer allow public postings concerning fee policy. Prodigy eventually revoked subscribers' memberships without notice. Applying the publisher metaphor, the nature of private ownership presumes that publishers may exclude any content (*Miami Herald Publishing Co. v. Tornillo*, 1974). According to Johnson and Marks (1993), the publisher metaphor fails to account for the lack of direct control over content.

Common Carrier

From the electronic communication media period, telecommunication regulatory approaches have been borrowed. Common carriers have a duty to carry all content, without discrimination (47 U.S.C. Section 202(a)(1988)) and are therefore immune from liability based on content. Statutory regulation of common carriers as defined by section 153 (h) of the Communications Act have been clarified through court interpretations from which a three-part test (*National Assn of Regulatory Comm'rs v. FCC*, 1976) has been fashioned to determine the existence of a common carrier. The carrier must be of a "quasi-public" character, must have uniform business practices and not operate where "individualized" decisions determine terms, and must allow the user to determine what is transmitted or carried (Johnson & Marks, 1993). Common carriers avoid liability when they simply made equipment available (*Restatement of Torts (Second)*, 1976). Here again Johnson and Marks (1993) note the implications of applying the common carrier metaphor to regulations of such postmodern media as electronic bulletin boards, noting the operators would impose an affirmative duty to make facilities available to all (47 U.S.C. Section 202 (a) (1988)) and would also require prior FCC approval before startup.

Distributor

Another metaphor, distribution, has been applied to cyberspace (Stuckey, 1994). The distributor metaphor raises issues of control or knowledge of content. Generally the distributor such as a bookseller, news vendor, or library is not liable for information created by others that creates harm (*Restatement of Torts (Second)*, 1976). Thus, in cases dating back to 1959, the Supreme Court has adopted as a First Amendment rationale to prevent the imposition of strict liability for distributors such as bookstore owners stocking obscene writing (*Smith v. California*, 1959) or television stations providing air time for political candidates exercising a right to reply time (*Farmers Educational and Cooperative Union of America v. WDAY, Inc.*,1959). Additionally, the Electronic Communications Privacy Act (Title 18) and related state statutes limit and may prohibit providers from reviewing communications made through their facilities again supporting the distributor metaphor (*Cubby v. CompuServe Inc.*, 1991). Yet, this metaphor is strained, however, in that most service provider agreements retain the right to review and control content (America On-Line Subscriber Agreement). Prodigy censors messages directly attacking other subscribers and uses what it calls "George Carlin" software that searches for and deletes messages containing objectionable words (Lewis, 1994b).

Contract Law

From the nonmediated perspective contract law has been favored as a regulatory approach to postmodern media, which it is argued would forestall direct government regulation while promoting growth of the medium (Johnson & Marks, 1993). The traditional concepts of public forum, in which rights and limitations on nonmediated discourse is regulated with regard to communication contexts, provides a particularly significant avenue of thought in search of a regulatory schemata for postmodern media.

SPATIAL METAPHORS, COMMUNICATION, AND THE LAWS OF ELECTRONIC SPACE

Words are what we make them, but they change and transform their origins. The landscape orientation of cyberspace is significant in that space has traditionally served as media of face-to-face (so called nonmediated) communication. Now a prior spatial identity has been applied to a nonterritorially defined medium. In this way metaphors from the laws governing free speech and privacy in physical space (that is, real property in legal terms) appears a logical extension of a body of well-established law. When the International Standards Organization adopted an Open System Interconnect reference model (somehow also linked with IBM's Systems Network Architecture) in order to assure compatibility among users, the language of architecture and urban planning had already provided a metaphorical lexicon to guide future development, usage, and regulation.

With the power of the spatial metaphor in mind, this portion of the chapter surveys the land use regulations that apply to the extension of the laws of physical public space to the ever-growing vistas of electronic space.

Public Space/Public Forum

On a very fundamental level the interaction of individuals in public space, without reference or presence of any other media of communication, involves regulation. Communication, particularly political communication, requires two types of sites: public fora and public places. The public forum is the platform for rhetoric and protest, the type of space traditionally devoted to programmed public expression. It is the forum of the designated site, the display piece of government, the stage for performance, the potential media event. Public oration and symbolic confrontation of demonstration is seldom, if ever, a spontaneous event. Rather, it is the climax of intricate development of communication relationships. It ideally represents a prior process of thought, deliberation, debate, discussion, dialogue, and talk circumscribed by culture and tradition that once occurred in the public place. The character of public streets, parks, and sidewalks have historically lent themselves to being considered natural sites for the public activity of dialogue. In the United States, access to both the public forum and the public space has been viewed as a corollary to the right to free speech enjoying special status in the law as court decisions have consistently recognized the "vital role for people who lack access to more elaborate (and more costly) channels of communication" (Tribe, 1978, p. 689).

Public places provide the site for interpersonal interaction as well. The public place is an environment such as a plaza, promenade, street, mall and park, cafès, pubs, coffeehouses, and community centers, which serve as sites for potential interaction. The public place is the catalyst for expression in the public forum; it is the backstage area for unstructured, informal social gatherings. These sites have become, according to Ray Oldenburg (1989), vital to the personal and political life of a society. "Public places for social interaction run counter to the type of political control exercised in totalitarian societies, so they are essential to the political processes of a democracy" (p. 67). The public forum without public place represents potential danger to a peaceful orderly democratic process. The public place offers a site where ideas may be exchanged and the blueprints for revolt designed.

Each is protected, defined, limited, by law. Public space is a far more difficult concept to legally define because so many jurisdictional issues are involved and because public space may or may not be both public or private, with public access an agreed-to component. So municipal regulations in the form of zoning laws will determine the kind of activities permitted (Drucker & Gumpert, 1991). Further Board of Health restrictions, drinking laws, smoking laws, building permits, and political activity in shopping centers and malls regulate communicative activity. A whole series of "newsstand cases" have gone through the court in which a municipality refused permission for publishers to place coin-operated newspaper dispensers on public property (*City of Lakewood v. Plain Dealer Publishing Co.*, 1988). In recent years in cases such as *City of Lakewood v. Plain Dealer Publishing Co.*, the high court has attempted to balance a municipality's legitimate interest in limiting the size, appearance, and placement of newspaper boxes on streets and pedestrian paths against the First Amendment rights to distribute and citizen rights to receive newspapers. These cases have ruled it an unconstitutional content regulation to ban newsracks in residential areas. So one of the interesting questions that arises is whether a publisher is engaged in a constitutionally protected speech activity in seeking to put a newspaper vending machine on a street corner.

Recently, several members of Congress were arrested by the District of Columbia police for protesting without a permit in front of the White House (*New York Times*, 1994). Licensing, within constitutional limits (those that do not vest "unbridled discretion in the hands of a government official or agency"), is a permissible prior restraint (*City of Lakewood v. Plain Dealer Publishing, Co.*, 1988, p. 750).

The Federal Courts have established characteristics "that a public space must possess if it is to be considered a public forum" (Naughton, 1993, p. 429):

> First, the property must have as a principal purpose the free exchange of ideas, and this purpose must be evidenced by a long-standing historical practice of permitting speech. Second, a public forum is not creation by inaction; a public forum is created only when the property is intentionally open[ed] . . . for public discourse. (p. 429)

With more and more activity once held to be a traditional function of the public space and/or forum domain being shifted over to an electronic form, what protection is afforded such functions as the shift occurs? That is, when a function is assumed by the newer medium, what legal protection is afforded the coopted activity? To some extent the implementation of the Fairness Doctrine, Equal Time, and Section 315 as developed by the Federal Communications Commission responded to a shift in which public activities had to be protected because the spectrum limitation of the medium required such protection. Because, in a pre-cable world, stations and channels were limited by the availability of space on the electromagnetic spectrum, the concept of public access to the channel was written into the law. It must be noted that, theoretically, at least, broadcasters had their license renewal application evaluated on the basis of whether they served "the public interest, convenience, and necessity."

However, it is the postmodern media period, a time in which the audiovisual landscape is being reshaped and reformulated, in which computers, fiber-optics, satellites, cellular phone, CD-ROM, and facsimile coalesce and converge, that the shift in functions of public interaction has accelerated and radicalized how we deal with each other in the public domain. It is in the postmodern media period that electronic space becomes a functional equivalent of public space, but in which such electronic space is primarily a construction rather than a reality confirmable in any kind of physical reality.

In many countries around the world, the kiosk has been a primary focal point for social interaction—the multifunctional stands where tobacco can be purchased, telephone calls made, where multiple newspapers are conveniently hung so that the strolling individuals can peruse the headlines and possibly engage others in conversation and discuss the state of the world or the problems of the community. Such public places play an important social and cultural role. In urban Greece, for example, such kiosks known as *peripiteros* are found on most major street corners and serve as a kind of community bulletin board. To some extent, similar kind of bulletin boards have existed in American life—with the village green and barber shop, soda fountain, pot-bellied stove serving such a function.

So it is interesting to note that a legal issue has emerged regarding computer bulletin boards in relationship to First Amendment rights. Advocates of a right of access to bulletin Boards contend that the public message areas of computer bulletin boards are the modern-day equivalents of the streets, parks, and commons of the 18th-century town, and just as the First Amendment guarantees access to those fora, it guarantees access to computer bulletin boards. The board operators respond by arguing that bulletin boards are not public fora, but rather the electronic equivalent of the press, and the operators may, in their editorial discretion, refuse to publish messages they deem inappropriate (Naughton, 1993).

Real Property and Cyber Property

From a legal perspective real property, physical space, is distinguished by possession and use and enjoyment. The laws of real property and access to that property in order to communicate produce distinct issues determined by whether the public space is publically or privately owned. Although title to real property is easily identifiable, who owns cyberspace? *Cyberspace* is described by CompuServe as "that nowhere space [electronic space] in the telephone line between you and where all things online happen, but it's also the 'room' or other expanse you're not really in when you're visiting any form of virtual reality" (*CompuServe Magazine*, 1994, p. 12). Bulletin Boards have been called the computer-age equivalent of a public forum (Naughton, 1993), but approximately 90% are operated by private individuals or organizations on privately owned computers (Feder, 1991).

Public Forum, Public Space and Property Rights

The public forum doctrine first developed in *Hague v. Committee for Industrial Organization* (1939) stated that the right to assemble and discuss national issues was a privilege of national citizenship secured by the Fourteenth Amendment. Justice Robert's dictum laid the foundation for the doctrine:

> Wherever the title of streets and parks may rest, they have immemorially been held in trust for the use of the public and, time out of mind, have been used for the purposes of assembly, communicating thoughts between citizens, and discussing public questions. Such use of the streets and public places has, from ancient times been a part of the privileges, immunities, rights and liberties of citizens. (p. 515)

This public forum doctrine developed to limit the legitimate power of the state to prohibit expression on *publically owned* property. *Marsh v. Alabama* (1946) began the expansion of this doctrine to some *privately owned* sites that were the functional equivalents of public property. The Supreme Court held that the fact that title may belong to a private corporation or individual is constitutionally insignificant with regard to the public forum doctrine as whether publically or privately owned there may be an identical interest in the functioning of the community in such a manner that the channels of communication remain free. Justice Black's opinion noted: "Ownership does not always mean absolute dominion. The more an owner, for his advantage, opens up his property for use by the public in general, the more do his rights become circumscribed by the statutory and constitutional rights of those who use it" (p. 506).

Private property was opened further to communicative activities in *Amalgamated Food Employees Union Local 590 v. Logan Valley Plaza, Inc.* (1968), when members of a union having been enjoined from picketing a supermarket in a private shopping center successfully appealed the injunction with the Court finding that shopping centers had become the functional equivalent of the "business block," particularly with the migration to the suburbs. The Court decision, limited to those situations in which the private property was open to the public, made clear that states can constitutionally regulate the exercise of First Amendment rights if the exercise interfered with the use to which the property was put (*Amalgamated Food Employees v. Logan Valley*, 1968). Ultimately, in *Hudgens v. NLRB* (1976) the Court held that if a shopping center is in fact the functional equivalent of a municipality, the First and Fourteenth Amendments would not permit content-based restrictions on speech, but that it is not automatically considered the functional equivalent of a municipality.

Cyberspace becomes cyberproperty when it is privately owned and operated. In attempting to extend the law of real property to access in cyberproperty, the concept of "municipality" enunciated in Marsh would have to be redefined in that although

> a computer network has many of the attributes of a traditional public forum . . . the network is analogous to a very large public place. This space is truly a marketplace of ideas and a public forum for the communication of ideas and information. Like city streets and parks, which have immemorially been . . . used for purposes of assembly . . . and discussing public question, computer networks since their inception have been used as a means of communication. Like a city street, a computer network is continually open, often uncongested, and . . . a place where people may enjoy..the company of friends . . . in relaxed environment. (Naughton, 1993, pp. 429-430)

Bulletin boards are designed to be opened for the purpose of communication, whereas sidewalks, streets, parks, and other traditional public fora were created for a variety of other public purposes as well: "For a substantial population, the electronic arenas of computer networks have displaced the nation's streets and parks as the quintessential public fora. Like streets and parks, computer bulletin boards provide individuals with a low-cost yet extremely effective means of communication" (Naughton, 1993, p. 431), a forum far larger than the real property counterpart. Yet in the *Georgetown Law Journal* article entitled "Is Cyberspace a Public

Forum?" Edward J. Naughton (1993) notes that despite the similarities between computer networks and traditional physical space public fora, the analogy is strained in that the bulletin boards have not "immemorially been held in trust for the use of the public and, time out of mind, . . been used for purposes of assembly . . . and discussing public questions, thus lacking the special status afforded the traditional historical concept of public forum. Furthermore, many bulletin boards (particularly commercial ventures) are governed by subscription agreements that for the most part expressly reserve the right to reject messages deemed inappropriate or to terminate the user's privilege to use the board. For example, America Online reserves the right, at its sole discretion, to immediately, without notice, suspend or terminate a member's access to and use of America Online upon any breach of the terms of service (America Online, 1994).

The public space arguments and spatial legal metaphors surrounding electronic bulletin boards were tested in the fall of 1990, when, as previously noted, Prodigy banned discussion of rate increases in public areas and canceled the accounts of 13 dissident users (Edelman, 1990). Prodigy later stated they conceived of the network as a newspaper publisher that would reject "grossly repugnant" messages and use editorial discretion to determine which posting fell into this category. This position was soundly criticized by groups such as the American Civil Liberties Union (Berman & Rotenberg, 1991).

Commercial bulletin boards are only open to a public able to pay fees, not the public at large. The contractual nature of the access strains the analogy to spatial access. Yet the majority of bulletin boards are open to the general public without limitations based in contract (Naughton, 1993). The status with regard to public access and use of this area of cyberproperty remains without a clear legal status or regulatory policy and is unregulated to date.

Non-Possessory Rights to Space

The nature of the relationship of parties interacting in electronic space includes not only cyberproperty or space but telephone connection as well. These relationships may be clarified through an analogy to legal concepts governing these relationships in physical space.

In the law of torts, the legal status of one who enters the land of another has been divided roughly into three categories: trespasser, licensee, and invitee. As the legal status changes, the obligations of protection owed the visitor by the possessor of the land increase, in other words, the categories have been used in determining liability for negligence. A trespasser, lowest on the scale, is defined as "a person who enters or remains upon land in possession of another without a privilege to do so, created by the possessor's consent or otherwise" (Prosser, 1971, p. 357), and generally no one has the right to enter without consent. Intruders have no right to demand protection from harm. In electronic space the unwanted e-mail message or the obscene or harassing phone call made for social purposes would be akin to the trespasser.

Thus the relationship of the sender of the obscene message may be viewed this way. A licensee includes anyone who has a privilege to enter the land, including those who enter for social visits or personal business dealings, tourists visiting at their own request, salesmen canvassing at the door of private homes, and those soliciting money for charity (Prosser, 1971). The licensee takes the premises as the occupier does, which suggests that at most the licensee is entitled to a warning of dangers on the land. Unsolicited commercial messages soliciting for charity or selling everything from investment opportunities to magazine subscriptions thus fall under this category. Invitees have been defined as those who "enter premises upon business which concerns the occupier, and upon his invitation express or implied" (p. 385), thus creating an affirmative duty to protect the invitee from all dangers known or discoverable. This category is also called the business invitee and includes customers entering a store, patrons of restaurants, theaters, and other commercial places open to the public. A social guest "however cordially he may have been invited and urged to come, is not in law an invitee. The guest is legally nothing more than a licensee" (p. 378) meaning that the possessor owes no affirmative duty of care for safety. If applied to electronic space the relationship created by a social or business contact made when one has given out an e-mail address or has an address posted on the directory would be considered that of invitee/possessor of land. In attempting to unravel the nature of the interpersonally mediated relationship formed in commercial telephone interaction, we return to the issue of power and control that has been significantly altered in the unique context of the 900 number. In a traditional noncommercial telephone interaction the caller (akin to a licensee status) is in a relationship in which the caller exercises some control vis-à-vis determining time and duration of the "visit," but the parties are essentially equals unless the underlying relationship dictates otherwise. But the consumer/caller of the 900 number has been invited for business purposes and the guaranteed economic benefit of the party called (in other words, the possessor of electronic space) and is therefore similar to the higher status invitee who enjoys a different position during the interaction rooted in the commercial nature of the customer/merchant relationship. The merchant is obligated to interact when and for however long the caller (able to pay) so wishes.

Nuisance Laws and Other Regulations of Real Property

Nuisance laws provide an alternative means of regulating land use and thereby interaction. Before the beginning of this century common law nuisance was a principle means of regulating use of real property. Private nuisance provides a tort action (civil liability) on which to litigate, focusing on the reasonableness of conduct while enjoying one's property as compared to the inconvenience and harm inflicted on others for activities such as excessive noise (Prosser, 1971). Private nuisance applies to the interest of a possessor of land in freedom from any unreasonable, nontrespassory interference with use and enjoyment of land, whereas public nuisance involves the public interest in freedom from activity that endangers health, safety, property, comfort, convenience, or offends public morals. Public nuisance provides criminal liability and has been directly linked with communicative activity in such circumstances as enjoining the operation of adult movie houses as public nuisances because of past exhibition of obscene films (*Vance v. Universal Amusement Co,,* 1980). Public profanity has also been found to create a public nuisance (*Wilson v. Parent,* 1961). Under these interpretations providing opportunities for interaction or open spaces for public gatherings could expose one to criminal liability if the interaction goes beyond controlled limits. Nuisances exist in cyberspace. Hate speech may be found on computer bulletin boards (Leroux, 1991). Prodigy has been criticized for allowing users to post anti-Semitic slurs in public area bulletin boards (Miller, 1991). Obscene and pornographic material may appear on bulletin boards. Once again issues of culpability may well rest in the determination of public versus private ownership—of whether a nuisance may be said to exist in public cyberspace or privately owned and operated cyberproperty.

Covenants are promises involving reality (*Blacks's Law Dictionary,* 1979). Restrictive covenants provide another alternative real property regulation that may have bearing on communication. Covenants are provisions in a deed limiting the use of property and prohibiting certain uses that may limit interaction by prohibiting certain activities on premises (*Black's Law Dictionary,* 1979). Restaurants, pubs, meeting halls, and other businesses that are open to the general public may be prohibited or the hours the property is open to the public could be restricted, thus affecting the opportunity for public interaction. Covenants may be personal between parties or may be said to "run with the land." Covenants that run with the land are not merely personal between the immediate parties, but are also intended to benefit and/or bind others in the future and cannot be separated from the [estate] [land], nor can the land be transferred without the covenant binding. These promises may directly circumscribe the communicative activities taking place on privately owned real property, functioning to limit activities of possessors and their guests. (*Black's Law Dictionary*, 1979, p. 329)

Restrictive covenants may provide a useful metaphor for privately owned and operated electronic space so that operators of not only more public arenas like bulletin boards, but those concerned with e-mail content and telephonic communication may find a mechanism for control. Such covenants might be extended to deal with cybersex or dial-a-porn if they are seen as a hazard.

EXPECTATIONS OF PRIVACY ON REAL PROPERTY AND CYBERPROPERTY

The laws of privacy represent an area of law that has advanced much further in addressing electronic nonphysical spaces of interaction. The evolution of the right to be left alone, or the right to privacy, and reasonable expectations of privacy often emerges from the nature of a particular geography location. Fourth and Fifth Amendment rights are implicated when considering search and seizure and freedom from self-incrimination associated with places in which there are reasonable expectations of privacy. Courts have explored these expectations in physical spaces ranging from cars to school lockers and, of course, homes and offices (Kamisar, LaFave, & Israel, 1986). Reasonable expectations of privacy are no longer restricted to the physical spatial realm. Back in 1967, in *Katz v. United States* (1967) the Supreme Court found "the emphasis on the nature of a particular targeted area deflected attention from the issue of Fourth Amendment infringement" (p. 351). Justice Steward wrote:

For the Fourth Amendment protects people not places. What a person knowingly exposes to the public, even in his own home or office, is not a subject of Fourth Amendment protection. . . . But what he seeks to preserve as private even in an area accessible to the public, may be constitutionally protected. (p. 351)

Congressional regulation of electronic surveillance of electronic spaces (originally wiretapping) was addressed in a comprehensive federal legislative action in 1968 entitled Title III of the Omnibus Crime Control and Safe Streets Act (18 U.S.C. Sections 2510-2520

(1982)). This act addressed both *wire communication* and *oral communication*, requiring government authorities to obtain a court-ordered warrant in order to conduct a surveillance. With the proliferation of methods of nonvoice communications, including electronic mail, cellular and cordless telephones, fax machines, video teleconferencing, paging devices, and digitized information networks, Congress was confronted with the need to revise Title III protections (Cutrera, 1991). Person-to-person interaction was subject to disparate legal treatment depending on the medium utilized. Congress responded in 1986 with the passage of the Electronic Communications Privacy Act (ECPA), which amended Title III to include electronic communications as a protected form of communications (18 U.S.C. Section 2510 (12) (1988)). Although the act clearly encompasses communication of the mediated period such as telecommunications, the amount of protection afforded computer messages is questionable. The ECPA does recognize protection of electronic communication storage such as the storage of bulletin board or e-mail messages (18 U.S.C. Section 2703, 1988). However, in *United States v. Miller* (1976) involving bank records,) information kept by a third party was not given Fourth Amendment protection because records were out of the possession of the originator producing no legitimate expectation of privacy concerning the information (Cutrera, 1991). This would indicate that stored electronic communication may not require a warrant in order to be seized and admitted in criminal court proceedings.

Since the early 1980s, more than half a dozen cases have ruled that private citizens do not have an expectation of privacy when conversing on a cordless phone (Marcus, 1989). Courts have emphasized the broadcast nature of the communication and thus the decreased expectation of privacy. In *Tyler v. Berodt* (1989, cert. denied 1990), the Eighth Circuit Court of Appeals held that users of cordless phones did not have a reasonable expectation of privacy that would apply to those participants in ordinary line telephone communication. Those aware that their conversation was being transmitted by cordless telephone were presumed to have no expectation of privacy when the conversation could be "broadcast by radio in all directions to be overheard by countless people" (*Edwards v. Bardwell*, 1986). Instruction manuals (packaged with the phones) alert owners to the fact that conversations could be transmitted to others, and thus there is no expectation of privacy (*State v. DeLaurier*, 1985). The remote scanning of private computer activity using CRT microspy devices are becoming available as an electronic surveillance technique. Computers monitors include an FCC warning notifying users that there are unintentional radiators: "The government, in an effort to conduct such scans without warrants, could analogize between computer monitors and cordless telephone receivers" (Cutrera, 1991, p. 163), finding no reasonable expectation of privacy so that remote scans could be conducted without warrants.

CONCLUSIONS

Cyberlaw pushes the envelope on existing legal doctrines, particularly those protecting First Amendment rights. Many legal metaphors and fields of extant law have been suggested as approaches for gaining a foothold on managing emerging questions of liability and rights. From treating postmodern media akin to publications, common carriers, or distributors to simply coping with the contractual nature of relationships, approaches that do not quite fit have been put forward. A state of confusion and gaps in the law have resulted from mixing legal metaphors to grapple with the legal issues emerging by the developments in cyberspace. The authors have suggested yet another metaphor, one that emphasizes the spatial dimension of the communicative event may well be emerging as a favored regulatory metaphor as it is the one most closely linked to the descriptive language being used about the medium to be regulated. The evolutionary process by which the laws governing the nonmediated and media periods have followed this path by which the descriptive terms used about the characteristics of a medium have been linked to the applicable law developed, suggesting the spatial terms and laws may well provide a useful source during a time marked by uncertainty.

The discussion of the application of the laws of real property to cyberspace should not be read as a recommendation but rather reflects not only a seemingly logical approach, but one in which the symbiotic relationship between the use of physical space (used for face-to-face interaction) and electronic space (offering options for mediated communication) is acknowledged.

If a regulatory approach borrowed from a noncommunicative orientation toward rights and liabilities forms the basis of cyberlaw, the future of free speech and privacy rights may be threatened. One may easily envision the need for a period of legal skirmishes and battles to reestablish the primacy of First Amendment rights in cyberspace.

It is significant that at a time when we seek refuge from the street, when the highway has been reduced to a connection between hostile zones, as we continue down the path of interiorizing and privatization, that the nomenclature of urban planning and architecture has been transformed into metaphors of cyberspace.

The significance of the landscape orientation of cyberspace and the regulations being brought to regulate this new frontier is not only that a prior spatial identity has been applied to a nonterritorially defined medium, but that the very process of naming redefines the earlier application. Developments in the law of electronic space are not only significant in and of themselves as a symbiotic relationship exists between physical and electronic space. As the law develops and focuses on communicative rights and liabilities in the mediated realm of cyberspace, the significance of the physical realm of social interaction will be deemphasized, portending serious implications for traditional expressive rights in that realm. Precedents being set in electronic space may well reflect and shape attitudes and rights with regard to physical space as well.

ENDNOTES

1. *Cubby v. CompuServe Incorporated* (1991) is the sole case to date in which a libel action was reportedly brought against an information service provider. In this case a plaintiff sued CompuServe on the basis of allegedly false and defamatory statements contained in an electronic newsletter available in CompuServe's Journalism Forum. The newsletter was published by a third party (not CompuServe). The court granted CompuServe's motion for summary judgment relying on CompuServe's actions as distributor, exercising no editorial control and acting as an electronic library.

2. Hate speech has become an issue faced by information providers. The Anti-Defamation League of B'nai B'rith cited anti-semitic notes sent via e-mail but rejected for public posting by Prodigy as an example of electronically networked hate speech (Miller,1991). For further discussion, see Leroux (1991).

3. Obscenity has received a good deal of attention within the context of cyberspace (Jackson, 1994). In a prominent case the operators of "Amateur Action" electronic bulletin board service were convicted under the federal law, criminalizing transmitting obscene images electronically from California to Tennessee (Landis, 1994).

4. Three students at Santa Rosa Junior College in California were offended by sexual comments on a computer bulletin board run through the school. In this case separate male and female bulletin boards were operated, and the students alleged sexual discrimination, bringing charges under Title IX of the Civil Rights Act prohibiting sexual discrimination in schools. Furthermore, it was found that one female student, Jennifer Branham, had been subjected to sexual harassment in that a hostile educational environment had been created with regard to the posting of the messages. A settlement was reached between the students and the college in the amount of $15,000. The case against the Education Department under Title IX remains open (A. Lewis, 1994).

5. The libel/slander distinction in law is particularly significant as damages for libel are generally larger than those for slander, and the elements required to be proven are generally less burdensome than those for slander as slander suits require plaintiffs prove actual monetary damages (*Restatement of Torts (Second)*, 1976).

6. The Internet began in the 1970s as a United States Defense Department network called ARPAnet. Slowly, corporations, universities, and information providers phased and dovetailed their networks into the system, agreeing on compatible connecting software (McNichol, 1994). And it is the Internet that is a focal point of the electronic data highway featured as a high priority in the Clinton-Gore Administration. Such a system includes digital libraries (making libraries accessible to everyone), database publishing, electronic mail, electronic communities (virtual or nonplace communities which that people with similar interests), software access, weather information, entertainment, and data exchange (Markoff, 1993).

REFERENCES

Amalgamated Food Employees Union Local 590 v. Logan Valley Plaza, Inc. 391 U.S. 308 (1968).

America Online. (1994). Subscriber agreement: Terms of service.

Becker, L. (1989). The liability of computer bulletin board operators for defamation posted by others. *Connecticut Law Review, 22*, 203-238.

Berman, J., & Rotenberg, M. (1991, January 6). Free speech in an electronic age. *The New York Times*, p. C13.

Black's Law Dictionary (5th ed.). (1979). St. Paul, MN: West Publishing.

Blankenship, J. (1980). The search for the 1972 Democratic nomination: A metaphorical perspective. In B. Brock & R. Scott (Eds.), *Method of rhetorical criticism: A twentieth century perspective* (2nd ed., pp. 321-345). Detroit: Wayne State University Press.

Bosmajian, H. (1982). Fire, snakes and poisons: Metaphors and analogues in some landmark free speech cases. *Free Speech Yearbook, 20*, 16-22.

Bosmajian, H. (1992). *Metaphor and reason in judicial opinion*. Carbondale: Southern Illinois University Press.

Burke, K. (1965). *Permanence and change: An anatomy of purpose*. Indianapolis, IN: Bobbs-Merrill.

City of Lakewood v. Plain Dealer Publishing Co., 108 S. Ct. 2138 (1988).

CompuServe Magazine. (1994, March 12).

Cubby v. CompuServe Incorporate, 776 F. Supp. 135 (S.D.N.Y.) (1991).

Cutrera, T.A. (1991). The Constitution in cyberspace: The fundamental rights of computer users. *University of Missouri-Kansas City Law Review, 60*(1), 139-167.

Daniel v. Dow Jones & Co., 520 N.Y.S. 2d 334 (1987).

Drucker, S.J., & Gumpert, G. (1991). Public space and communication: The zoning of public interaction. *Communication Theory, 1*(4), 296-310.

Edelman, L. (1990, November 20). Is this man invading your privacy? *Boston Globe*, p. 25.

Edwards v. Bardwell, 632 F. Supp. 584 (1986).

Farmers Educational and Cooperative Union of America v. WDAY, Inc. 360 U.S. 525 (1959).

Feder, B.J. (1991, November 3). Toward defining free speech in the computer age. *The New York Times*, p. D5.

Hague v. Committee for Industrial Organization, 307 U.S. 496 (1939).

Hudgens v. NLRB, 424 U.S. 507 (1976).

Internet Society. (1994, August 4). *Latest Internet measurements reveal dramatic growth in 1994* [press release].

Jackson, D. S. (1994, July 25). Battle for the soul of internet. *Time*, pp. 50, 56.

Johnson, D.R., & Marks, D.A. (1993). Mapping electronic data communications onto existing legal metaphors: Should we let our conscience (and our contracts) be our guide? *Villanova Law Review, 81*(2), 487-516.

Kamisar, Y., LaFave, W. R., & Israel, J. H. (1986). *Modern criminal procedure* (6th ed.). St. Paul, MN: West Publishing.

Katz v. United States, 389 U.S. 347 (1967).

Landis, D. (1994, August 9). Regulating porn: Does it compute? *USA Today*, p. D1.

Layne v. Tribune Co.,146 So. 234 (Fla. 1993).

Leroux, C. (1991, October 27). Hate speech enters computer age. *Chicago Tribune*, p.C4.

Lewis, A. (1994, October 14). Time to grow up. *The New York Times*, p. A35.

Lewis, P. (1994a, June 19). Getting down to business on the Net. *The New York Times*, p. C.1.

Lewis, P. (1994b, June 29). No more "anything goes": Cyberspace gets censors. *The New York Times*, p. A.1.

Marcus, A.D. (1989, November 29). Callers on cordless phones surrender privacy rights. *Wall Street Journal*, p. B4.

Markoff, J. (1993, September 5). The Internet. *The New York Times*, p. 11.

Marsh v. Alabama, 326 U.S. 501 (1946).

McNichol, T. (1994, January 21). Fellow travelers on the Info Highway. *U.S.A. Weekend*, p.4.

Miami Herald Publishing Co. v. Tornillo, 418 U.S. 241 (1974).

Miller, M.W. (1991, October 22). Prodigy network defends display of Anti-Semitic Notes. *Wall Street Journal*, p. B1.

Naughton, E.J. (1993). Is cyberspace a public forum? Computer bulletin boards, free speech, and state action. *The Georgetown Law Journal, 81*, 409-441.

The New York Times. (1994, April 22). P. 1.

Oldenburg, R. (1989). *The great good place: Cafes, coffee shops, community centers, beauty parlors, general stores, bars, hangouts, and how they get you through the day.* New York: Pergamon Press.

Ong, W. (1977). *Interfaces of the word: Studies in the evolution of consciousness and culture.* Ithaca, NY: Cornell University Press.

Prosser, W.L. (1971). *Handbook of the law of torts* (4th ed.). St. Paul, MN: West Publishing.

Resnick, R. (1991, September 16). The outer limits. *National Law Journal*, pp. 1, 19.

Restatement Of Torts (Second). (1976). St. Paul, MN: West Publishing.

Smith v. California, 361 U.S. 147 (1959).

State v. DeLaurier, 488 A. 2d 688 (R.I. 1985).

Strauber, I.L. (1987). The rhetorical structure of freedom of speech. *Polity, 19*, 507-28.

Stuckey, K.D. (1994). Rights and responsibilities of information service providers. In E. Kirsh, L. Rose, & S. Steele (Eds.), *Business and legal aspects of the Internet and online services* (pp. 407-450). New York: Law Journal Seminars Press.

Tribe, L. (1978). *Constitutional law.* Mineola, NY: Foundation Press.

Tyler v. Berodt, 877 F. 3d 705 (8th Cir. 1989, cert. denied.110 S.Sct. Rptr.____ (1990).

United States v. Miller, 425 U.S. 435 (1976).

Vance v. Universal Amusement Co. 445 U.S. 308 (1980).

Wilson v. Parent, 365 P. 2d 72 (1961).

5

ECONOMICS AND THE INTERNET: NO FREE RIDES ON THE INFOBAHN
THE INFORMATION SUPERHIGHWAY BECOMES A TOLL ROAD

HOWARD M. COHEN

What drives regulation? Does a regulatory system drive media development? Or does cyberspace and computer development shape regulation? Howard Cohen provides a clear overview of the complex history and infrastructure of the developing business environment known as cyberspace. He explores the question of appropriate models for conceptualizing the economic structure emerging and grapples with the question of how the growing integration of the Internet creates and promotes a new system of haves and have-nots—differentiating between those who have immediate, moderate, or no access at all.

The development of the Internet has been one of the most remarkable technical and social achievements in the history of federally funded projects. Now, as the expansion of commercial Internet use continues to grow exponentially, it becomes vital to understand and to examine how privatization and the new economics of our connected society will impact the way in which we use this global network infrastructure. As commercial interests require new investments and new regulation of those investments, we will almost certainly see changes not only in how we use the network, but also in who has access and who does not.

How was the initial development of the Internet funded? What is the financial structure supporting the physical and technical infrastructure today? Who is paying, for what, and who is profiting? The development of cogent answers to these questions, answers that are still unfolding, helps us to envision how the Internet will serve us in the years to come.

The Internet is becoming to data transmission what the public telephone network has been to voice communications. To use the public telephone network, an individual wishing to speak to another individual turns instinctively to the telephone, dials a phone number, connects and converses. Similarly, individuals wishing to access needed information are learning to turn to their computer, click a mouse or press a key, and find themselves connected to a vast wealth of useful resources on the Internet.

There are economic drivers that suggest that, in addition to data, the Internet will also compete with the public telephone network as a primary voice transport as well, utilizing, integrating with, and perhaps replacing much of that infrastructure. Ultimately, the Internet has and will continue to become a medium for new interactive transmissions based on converging computing and communications technologies, including collaborative full-motion video, high-fidelity stereo sound, and secure commercial transactions. Of course, as the Internet infrastructure becomes or replaces today's commercial tariff-bearing voice and data networks, the governmental agencies who levy those tariffs must increase their regulation of this medium.

The public telephone network is funded by rate payers who pay for time and distance. Their charges are computed based on how much time they spend conversing and how far they are from the recipient of their call. Regulatory tariffs are then added to complete the computation. The public telephone network started as one system, in which one monopolistic entity owned the entire infrastructure from end to end. As a result of divestiture and the ensuing competitive opportunities, today's public telephone network is comprised of many local, regional, national, and global networks all interoperating and charging each other access fees that ultimately are charged back to originating caller/rate payers.

The Internet, by contrast, has developed in precisely the opposite direction. From its inception the Internet has been a network of networks conceived, designed, and developed to provide a common communications medium for dissimilar computing platforms. This is not only an important technical distinction but a critical economic component as well.

AT FIRST, GRANTS PAVED THE WAY

When Vinton G. Cerf, commonly referred to as the founder of the Internet and today Senior Vice President of the Data Services Division of MCI Telecommunications Corporation, set out in 1972 with his colleagues from UCLA to assemble a computer communications network for advanced research projects, they enjoyed federal funding from the Department of Defense's Advanced Research Projects Agency (ARPA), as well as the patronage of a variety of educational and governmental institutions (Aboba, 1993).

Originally conceived by the Rand Corporation think-tank as a strategic network that would provide continued communication for remote computing during a nuclear attack (Sterling, 1993), the ARPANet grew into an informal channel for the academic community to share research and ideas. Rules and regulations, if there were any, were created by consensus. Anyone wishing to add new functionality to the network would issue an informal "RFC," a Request For Comment, which would then receive multiple responses shared throughout the community. Ultimately, whichever central organizing body was currently "in charge" would take the initiative to generate a final specification based on the original RFC and its responses. This specification would be circulated and, if there were no dissenting comments, implemented.

The original Rand concept called for a network with no central control. Instead, information would be organized into "packets," each of which would contain "header" information identifying its origin and its destination. Each packet would travel from one "gateway" to another. These gateways would route the packet to the next gateway, which would be closer to the destination until, ultimately, the packet arrived at the intended "host" computer. Because each gateway automatically computed the best route based on a variety of parameters, each packet could travel any of dozens or hundreds or thousands of ways. As such, even if large sections of the network were destroyed, the gateways would retry other routes until a successful path was found. This strategy might not be as efficient as others, but it certainly was durable.

Starting with "nodes" at only four academic and research locations in late 1969, within two years the Internet connected more than 30 ARPA-funded university sites. Originally created to provide remote computing capability, ARPA soon found that the academic community had seized on this infrastructure as a convenient medium for the exchange of research information, informal electronic mail communications, and simple gossip.

After 10 years of modest growth and experimentation, ARPA created the Internet Configuration Control Board (ICCB) to coordinate and control the effort of managing the network, which now numbered over 200 nodes. By 1982, the ICCB was renamed the Internet Activities Board (IAB). IAB supervised the incorporation of many more networks into the Internet. BITNET, the "Because It's Time" Network, began as a cooperative network between the City University of New York and Yale University. At the same time, CSNet, the Computer Science Network, was created as the collaboration of computer scientists at the Universities of Delaware and Wisconsin, Purdue, the RAND Corporation, and the engineering firm Bolt Beranek and Newman through seed money granted by the National Science Foundation to provide electronic mail and other networking services to university scientists who had no access to ARPAnet (Zakon, 1993). In 1987, these two networks merged to form CREN, the Corporation for Research and Educational Networking. Dues paid by the member organizations fully defray all of CREN's operating costs (Cerf, n.d.). Regional networks including BARNET, SURANET, JVNCNET, CICNET, NYSERNET, and others were connected as well (Cerf, 1995).

In the end result, the Internet was truly a network of networks, with no one organization owning or controlling any substantial portion of the infrastructure. In 1991, Vinton Cerf (n.d.) observed:

> "Regional" support for the Internet is provided by various consortium networks and "local" support is provided through each of the research and educational institutions. Within the United States, much of this support has come from the federal and state governments, but a considerable contribution has been made by industry.

POST NO BILLS

Commercial use was not part of the plan and, as such, was strictly forbidden. The Acceptable Use Policy for the NSFNet, a primary backbone for the Internet, named for the National Science Foundation, states:

> NSFNET Backbone services are provided to support open research and education in and among U.S. research and instructional

institutions, plus research arms of for-profit firms when engaged in open scholarly communication and research. Use for other purposes is not acceptable. (Office of Inspector General/NSF, 1993)

"Other purposes" referred directly to commercial traffic. In fact, the Internet community tacitly forbid even the hint of a profit motive and actively condoned retribution. Anyone found "spamming," or posting messages with commercial, profit-motivated intent on the Usenet bulletin boards or Listserv electronic mailing lists, would likely find themselves "flamed" by members of the community, bombarded with thousands of angry messages insisting that he or she cease and desist this detestable behavior.

Several for-profit organizations, most of which were started by the academics who had been originally involved in the development of ARPANet, including Advanced Networks & Service (ANS), Performance Systems International (PSI), and UUNET, began construction of a Commercial Internet Exchange in an effort to create a parallel infrastructure that would not violate the NSF's Acceptable Use Policy. With commercial involvement, utilization of the infrastructure began to grow dramatically. Cerf (1995) describes the privatization of the NSF regional networks:

NYSERNET (the New York State regional network) was the first to spin out a for-profit company, Performance Systems International, which now is one of the more successful Internet service providers. Other Internet providers actually began as independent entities; one of these is UUNET, which started as a private non-profit but turned for-profit and began offering an Internet service it calls ALTERNET; another is CERFNet, a for-profit operation initiated by General Atomic in 1989; a third is NEARNet, started in the Boston area and recently absorbed into a cluster of for-profit services operated as BBN Planet (recall that BBN was the original developer of the ARPANet Interface Message Processor; BBN also created the Telenet service, which it sold to GTE and which subsequently became Sprintnet).

In 1988, in a conscious effort to test Federal policy on commercial use of Internet, the Corporation for National Research Initiatives approached the Federal Networking Council for permission to experiment with the interconnection of MCI Mail with the Internet. An experimental electronic mail relay was built and put into operation in 1989, and shortly thereafter CompuServe, ATTMail and Sprintmail followed suit. Once again, a far-sighted experimental effort coupled with a wise policy choice stimulated investment by industry and expansion of the nation's infrastructure. In the past year, commercial use of the Internet has exploded.

By 1989, with tens of thousands of nodes internetworked together, the need arose for some central body to coordinate the technical development of the network. Continuing the tradition of Internet governance by consensus, the IAB created the Internet Engineering Task Force (IETF). Today, the IETF is part of the Internet Society, which was established in 1992 "by a group of individuals involved with the IETF, who saw a need to provide an institutional home and financial support for the Internet Standards process" (Burack, 1996). In its welcoming message on the IETF World-Wide Web homepage, the IETF describes itself in the context of the various Internet governing organizations as follows:

The IETF is the protocol engineering and development arm of the Internet. The IETF is a large open international community of network designers, operators, vendors, and researchers concerned with the evolution of the Internet architecture and the smooth operation of the Internet. It is open to any interested individual.

The internal management of the IETF is handled by the area directors. Together with the Chair of the IETF, they form the Internet Engineering Steering Group (IESG). The operational management of the Internet standards process is handled by the IESG under the auspices of the Internet Society. The Internet Architecture Board (IAB) is a body of the Internet Society responsible for overall architectural considerations in the Internet. It also serves to adjudicate disputes in the standards process.

The Internet Assigned Numbers Authority is the central coordinator for the assignment of unique parameter values for Internet protocols. The IANA is chartered by the Internet Society (ISOC) and the Federal Network Council (FNC) to act as the clearinghouse to assign and coordinate the use of numerous Internet protocol parameters. (Welcome to the Internet Engineering Task Force, 1997)

Also in 1989, working at the European Center for Particle Research (CERN), Tim Berners-Lee introduced World-Wide Web software to the Internet, designed to allow high-energy physicists to share and exchange graphical data as well as text, using "hypertext" technology. In his summary vision statement for the W3 project, Berners-Lee (1997) explains:

The WWW project merges the techniques of networked information and hypertext to make an easy but powerful global information system. The project represents any information accessible over the network as part of a seamless hypertext information space.

W3 was originally developed to allow information sharing within internationally dispersed teams, and the dissemination of information by support groups. Originally aimed at the High Energy Physics community, it has spread to other areas and attracted much interest in user support, resource discovery and collaborative work areas. It is currently the most advanced information system deployed on the Internet, and embraces within its data model most information in previous networked information systems.

In fact, the web is an architecture which will also embrace any future advances in technology, including new networks, protocols, object types and data formats.

The new object types and data formats Berners-Lee referred to included graphics such as drawings, photographs, or maps that a user could point at with his or her mouse and click on specific areas that would then cause new information to be displayed on the screen. This "hypertext" technology had been introduced in the mid-1980s with limited success in the "HyperCard" software product on the Apple Macintosh computer. Part of the problem with the Macintosh implementation was that most users were working with data that were located on their own computer. The hypertext concept suggested that links could be formed between any data anywhere on a highly dynamic network of sources.

Up until Berners-Lee's introduction of hypertext technology into his Web project, the Internet had been a fairly private communications channel for the academic and technical community that was generally self-regulated. Because the data shared were mostly text documents, the commercial world with its inherent hunger for eye-catching graphics remained unimpressed. Now, with the ability to incorporate all manner of graphics, the commercial world began to take note. Within just a few years, even Mr. Berners-Lee realized that the W3 could not live by grants alone. In a July 1995 interview with *Information Week* magazine, he observed: "The Internet, specifically the Web, is moving from appearing as a neat application to being the underlying information space in which we communicate, learn, compute, and do business" (Lange, 1995).

By this time, the commercial world had truly discovered the World-Wide Web. Combining Berners-Lee's W3 server system with the "browser" software known as Mosaic, developed separately in 1992 by Marc Andreesen and colleagues at the University of Illinois National Center for Supercomputing Activities, innovative retailers such as Pizza Hut, 1-800-Flowers, and Virtual Vineyards had already erected their billboards on what was already being referred to as the "information superhighway." Vinton Cerf (1995) explains the impact of the introduction of the Mosaic browser:

It took the world by storm. The excitement of being able to provide images, sound, video clips and multifont text in a hypertext system was irresistible. Between 1992 and 1995 a number of commercial versions of Web browsers and servers emerged, among them Netscape Communications, which was founded by the former chairman of Silicon Graphics, Inc., who instantly realized that the Web would dramatically magnify the utility of the Internet by replacing its rather arcane interface with something anyone could do—point and click!

"Mosaic" would become the foundation of the Netscape Navigator browser, which would transform its $6.85 an hour programmer/progenitor Andreesen into a multimillionaire industry visionary by age 26, courtesy of a very successful initial public offering to a market hungry for Internet entrepreneurialism.

These early efforts at marketing on the Internet had some obvious limitations, the greatest of which was the limited audience available to consume the message. It was anticipated, however, that the burgeoning demand for home computers would combine with the growing number of corporations connecting their entire internal computer network to the Internet to create an enormous consumer community within just a few years. This anticipation drove, and continues to drive, the progenitors of the Commercial Internet Exchange backbone, ANS, PSI, UUNET, and others to pour stratospheric investments into additional infrastructures.

THE NEED FOR SECURITY

More limiting than the small initial market, however, was the insecure nature of communication across the Internet. Because the system was designed for use by the research community, it was assumed that all participants would always remain altruistic and, therefore, there was little need to protect information traveling from one point to another. Even the most casual commercial user, however, exhibited no such trust or confidence.

If merchants were going to sell their products and services over the Internet, however, customers would have to transmit their credit card or other account information. This information would have to be protected. Of course, the likelihood of someone intercepting a credit card number transmitted over the Internet paled in comparison to the likelihood that a restaurant waiter taking payment for an evening supper, or a gas station attendant ringing up a fill, might duplicate the credit card information. Is it not ironic, then, that the customer who paid for lunch with his credit card and then gassed up the family car on the way home sat down at his PC to order up some pizza, wine, and flowers for his loving wife but could not imagine typing in that account number?

The perceived need for enhanced security on the now commercialized Internet spawned an entire new industry ready to provide the technical infrastructure required to enable electronic commerce. Privacy for these transactions could only be accomplished if the following technologies were assured.

Authentication

Merchants receiving requests for purchases require assurance that requesters are actually who they say they are. In a face-to-face transaction this is accomplished by providing signed identification such as a driver's license. Similarly, the consumer needs assurance that he or she is sending a request for purchase, along with assurance of payment, to the actual merchant and not some other organization posing as the merchant.

Encryption

Once identities have been established and assured, the transaction may take place in the form of transmissions of data between the consumer and the merchant. Because these data to be transmitted include the consumer's personal account information, it is important to assure that the transmission cannot be monitored and recorded in transit. This is accomplished by establishing a mutually agreed secret code into which the data will be encrypted at one end and deciphered at the other.

Nonrepudiation

Finally, the transaction system must provide assurance that a request, confirmation, or any other message exchanged between the parties has not been altered between transmission and reception. This digital signature assures that the message is genuine and cannot be questioned later should a dispute over the transaction arise.

ENTER VISA AND MASTERCARD

Setting such security standards in an environment in which dozens of companies mighty and small were competing soon became daunting. The critical mass required to set a standard was only achieved when the two behemoths of the bank card industry, the two corporations with the most to gain from the institution of a standard, established a standard. Visa and MasterCard introduced their joint plan for the Secure Electronic Transaction (SET) standard in February 1996, with American Express joining their initiative less than a month later. The press release announcing the introduction of the SET standard clearly indicates the importance of this development:

> Addressing consumer concerns about making purchases on the Internet, MasterCard International and Visa International joined together today to announce a technical standard for safeguarding payment card purchases made over open networks such as the Internet. Prior to this effort, Visa and MasterCard were pursuing separate specifications. The new specification, called Secure Electronic Transactions (SET), represents the successful convergence of those individual efforts. A single standard means that consumers and merchants will be able to conduct bankcard transactions in cyberspace as securely and easily as they do in retail stores today. ("Visa and MasterCard combine security," 1996)

Although they estimate 50 million users on the Internet today, with projections of over 100 million by the end of the decade, it is interesting to note that none of the SET bank card participants provide any estimate of anticipated Internet purchasing volume in the information they present at their World-Wide Web sites. Still, by investing such a significant level of time, energy, and resources to the establishment of a unified standard for secure electronic transactions, Visa, MasterCard, and American Express signal their acceptance of the Internet as a viable channel for moneymaking, which will grow dramatically over the next few years.

MONEY-MAKING MODELS ON THE INTERNET

Since the 1992 introduction of hypertext and the World-Wide Web, several economic models have emerged from the minds of enterprising entrepreneurs. A discussion of some of these models follows.

The Advertising Model

The earliest money-making model on the Internet was the most obvious one: Create a high-demand Web site and sell advertising space on it. The earliest adopters of this model were the Web directory services. These sites, epitomized by the wildly successful Yahoo!, which is widely rumored to be an acronym for "Yet Another Hierarchically Organized Oracle" (Larsen, 1995), became a roadmap for all new visitors to the World-Wide Web. Here they could find listings of sites organized by subject, which would guide them to new worlds of information. Widely heralded as the most comprehensive guide to the Web, Yahoo! enjoys a tremendous "hit rate," a key measure of how many times users "click" their mouse button on a "link" somewhere on a web site.

Yahoo! leveraged this high "hit rate" on its Web site into advertising sales. Computer manufacturers, publishers, beverage companies, and others clamored to pay thousands per month to Yahoo! for the opportunity to have their banner, an inch-high rectangular ad approximately the width of a typical computer screen, displayed prominently on popular Yahoo! Web pages. Others followed suit, including *Wired* magazine's HotWired site, which advertised everything from Stolichnaya Vodka to Volvos.

The Merchant Model

Some of the earliest jokes about the World-Wide Web referred to the fact that one could use this powerful new medium to accomplish the most important business functions such as buying pizza, wine, and flowers. Merchants such as Pizza Hut, Virtual Vineyards, and 1-800-FLOWERS were among the first to embrace this new opportunity, this new channel through which new customers could flow.

They faced significant obstacles, not the least of which was the lack of a secure payment methodology. Although some customers did not hesitate to enter their credit card number into the system, and others accepted the idea of a special account with CyberCash or DigiCash, to be used only for spending on the Web, many were not ready for electronic commerce. With the agreement between Visa and MasterCard for a standard for Secure Electronic Transactions (SET), merchants and customers gain the ability to authenticate each others' identities for the purpose of consummating transactions for products and services with confidence. This signals both the acceptance of the validity of electronic commerce and the understanding on the part of the largest bank card service providers that once consumers are assured of security, they will begin shopping actively on the Internet:

> Secure Electronic Transaction (SET) is an open specification for protecting payment card purchases on any type of network. The SET specification incorporates the use of public key cryptography from RSA Data Security to protect the privacy of personal and financial information over any open network. The specification calls for

software to reside in the cardholder's personal computer and in the merchant's network computer. In addition, there is technology residing at the acquirer's (the merchant's bank) location to decrypt the financial information, as well as at the certificate authorities location to issue digital certificates. It is anticipated that software vendors will incorporate SET into existing browsers and merchant servers as soon as Visa's testing is completed. (Visa, 1997)

Software companies such as Netscape, Open Market, O'Reilly, and the software industry's largest player, Microsoft, have all introduced "merchant servers" or "commerce servers," software intended to help merchants build a new electronic sales channel. Such systems allow the merchants to construct their online "store," offering an interactive shopping experience highlighted by photographic images and complete descriptions of products. The system keeps track of shoppers' sizes, preferred styles, and colors, as well as those of friends, relatives, and other associates. The shopper merely needs to point at a product and click on the mouse, causing the product to be "dropped" into a "market basket." At the end of a shopping session, the customer is presented with an on-screen listing of the order. The customer may adjust quantities, sizes, colors, styles, and add or delete items. When finished, the customer is shown the total price of the order, including applicable taxes, shipping, and other charges. He or she may then select a preferred payment method at which point the merchant server utilizes its SET capabilities to complete the sale.

The "Cash by the Click" Model

Target of legislation and derision, the pornographer has nonetheless staked a claim in the Internet rush to gold. Many pornographers have engaged a form of multilevel marketing to attract more potential buyers to shop at their Web site. In this structure, the commercial seller of pornographic images enlists amateurs to include an advertising banner on their own Web site or sites. These amateurs in turn become very active trying every way they can to attract new visitors. Every time a visitor points at the advertiser's banner and clicks the mouse to link to the commercial site, the amateur is paid some small amount of money. Once at the commercial site, the visitor finds him- or herself in a well-organized, highly polished shopping environment.

Armed with a high-demand product, the pornographers wasted no time in preparing their sites to accept whatever form of payment a visitor would consider using. Credit cards, specialized Internet accounts such as CyberCash and DigiCash, and prepaid "wallet" accounts that an Internet user could spend from electronically were all available early on in the rush to electronic commerce. Many of these sites feign some level of credibility by including links to filtering products such as Net Nanny, CyberPatrol, and SurfWatch, all of which are designed to give parents the ability to limit their children's access to these inappropriate materials. Several of these products also herald their ability to provide the same level of control within a corporate community.

The "Making More Money by Spending Less Money" Model

Perhaps the most obvious example of a company successfully reducing costs by automating necessary business functions is the package-tracking function introduced by Federal Express. Visitors to its Web site can enter their Federal Express waybill number to obtain information about the whereabouts of their shipment, including the name of the person who signed for it and the time of delivery. Providing this function on the World-Wide Web allowed FedEx to reduce the load on the customer service representatives, who traditionally provided this information by telephone. This, in turn, allowed them to decrease expenses by reducing the number of customer service representatives and the associated overheads.

Other companies are employing Internet-based services such as fax services, data distribution services, research services, and more to offset traditional internally administered supports. By spreading the cost of maintaining these services among many clients, Internet entrepreneurs are creating a revenue flow for themselves while creating attractive cost-reducing offerings for their clients.

INTERNET SERVICE PROVIDERS

Internet Service Providers (ISP) such as NetCom, PSI, UUNET, Earthlink, Digex, and ANS are the "telephone companies" of the Internet. A user wishing to connect to the Internet will open an account with one of these companies. The individual user will be given a list of local "point-of-presence" phone numbers in his or her area along with software to use for dialing in. This differs from online services such as America Online, CompuServe, and the Microsoft Network (MSN), which offer access to their own "content" databases along with a gateway connection to an ISP. The online service focuses on revenue generation from the online "publication" of their content, whereas the ISP focuses only on generating revenue by providing Internet access service.

Instead of a dialup connection, corporations may lease a dedicated line from their local telephone provider to connect between their company's local network and the ISP's point-of-presence. The ISP charges users for access time and speed or bandwidth, how much data they need to push or pull through this connection on a sustained basis. What the customer does not pay for is distance. Unlike the long-distance telephone carriers, who own or lease all the infrastructure they use to provide connections, the Internet Service Providers such as PSI, UUNET, ANS, BBN Planet and others, each own regional portions of the infrastructure. As such, they cannot charge for the mileage or duration of a particular connection. Because a dedicated line is a full-time connection, and there is no variability of cost based on distance, the customer benefits from the advantage of a fixed and predictable monthly cost, which is based on the speed or bandwidth of the connection.

Because this cost is fixed, and is generally lower than the cost of maintaining long links between cities, many corporations have begun to move much of their data to "virtual private networks," using the Internet to replace their existing long-distance leased lines. By placing similar security devices, or firewalls, at each end of the connection, these companies have been able to transmit and receive business data inexpensively and in a relatively secure fashion. The firewalls encrypt the data on its way out of the originating computer and decrypt the data on the way in to the destination computer so that anyone eavesdropping on the transmission will end up with unintelligible data.

Some ISPs and online services have offered fixed monthly rates for unlimited dialup access time as well, with mixed results. At least one public online service has already announced a competitive offering, eliminating its traditional program of base price for a minimum number of usage hours monthly plus additional charges for additional utilization. Although flat-rate unlimited use billing sounds like a great deal for the user, there is a considerable downside for the network, as Cerf observes:

> I think this kind of phenomenon is going to exacerbate the need for understanding the economics of these systems and how to deal with charging for use of resources. I hesitate to speculate; currently where charges are made they are a fixed price based on the size of the access pipe. It is possible that the continuous transmission requirements of sound and video will require different charging because you are not getting statistical sharing during continuous broadcasting. In the case of multicasting, one packet is multiplied many times. Things like this weren't contemplated when the flat-rate charging algorithms were developed, so the service providers may have to reexamine their charging policies. (quoted in Aboba, 1993)

Several companies that were involved in the creation of the Commercial Internet Exchange in the late 1980s and early 1990s, such as UUNET, ANS, and others, very successfully went public or were purchased in the mid-1990s, and then proceeded to very publicly lose millions. These builders of the infrastructure clearly recognized the opportunity coming toward them and were prepared to invest. They continue to invest in building more and more infrastructure, adding more reach and capacity to the Internet as they do. They anticipate that the next few years will bring them past the stage of the early adopters and on into the general acceptance that will more than compensate them for their infrastructure investments, if they can survive the predatory survival tactics of the major carriers such as AT&T, MCI, MFS, and Sprint.

THE BANDWIDTH WAR

Contrary to popular perception among Internet users, bandwidth is not infinitely elastic. One of the most popular ways to breach the security of a network server is called a "denial of service" attack, which is created by bombarding that server with requests. This has the effect of overloading the server and, often, causing it to halt function completely. This is happening inadvertently on the network on a regular basis. A novice user may decide to download several enormous files simultaneously, at the same time that another user is sending a large multimedia file. The result is denial of service to all other users of that segment of the network for a protracted period of time.

Expand this idea to encompass the growing Internet community. As more users are enjoying more richly varied data types across the Internet, so grows the likelihood of grinding larger and larger segments to a complete halt. Flat-rate unlimited access promotes this activity by actually creating an incentive for increased casual use. If a user does not have to worry about additional charges, the tendency is to "nail up the connection" all day long, instead of disconnecting during periods of nonuse. One solution to this, of course, is to eliminate flat-rate unlimited access charges, which is a course recommended by most members of the Internet community. The online services and ISPs, however, in the drive to swell their subscriber ranks, are moving in exactly the opposite direction.

Another obvious solution calls for the Internet Service Providers to build more and more bandwidth availability. The very public losses suffered by the ISPs are testimony to the fact that they are indeed doing just that. However, increased traffic incented by flat-rate access pricing, coupled with the exponentially growing user community, stands to outpace the growth of infrastructure for some time to come. This being the case, the only other available variable is time, meaning that users will continue to wait longer and longer for data to traverse the available bandwidth if the current condition continues.

The waiting time will not discriminate. Corporate users transmitting strategic data will wait just as long as the college undergrad waiting for an e-mail response from her parents about the need for another cash advance. The audio stream of the President's speech will be delayed just as much as the sampler sound bite from the latest "Snoop Doggy Dog" release.

This indiscriminate waiting time is based on the fact that the basic TCP/IP transport technology of the Internet is a "first-come, first-served" design with no provisions for prioritization based on type or source of information transmitted. TCP/IP is the combination of Transport Control Protocol (TCP) and Internet Protocol (IP). TCP is a connectionless protocol that breaks data down into packets of information. Each packet has an address header that describes its destination. IP sends each packet from the originating host computer to a router, which is programmed to decide where to send it next. Usually it is sent, along with many other packets from many other computers, to another router, and then another, until it reaches a router that knows what destination host computer to ultimately send it to. At no time is an actual connection made between the originating host and the destination. This design is highly economical and flexible, but does not really facilitate transport of anything but fundamental text information because the flow of data is predicated on how busy each router is when the data arrive. If the router is too busy, incoming packets may be delayed or even discarded, requiring retransmission from the source. Streaming data types such as audio or video must have smoothly continuous transport to deliver properly.

Multimedia data types are far better served by connection-oriented technologies similar to our circuit-switched telephone system, in which the exchange of data begins with the negotiation of a dedicated circuit connection between origin and destination points. Throughout the transaction, the bandwidth is dedicated to this communication. New proposed protocols combine the advantages of a connection-based transport with the economies of packet-data transmission, but these may take months if not years to be agreed on, much less implemented in usable products.

Wars inevitably lead to the consolidation of factions, and the bandwidth war is certainly no exception. As traditional voice circuits now carry data and video, so will traditional video circuits carry more text and voice. The cable television providers, the Regional Bell

Operating Companies (RBOCs), and the long distance carriers are all jockeying for position in a battle to provide the best integrated digital service. Physical media purists have even begun to formulate a war between photons carried on fiber-optic cable and the electrons that traverse copper wire. Ultimately, the beneficiary should be the end-users who will vote with their dollars who should win this battle. Increased bandwidth at reduced rates with more reliable service will be the spoils.

THE HAVES, THE HAVE-NOTS, AND THE HAVE-SOMES

The basic issue of having a connection to the Internet is not trivial, nor is it polar. In fact, the relationship of an individual to the Internet experience, and to communicating via this medium, is in many ways proscribed by the nature of his or her connection or connections to the Internet.

Many corporations have elected to lease full-time connections to the Internet. This involves the provisioning of a dedicated line leased from a local carrier running from the corporate site to the nearest Internet point-of-presence (POP) maintained by an Internet Service Provider (ISP). Although this connection may cost the company anywhere from a few hundred to a few thousand dollars each month to maintain, it is usually connected to the corporate local computer network, thus allowing dozens or even hundreds of employees to share access to the Internet.

Individual users have generally elected to use their regular telephone line to dial into a connection to the Internet in one of two fundamental ways. Many have subscribed to popular online services such as America Online, Prodigy, CompuServe, or the Microsoft Network. These services, delivered via a computer system that all users dial into with their computer modems, then provide a gateway to dedicated leased connections into the Internet. Generally, browser and other Internet software to be used is determined by the online service, and the user shares the connection with all other users of that service. This creates an additional level of delay during peak utilization times.

Other individual users have elected to obtain a "point-to-point" (PPP) connection to an ISP. This removes the additional layer of management, selection, and latency introduced by the online service, giving the user better performance and flexibility of choice of software. The most important benefit is that a PPP connection is generally faster and more responsive than an online service connection. Many ISPs offer fixed monthly rates, although most have a package that, like the online services, offers a base number of monthly access hours for a base price with incremental charges for additional utilization and services.

The measurement of the efficiency of these connections is referred to as "bandwidth," which refers generally to how much data can move through the connection each second. The bandwidth of a dial-up connection is limited by the speed of available modems. Measured in "bits" of information transmitted per second (bps), the fastest modems available today can transmit more than 33,000 bps. One modem manufacturer has announced the introduction of modems capable of transmitting and receiving 56,000 bps, but popular use of these will have to wait until ISPs have deployed these at their points-of-presence, and consumers have begun to replace their current modems with the new models.

By comparison, dedicated leased-line connections begin at 56,000 bits per second and run all the way up to 1,544,000 bps, which is referred to as T1 speed. Even faster T3 connections provide 45,000,000 bps of bandwidth. The Integrated Systems Digital Network (ISDN) combines two channels, each of which is capable of carrying 64,000 bps for an effective bandwidth of 128,000 bps. In some markets, ISDN has become a popular way to access the Internet for consumers and corporations alike.

As discussed earlier in this chapter, the ultimate outcome of the activities of the various interested parties will invariably result in some form of integrated digital service network providing highly flexible bandwidth options to support multimedia transmission requirements.

BANDWIDTH AND THE INTERNET EXPERIENCE

Users may approach their Internet activities very differently depending on the bandwidth of their connection and whoever is paying the access bill. For example, corporate users whose computers are connected to their company's local area network will experience the World-Wide Web much as they would any other application running on their computer. That is, they will click their mouse on the browser application, enter a universal resource locator (URL) address, or select from a list of favorite Web sites, which will result in the display of desired information on their screen. They may read the text, observe the graphics, even copy and paste them into documents they are editing using word processing or other software. They may also get up from their desk and go get a cup of coffee, talk to a co-worker, or have some lunch. They may even go home. The temporal element is inconsequential. The data obtained from the Web may remain on the screen for days. The intercourse with the Internet is informal, casual, unburdened.

Users move deftly through their session on the Internet, shutting down the automatic loading of graphics to save time while browsing for desired information, downloading that information to a local storage device once found, and terminating the connection as quickly as possible. Their rapid interaction is economically motivated. The clock is ticking. They are paying for access by the minute to both the ISP and the telephone company through whose network they are making their connection.

Some savvy users have found their way around the system. They have identified an ISP with a fixed monthly rate whose point-of-presence telephone exchange exists within their unlimited calling area, and they have signed up for their local loop carrier's unlimited calling program. But they still shut down the autoloading graphics and find every shortcut possible because their dial-up connection is still so slow. One enterprising Web site developer who understood this dynamic required his Web site development staff to work only on a 14,400 bps dial-up connection because he wanted them to experience the Web sites they were building the way a "typical user" would.

THE BROWSER WAR

Browsers are the software a computer user uses to look at information provided by Web servers over the World-Wide Web. As has been previously mentioned, the first browser, Mosaic, produced by Marc Andreesen and friends at the University of Illinois National Center for SuperComputing Activities, became the foundation for what would become the category killer for browsers: Netscape Navigator.

By literally giving Navigator away over the Internet for the first few years of its existence, Netscape bought itself overwhelming market share. Some estimates suggest that more than 85% of people using the World-Wide Web browse it with Netscape Navigator. Today, a customer can still download "beta" or prerelease versions of Navigator from the Netscape Web site, which cease to function after a specified date, or purchase a permanent copy for $79.

This success would also make Netscape the latest target in the crosshairs of the Microsoft Corporation, which signaled its entry into the market with the introduction of its forever-free-of-charge browser, the Microsoft Internet Explorer. Obviously, the consumer is the winner in this David and Goliath confrontation. Users can own and use both browsers over their point-to-point direct connection, switching when one or the other adds new functionality, repeatedly leapfrogging each other on a regular basis.

There are far more overriding and compelling implications, however, to this war of the browsers. To observe them, one need only to examine the motives of Microsoft. Why would a multibillion dollar corporation of almost 20,000 employees with all but complete control over the personal computer desktop operating system and application environment suddenly switch all of its gears to compete with a startup company marshalling fewer than 500 employees struggling to achieve a fraction of its inflated initial market value?

The answer can be found in the very publicly shared vision of several industry giants, including Microsoft's chairman, Bill Gates, along with Sun co-founder Bill Joy and Oracle CEO Larry Ellison. All share a common vision of the browser as a complete replacement for the desktop graphical user interface with an important new advantage. In their vision, the browser becomes a multiplatform "lingua franca" for all software applications and information transfer. Fundamental applications such as word processing, spreadsheets, and other productivity tools will be "rented" by the millisecond using inexpensive "network computers" consisting of little more than a keyboard, a monitor, a processor, and a connection to the Internet.

In this vision, the Internet becomes a massive storage facility for all connected computers and, in the completion of a cycle started in the mainframe age, these connected computers become little more than terminals providing access to the resources presented by the Net. Gates's Microsoft, which earns its billions selling software to the enormous installed base of fully configured computers, would have to completely overhaul its strategy to survive in such a completely connected computing future. Netscape, by contrast, has designed itself and its products to support such an outcome.

And so the real war begins, the war of the desktop computing paradigm.

OPEN STANDARDS AND MANAGEMENT BY CONSENSUS

No single entity—academic, corporate, governmental, or non-profit—administers the Internet. It exists and functions as a result of the fact that hundreds of thousands of separate operators of computers and computer networks independently decided to use common data transfer protocols to exchange communications and information with other computers (which in turn exchange communications and information with still other computers). There is no centralized storage location, control point, or communications channel for the Internet. (ACLU v. Reno, 1996)

From its inception, management of the Internet has been by conducted by those who have volunteered to participate, with some eventually receiving funding for ongoing support. In the earliest days, despite the ominous overtones of "a network that would survive nuclear attack," the stakes were relatively low, and assignments of responsibility were based on trust. As an example, the Internet Assigned Numbers Authority (IANA), the organization responsible for the distribution and management of unique Internet protocol parameters, consists of the Director of the Information Sciences Institute at the University of Southern California, Jon Postel, working with a few interns. Postel has held this position since IANA's inception in 1984, although he has been doing the job considerably longer. Describing Postel's "appointment" to this role, Sharon Eisner Gillett and Electronic Frontier Foundation's Mitch Kapor explain that "Postel picked up the role of number coordinator because it needed to be done when he was a graduate student involved in the birth of the ARPANet, and he never quit doing it" (Eisner, 1996).

In describing the risks faced as various government, industry, and other stakeholders work to determine the future direction of the coordination of the Internet, Gillett and Kapor explain:

> This risk is especially great for the many people who, because of the realities of exponential growth, have not grown up with the Internet (so to speak) but will help to chart its future. Although the Internet looks quite different from traditional communications infrastructures (such as the telephone system, and the mass media of print, radio and TV), there is a natural tendency to apply the better understood, more centralized mindset associated with these systems to the Internet's coordination problems. . . . This system relies much more heavily on automation and loosely-unified heterogeneity than on institutions and centrally-dictated uniformity. (Eisner, 1996)

Continuing to describe the development of the Internet's protocols, the rules by which all of the computing devices on the network actually exchange information, they point out that:

> The Internet protocols became widely-accepted standards in an unconventional way. Unlike ISO's OSI, they did not have the official imprimatur of an internationally-recognized standards authority. Unlike commercial networking protocols developed contemporaneously, such as IBM's SNA, Digital's DECNET, and Xerox's XNS, they did not have the marketing resources of a large company behind them, nor was their design oriented toward any particular vendor's hardware. Instead, they were developed by researchers funded by the U.S. government, and consequently made freely available to anyone who wanted to use them—in other words,

they became open standards. They were developed in an iterative fashion and improved over time in a process that was not controlled by financial interest, leading to a free and quality product that people wanted to adopt. The seemingly ironic outcome of this process is that the free choices of millions of individuals led to much more universal adoption of the common Internet protocols than any of the other more centrally-mandated alternatives. (Eisner, 1996)

The design decisions made by Vinton Cerf and colleagues in the early 1970s have led to the development of an open set of protocols so simple and so robust that they continue to provide a viable platform for profound advancement nearly 30 years later. When Tim Berners-Lee wanted to share hypertext-based data with his community of high-energy physicists, he was able to layer HTTP, the hypertext transport protocol, atop TCP/IP, the fundamental protocol suite of the Internet. Intel has recently proposed RSVP, Resource Reservation Protocol, which would allow for interactive videoconferencing over the Internet, fully supported by TCP/IP. Similarly, streaming audio, three-dimensional "virtual reality," and other multimedia types have all been supported by this decentralized technical infrastructure. In technical parlance, it can be said that the design and implementation of TCP/IP have "scaled" well. That is, they have continued to provide significant value even as the network has grown from 4 nodes to 40 million.

THE STAKES AND THE STAKEHOLDERS

Of course, the meteoric growth of the Internet since the introduction of the World-Wide Web has pushed this scalability to its natural limit. If scarcity is the progenitor of precious value, there are three commodities that will drive up the costs associated with Internet utilization with significant and, conceivably, deleterious results.

Bandwidth

A 1983 FCC ruling exempted local calls to "enhanced service provider" data networks from per-minute access charges in an effort to stimulate the growth of the data access service market. One of the indirect results of this action has been flat-rate unlimited access fees offered to consumers by ISPs such as NetCom and online services such as America Online. Bill Frezza (1996), President of Wireless Computing Associates, points out:

Back in 1983 this was not a big deal because there were so few data users. But today, thanks in part to the stimulus of flat-rate pricing, we are awash in exponentially growing waves of demand. This is crashing down on an inflexible, highly regulated system that is getting crushed under the load. The uncomfortable truth is that the biggest single threat to the future of the Internet is not a slackening in the growth of demand, but chronic overload caused by failed pricing mechanisms. (Frezza, 1996, p. 41)

When the FCC finally decides to remove this exemption, the pricing algorithm for the entire ISP market will change, and the most marked impact will be on the individual user. Current flat-rate pricing programs offer unlimited access to the Internet and all of its services for approximately $20 per month. Without the FCC exemption, regional local phone access providers will begin charging the ISPs about a penny a minute for local data access. These charges will almost invariably be passed directly through to the consumer. As a result, the user who spends one hour per day on the Internet will almost double his or her monthly payment. Business users will incur even more expense. So much, in fact, that they may cease using the Net altogether. Quoted in an industry publication, Concentric Network Corp. executive James Isaacs observed, "if ISPs passed the access fees on to customers, the consumer side of the (Internet access) business might dry up" (Rafter, 1997, p. 51).

Alternatives to flat-rate pricing include time-based, distance-based, and per-packet-based pricing. Time-based pricing is today used by many ISPs, although they face competitive pressure from flat-rate providers. Distance-based pricing requires "settlement" arrangements between the various regional networks that comprise the Internet. As yet, there is not sufficient metering technology available to support proper settlement systems. Similarly, the cost of measuring packets flowing through the various routers used by ISPs to connect their customers would be dramatically higher than the revenue available from them.

Another alternative would be to establish classes of service, giving preference to higher, more expensive classes. Properly devised, this system would permit individual users to keep dollar costs down while incurring potential delays due to lower classification, whereas larger business users would subsidize the system through higher fees paid for superior responsiveness and throughput.

Internet Protocol Address Numbers

As one example of unanticipated scarcity creating artificial value, the Internet seems to be running out of addresses. Certainly, the one-man organization set up to assign the 20 or so numbers per month required to manage ARPANet in the early 1970s cannot keep up with the 20,000 or more requests processed monthly today. Jon Postel explains:

> Part of the problem is that what might be an appropriate authority when the Internet has a certain size and scope might not be appropriate when the Internet is much larger. The IANA took on the kinds of tasks it carries out in the early days of the ARPANET, supported by funding by DARPA. This was clearly the appropriate authority relationship at that time. (Biederman & Murphy, 1997)

Postel, director and sole full-time participant in the Internet Assigned Numbers Authority, has proposed an ambitious plan to reorganize his process by creating a series of privatized registries similar to those responsible for assigning IP numbers in Asia and Europe, organized into a new body called the American Registry for Internet Numbers (ARIN):

> For more than a year, there have been discussions involving IANA (see IANA Statement), IETF, RIPE, APNIC, NSF and FNC concerning a proposal to manage IP number assignments separate and apart from the registration of Internet domain names. The stability of the Internet relies on the careful management of the IP addresses.

> Recommendations have also been made that the management of the IP space should be placed, as it is with RIPE and APNIC, under the control of and administered by those that depend upon and use it— the end users. Those end users include ISPs, corporate entities, universities, and individuals.

> Consistent with the RIPE and APNIC models, a non-profit organization has been suggested by representatives of the Internet community as an appropriate organization to manage the IP address space for assigned territories, similar to the RIPE and APNIC regional IP registries (ARIN Background Information, 1997). A proposed, independent, non-profit corporation, The American Registry for Internet Numbers (ARIN), is described in the proposal.

> Similar to other non-profit organizations, funding for ARIN would come from membership dues and fees for registration and maintenance. Membership would be open to anyone with an interest in IP-related activities. Members would be responsible for determining the goals of the registry and how it would best meet those goals.

> The fee schedule outlined is similar to that of the RIPE and APNIC models. [http://www.ripe.net and http://www.apnic.net]. All registration fees described would apply only to those IP number allocations received directly from ARIN. IP address space allocated

prior to the incorporation of ARIN is not subject to the proposed fees, and those individuals/entities who have received IP address space prior to the incorporation of ARIN will not be affected by the registration fees.

It is also important to note that almost all Internet users will receive IP addresses from their upstream service provider, rather than directly from ARIN. Those individuals/entities who do not receive address space directly from ARIN will not be charged any registration fees by ARIN.

While we recognize that some Internet Service Providers may need to pass on the costs of ARIN's registration services to their end users, the fees have been structured so that they will produce the most minimal impact possible on the individual end user of an IP address.

Above all else, it should be stressed that ARIN will not be "selling" IP numbers. All requests for IP address space must meet pre-determined criteria currently followed by all IP registries [RFC2050]. These criteria will be the basis for all allocations. The fees that ARIN will collect do not represent charges for the IP numbers. The registration fees are for the registration services rendered by ARIN— review and verification of requests and reassignment information, help desk support, allocation guidelines, whois and other information servers, in-addr.arpa service, record upkeep and database maintenance—and will support the administration and operational requirements of running the registry and managing the IP address space for the assigned territories."

The proposal includes recommendations for a schedule of annual fees to be charged for acquisition and maintenance of IP address blocks. These fees, which might range from $2,500 to $20,000, would dramatically alter the Internet value proposition. Quoted in an industry publication, Doug Humphrey, founder of ISP Digex, Inc., said: "Unless they do this in an equitable manner and it is administered carefully, this could become a nightmare. This is a public trust, but now you have a profit incentive when you start selling addresses." Darrin Wayrynen, a vice president at ISP GoodNet, added: "They're taking advantage of a monopoly situation because the fees are way more than the cost of allocating addresses." Jon Postel, in support of the for-fee registry concept, responded in the same article, "If you're a real company, you pay fees all over for things like business licenses. But I understand that any time you go from a fee service that's been subsidized to some other activity, there will be a large number of people who'll be upset" (quoted in Masud, 1997).

Internet Domain Names, Particularly in the ".com" Top-Level Domain

The Domain Name System (DNS) has been a key to the scaling of the Internet, allowing it to include non-Internet email systems and solving the problem of name-to-address mapping in a smooth scalable way. Paul Mockapetris deserves enormous credit for the elegant design of the DNS, on which we are still very dependent. (Aboba, 1993)

In 1984, the Domain Name Service was introduced to the Internet in an effort to improve mapping hard-to-remember IP address numbers to easier-to-remember names. It soon became obvious that domain names would have to be administered in much the same way as numbers were. In early 1993, the National Science Foundation (NSF) awarded what amounts to a monopoly on the assignment of internet domain names to Network Solutions, Inc., forming the Internet Network Information Center, or InterNIC.

Again, what was not foreseen was the tremendous growth of the Internet, except perhaps by enterprising Internet entrepreneurs such as journalist Josh Quittner, who registered the domain name "mcdonalds.com" and later sold it to the giant hamburger chain for a substantial premium. Subsequently, the InterNIC has instituted rules that require that registrants actually use the names they register and be prepared to demonstrate trademark ownership in event of challenge, but the rush for recognizable domain name continues nonetheless. Especially when the registrant is a commercial enterprise, there is a desire to obtain a domain name that is clearly indicative of the identity of its owner. Commercial enterprises remain very concerned about how prospective visitors will find their World-Wide Web site. Their anticipation is that many users will simply put "www." before their company name and ".com" after it in their first attempt to find them. The commercial enterprise wants to make sure these users successfully find them. This becomes difficult when ABC Appliances, ABC Automobiles, ABC Bakeries, and ABC Television all compete for "abc.com" because only one can register it.

Most recently, the Internet Ad Hoc Committee formed by the Internet Society is attempting to mitigate the competition by introducing new "top level" domains in addition to the "commercial" or ".com" top-level domain. Their suggested additions include.firm for business firms,.store for businesses that advertise goods for sale,.web for world-wide web service organizations, .arts for cultural and entertainment Web sites, .rec for recreation and entertainment, .info for providers of information services, and.nom for individuals. Thus, ABC Appliances might have www.abc.store for its Web address, whereas ABC Accounting might use www.abc.firm.

It is interesting to note that part of the InterNIC's registration revenues are deposited into a fund for "internet infrastructure development." As of December 1996, the InterNIC reports deposits of more than $12 million, which go unspent largely because nobody knows exactly what the funds should be spent on.

CHALLENGES TO THE INTERNET SOCIETY AND INTERNET SOCIETY

Writing in *The New York Times*, writers Christine Biederman and Jamie Murphy crucified the Internet Society and its related organizations such as the IETF, the IANA, and the InterNIC, casting them as "a small band of nonprofit organizations with murky ties to the United States Government [who] floated a master plan for the further colonization of cyberspace" (quoted in Biederman & Murphy, 1997). They go on to pose the question:

And beneath all the squabbles over details there simmers a much more fundamental and disturbing question: Will these founding fathers of cyberspace now willingly yield their brainchild to the oversight of an appropriately constituted international body? Or will a small band of United States Government contractors continue to rule cyberspace, assuming as their only mandate a fast-fading cold war legacy? (quoted in Biederman & Murphy, 1997)

Challengers include former Internet Society office Tony Rutkowski:

What is new here is the amazing apparent belief that they still are—or should be—in control of key components of the Internet," says Tony Rutkowski, a former member of the Internet Society and now the group's most outspoken critic. "It's a case study in how a small group of people who one time had absolute control over the Internet when it was a DARPA/research and academic infrastructure, and operated through their own closed processes, and provided mutual assistance, carefully constructed an institution that they believed could give them significant permanent global control over key components of the Internet, and a significant revenue stream to sustain the effort. (quoted in Biederman & Murphy, 1997)

The rising desire to wrest control of the Internet from the Internet Society-related organizations is also clearly evidenced in reactions to the ARIN proposal:

IANA's proposal was viewed by many as a cyberspace land grab to rival the Homestead Act—but with no "act" by any sovereign recognizing or creating the group's authority. As a result, a wide spectrum of critics, ranging from anarchist groups to foreign citizens to United States Government bureaucrats, have accused IANA and two closely-related groups—the Internet Society (ISOC) and the Internet Architecture Board (IAB)—of committing an equally broad range of sins, from arrogating power to being too United States-centric to the ultimate high crime of the information revolution: attempting to control the Internet. (quoted in Biederman & Murphy, 1997)

Martin Burack, Executive Director of the Internet Society Secretariat, along with Donald M. Heath, President of the Internet Society, George Sadowsky, Vice President of Education for ISOC, and Brian Carpenter, Chair of the Internet Architecture Board, responded in *The New York Times* to the Biederman and Murphy article, explaining the structure of the various organizations that currently govern the Internet:

The Internet Society was established in 1992 by a group of individuals involved with the IETF, who saw a need to provide an institutional home and financial support for the Internet Standards process. It consists of approximately 7,000 individual members and 130 organizational members from more than 150 countries. . . . The members elect the Board.

The Internet Engineering Task Force (IETF) . . . approves the (de facto) standards for the Internet. Its actions are accepted because its membership is made up of thousands of people from throughout the worldwide Internet community. About 90% of the attendees at recent IETF meetings have been from companies such as MCI, AT&T, Netscape, Microsoft, the German and French telephone companies, Sun Microsystems, and a host of other non-academic, non-U.S. governmental operations. Anyone can join the IETF, come up with an idea, gain support from other members, and eventually bring it to a vote. The members nominate and elect their leadership. (quoted in Burack, 1996)

Burack continues by offering a glimpse into the future:

I don't know where you can find a more classic example of good government activity than the Internet. The U.S. spent hundreds of millions (or more) to develop technology, nurtured an embryonic industry, and is turning the results over to private enterprise and the rest of the world. (quoted in Burack, 1996)

So, if management of the Internet is indeed being turned over to private enterprise and the rest of the world, who will end up in charge, and what impact will that have on the millions of users who share the infrastructure today?

It seems unlikely that all the large corporations that have gained an interest in the Internet recently will allow a group of academics to continue to manage an infrastructure that becomes more critical to their mission every day. Ultimately, the Internet becomes a common carrier for commercial enterprise, requiring economic regulation and increased fiduciary responsibility. It will be funded perhaps by taxes and tariffs in some locales and certainly by rate payers throughout the world.

Perhaps the most profound impact on tomorrow's Internet will be created by the burgeoning popularity of the implementation and incorporation of intranets in corporations, particularly multisite corporations. To create an intranet, a corporation will employ the same technology used on the World-Wide Web. This involves the creation of a "Web server," a computer with enough memory, storage, and the appropriate software to allow it to present the text, graphics, and other media available to World-Wide Web users. Were the corporation to attach this Web server computer to the Internet, through its ISP, it could then host Web sites on the World-Wide Web. Instead, however, the Web server is attached only to the company's internal computer network. This internal network may be a local area network (LAN) consisting of only one location or a wide area network (WAN) using dedicated leased communications lines to connect physically disparate sites.

The information served up by this Web server may include such fundamental private information as the company's personnel directory or policies and procedures manuals. Commonly selected for intranet inclusion is information that must be updated and redistributed regularly. In fact, at least one company that mounted an intranet initiative saved over US$1million in its first year in paper production and distribution costs. This return on investment potential is compelling and has driven thousands of corporations to implement Web servers and browsers on their internal networks.

This rush to intranets next impacts Internet economics as multisite corporations begin to compare the monthly recurring cost of their leased-line networks to the cost efficiency of using the public Internet to connect their various locations. The obvious challenge to this method is the lack of privacy. Because the Internet is indeed public, there is no guarantee of privacy for information traveling from one corporate site to another. The solution is to install similar firewalls at each corporate location. Then the firewalls can encrypt all outbound information and decrypt the data as they come into their locale. This assures that anyone attempting to eavesdrop or intercept the data in transit will only receive garbled nonsense. Without the appropriate key they will not be able to interpret the data in any intelligible way.

Intranet users will also want to incorporate voice technology, which will allow them to conduct the rough equivalent of Internet telephone calls to and from anywhere in the world. Because they only pay for access to the Internet, and not mileage, international calls can be achieved for the price of local calls. The Internet now becomes a viable alternative to what is today a substantial source of revenue for the common telephone carriers, who will not ignore the import of this development. Already, MFS has acquired UUNET, World Com has, in turn, acquired MFS, and America Online now owns ANS. The feeding frenzy to own the new information infrastructure has barely begun. The war that will ensue can only be envisioned as local and long distance providers contend with each other, and with cable television providers, to own the most connections to the Internet.

This presumes that there will continue to be only one Internet.

In 1995, the Novell Corporation, which at that time enjoyed 80% market share for local area network operating systems, teamed with AT&T to create AT&T NetWare Connect Services (ANWCS). In their joint presentation to resellers and integrators of the Novell NetWare operating system, they introduced ANWCS as "A Secure Business Internet." Few if any observed that if ANWCS was a secure business Internet, there was, by implication, *another* Internet somewhere. This should not be casually dismissed. ANWCS may have been a failed initiative, but the concept that AT&T or any of the major long distance carriers might offer a separate Internet infrastructure is strategically likely. Some of the major Internet Service Providers claim that anywhere from 60% to 80% of the traffic that crosses their own network infrastructure never leaves that infrastructure. As such, this "Internet" traffic never actually reaches the "inter" of the Net. This can truly be considered multiple parallel infrastructures, or multiple Internets.

And perhaps this is the healthiest environment that can be established. The growth, divestiture, and dismantling of AT&T's monopoly on the voice telephone infrastructure reinforces the idea that many Internet choices is a good thing, assuming that all the providers remain true to the Internet founders' dedication to open standards of interoperability.

In the mid-1970s, Smalltalk progenitor Alan Kay, who was first to describe a windowed computer interface with a point-and-click mouse device, drop-down menus, and icons while working at Xerox's Palo Alto Research Center (PARC), described his vision of a handheld device that would deliver any information instantaneously to its user from some vast knowledge base. Kay's original PARC vision of the DynaBook will soon be completely realized in handheld personal digital assistants (PDAs), which will allow their users to instantly access a world wide web of information with verbal or point-and-click requests understood, parsed, and fulfilled in context. PDAs such as Apple's Newton, or US Robotics' Pilot, provide the device. Satellites provide the connection medium. The Internet, which was just a fledgling little ARPANet of a few dozen academics and defense contractors when Kay posited the idea, provides the global information resources with search engine-driven access to hundreds of thousands of information servers.

Released from the limits of hardwire connections by advanced and readily available satellite access, the Internet will become a truly global mesh of digital data connecting everyone and everything in every way at all times. Internet technology will be embedded in computers, clock radios, cellular phones, billboards, wristwatches, virtual reality headsets, office doors, elevators, desks, chairs, badges, pens, and pads. The implications are staggering, and we will be challenged once again by the need to keep the pace of our technological advance in step with the wisdom of our political logic.

Once again, the overriding, or underwriting, question will be "who will pay for all of this, and how?" Ultimately, the answer may be far simpler than the blistering rhetoric of Microsoft's Bill Gates, Oracle's Larry Ellison, Sun's Scott McNealy and Bill Joy, and Netscape's Jim Barksdale combined. The market will prevail. Information will be sold and bought by the byte, with value determined by the buying public. The information industries will give away the razors, the Network Computers, personal digital assistants, virtual reality headsets, or whatever, just to have the opportunity to sell the blades of useful information. And "useful" will be in the value-setting eye of the beholder.

In the process, Gates's fortune will rise another few dozen billion, more nascent Marc Andreesens will parlay a few bug-eyed nights of coding into the next few killer Net applications, more chief executives will leave their megacorporations to take up posts at small startup Web developers, and more startups will go belly-up. As a result of all of this, hopefully, the rest of us will have experienced a revolution as profound as Gutenberg's introduction of movable type; a revolution of mutable data—an interactive data-sharing environment in which all participants may publish and subscribe. Artists, journalists, entrepreneurs, academics, craftspeople, and hacks will all find their voice on it. It will convey value, and valuelessness. It will give audience to the most lofty aspirant, and to the most depraved.

But, perhaps best of all, in the final analysis the revolution will have been funded by a broad cross-section of businesses and individuals in direct proportion to the degree of benefit each has enjoyed from using it. As such, thanks to the economics of the Internet, this will be the most egalitarian revolution in the history of humankind.

REFERENCES

Aboba, B. (1993, November). How the Internet came to be, Vincton Cerf. *The Online User's Encyclopedia.* Reading, MA: Addison-Wesley. http//:www.forthnet.gr/forthnet/isoc/how.internet. came.to.be.cerf.

ACLU v. Reno, ALA v. U.S.(1996). *Communications Decency Act: CDA ruled unconstitutional.* http://www.epic.org/free-speech/CDA.

Berners-Lee, T. (1997). World-Wide Web Consortium (W3C). http://www.w3.org/pub/www/summary.html

Biederman, C., & Murphy, J. (1997). Rebellion over who controls the net. *The New York Times.* http://www.nytimes.com/library/cyber/week/1123rebel.html.

Burack, M. (1996). Internet Society says it was attacked unfairly. *The New York Times.* http://www.nytimes.com/library/cyber/week1205 response.html.

Cerf, V. (n.d.). *A brief history of the Internet and related networks.* http://www.skywriting.com.

Cerf. V. (1995). *Computer networking: Global infrastructure for the 21st century.* http://www.cs.washington.edu/homes/lazoska/cra/networks.htm.

Eisner, S. (1996, September). *The self-governing Internet: Coordination by design.* http://icg.stwing.upenn.edu/cgi-bin/mfs/02/3620.html.

Frezza, B. (1996, November 11). Does flat-rate unlimited user access threaten the Internet? *Communications Week,* p. 41.

Lange, L. (1995, July 17). The Internet—Where's it all going? *Information Week.* http://techweb.cmp.com/iw/center/default.html.

Larsen, K.R. (1995, December). *Finding information on the World Wide Web.* http://www.ctg.albany.edu/-klarsen/case2te3.html

Masud, S. (1997, January 20). Vars concerned over IP payment plan. *Computer Reseller News.* http:192.215.107.71/wire/news/0120payment.html.

Office of Inspector General/NSF (report on NSFNet). (1993, April 23). http:// www.nsf.gov/ftp/OIG/reports/oig9302.txt-

Rafter, M.V. (1997, January 20). ISPs could owe new fees to Telcos if FCC gives its OK. *Web Week*, p. 51.

Sterling, B. (1993, February). Short history of the Internet. *The Magazine of Fantasy and Science Fiction*. http://www.forthnet. gr/isoc/short.history.of.internet.

Visa International. (1997). http://www.visa.com/cgi-bin/vee/nt/ecomm/set/main-html?2+0#leads.

Visa and Mastercard combine security specifications for card transactions on the Internet [press release]. (1996, February 1). http://www.visa.com/cgi-bin/vee/vw/news/PRelco020196. html?2+0.

Welcome to the Internet Engineering Task Force. (1997). http:// www.ietf.org.

Zakon, R.H. (1993). Hobbes' Internet timeline. http://info.isoc./org/ svest/zakon/internet/history/hit.html.

PART 2

COMMUNICATIONS DECENCY ACT

Communications Decency Act: Editors' Comments

Susan J. Drucker and Gary Gumpert

OVERVIEW

Throughout history, sexually oriented uses are present in an early phase in the process of introduction, examination, experimentation, and acceptance of new communication technologies. So it is not unusual or unexpected that there is currently concern over the computer-mediated transmission of "indecent" materials, particularly available to minors. Various nations have attempted to address these concerns. While nations around the world consider the need to impose restrictions on a new source of sexually oriented material, netizens around the globe are waging wars to ensure cyberspace remains unregulated.

On April 24, 1996, at the informal Council meeting held in Bologna, Italy, the European Telecommunications and Culture ministers identified the issue of illegal and harmful content on the Internet as an urgent priority. The Telecommunications Council of the European Union (EU), for example, expressed concern with regard to offensive material accessible via the Internet, noting that the exact definition of offenses varies from country to country. Within the EU, even child pornography, for example, in which a high degree of consensus exists, is covered by specific legislation in some member states and by more general rules relating to obscenity in others. On September 27, 1996, the Telecommunications Council of the European Union adopted a resolution on preventing the dissemination of illegal content on the Internet, in particular, child pornography. To date these concerns have been left to member states to address, but it may justify community intervention at a later date. The Council noted it is indispensable that international initiatives take into account different ethical standards in different countries in order to explore appropriate rules to protect people against offensive material while ensuring freedom of expression (see chap. 1 for a greater discussion of specific international initiatives taken in this regard).

In the United States vast changes in telecommunications prompted sweeping changes in telecommunications law, embodied in the Telecommunications Act of 1996. The section of the law being closely watched (and hotly debated) throughout the world is the provision for controlling sexually explicit material on the Internet embodied in the so-called Communication Decency Act (otherwise known as the CDA), which was attached to the Telecommunications Act. The Communications Decency Act, 47 U.S.C. § 223 et.seq., states that any person in interstate or foreign communication who, "by means of a telecommunications device, knowingly . . . makes, creates, or solicits" and "initiates the transmission" of "any comment, request, suggestion, proposal, image or other communication which is obscene or indecent, knowing that the recipient is under 18 years of age, . . . shall be criminally fined or imprisoned."

This act prohibits transmission of obscene or indecent communication by means of a telecommunications device (including a modem), as well as sending patently offensive communications through the use of an interactive computer service to persons under age 18. Congress passed the law as a last-minute addition to the major telecommunications bill, making it a crime to display indecent material on an interactive computer network "in a manner available to a person under 18 years of age." A violation carries penalties of up to $250,000 and two years in prison.

This measure sparked intense debate over issues of free speech and government regulation on the Internet. A diverse group of Internet users joined forces in an effort to overturn the CDA, including publishers, librarians, content and access providers, and civil liberties organizations, arguing that the measure severely restricts the First Amendment rights of all U.S. citizens and threatens the very existence of the Internet itself. On the other side, pro-family groups supported and defended its passage, emphasizing the threat to minors and arguing that without the strong provision to combat cyberporn, adults could freely send indecent material to minors on the Internet. Within days of the bill being signed into law, several actions were filed challenging the law. The Consumer Internet Empowerment Coalition, CIEC as it has become known, filed a complaint in federal court requesting that a temporary injunction be granted against the implementation of the CDA.

One action, brought by lead plaintiff the American Civil Liberties Union, and filed in the United States District Court for the Eastern District of Pennsylvania, resulted in the issuance of a temporary restraining order by Judge Ronald Buckwalter. This TRO was issued on the grounds that the indecency provision of the CDA was unconstitutionally vague. Chief Judge Dolores K. Sloviter, Chief Judge for the Third Circuit Court of Appeals, agreed to convene a three-judge court, pursuant to section 561(a) of the Telecommunications Act, for review of the law. The three-judge court consisted of Judge Sloviter, Judge Buckwalter, and Judge Stewart Dalzell. Attorney General Janet Reno then agreed to halt any investigations or prosecutions under the CDA until the three-judge court had decided on a more general plaintiff's motion for a preliminary injunction.

At that point, the American Library Association and others filed a similar action against the CDA, and eventually their action was consolidated with the original ACLU action, all to be heard by the same three-judge court. The case heading has come to be known as *Reno vs. American Civil Liberties Union*, No. 96-511. In June 1996, the three-judge court handed down a unified decision but authored three separate opinions. On June 12, 1996, a federal court in Philadelphia ruled on behalf of the coalition. The judges ruled that the CDA would unconstitutionally restrict speech on the Internet. Said Judge Stewart Dalzell, "These findings lead to the conclusion that Congress may not regulate indecency on the Internet at all." In a statement the same day, President Clinton said, "I remain convinced, as I was when I signed the bill, that our Constitution allows us to help parents by enforcing this Act to prevent children from being exposed to objectionable material transmitted through computer networks. I will continue to do everything I can in my Administration to give families every available tool to protect their children from these materials." The administration counts among its allies such organizations as the U.S. Chamber of Commerce and the Association of National Advertisers. In a statement the following day, CIEC lead attorney Bruce Ennis said, "This court is the first to fully grapple with and grasp the unique nature and potential of the Internet." This intermediate decision is quite noteworthy in its own right as an illustration of the necessity to develop unique innovations in rules concerning new information technology and freedom of speech.

In July another three-judge federal court, in New York, ruling in a separate lawsuit, also blocked enforcement of the law. That panel, consisting of Judge Jose Cabranes of the 2nd U.S. Circuit Court of Appeals and two federal district judges, Leonard Sand and Denise Cote, did not find the law unconstitutionally vague, but they did find it fatally overbroad as a "ban on constitutionally protected indecent communication between adults." The New York panel said it was "inescapable" that the Communications Decency Act "will serve to chill protected speech." The Clinton administration appealed both rulings. The Supreme Court court did not act in the New York case, *Reno vs. Shea*, No. 96-595, and will evidently hold that case for decision in light of its resolution of the Philadelphia case, *Reno vs. American Civil Liberties Union*, No. 96-511.

On July 1, 1996, the Department of Justice filed an appeal of the Philadelphia federal court ruling. On December 6, 1996, the Supreme Court agreed to hear the government's appeal of the Philadelphia court decision. On March 19, 1997, oral arguments were heard by the Supreme Court in the case of JANET RENO, ATTORNEY GENERAL OF THE UNITED STATES, ET AL., Appellants v. AMERICAN CIVIL LIBERTIES UNION, ET AL. (No. 96-511). Oral argument on behalf of the appellants was made by Seth P. Waxman, Esq., whereas Bruce J. Ennis, Esq., represented the appellees. Waxman, Deputy Solicitor General, presented the Clinton administration's defense of the Communications Decency Act of 1996, characterizing the Internet as a danger, "a revolutionary means for displaying sexually explicit, patently offensive material to children in the privacy of their own homes." Ennis, the lawyer for a coalition of civil liberties and computer industry groups that successfully challenged the new law in a lower federal court, described the Internet as "democratizing and speech enhancing," distinctive as a forum for worldwide conversation at little or no cost.

On June 26, 1997, the United States Supreme Court handed down its ruling in which it rejected almost every argument advanced in support of the CDA. All nine justices signed the 40 page majority opinion authored by Justice John Paul Stevens. Chief Justice William Rehnquist and Associate Justice Sandra Day O'Connor issued a separate opinion dissenting in part. The majority opinion emphasized that the law would place undue barriers on adult communications and said its blanket prohibitions on "indecent" and "patently offensive" online content were *overbroad*. The justices acknowledged that the law's goal of protecting children from indecent material was a legitimate and important one but concluded that the "wholly unprecedented" breadth of the law threatened to suppress far too much speech among adults as well as between parents and children. The Internet is encouraging freedom of expression in a democratic society outweights any theoretical but unproven benefit of censorship." The opinion of the court also found the *vagueness* of the CDA a matter of "special concern," noting that vagueness in a content-based regulation of speech raised special First Amendment concerns for a chilling effect and that as a criminal statue this was especially troubling. The concept of "indecency" was soundly rejected as applied to the Internet. The opinion noted, "We are persuaded that the CDA lacks the precision that the First Amendment requires when a statute regulates the content of speech. In order to deny minors access to potentially harmful speech, the CDA effectively suppresses a large amount of speech that adults have a constitutional rights to receive and to address to one another."

The opinion of the court strongly rejected the government's argument that its "significant interest in fostering the Internet's growth provides an independent basis for upholding the CDA's constitutionality." Supporters of the CDA had argued that development of the Internet would be supressed by parents' fears about having online access if they could not shield their children from indecent material and thus would be driven away from the medium all together. This argument was characterized as "singularly unpersuasive." Justice Stevens added that "the dramatic expansion of this new marketplace of ideas contradicts the factual basis of this contention."

The dissenting opinion maintained that "the CDA can be applied constitutionally in some situations." Specifically the analogy was made to the creation of "adult zones" and the use of zoning laws as an appropriate and constituonally sound way to protect minors without unduly restricting adult access to the material. Justice O'Connor noted that two characteristics of the physical world which made "adult zones" a workable approach to limiting access to sexually explicit material were two characteristics of "geography" and "identity." Thus, the twin characteristics of georgraphy and identity enable the establishment's proprietor to prevent children from entering the establishment, but to let adults inside. The electronic world is fundamentally different. Because it is no more than the interconnection of electronic pathways, cyberspace allows speakers and listeners to mask their identities. Acknowledging that "gateway" technology which would assist in the identification process is available, it is not yet ubiquitous and therefore "cyberspace still remains largely unzoned and unzoneable." However, when addressing the CDA's provision banning transmission of "indecent" material to "specific minors," she argued that when an adult speaker sends an indecent e-mail message knowing the recipient is a minor or converses in a chatroom with minors only, then the "indecency transmission" and "specific person" provisions of the law do not infringe on adults' speech and the provisions are not overbroad in the sense that they restrict minors' access to a substantial amount of speech that minors have the right to read and view.

Legal scholars' and critics' reactions to this ruling emphasized the implications of the "sweeping endorsement of free speech on the Internet" in the Court's first endeavor extending the principles of the First Amendment into cyberspace. Further, of great interest are the ramifications with regard to the legal concept of "indecent speech" when applied to other media (i.e., broadcasting, cable television, telephonic communication).

The debate over the CDA and the ultimate ruling by the Supreme Court with regard to its constitutionality are of great significance in terms of establishing precedent in the area of sexually oriented messages. More significant, perhaps, is the precedential value of this controversy on the frontline of a new endeavor of drafting and interpreting the laws of cyberspace. What follows are four chapters that explore the Communications Decency Act from distinct vantage points. It is our hope that focusing on separate dimensions of the act and various interpretive frameworks will yield a greater, more comprehensive understanding of the whole.

6

FIRST AMENDMENT CHALLENGES TO RESTRICTIONS ON INTERNET EXPRESSION: WHICH STANDARD FOR JUDICIAL REVIEW?

DOUGLAS FRALEIGH

When deciding whether legislation affecting First Amendment rights is constitutional, reviewing courts employ several different tests. If the challenged restriction impacts a fundamental right, a stringent form of analysis referred to as strict scrutiny is used. This text is the appropriate standard of review for laws that restrict freedom of expression. In this chapter Douglas Fraleigh examines several different standards that could be used to review the Communications Decency Act of 1996 and advances the argument that strict scrutiny should be applied to protect expression in this case.

Indecency and obscenity are not synonymous concepts in First Amendment law. The Supreme Court settled on the criteria for obscenity in *Miller v. California* (1973), and subsequent decisions have made it clear that material must depict patently offensive hard core sexual conduct (*Jenkins v. Georgia*, 1974) and lack serious literary, artistic, political, or scientific value. Obscenity is not protected by the First Amendment (*Roth v. United States*, 1957), and the Communications Decency Act's ban on obscene cyberspace communication has not been challenged.

Indecency is a broader term than obscenity. It refers to material that does not conform with accepted standards of morality (*FCC v. Pacifica Foundation*, 1978). Communication that does not describe "hard core" sexual conduct may nevertheless be indecent because it contains offensive words dealing with sex or excretion (*FCC v. Pacifica*, 1978) such as comedian George Carlin's "Filthy Words" monologue that was at issue in *FCC v. Pacifica*. Sexual expression that is indecent but not obscene is protected by the First Amendment (*Sable Communications of California, Inc. v. FCC*, 1989).

The constitutionality of the *indecency* provisions of the Communications Decency Act (CDA) was challenged in lawsuits filed February 8, 1996, the day President Clinton signed the CDA into law. Two federal district courts issued preliminary injunctions against the enforcement of the CDA (*ACLU v. Reno*, 1996; *Shea v. Reno*, 1996) The Supreme Court is expected to hear an appeal of one of these cases, *ACLU v. Reno*, in Spring 1997.

When the Supreme Court decides this case, it will need to decide what level of scrutiny to employ in analyzing the government's justification for restricting the content of speech in cyberspace. Historically, the level of scrutiny applied to restrictions on expression by the Supreme Court has varied, depending on the medium of communication at issue. The standard the Court decides to use when evaluating restrictions on cyberspace expression could have a pivotal effect on the outcome of the case because the burden of justification placed on the government varies greatly under these different tests.

This chapter discusses four different standards by which restrictions on the content of expression in cyberspace could be judged. At opposite ends of this spectrum are strict scrutiny (applied to the most favored channels of communication) and the rational basis test (applied when low value speech such as obscenity is regulated). Two other standards that are analyzed are the test applied to broadcasting in Pacifica and a new criteria which was recently applied to cable television in *Denver Area Educational Telecommunications Consortium, Inc. v. FCC* (1996). The Communications Decency Act is used as a case study in this chapter when examining the application of each standard, but the same principles are relevant if other restrictions on cyberspace expression are imposed in the future.

STRICT SCRUTINY OF RESTRICTIONS OF SPEECH

The Strict Scrutiny Test

Strict scrutiny is the standard of review that is most difficult for the government to meet. This level of scrutiny applies to content-based restrictions on traditional modes of communication such as newspapers, pamphlets, and public speeches. It has also been applied to restrictions on telephone communication that is indecent but not legally obscene (*Sable v. FCC*, 1989).

When strict scrutiny is applied to a restriction on speech, the Court analyzes whether the regulation promotes a compelling state interest and whether it constitutes the least restrictive means to further that interest. The means by which the government interest is served must be carefully tailored (or narrowly tailored) to achieve those ends, and the law must be reasonably restricted to the evil with which it is said to deal (*Sable v. FCC*, 1989).

The protection of minors' physical and psychological well being will satisfy the compelling state interest portion of the test. The Supreme Court has upheld legislation protecting the well being of youth, "even when the laws have operated in the sensitive area of constitutionally protected rights" (*New York v. Ferber*, 1982, pp. 756-757). However, it is not sufficient for the government to simply assert that the nation's youth are in need of protection. The government cannot "posit the existence of the disease sought to be cured," instead it must "demonstrate that the recited harms are real, not merely conjectural" (*Turner Broadcasting System v. FCC*, 1994, p. 531).

Even if the state interest is compelling, legislation aimed at indecency may also be found unconstitutional because the means by which the government attempts to protect children cannot survive strict scrutiny. One question asked is whether the government's interest can be served by a law that is less intrusive on First Amendment freedoms? For example, in *Sable v. FCC*, the Court held that a ban on indecent commercial telephone messages was not needed to prevent children from accessing the messages. Less intrusive means to protect children would include requiring a credit card or access code before one could receive a message. The government could not prevail by asserting that these alternatives to a ban would be ineffective; instead, it would be the state's burden to prove that enterprising minors would be able to circumvent the rules (*Sable v. FCC*, 1989).

A second concern is whether the regulation will be successful in serving the asserted state interest. This principle was applied in the dissent of Justices Kennedy in *Denver Area v. FCC* (1996). In that case, the Supreme Court upheld a federal law allowing cable system operators to prohibit the broadcasting of patently offensive broadcasting on those channels that they are required by law to lease to third parties. The dissenting justices applied strict scrutiny and came to a different result. Their opinion noted that children could still see offensive programming in any locality in which the cable operator opted not to ban such programming. Hence, this law was at most "partial service of a compelling interest" (p. 943) and could not survive strict scrutiny.

A third issue is whether the costs to free expression imposed by the means chosen by the government are outweighed by any benefits achieved by the restriction. In *Butler v. Michigan* (1957), a unanimous Supreme Court invalidated a statute that prohibited distribution to the general public of materials found to have a potentially harmful influence on minors. The Court reasoned that the law denied adults their free speech rights by allowing them to read only what was acceptable for children. Justice Frankfurter's opinion in Butler analogized the effect of this provision to "burn[ing] the house to roast the pig" (p. 383).

Application of Strict Scrutiny to the CDA:
The Compelling State Interest

The federal government has argued that the compelling state interest served by the Communications Decency Act is shielding minors from access to indecent materials (*ACLU v. Reno*, 1996). Protecting the physical and mental well-being of this nation's youth is clearly a compelling interest (*New York v. Ferber*, 1982). Under a strict scrutiny analysis, the Court should also question the extent to which children are harmed by the existence of indecent materials on the Internet. In his dissent in *Action for Children's Television v. FCC* (1995), Chief Judge Harry Edwards of the U.S. Court of Appeals, District of Columbia Circuit applied strict scrutiny and reached the conclusion that harmful effects of indecent material on children were not proven. He noted that "there simply is no evidence that indecent broadcasts harm children," and that during an oral argument of that case, the counsel for the FCC was "unable to cite any study that found a causal connection between exposure to indecent broadcast and psychological or other harm to children" (p. 682).

The government would also be likely to argue that children's viewing of immoral material is itself harmful. According to this perspective, the majority of society has the right to establish a moral code for children, and a violation of this code is an evil the state may prevent. For example, in 1968, the Supreme Court held that a statute that protected children from exposure to materials that would impair their ethical and moral development was constitutional

(*Ginsberg v. New York*, 1968). A good argument can be made that such a harm is no longer sufficient to survive strict scrutiny. In the context of legislation regulating obscenity (expression that is less protected than indecency), Franklyn Haiman (1993) noted that protection of the public morality is "a far cry from the kind of direct, immediate, and irreparable harm that the Supreme Court has required before other kinds of speech can be suppressed" (p. 53). He likens the obscenity exception to the First Amendment as "an anachronistic relic of the Victorian era" (p. 53), and the same argument can made about the attempt to control the moral standards of society by regulating indecent expression.

Even if the prevention of children's exposure to indecent materials is a compelling state interest, the Communications Decency Act is not a means of serving that interest that is likely to survive strict scrutiny.

Application of Strict Scrutiny to the CDA: The Means of Achieving the State Interest

When using strict scrutiny, the Court asks whether the state interest could be served through legislation that is less restrictive to freedom of expression. Several less intrusive means for restricting children's access to indecent materials on the Internet were described in the federal district court's opinion in *ACLU v. Reno* (1996). There is an expanding market for software that will enable parents or schools to limit the Internet access of children. One example is Cyber Patrol, which allows adults to block access to 12 categories of rated sites. These categories include sexually explicit material, as well as racist texts, materials that glorify illegal drug use, and those promoting militant political groups (*ACLU v. Reno*, 1996). America Online hosts an online area designed specifically for children and allows parents to set up accounts for their children that limits access to the Kids Only channel. The federal district court concluded that "currently available user-based software suggests that a reasonably effective method by which parents can prevent their children from accessing . . . material which parents believe is inappropriate for their children will soon be widely available" (p. 842).

Thus, technologies exist that helps adults to prevent minors from utilizing materials deemed inappropriate. Parents could also decide not to allow their children to access the Internet at all. Approaches that place the choice of what material will be viewed into the hands of parents are less restrictive alternatives to the Communications Decency Act. They allow all expression that is protected by the First Amendment to be on the Internet and let individual parents decide what limitations should be placed on their children. This decision is much like the one that a parent must make if he or she keeps sexually explicit books on the shelf. Parental responsibility for controlling children's access to materials they find objectionable has been a judicially preferred alternative to censorship (*Fabulous Associates, Inc. v. Pennsylvania Public Utility Commission*, 1990).

In addition to analyzing less restrictive alternatives, strict scrutiny requires the reviewing court to question how effectively the regulation will achieve the state interest. In his opinion in *ACLU v. Reno* (1996), Judge Dalzell noted that about half of the Internet communications originate outside of the United States. Individual communicators with no physical presence in the United States cannot be prosecuted under the Communications Decency Act, and commercial pornographers might simply relocate to a foreign country. Hence, the act constitutes at most a "partial service of a compelling interest" (*Denver Area v. FCC*, 1996), making it less likely to survive this component of strict scrutiny.

A third question applied to the means of achieving the state interest is asking whether the legislation in question imposes too high a cost on free expression in relation to the benefits. The Communications Decency Act would be unlikely to survive this analysis. One of the virtues of the Internet is that ordinary citizens who have access to a personal computer and a modem can access a worldwide audience. Unlike broadcasting, publishing, or cable television, a large investment is not required to participate in this medium of communication. It would be technologically or economically impossible for many of the persons using the Internet to determine the age of all those who might see the material they post (*ACLU v. Reno*, 1996). Consequently these persons would need to "reduce the level of communication to that which is appropriate for children" to be protected under the decency act (p. 854). When strict scrutiny has been employed, the Supreme Court has been cautious not to "burn the house to roast the pig" (*Butler v. Michigan*, 1957, p. 383). As with the ban on indecent commercial telephone messages in *Sable v. FCC* (1989), the CDA would likely be found unconstitutional because it reduces the level of communication on the Internet to that which is acceptable for children.

Therefore, the Communications Decency Act would be unlikely to survive a strict scrutiny analysis. Even if the act were found to serve a compelling interest in shielding minors from indecent material, the law would not serve that interest in an acceptable way. There would be an excessive burden placed on the rights of adults to send and receive information, the law would not shield minors from indecent material that originated overseas, and parental control would be a less intrusive means of protecting children than government censorship. The favorable treatment afforded Internet expression under strict scrutiny can be contrasted with the limited protection that would be available under the rational basis test.

THE RATIONAL BASIS TEST

The rational basis test lies at the opposite end of the spectrum from strict scrutiny. Under this standard, a government restriction of speech is constitutional if there is some rational basis for the restriction. Courts utilizing this type of analysis will ordinarily defer to a legislative judgment that there a need to restrict speech, and that the regulation chosen is an appropriate solution.

Rational basis analysis is ordinarily not used to review content-based limitations on speech. However, it has been used to review regulations on low value speech such as obscenity, which is not protected by the First Amendment. For example, in *Paris Adult Theatre I v. Slaton* (1973), the Supreme Court upheld a Georgia law banning the exhibition of obscene materials. The Court did not rigorously examine the state interest in precluding consenting adults from viewing an obscene film in a theater. Instead, the Court noted that "although there is no conclusive proof of a connection between antisocial behavior and obscene material, the legislature of Georgia could quite reasonably determine that such a connection does or might exist" (pp. 60-61). Although a strict scrutiny analysis would not allow a regulation of expression to be based on conjectural harms (*Turner v. FCC*, 1994), a rational basis analysis candidly allows for regulation based on harms that might exist.

Application of the Rational Basis Test to the CDA

Under a rational basis analysis, the Communications Decency Act would be held Constitutional. In *Ginsberg v. New York* (1968), the Supreme Court upheld a New York law making it unlawful to knowingly sell to a person under 17 any picture or magazine that depicts nudity and is harmful to minors. The Court's rational basis analysis required "only that we be able to say that it was not irrational for the legislature to find that exposure to material condemned by the statute is harmful to minors" (p. 641).

Regardless of one's judgment as to the best arguments on this issue, it would not be irrational for Congress to accept the arguments of those who contend that indecent materials are harmful to minors. Prior to passage of the CDA, there were abundant statements before Congress by persons such as the National Coalition for the Protection of Children & Families (1995), who argued that the act was "vital to the well being of our nation's most important resource, its children" (p. S8337). Because "Congress does not need the testimony of psychiatrists and social scientists in order to take note of the coarsening of impressionable minds that can result from persistent exposure to sexually explicit material" (*Action for Children's Television v. FCC*, 1995, p. 662), the opinions of concerned citizens and members of Congress themselves (*Paris Adult Theatre I v. Slaton*, 1973) would provide a rational basis for sustaining the Communications Decency Act.

The Supreme Court has never assumed that there is a forced choice between a stringent strict scrutiny evaluation or the permissive rational basis test. For newer media, intermediate forms of scrutiny have been often been utilized. The next section analyzes the Communications Decency Act under one such standard that was applied to broadcasting.

THE BROADCAST STANDARD

The Pacifica Ruling on Broadcast Indecency Regulation

The landmark decision holding that the government has a lower burden of justification when regulation of indecent expression in the broadcast medium is challenged was *FCC v. Pacifica Foundation* (1978). In *FCC v. Pacifica*, the Supreme Court upheld the Federal Communications Commission's power to impose sanctions when a radio station broadcast George Carlin's "Filthy Words" monologue at 2 o'clock in the afternoon. The case arose when a father complained to the FCC because he heard the broadcast while driving with his son. The Carlin monologue was not legally obscene, but it was found to be "indecent."

The *FCC v. Pacifica* opinion did not articulate a particular level of scrutiny for reviewing regulations directed at the content of broadcasting. Instead, the Court began by discussing two reasons for giving the government greater power to punish indecent messages on the airwaves. First was the fact that the "broadcast media have established a uniquely *pervasive* presence in the lives of all Americans" (p. 748; emphasis added). The Court noted that indecent material on the airwaves can confront the citizen in the privacy of the home. An individual could turn on his or her radio and be subjected to indecent programming of which he or she had no prior notice. Justice Stevens's majority opinion rejected the argument that the harm of indecency could be remedied by turning off one's radio, analogizing this claim to "saying that the remedy for an assault is to run away after the first blow" (pp. 748-749).

Second, the Court noted that broadcasting is uniquely accessible to young children. The "government's interest in the 'well being of its youth' and in supporting 'parents' claim to authority in their own household" (p. 749) justified a ban on indecent broadcasting, at least during times when children are likely to be awake.

The detriment to the communicator is substantial when the constitutionality of government restrictions is determined by the broadcasting standard rather than strict scrutiny. First, for highly protected communication channels, the less restrictive alternative of turning one's head is the remedy to offensive expression (*Cohen v. California*, 1971, p. 21). For pervasive modes of communication, if the receiver can be surprised by offensive words, the receiver's right not to be offended in the home trumps the free expression rights of the source.

Additionally, in a highly protected communication media, the government has a burden to prove that alternatives to a ban on indecent expression would fail. In *FCC v. Pacifica* (1978), it was assumed that alternatives to a ban would fail. The government was not required to prove that radio station warnings would be unable to keep most children from hearing offensive programming. Alternatives such as parental programming of the radio buttons in the car, or a parental rule that only adults may tune in a station, were not considered.

Finally, the *FCC v. Pacifica* court did not ask whether the gains from banning indecent programming outweighed the cost. The majority opinion expressed concern that the listener could not be *completely* protected from offensive expression. The interest of the offended listeners was the only one considered. It was assumed that any harm caused by exposure to indecency was sufficient to outweigh the freedom of speech that is lost. The free expression right of the communicator and the right of willing listeners to hear the Carlin monologue were not even placed into the equation.

Application of the Broadcast Standard to the CDA

If cyberspace communication was analogized to broadcasting, the *FCC v. Pacifica* reasoning could be used to justify control of indecent communication on the Internet. Pervasiveness and accessibility to children, the two special circumstances used to justify the less stringent standard of review in *FCC v. Pacifica*, are arguably present when cyberspace is the medium of expression.

Personal computers are often located in the home, the domain in which the *FCC v. Pacifica* majority found the rights of the potentially offended listener to be paramount. Imprecise searches may lead to accidental viewing of indecent material (*Shea v. Reno*, 1996). Although the risk of accidentally discovering an indecent Web site may be less than that of accidentally tuning the radio to an indecent broadcast, *FCC v. Pacifica* did not turn on the degree of risk to children. The Court emphasized the listener's inability to be completely protected from unexpected indecent program content.

Furthermore, the Internet is accessible to children. Teenagers and precocious preteens are able to log on to the Internet on their own. Beyond the possibility of an accidental indecency sighting, there is certainly a risk that unsupervised children will intentionally uncover sources containing words and/or pictures that their parents would prefer them not to see. To date, there is no software that can guarantee that all indecent sites can be blocked by parents (*Shea v. Reno*, 1996). Because Internet sites are accessible 24 hours a day, a safe harbor compromise (permitting indecent expression on the Internet during hours children are not likely to be online) is not feasible. The courts will need to choose between the First Amendment rights of adults and the government's interest in keeping children from accessing indecent materials.

In addition, the *FCC v. Pacifica* opinion did not require proof of a significant harm to children before indecency could be regulated. Rather than scrutinizing whether the injuries are conjectural (*Turner v. FCC*, 1994), the fact that indecent communication adversely affects children is likely to be taken as a given. For example, in *Action for Children's Television v. FCC* (1995), the D.C. Circuit Court of Appeals noted that: "The [Supreme Court] has made it abundantly clear that the Government's interest in the well being of its youth justified special treatment of indecent broadcasting" (p. 662).

The Communications Decency Act could survive judicial scrutiny under the broadcast standard established in *FCC v. Pacifica*. This level of review is far less demanding than strict scrutiny. Although the Court analyzes the restriction at issue in more detail than it does when using the rational basis test, the outcome could be the same because both tests accept the assumption that shielding children from indecency is more important than protecting freedom of expression.

The broadcasting standard is not the only intermediate level of review that the Supreme Court could employ when examining restriction of expression in cyberspace. In *Denver Area v. FCC* (1996), the Court created a test for cable television regulations that could have very unpredictable results if applied in cyberspace cases.

THE DENVER AREA STANDARD

The Denver Area Test for Cable Regulation

One of the statutory provisions at issue in *Denver Area v. FCC* was Section 10a of the Cable Television Consumer Protection and Competition Act of 1992. That provision permitted the operator of a cable system to regulate certain offensive expression on those channels that the operator is required by law to lease to third parties. Specifically, an operator could prohibit the broadcasting on leased access channels of programming that he or she reasonably believed to describe or depict sexual or excretory activities in a patently offensive manner.

The Supreme Court ruled that Section 10a did not violate the First Amendment, although the justices were sharply divided in the reasoning they used to reach that result. Three justices (Thomas, Rehnquist, and Scalia) did not consider the indecency issue, instead basing their holding on the fact that the expression rights of cable system operators generally took primacy over the rights of those who leased channels from the operators.

Justice Breyer's plurality opinion (joined by Justices Stevens, O'Connor, and Souter) created a standard that would be unpredictable if applied to cyberspace regulation. The plurality declined to apply strict scrutiny and instead said Section 10a was constitutional if it "properly addresses an extremely important problem, without imposing, in light of the relevant interests, an unnecessarily great restriction on speech" (p. 902).

Applying this new standard of scrutiny, Justice Breyer concluded that Section 10a did not violate the expression rights of those who leased cable channels. First, the provision had an "extremely important justification," namely, protecting children from "exposure to patently offensive sex-related material" (p. 902). Second, the context of this provision was unique, involving the allocation of expression rights between system operators and those who leased channels from them, rather than a government ban on offensive programming. Third, the plurality held that the problem in this case was "remarkably similar to the problem addressed by the *FCC in Pacifica*" (p. 903). The *FCC v. Pacifica* restriction was constitutional because broadcasting is uniquely accessible to children, and cable broadcasting is "as accessible to children as over the air broadcasting if not more so" (p. 903). Finally, because Section 10a only permitted cable operators to limit offensive programming, the loss of expression would probably be less than that which would be imposed by a governmental ban.

Application of the Denver Area Standard to the CDA

The Communications Decency Act contains relevant differences from Section 10a of the 1992 Cable Television Act; hence, it could be found unconstitutional even if the *Denver Area v. FCC* test was applied. Most significantly, the CDA is a government restriction on indecent online communications, rather than a government allocation of expression rights to private owners of a communications system rather than system users. Furthermore, the CDA does not simply permit the exclusion of indecent communications, it prohibits that communication. Hence, two of the four factors that justified the constitutionality of Section 10a are not present in the case of the Communications Decency Act.

However, other components of the *Denver Area v. FCC* plurality's standard of review point to the conclusion that the CDA would be found constitutional. The decency act is premised on the same justification as Section 10a, the protection of children from offensive material. Furthermore, much as the *FCC v. Pacifica* majority did not seriously consider the possibility of less restrictive alternatives to a ban on broadcast indecency, the *Denver Area v. FCC* plurality assumed that offensive cable broadcasts would be accessible to children. Justice Breyer's opinion did not discuss the use of a lockbox or parental key (*Cruz v. Ferre*, 1985) to limit children's access to objectionable cable channels. If this *Denver Area v. FCC* analysis was applied to the CDA, the Court would not consider whether parental control software would be an acceptable less restrictive alternative to a ban on broadcast indecency.

Although the *Denver Area v. FCC* standard may not lead to a finding of constitutionality if applied to the CDA, it is troubling for another reason. It shows that the appropriate standard for restrictions on cyberspace (and other future communication media) may be decided on an ad-hoc basis. The plurality's standard focused on two issues. First, does the restriction focus on an extremely important problem? Second, does the restriction impose an unnecessarily great restriction on speech in light of the relevant interests? Justice Breyer's opinion cited no case law in support of these standards. The plurality gave no definition of these terms and failed to compare or contrast them to strict scrutiny, the rational basis test, or the *FCC v. Pacifica* rule.

The novel analysis used by the *Denver Area v. FCC* plurality portends a very unpredictable outcome when the constitutionality of the Communications Decency Act (and future restrictions on expression in cyberspace) are considered. Justice Kennedy suggested that the plurality "clutter[ed] our First Amendment case law by adding an untested rule with an uncertain relationship to the others we use to evaluate laws restricting speech" (*Denver Area v. FCC*, 1996, p. 930). In a dissent joined by Justice Ginsberg, he noted the uncertainty that will plague lower courts and communications lawyers who must account for the Denver Area precedent in future cases. The plurality's holding provides one more lesson about the possible fate of the CDA and future legislation. In the absence of clearly defined standards for adjudication, the outcome will be highly unpredictable.

CONCLUSION

When the Communications Decency Act and future legislation restricting expression in cyberspace are challenged on First Amendment grounds, the Supreme Court will need to establish a standard of review by which the justification for the restriction will be evaluated. This chapter has considered four such standards: strict scrutiny, the rational basis test, the broadcast standard, and the standard for cable television used by the *Denver Area v. FCC* plurality.

The choice of which standard to use has significant implications for freedom of online expression. Using the example of the Communications Decency Act, this chapter has analyzed how speech restrictions can have different constitutional outcomes, depending on the standard of review utilized. Because the tests differ greatly in the importance placed on shielding minors from indecent communication relative to freedom of expression, the choice of a standard could easily dictate the outcome of the challenges to the Communications Decency Act.

REFERENCES

Action for Children's Television v. FCC, 58 F.3d 654 (D.C. Cir. 1995).
American Civil Liberties Union (ACLU) v. Reno, 929 F. Supp. 824 (E.D. Pa. 1996).
Butler v. Michigan, 352 U.S. 380 (1957).
Cohen v. California, 403 U.S. 15 (1971).
Cruz v. Ferre, 755 F.2d 1415 (11th Cir. 1985).
Denver Area Educational Telecommunications Consortium, Inc. v. FCC, 518 U.S. _____, 135 L. Ed. 2d 888, 116 S. Ct. 2374 (1996).
Fabulous Associates, Inc., v. Pennsylvania Public Utility Commission, 896 F.2d 780 (3rd Cir. 1990).

Federal Communications Commission (FCC) v. Pacifica Foundation,
    438 U.S. 726 (1978).
Ginsberg v. New York, 390 U.S. 629 (1968).
Haiman, F. (1993). *"Speech acts" and the First Amendment.*
    Carbondale: Southern Illinois University Press.
Jenkins v. Georgia, 418 U.S. 153 (1974).
Miller v. California, 413 U.S. 15 (1973).
National Coalition for the Protection of Children and Families, 103
    Cong., 1st Sess., Cong. Rec. S8337 (1995).
New York v. Ferber, 458 U.S. 747 (1982).
Paris Adult Theatre I v. Slaton, 413 U.S. 49 (1973).
Roth v. U.S., 354 U.S. 476 (1957).
Sable Communications of Cal., Inc. V. FCC, 492 U.S. 115 (1989).
Shea v. Reno, 930 F.Supp. 916 (S.D.N.Y. 1996).
Turner Broadcasting System, Inc. v. FCC, 512 U.S. _____, 129 L. Ed.
    2d 497, 114 S. Ct. 2448 (1994).

7

THE OLD RULES MAY NOT APPLY ANYMORE: TECHNOLOGY AVERSION, VIRTUAL COMMUNITIES, AND THE NEED FOR INNOVATION IN EVALUATING RESTRICTIONS OF CYBERSPACE

JOSEPH S. TUMAN

By examining the decision making and reasoning behind the three-panel federal district court of Philadelphia's decision holding the CDA unconstitutional on its face, Joseph Tuman explores existing standards of review and argues for the technologically driven need to construct new laws tailored to new media developments. Although admitting the danger of regulating the Internet, he also examines the public interest in protecting children.

In this chapter I explore the fragmented yet consolidated approach of the federal district court of Philadelphia in resolving the constitutional questions raised by the Communications Decency Act (CDA). Although I am interested in the specifics of this legislation, I am also concerned with the larger implications it raises about trying to regulate the Internet and how we balance this against a valid public interest in protecting children. Equally so, I am interested in what this case says about the level of technical and technological competence we have in this country and how that may vary by generation.

My own ignorance about the Internet is a perfect example. I know a bit about computers and have been exposed to them since my time in college nearly 20 years ago. But what I know about computers is minor compared to my students, and what they know will be nothing compared to the generation that follows them (like my children). With technology changing and constantly reinventing itself and the way we communicate, what happens when judges, brilliant and educated in their own right, are asked to make decisions about First Amendment concerns from a technology they may not understand or be averse to learning about?

Finally, I also consider the nature of the Internet itself, as seen in light of the Marketplace of Ideas metaphor for freedom of speech.

ACLU V. RENO

The above-mentioned case was simply referred to as *ACLU v. Reno* (1996) by the three-judge court, and in addition to reviewing the language of section 223 (a)(1)(B) of the CDA, the court also agreed to consider section 223 (d)(1), which made it a crime to use an "interactive computer service" to "send" or "display in any manner available" to a person under the age of 18 "any comment, request, suggestion, proposal, image, or other communication that, in context, depicts or describes, in terms patently offensive as measured by contemporary community standards, sexual or excretory activities or organs, regardless of whether the user of such service placed the call or initiated the communication."

Additionally, the court agreed to review the viability of the three chief defenses offered in the CDA, which would supposedly make for a "safe harbor" from prosecution under the law. As embodied in section 223 (e), these defenses allowed for good faith efforts made by service providers who made "reasonable, effective and appropriate actions under the circumstances to restrict or prevent access by minors," "by requiring use of a verified credit card, debit account, adult access code, or personal identification number" (see 47 U.S.C. 223(e) (5) (A-B)).

Before getting to the questions of law (about which there were to be different views by the three judges), the court opinion spent 18 pages, in a somewhat self-conscious exercise of over-explanation, on the background to the Internet. As I discuss in a later section, the court's review of the factual nature of this case was exhaustive and at one level intended to evidence a thorough mastery of the technology behind the constitutional controversy. At another level, however, the review and the conclusions it led the court to also suggested a potential problem with technology aversion in people.

In this section, the court felt compelled to discuss the creation of the Internet and the development of cyberspace (*ACLU v. Reno*, 1996) as well as how individuals can access the Internet, the use of "free nets," "computer coffee shops,"[1] commercial and noncommercial Internet providers, commercial online services,[2] "bulletin board systems,[3] one-to-one messaging (such as email), one-to-many messaging,[4] distributed message databases,[5] real-time communication,[6] real-time remote computer utilization,[7] remote information retrieval,[8] the intricacies of the World-Wide Web, and the variety of devices and procedures for preventing unwanted online material.[9]

Dispensing with a discussion of the technology, the judges then felt compelled to take different yet parallel directions with their decisions. I consider their opinions separately.

Chief Judge Sloviter: A Strict Scrutiny for CDA

Chief Judge Sloviter's opinion quickly asserted that the CDA's provisions in question amounted to content-specific regulation, writing: "The CDA is patently a government imposed content based restriction on speech, and the speech at issue, whether denominated 'indecent,' or 'patently offensive,' is entitled to constitutional protection" (p. 851).

This rather hasty assessment of the CDA language as content based thus allowed Sloviter to trigger a strict scrutiny analysis. She added: "The regulation is subject to strict scrutiny, and will be upheld if it is justified by a compelling government interest and if it is narrowly tailored to effectuate that interest" (citing *Sable Communications of California, Inc. v. FCC*, 1989).

I argue later that this may not have been the appropriate standard for review for cases involving a medium like the Internet. Of course, once this standard of review was triggered, the government's burden of proof became considerable. The government had hoped for a lesser standard of review, arguing that this was akin to broadcasting, and that the test for review in broadcasting cases should be employed here (see, e.g., *FCC v. Pacifica Foundation*, 1978). Sloviter disagreed, rationalizing her selection of a strict scrutiny standard thusly:

In any event, the evidence and our Findings of Fact based thereon show that Internet communication , while unique, is more akin to telephone communication, at issue in Sable, than to broadcasting, at issue in Pacifica, because, as with the telephone, *on the Internet we must act affirmatively and deliberately to retrieve specific information on line. Even if a broad search will, on occasion, retrieve unwanted materials, the user virtually always receives some warning of its content, significantly reducing the element of surprise or "assault" involved in broadcasting.* Therefore, it is highly unlikely that a very young child will be randomly "surfing" the Web and come across "indecent" or "patently offensive" material. (pp. 851-852; emphasis added)

With the stricter standard, Judge Sloviter then reviewed the government's asserted interest—"shielding minors from access to indecent materials."[10] In Sloviter's calculus, however, that interest was best asserted in situations in which the "potential harm for children is evident" (p. 852). Here, however, it was not quite so obvious what the harm might be. Sloviter then veered slightly off consideration of the harm to assess how narrowly drawn the CDA language might be. Sloviter was concerned with how the rule might affect "valuable literary, artistic or educational material," (p. 852). Sloviter then openly speculated about the impact of this on an online discussion about *Angels in America* (a Broadway play concerning AIDS and homosexuality in America), online newspaper articles concerning FMG (female genital mutilation) in the African continent, a written discussion about brutal prison rape (recall that one of the plaintiffs to the original case was Stop Prisoner Rape), or even an online service for discussion of HIV and AIDS (e.g., the Critical Path AIDS Project).

Sloviter concluded by declaring that the CDA thus reached more speech than it constitutionally should, and that despite government protests to the contrary, there is no foolproof current technology to insure age verification. Sloviter noted:

With the possible exception of e-mail to a known recipient, most content providers cannot determine the identity and age of every user accessing their material. . . . [N]o technology exists which allows those posting in the category of news groups, mail exploders, or chat rooms to screen for age. . . . If it is not feasible for speakers who communicate via these forms of communication to conduct age screening, they would have to reduce the level of communication to that which is appropriate for children in order to be protected under the statute. This would effect a complete ban even for adults of some expression. (p. 854)

Sloviter felt the same was true even for the Web, where technology such as Common Gateway Interface (GGI) scripting exists,[11] but is an unaffordable option for all noncommercial organizations—and even many commercial providers. The CDA, thus, was deemed overbroad.

A finding of overbreadth should have ended the discussion, but Judge Sloviter felt compelled to play out the rest of the strict scrutiny test, attempting to determine just how "narrowly drawn" the CDA language was. Here, the Chief Judge reasoned that the CDA's proposed defenses for providers who acted in good faith were not adequate.[12]

Judge Buckwalter: Defining "Indecency" on the Internet

By comparison, Judge Buckwalter's opinion was considerably shorter, focusing less on a full discussion of strict scrutiny (he endorsed Chief Judge Sloviter's reasoning) and more on his fear of vagueness in the language of the CDA provisions in question. Chiefly, Buckwalter addressed the use of "indecency" and "patently offensive." He made a series of arguments, the first of which complained of the degree to which Congress inferred in the CDA that both terms mean the same thing.

> The fundamental constitutional principle that concerns me is one of simple fairness, and that is absent from the CDA. The Government initially argues that "indecent" in this statute is the same as "patently offensive." I do not agree that a facial reading of this statute supports that conclusion. The CDA does not define the term "indecent," and the FCC has not promulgated regulations defining indecency in the medium of cyberspace. (p. 861)

Begrudgingly reading a conference report, Buckwalter was willing to allow that perhaps the government intended that the two terms mean the same thing, but he still argued that the terms did not pass constitutional muster:

> The Government attempts to save the "indecency" and "patently offensive" provisions by claiming that the provisions would only be used to prosecute pornographic works which, when considered "in context" as the statute requires, would be considered "indecent" or "patently offensive" to any community. The Government thus contends that plaintiffs' fears of prosecution for publishing material about matters of health, art, literature or civil liberties are exaggerated and unjustified. The Government's argument raises two issues: first is the question of which "community standards" apply in cyberspace, under the CDA; and second is the proposition that citizens should simply rely upon prosecutors to apply the statute constitutionally. (p. 863)

Buckwalter's first question seemed to go to the heart of the controversy because indecency was deemed to be something just beneath obscenity—a recognized categorical exception to the First Amendment—but still a form of expression that might be judged by community standards. Observing that in other similar cases the traditional community for the purposes of "community standards" is the community in which the information is "accessed and where the jury sits" (see, e.g., *Sable v. FCC*, 1989, p. 125), Buckwalter still noted that the Conference Report for the CDA had suggested a desire on the part of Congress to establish "a uniform national standard of content regulation" (*Sable v. FCC*, 1989, p. 191). Clearly, a national standard conflicted with the application of whatever local standard a community employed. How, Buckwalter wondered, was an online provider to know which standards to follow—especially when the so-called "national standards" for "indecency" were never clearly articulated?

Additionally, he worried that the use of "indecency" language would allow government prosecutors to do the opposite of what had been claimed because the various definitions of "indecency" by the Supreme Court have not traditionally made allowances for works of serious literary, artistic, political, or scientific value, as they had for obscenity. Said the Judge:

> The thrust of the Government's argument is that the court should trust prosecutors to prosecute only a small segment of those speakers subject to the CDA's, and whose works would reasonably be considered "patently offensive" in every community. Such unfettered discretion to prosecutors, however, is precisely what due process does not allow. (p. 861)

Judge Dalzell: Defining Community Standards

Finally, Judge Dalzell addressed a slightly different set of issues in considering the constitutional reach of the CDA, arguing that any standard of review by the court must address the specific medium to be regulated. Acknowledging that the Internet presented the court with a new medium, Dalzell asserted that the old models for review suggested in cases such as *FCC v. Pacifica* would not apply here—chiefly because of the difference in the mediums. (Recall from an earlier passage that the government had argued for the application of the Pacifica rationale to support the challenged CDA language.) Citing *Turner Broadcasting Systems Inc., v. FCC* (1994) Dalzell correctly pointed out that the Supreme Court had in that case declined to extend the rationale of Pacifica—which validated the right of government to regulate the airwaves because of the *scarcity* of bandwidth—to cable television, in which no such scarcity problems existed. The scarcity theory had been limited by the specific medium to be analyzed.

By that rationale, Dalzell argued, the same must now apply to the Internet: "I conclude that Pacifica's holding is not persuasive authority here, since plaintiffs and the Government agree that Internet communication is an abundant and growing resource" (*ACLU v. Reno*, 1996, p. 877).

Summary of the Three-Judge Court

In sum, the three individual opinions led to a unanimous decision, granting the plaintiff's motion for preliminary injunction, but for different reasons. For Chief Judge Sloviter, the CDA's challenged provisions failed strict scrutiny, both because they reached constitutionally protected speech and because they were not narrowly drawn to achieve the desired result. For Judge Buckwalter, the constitutional problems grew out of the imprecision of the terms *indecency* and *patently offensive* and the difficulty in applying community standards with what appeared to be a Congressional attempt at national uniform standards. For Judge Dalzell, the issue was approached differently, focusing on a failed justification for the CDA, grounded in Pacifica's dated "scarcity" rationale—a rationale that does not always apply to new and developing mediums like cable television—or now the Internet.

BROADER IMPLICATIONS OF *ACLU V. RENO*

After reading this decision I am led back to some of the questions I hinted at in the beginning of this chapter. The civil libertarian in me was and is happy that a fairly Draconian piece of legislation like the CDA did not withstand a first brush with constitutional scrutiny. There is a sense of comfort in the recognition that mass communication mediums are not all homogeneous and deserving of the same kind of treatment and regulation.

Still, a nagging voice stayed with me as I considered the reasoning of this three-judge panel—and in the end, although I was comfortable with the preliminary injunctive relief, I was uncomfortable with the notion that this three-judge court may have done the right thing for the wrong reasons.

TECHNOLOGY AVERSION AND JUDICIAL DECISION MAKING

I begin this section by elaborating on a point I hinted at earlier: I am concerned about the level of technical/technological competence in this country. For me, *technical* and *technological* are not the same terms. By technical competence I refer to the ability and skill that one possesses to operate a given technology such as the ability to operate and work with a computer wired onto the Internet. By technological competence, correspondingly, I refer to a conceptual understanding of that same technology—what it is, what its rules are, how its affects us, and what its significance might be.

We are in the midst of a technological boom that parallels the invention of the wheel, the development of gun powder, and the mastering of flight. Our technological boom is fueled by advances in computer science, programming, and engineering—not just for their own sake, but primarily because of their very connection to information technology. Is it any surprise that the dramatic levels to which Western stock markets have climbed have been driven by the strength of U.S. companies in computer technology?[13] This technological boom is changing the way we live, consume, educate, govern, and do business in this country. Inside the classroom today, the computer is as desired a tool as a book or paper. Businesses require this technology for operations, data storage, and communication. Government relies on this for efficiency of operation, and politicians continually turn to this for communication with those they represent.

At the individual level, the possession of a computer for individuals and families has become commonplace. In 1995, it was reported that 35% of all U.S. households had at least one personal computer (Negroponte, 1995). More to the point, 70% of new sales in computers were for the home market, as families with children began to buy computers, creating the possibilities for successive generations of computer-literate people—at least for those who could afford this technology.

When Doug Fraleigh and I finished the manuscript for our book, *Freedom of Speech in the Marketplace of Ideas* (Fraleigh & Tuman, 1996), the estimates for the number of people employing information technology with online use of their computers was 10 million in this country alone, and 25 million worldwide, in over 100 countries. In less than a year, that estimate grew to 40 million worldwide, with estimates of 200 million by the end of the century. It is no understatement to suggest that this technological boom has in many ways shrunk our world.

So much, so good—but no global change of this magnitude ever occurs without costs. One obvious cost in our society is the potential widening of the gap created by those with the resources and skill to operate this technology and those with the lack of either or both of the same. Public schools without computers continue to fall behind the performance standards of public schools with computers for students. And both of these continue to trail the efforts of private schools boasting not only computers and online access, but also more modern and contemporary equipment.

In almost Darwinian terms, businesses grow and survive with these same skills, and those lacking the capital, or the acumen to embrace change, fall behind or disappear. Politicians argue about a "bridge to the future," with explicit reference to computer technology, whereas those lacking such competence fall behind and lose political contests.

Some of what I have described as a widening of this gap is driven by the harsh realities of economics—as some do not compete because they lack the financial resources to play the game. Sometimes, however, the gap occurs because of attitudinal reasons— in this instance, an aversion, or what I call *technology aversion*. In this respect I am talking about an aversion or resistance to learning about this new computer and information technology. I have observed this aversion in many forums—business, political, academic, and even in private life—as many of us (myself included) struggle with a strong desire to avoid technology.

Initially, I thought this aversion was purely generational— meaning that as one got older, one was less inclined to embrace technological advances. To some degree I think this is still the case, but not because of anything specific to age. Rather, I believe what drives this aversion or resistance is our dislike, on the one hand, of the incredible (almost alarming) rate with which this technology has developed and evolved,[14] as well as the fact that for many of us as baby boomers or older, we are not part of the group advancing this technology, and we most certainly are not in the majority of those developing the rules and shaping the culture for cyberspace. The average age of an online subscriber or user is 23, and the research suggests that number is dropping and will continue to drop (see Negroponte, 1995).

What this means is that the technology, the customs, the culture, and the communication itself are continually evolving, and the innovators of this change are of a gradually younger age. The technology, however, affects all of us.

The presence of a technical/technological competence gap becomes more problematic once we consider some of these influences in our lives—perhaps in the area of free speech as an example. Information technology and communication in cyberspace implicates numerous free speech issues, many of which I have discussed earlier in this chapter. What happens, however, when the adjudicators of Constitutional disputes are called on to resolve questions about cyberspace? How many members of our judiciary are 23 and younger? Regardless of age, how many openly or quietly are touched with the same sense of technology aversion I have described here?

STANDARD OF REVIEW IN *ACLU V. RENO*

One manifestation of this may be observed in the aforementioned case. As Judge Sloviter reviewed the challenged language in the CDA, she quickly decided that this was a content-based restriction and imposed a strict scrutiny standard of review. Although the government argued for a more lenient standard akin to some the Supreme Court had employed in broadcasting cases, Judge Sloviter demurred, arguing instead that the Internet was closer to telephone technology because of the steps involved with using the technology. As Sloviter noted: "An Internet user must act affirmatively and deliberately to retrieve specific information on-line" (*ACLU v. Reno*, 1996, p. 851). In Judge Sloviter's calculus, the extra steps required of a user protected that user from casual or surprise contact with unwanted information. Just as a child would have to initiate a dial-a-porn call, get past the age-screening question, and produce a credit card number, so too on the Internet would a child have to go through several steps (user code, screening questions, credit card numbers) to reach the questionable information.

Judge Sloviter's reasoning, however, misses the mark here—and perhaps illustrates the point I was making earlier about judges who may not understand this technology making decisions about its use. The Internet is more akin to telephones than broadcasting—true enough, but more for a reason Sloviter fails to articulate: namely, the element of *interaction* present in both. What makes the mediums of telephones and computer networks parallel is the ability both afford a user to *interact* with the medium or with another user. When an individual employs a sex calling telephone service, that person interacts with the person on the other line, or makes choices (by pressing buttons on the touch tone phone) about what he or she wants to hear—both being examples of interaction. The same is true of a user of the Internet, whether he or she accesses a list, a bulletin board, a chat room, electronic mail, or simply surfs the Net. All of it is an act of interaction. The prefix *inter-* in Internet should suggest more than a sense of connection between the parts of the Net, that connection requires activity.

If anything, the Internet is perhaps the next evolution of telephone interaction. Although it is parallel in many respects to the telephone, I am not convinced that both are similar enough to justify Judge Sloviter's conclusion that a strict scrutiny standard should be employed. Contrary to her assertion about the affirmative and deliberate steps required, and contrary to my own point about both being examples of interaction, the Internet is also sufficiently different from telephone use in ways that ought to concern us. It is not the case, as Judge Sloviter carelessly asserts, that it is "highly unlikely that a very young child will be randomly 'surfing' the Web and come across 'indecent' or 'patently offensive' material" (pp. 851-852). Rather, it is extremely easy for children or anyone to encounter commercial sex sites—with plenty of graphic advertisements and teases prior to entry into the site, simply by employing a word search with any sexual reference in it. Equally so, access to chat rooms or talk sites make it possible to talk to nameless, faceless strangers who may be adults and have more in mind than casual conversation. There are other possibilities, with noncommercial providers as well. As each generation of children behind us becomes more computer literate than their parents, the ease with which they can access this material grows.

At the same time, whereas both the telephone and the Internet are examples of interactive technology, I am not certain they are interactive in the same way. Telephone interaction allows one person to one person voice communication, and sometimes (if through mass voice mail, or the old "party lines") one person to many people voice communication. The Internet allows verbal communication and interaction as well, but with a potential audience that is vastly larger than anything on the telephone. Moreover, the Internet also allows for data storage and transfer— meaning much more information than anything the telephone could offer, unless something was faxed, or a user had the patience to read information to a listener. The capacity or volume of information that can be transferred is greatly more than what a telephone can accommodate, and the speed in accessing this material is enhanced by the medium of the Internet itself—something a simple telephone could never match. In these ways, the Internet offers more possibilities for potential interaction with unwanted information than anything a telephone could offer.

In that sense, it is not clear that a strict scrutiny standard of review should necessarily have been employed against the CDA language—even though, admittedly, this was not a well-written law. Perhaps something less than strict scrutiny, but greater than giving the government a free pass, was called for. For example, Sloviter could have employed a standard that looked for a government interest, without having to test for how compelling it was; or conversely, she might have looked more broadly at the question of how narrowly drawn the language was.

My point is, on this most crucial link of her opinion (which standard of review?), Judge Sloviter's failure—even after so many pages of the opinion devoted to explaining cyberspace—to understand the Internet meant that she used the wrong standard, or at the least, failed to be innovative in articulating a standard that would apply to the CDA and cyberspace.

COMMUNITY STANDARDS IN CYBERSPACE

I think the same argument can be made about Judge Buckwalter's analysis of the community standards necessary to evaluate "indecency" and "patently offensive." Although he hints at considering a cybercommunity, Buckwalter ultimately rests his conclusion on the notion that Congress was attempting to develop a "uniform national" standard, which would defy the approach of local, case-by-case, community-by-community standards in evaluating something like indecent material. Buckwalter's analysis is consistent with existing law, but shows little understanding of the complexity of cyberspace.

Another dynamic of something like the Internet is its ability to blur or completely obliterate geopolitical boundaries. At any given moment, a user may be interacting with other users from other parts of the country, or from around the world. In cyberspace, our real-world sense of "communities" do not apply; rather, because of the high volume of interactivity, what we often see are *virtual communities*, made up of users, subscribers, and interested parties, usually sharing a common interest in a given subject matter, whether that be dog grooming or the politics of nuclear proliferation. As suggested earlier, these individuals can come from anywhere in the world, let alone anywhere in the United States.

Buckwalter suggests that it is perfectly acceptable to use the standards of whatever community the information is accessed in (or wherever the jury may sit) as the community of record for community standards—but such dated reasoning ignores this dynamic of the Internet. Why should the community in which information is accessed be the community of record? Especially when there may be users from around the world? By what right do any of us impose standards in this situation? One answer here may be that it is perfectly lawful for our government to impose restrictions on the foreign importation of pornography from countries with different standards (e.g., Denmark), so why not do the same for the Internet? A valid question, but I think the difference here is that the medium of the Internet is again interactive in ways that simple mailing of pornographic material could not be. This interaction allows all users to develop the culture and rules of use in the Internet, so that each user becomes part of the virtual community and "owns" a piece of that culture.

For that reason, traditional community standards analysis does not—and, I would argue, cannot ever—apply in the context of cyberspace. Again, we reach this result because of a judicial failure to be innovative in thinking about the Internet.

THE INTERNET AND THE MARKETPLACE OF IDEAS

Both of the examples I cited previously, as well as the court's tortured and self-conscious display of the history and background of the Internet, illustrate the premise I was arguing before about technology aversion and the risk in having people who do not understand the technology make rules about its use. I admit that I have no personal knowledge of any of these judges and their involvement with this technology; I base my observations on their writing and their reasoning—and on the assumption (a defensible one, I think) that they are no different than many of us who feel a sense of distance and a fear of falling behind a technology that changes so fast. I do not intend to conclude things this way, however, suggesting that nothing can be done to protect people— especially minors—from unwanted expression without harsh measures like the CDA.

How do we then resolve this problem if the technical/technological gap I have described continues, driving aversion to the technological medium and creating great difficulty in fashioning judicial rules about the constitutional use of cyberspace?

I believe the answer may come in returning to metaphorical interpretation for freedom of speech in the *marketplace of ideas.* Judge Dalzell hinted at this near the end of his opinion as he referred to the Internet as "the most participatory marketplace of mass speech that this country—and indeed the world—has yet seen" (*ACLU v. Reno,* 1996, p. 881). I concur with this assessment of the Internet. I argue that the Internet is the purest form of a true marketplace of ideas possible (Fraleigh & Tuman, 1996). When first articulated by Justice Holmes, this description of free speech operated under the assumption that speech could be traded freely, like commodities in a free marketplace. Speech and the ideas and thoughts it communicates can be judged by the standards of the marketplace, and if necessary regulated by the marketplace and not the government.

This concept has often proven controversial in practice for numerous Supreme Courts, which have not always agreed with Justice

Holmes, as well as for numerous observers of the concept who object to its logic. Some argue that the marketplace metaphor only applies if we have a truly free marketplace, where everyone has equal access. The last part of this has proven problematic in real life; not every citizen in our democracy always has equal access to free speech. Sometimes, wealth and class status determine this as much as anything.

Of course, that only demonstrates a difficulty with using this metaphor to describe freedom of speech in our real-world situation. In a virtual world, however, where everyone has equal access, and where currently government does not really regulate or restrict, the marketplace metaphor is more than apt as a description.

Because it is the case that the Internet was born as the product of a union between people—scientists and researchers—who wanted to share ideas, and which has now grown to incredible proportions by people around the world who have developed its culture, its rituals, and its customs, maybe the solution to difficulties with encountering unwanted speech here resides in allowing this marketplace to regulate itself. Most of the innovations in security and age verification technology—although far from perfect—have come from people within this technical community—and well in advance of legislation like the CDA. Given time to work things out, I have confidence that this marketplace will indeed develop solutions to this problem. Because we cannot really ask 23-year-olds to be legal judges, it may be better to leave this issue out of the courts of the real world and within the virtual courts of virtual communities in cyberspace.

Given the fact that the Internet has grown to be a global network, there is something logical in such a marketplace approach because it would encompass the views of people from other countries and cultures, who have come together in cyberspace. As technology continues to shrink our planet, there is indeed something comforting in such a sentiment.

ENDNOTES

1. These are establishments that provide Internet access for a small hourly fee.
2. Examples include America Online, Compuserve, The Microsoft Network, and Prodigy.
3. With an investment of as little as $2000, bulletin boards can be created in which friends, members, subscribers, or customers can exchange ideas and information—much like leaving notices on a real bulletin board.
4. Automatic Mailing List Services, such as "listservs," enable communication about particular subjects among a group of people.

5. This is similar to listservs, but different in the sense that most of these are open discussions and exchanges about particular subjects. They do not require advance membership or subscription.

6. This allows one-to-one or one-to-many communications, which can occur instantaneously and appear on screen. These are sometimes referred to as "chat" or "talk" functions.

7. This refers to using information on the Internet to access and control remote computers in real time.

8. This involves searching for and retrieving information located on remote computers. These include methods like "ftp" or file transfer protocol; "gopher," a program and format that guides a search through available resources; and the "World Wide Web," a system originally designed to share information between researchers and engineers at the European Particle Physics Laboratory, which today extends to communications between individuals, groups, and businesses. The Web is nothing but a series of documents stored in different computers all over the Internet.

9. Examples include PICS (Platform for Internet Content Selection) software such as Cyber Patrol, CyberSitter, The Internet Filter, Net Nanny, Parental Guidance, SurfWatch, Netscape Proxy Server, and WebTrack.

10. See also *New York v. Ferber* 458 U.S. 747 (1982): "It is evident beyond the need for elaboration that a State's interest in safeguarding the physical and psychological well being of a minor is compelling" (pp. 756-757).

11. These enable creation of a document that can process information by a visitor.

12. Sloviter found that credit card verification was not economically or always technologically feasible and that adult verification services were not technically sound. Even a future technology for age verification—like "tagging" (this would imbed a string of characters in all indecent or patently offensive material)—is not feasible at this time. Said Sloviter: "The government's tagging proposal is purely hypothetical and offers no operative defense to Internet content providers" (p. 856).

13. As of the day of this writing, the Dow Jones Industrial Average had topped the 9000 mark, an all-time high, largely led by advances in technology stocks, most of them located in California's computer technology wealthy Silicon Valley.

14. I would invite you to think about your own computer, if you own one, and whether you grimaced about the fact your machine was already "obsolete" less than a year after you purchased it?

REFERENCES

ACLU v. Reno, 929 F. Supp. 824 (E.D. Pa 1996).

FCC v. Pacifica Foundation, 438 U.S. 726 (1978).

Fraleigh, D., & Tuman, J. (1996). *Freedom of speech in the marketplace of ideas*. New York: St. Martin's Press.

Negroponte, N. (1995, February 11). Homeles@info.hwy.net. *The New York Times*, p. 15.

New York v. Ferber, 458 U.S. 747 (1982).

Turner Broadcasting Systems, Inc. V. FCC, 114 S.Ct. 2445 (1994).

Sable Communications of California Inc. v. FCC, 492 U.S. 115 (1989).

8

HISTORY AND DECENCY: OVERCOMING THE THREAT OF AN INSIDE-OUT APPROACH*

ERIC M. FREEDMAN

In a comprehensive law review article recently published in the Iowa Law Review, Eric Freedman argued for the repudiation of the so-called "inside-outside" approach to which types of expression receive the protection of the First Amendment. In "A Lot More Comes into Focus When You Remove the Lens Cap: Why Proliferating New Communications Technologies Make it Particularly Urgent for the Supreme Court to Abandon its Inside-Outside Approach to Freedom of Speech and Bring Obscenity, Fighting Words and Group Libel Within the First Amendment," Freedman called on the Supreme Court to reject this longstanding approach, under which certain categories of expression are viewed as being of such low value as to be "outside" the protection of the First Amendment. He persuasively contended that adherence to this view renders free speech interests vulnerable to

---

*The first section of this chapter is an edited excerpt from a work originally published in 81 *Iowa Law Review* 1 (1996) pp. 1-86. Reprinted with permission. For this reason we have maintained the original *Bluebook Citation* format where appropriate.

attacks. What follows is an excerpt reprinted from this article followed by Professor Freedman's application of his argument to the issue of Internet indecency, most particularly, the Communications Decency Act of 1996.

PART I: THE PROBLEM

Current free speech law resembles the Ptolemaic system of astronomy in its last days. Just as that theory grew increasingly incoherent in an attempt to incorporate new empirical observations that were inconsistent with its basic postulates, so is First Amendment doctrine disintegrating as cases reviewing restraints on speech strive to paper over the fact that analyses based on presuppositions as to the value of particular kinds of expression are inconsistent with the premises of the First Amendment itself.

Most readers of the opinions in *R.A.V. v. City of St. Paul*,[1] for example, will surely find it difficult to shake the feeling that all nine Justices are missing the forest for the trees, disputing hoary categories like "fighting words"[2] in a case whose true conflict bears no relationship to those categories (see Alexander, 1993).

The explanation for the Justices' performance is that they are viewing the free speech universe through the distorting lens of an outmoded paradigm, one in which only certain speech is "within" the First Amendment. When the state seeks to regulate such speech, the key questions are:

1. *Is the purpose of the regulation to restrict speech?*

In some cases, the answer may be no. For example, the regulation's purpose may be to suppress nonspeech conduct (e.g., heroin sales, consumer fraud) with the restraint on speech being merely incidental.[3] Because, in many areas, simply asking the question comprehensively[4] goes a long way toward answering it, this issue rightly plays a central role in traditional First Amendment analysis (see, e.g., BeVier, 1978; Post, 1990).

2. *If so, has the state demonstrated a compelling reason consistent with First Amendment values for restricting this speech?*

This inquiry is inevitably the controversial one. But asking it focuses discussion on the right subject, making explicit the policy choices that close cases will necessarily involve.[5]

3. *If so, has the state demonstrated that the regulation has been narrowly tailored towards achieving its permissible purpose?*

As the Supreme Court has long recognized, this standard plays an important practical role in keeping the government within whatever boundaries the legal system has determined are legitimate.[6]

In contrast, according to the Court, speech that falls into the categories of group libel, fighting words, and obscenity is "outside" the First Amendment.[7] Although the Justices disagree about precisely what it means for speech to be "outside" the First Amendment,[8] the underlying concept is clear: The speech categories "outside" the First Amendment are less socially valuable than the ones "inside" it, so governmental restraints on the former are free of the rigorous judicial scrutiny given to governmental restraints on the latter.

There are at least three major problems with this vision of the First Amendment.

First, its simplistic dualism is empirically false as a description of the legal landscape. All libel is plainly "within" the First Amendment.[9] Fighting words, although formally remaining outside it, are for all practical purposes within it. That is, the Court, in addressing the problems posed by those categories of speech, has demonstrated a commendable focus on the three questions listed earlier. Only obscenity (and a widening sphere of erotically oriented speech that is not technically obscene) remains truly "outside" the First Amendment,[10] in the sense that the Court has relieved itself of the obligation to address those questions.

Second, the "inside-out" model of the First Amendment, and the obsolete doctrine it perpetuates, clouds clear thinking and reduces the likelihood of correct results on numerous free speech problems. The issue goes far beyond the logical desirability of improving doctrinal tidiness.[11] The current disarray in the law provides ammunition for a variety of attacks on free expression.

As long as certain categories of speech may be defined as "outside" the First Amendment because judges believe them to be unworthy of its noble protections, there is no logically consistent reason why any number of other forms of socially unpopular expression should not be similarly categorized.[12] This would allow their summary suppression without the need for serious consideration of the issues at stake.[13]

Third, the ability to cast certain forms of expression beyond the First Amendment pale poses a special danger to technologically novel communications media. Thus, for example, just as movies originally were placed "outside" the First Amendment because they were thought to be such a threateningly powerful medium of expression,[14] so it is now proposed that the unique characteristics of computers justify imposing special restraints on the communications they transmit.

In response to these problems, the Supreme Court should repudiate the view that some forms of expression, whether defined by their content or by their mode of delivery, are "outside" the First Amendment. This proposal is not designed to provide a "theoretical basis for free speech that is at once true and elegant" (Fried, 1992). In particular, it assumes *arguendo* a continuation of the current proliferation of judicially recognized subcategories of speech "within" the First Amendment.[15] The merits of that development have been much debated elsewhere,[16] and are not addressed here. For the categorization questions only arise with respect to speech that is already "inside" the First Amendment (Tribe, 1988, p. 895). Once it has achieved that status, judicial definition of the extent of legal protection requires an explicit discussion of First Amendment values. Thus, just as freedom of expression was enhanced when libel and commercial speech were moved from "outside" the First Amendment to "inside" it, albeit each in its own category and subject to its own rules, so too will freedom of expression be enhanced when all speech is "inside" the First Amendment.

PART II: THE COMMUNICATIONS DECENCY ACT AND THE INSIDE-OUTSIDE APPROACH

Specifically, and of special importance for the concerns of the present volume, a rule that all forms of speech are within the First Amendment will insure the nondiscriminatory coverage of all current or future methods by which expression may be conveyed. A glance at current developments in light of history demonstrates the importance of this advantage. Early in 1996, President Clinton signed the Communications Decency Act. This legislation subjects to fines and imprisonment for up to two years.

1. the knowing transmission of "any comment, request, suggestion, proposal, image, or other communication which is obscene or indecent, knowing that the recipient of the communication is under 18 years of age, regardless of whether the maker of such communication placed the call or initiated the communication; and

2. the knowing use of "any interactive computer service to display in a manner available to a person under 18 years

of age, any comment, request, suggestion, proposal, image, or other communication that, in context, depicts or describes, in terms patently offensive as measured by contemporary community standards, sexual or excretory activities or organs, regardless of whether the user of such service placed the call or initiated the communication."

By all ordinary First Amendment standards, these provisions are manifestly invalid.

First, regulation on the basis of indecency (as opposed to the much narrower category of "obscenity") was pointedly limited by the Supreme Court in *FCC v. Pacifica Foundation* (1978) to the broadcast media, a context in which it was claimed to be justified on the basis of spectrum scarcity and the special intrusiveness of those media (Kim, 1995). The Internet is not a physically limited medium; on the contrary, it is infinitely expandable as people set up additional nodes (Berman & Weitzner, 1995). Nor is the medium intrusive; on the contrary, one has to search with considerable diligence to find what one is seeking (Rigdon, 1996).

Second, assuming regulation on the basis of indecency were permissible, the term is not defined in the first provision quoted while the definition in the second provision does no more than reiterate that of the FCC in the broadcast context—which has been universally denounced on the grounds of vagueness, overbreadth, and potential for selective enforcement (Goldsamt, 1995; Phelan, 1995).

In any event, in contrast to the broadcast media (and analogously to the case of dial-a-porn services, which the Supreme Court refused to allow Congress to outlaw—*Sable Communications v. FCC*, 1989) there are less restrictive alternatives to a total ban available in the form of a variety of access control and content-labeling systems (Lewis, 1996; Markoff, 1996).

Third, technical considerations make the statute so extremely unlikely to achieve its stated purpose—while so extremely likely to suppress speech that is protected by any standard—as to render it invalid under the First Amendment on the grounds of simple irrationality, like the alcohol-content labeling statute at issue in *Rubin v. Coors Brewing Company* (1995). This challenge is particularly strong in a context in which pursuit of the unattainable goal of keeping the targeted material out of the hands of minors will necessarily restrict all communications on the Internet to a level suitable for children, because the Supreme Court has repeatedly condemned statutes having that effect on the adult population (*Butler v. Michigan*, 1957; *Virginia v. American Booksellers Association*, 1988).

In light of the overwhelming force of this attack (which I predict will, in fact, prevail), how could anyone give even a moment's credence to the possibility that the Supreme Court might uphold the statute? The answer is that historical experience—with, among others, printing presses (Ringel, 1970, pp. 148-149; Shackelton, 1975, p. 11), secular dramatic troupes (Heinemann, 1993), rock music (Hill, 1991), comic books (and before that dime crime novels; Johnston, 1994; Klapper, 1960, pp. 143-159), sexually explicit telephone services (Woolfall, 1994), and video games (Zito, 1993)— shows that each new medium is seen at first as uniquely threatening because it is uniquely influential and therefore a uniquely appropriate target of censorship.

Thus, "when Thomas Edison started making short films around the turn of the century, patrons ran from theatres in horror when they saw a steam engine barreling directly toward the front row seats" (Zito, 1993, p. 25). It was in this context that, as already noted, the Supreme Court held in 1915 that there was no First Amendment violation in the creation of a government system for the censorship of movies because movies formed no part of the "press" (*Mutual Film Corp. v. Industrial Commission of Ohio*, 1915). In other words, movies—like pornography—were defined as "outside" the First Amendment.

This is the backdrop against which we currently find governments reacting with near hysteria to the possibility of the creation, dissemination, and viewing through the use of computer technology of messages even vaguely related to sexuality (Freedman, 1996, p. 959). To be sure, computers are already covered by the existing statutory prohibition on the interstate distribution of obscene materials, and 18 U.S.C. 2252 (a)(2) already specifically criminalizes computer dissemination of depictions of minors engaging in "sexually explicit" conduct. The existing general federal prohibition on the possession of child pornography already extends to one's home computer, and prosecutions in computer-related cases are already regularly brought under such statutes. But unfamiliarity makes this new medium seem particularly dangerous, and governments are haunted by the fear that the mechanisms of communications may be outrunning those of control (Human Rights Watch, 1996; Knoll 1996).

Hence, there arises a widespread view that neither the doctrinal categories nor the substantive content of current First Amendment law are adequate to deal with emerging problems. Thus, to take just one example, in an effort at thought control that flatly defies the First Amendment as understood to date, the 104th Congress buried in the omnibus budget bill that it passed just before adjourning the Child Pornography Prevention Act of 1996.

Introduced by Senator Orrin G. Hatch of Utah, this legislation broadly criminalizes the dissemination of all visual images that "appear to be" ones of children engaging in "sexually explicit" conduct, notwithstanding that the images were generated purely electronically, without the use of any children (or adult actors, for that matter) at all. According to the legislative findings contained in § 121(1)(4) of the Act, viewing such images "can desensitize the viewer to the pathology of sexual abuse or exploitation of children, so that it can become acceptable to and even preferred by the viewer." Moreover, according to §121(1)(11)(B), such images create an unwholesome moral environment.

How can these rationales can be reconciled with such classic cases as *Kingsley International Pictures Corp. v. Board of Regents* (1957), which held that the State "struck at the very heart of constitutionally protected liberty" under the First Amendment by censoring movies portraying adultery as attractive, notwithstanding that such relationships were "contrary to the moral standards, the religious precepts, and the legal code of its citizenry," or such modern ones as *New York v. Ferber* (1982, p. 763), which, in upholding a New York ban on "child pornography," relied on the fact that the challenged statute left open the alternatives of using older actors or simulating the performance?

There is no explanation to be found in the supporting committee report, which simply declares that the legislation "is needed due to technological advances" in the creation of visual images, "particularly through the use of computers," that have "made possible the production of visual depictions that appear to be of minors engaging in sexually explicit conduct" (Senate Report, 1996, pp. 1189-90). The authors of this rationalization are either ignorant of, or choosing to ignore, history: "Photography became a frequent censorship target in the late nineteenth century because it was supposedly more graphic and realistic than painting" (Meyer, 1994). Around the same time, magic lantern shows were often so shocking to audiences that, historian Peter Bacon recounts, "they fainted, cried, or talked back to the lantern-slide screen" (quoted in Roberts, 1995. p. 28). Are we now supposed to believe that images that could no longer be banned if shown in those media can be suppressed if generated by computer animation software because the latter are too vivid?

The reality is that new media achieve their initial marketplace success precisely because they are for some purposes a more effective form of communication than preexisting ones. This should be seen as an advance in human enlightenment, rather than an excuse for otherwise impermissible state censorship.

The courts should enforce the First Amendment in the context of new media just as they do in the context of old ones—with an awareness that, historically, erring on the side of freedom of speech under conditions of uncertainty, whether technological, political (as during World War I or the Cold War), or empirical (as in the case of the Pentagon Papers), has proven in retrospect to be the wiser course. Thus, for example, just as the Supreme Court eventually overruled its earlier decision and held in *Joseph Burstyn, Inc. v. Wilson* (1952) that movies were entitled to First Amendment protection, in time a consensus will arise that the first reaction to the perceived threat of cyberspace was as overblown as with other new media.

As in all of First Amendment law, though, the danger is in the meantime—when the ability to declare certain technologically defined categories of speech "outside" the First Amendment provides the courts an ever available escape hatch from the need to provide coherent justifications for imposing otherwise impermissible regulations on just those communications formats in which the public has the liveliest interest.

Such discrimination against new technologies is not only unjustifiable but unnecessary, for the marketplace will tend to do effectively—perhaps too effectively—that which would be a threat to civil liberties if done by the government. Today, for example, as all consumers know, standards for sexual explicitness differ among the commercial broadcast, cable, and movie industries, and, within the movie industry, between productions designed to be seen in movie theaters and in hotel rooms. So, too, there was greater reluctance among the long-distance telephone carriers than the local ones to carry "dial-a-porn" services, even though the latter were subject to more stringent legal regulations. In all of these cases, marketplace considerations, not legal ones, have determined the outcomes.

However distressing those outcomes may be to some aesthetic or political tastes, this process represents the First Amendment working as it usually does in fact. Just as the Constitution provides a quite lax outer framework within which day-to-day politics operates to produce policy results that, whatever one may think of their substance, have been determined after a generally unimpeded contest between political groups of varying power, so does it provide very broad limits within which the marketplace operates to disseminate that which the public—often making its desires known through aggressive political and media campaigns—wishes to obtain. (Collins & Skover, 1993; Price, 1994). The key constitutional concern is that control rest with the people, not the government.

To be sure, there is implicit in this view the realization (which one may, according to taste, label realistic or cynical) that the political/economic marketplace, not the legal system, will determine the ultimate extent of speech regulation, a conclusion that may initially cause all of those sparring over First Amendment standards to wonder why they are bothering. The Supreme Court does not exist apart from the culture that it both shapes and reflects (Marshall & Ignagni, 1994), and in the long run Americans will have just as much freedom of speech as the majority desires.

But "in the long run we are all dead" (Keynes, 1923, p. 80). As the now-vanished flag-burning uproar illustrates, First Amendment doctrine makes a difference in keeping the channels of discourse—and hence the possibilities of change—open during the interval that elapses between the initial urge toward suppression and the time, if ever, that the majority overcomes the Constitutional obstacles to the exercise of its will. As the rapid pace of modern communications works to shorten that interval, the importance of robust First Amendment standards increases.

ENDNOTES

1. 505 U.S. 377 (1992). For a full-length account of the case by counsel for the defendant, see Cleary (1994). See also *United States v. Juvenile Male* (1994) (affirming conviction of R.A.V. and others on federal civil rights charges arising out of the same incident that led to state charges in R.A.V.).

2. See Greenfield (1994); Shiffrin (1994; commenting that the "Court simply bungled the first amendment job"); Trollinger (1994); Degan (1993; "The fundamental flaw in R.A.V. is the Court's attempt to analyze the St. Paul ordinance under the fighting words doctrine."). The bankruptcy of the "fighting words" doctrine is discussed Part III.A of the *Iowa Law Review* piece—editor's note.

3. For more controversial examples than those in the text, see *Arcara v. Cloud Books, Inc.* (1986); *Konigsberg v. State Bar of California* (1961).

4. In particular, the Court must assess the state's real purpose as well as its articulated one. See *Edwards v. Aguillard* (1987); *Cornelius v. NAACP Legal Defense and Educ. Fund* (1985).

5. See Post (1991); Shiffrin (1978). Volokh (1996) rightly emphasizes the importance of the inquiry into constitutional values in answering this question.

6. See, e.g., *Sable Communications v. FCC* (1989); *Schad v. Mount Ephraim* (1981); *Martin v. Struthers* (1943); *Jamison v. Texas* (1943); *Schneider v. State* (1939); *Lovell v. Griffin* (1938).

   Thus, in *Ladue v. Gilleo* (1994), the Court, in a case involving an individual who had posted an antiwar sign in the front window of her house, indulged in the entirely implausible assumption that the municipality's ban on residential signs was content-neutral (an assumption that saved the ban from summary invalidation under tests deriving from the second question), but went on to hold the ordinance unconstitutional because "more temperate measures could in large part satisfy Ladue's stated regulatory needs without harm to the First Amendment rights of its citizens" (pp. 58-59). See generally Cordes (1995).

7. See *R.A.V. v. City of St. Paul*, 505 U.S. 377, 382-383 (1992); New York v. Ferber (1982).

8. In R.A.V., Justice Stevens (speaking on this point for himself alone) announced that he would conduct a holistic analysis of the speech in question and the regime of regulation being applied to it in order to determine the First Amendment issue (R.A.V., 505 U.S. at 427-31). Justice White (whose views were joined by Justices Blackmun and O'Connor) wrote that the proper approach was to determine whether the speech fell within a category traditionally unprotected because of its absence of social value (e.g., obscenity, fighting words) and to permit or prohibit regulation accordingly. The Court, in an opinion by Justice Scalia (joined by Chief Justice Rehnquist and Justices Kennedy, Souter, and Thomas), explained that the classification of the speech as protected or unprotected bore on, although it was not dispositive of, the issue of the degree of permissible government regulation.

9. See *New York Times v. Sullivan* (1964); see also R.A.V., 505 U.S. at 382-83.

10. Although the issue of definition is one of some independent importance, the argument presented here does not depend on how the legal system may choose to demarcate the material at issue. Hence, for present purposes, I use the terms *pornography* and *obscenity* interchangeably to mean any sexually explicit expression that the state seeks to suppress (See Collins & Skover 1994, adopting same approach); Gey (1988, same); Schauer (1978-79, distinction between "obscene" and "pornographic" is "constitutionally uninteresting") cf. de Grazia (1992, stating that at the time of *Roth v. United States*, 354 U.S. 476 (1957), "everyone realized—even if no one could define either term—that there *was* a difference between them," and although reputable people could fight for an end to controls on obscenity, "'pornography' was very widely thought of as abominable stuff that no reputable lawyer or judge would care to be found defending"); Schauer (1976, "Obscene' refers to that which is repugnant or disgusting. . . . Except as used in the law, it does not necessarily have any sexual connotations. `Pornography,' on the other hand, . . . is limited to depictions of sexual lewdness. . . . Definitionally, obscenity may or may not be pornographic, and pornography may or may not be obscene." See generally Wolfson (1994); and Safire (1991).

11. See Kalven (1960, pp. 25-26: "It is abundantly clear that the effort of the Court to deal with obscenity within its commitment to free speech has opened issues about free speech which transcend in importance the limited problem of obscenity").

12. See Abrams (1992): "Every major new doctrinal exception to the general rule that speech may not be infringed leads in turn to new demands for further exceptions. What else would one expect?" Thus, various authors have deployed the inside-out approach to support proposals to

curb violent entertainment, rap music, and "morally abhorrent speech" (Freedman, 1996, pp. 946-947).

13. See Mincberg (1993): "In other words, if before reaching the question of whether a restriction is valid under one of the demanding First Amendment tests, such as strict scrutiny, the Court decides *a priori* that the First Amendment does not apply . . . then the conflict is resolved because the Court does not have to get into the First Amendment and strict scrutiny at all. . . . [W]e often say that application of the First Amendment 'triggers' strict scrutiny. This method of analysis puts a trigger lock on the First Amendment."

14. See *Mutual Film Corp. v. Industrial Comm'n of Ohio* (1915), *overruled* by *Joseph Burstyn, Inc. v. Wilson* (1952).

15. These legal subdivisions are multiplying at a rate that almost insures that any description will be obsolete by the time it sees print. As helpfully summarized in Haggerty (1993), the Court first decides: (a) that a certain activity is "speech," (b) that it is "within" the First Amendment, and (c) that it should not be shunted off to one of a number of special tracks reserved for such matters as:

(i) commercial speech, see *Virginia State Bd. of Pharmacy v. Virginia Citizens Consumer Council* (1976)—comparing and contrasting special track categories to each other and to political speech); Tribe (1988, pp. 929-934)—describing how commercial speech moved from "outside" the First Amendment to within it but in a lower-value category); and Simpson (1994)—criticizing the Court for analyzing such cases by deciding for itself the social utility of the speech, instead of treating "free speech as a right, rather than a privilege"): see also Wilson (1993; reviewing recent decisions); or

(ii) speech in one of three distinct categories of public forum, see Farber & Nowak (1984)—criticizing the Court for diverting cases at this point, rather than proceeding to remainder of analysis).

The Court then places the speech onto one of two main tracks:

(a) On what the commentators label Track One are content-based restrictions on speech, which are supportable only if "necessary" to the achievement of a "compelling" state interest and if they are no broader than necessary to serve that interest (e.g., *National Bank of Boston v. Bellotti,* 1978);

(b) On Track Two are content-neutral regulations, which will be upheld if the state interest is "important" or "substantial" or "significant," and the regulation is "narrowly tailored" to achieve this interest (See *Ward v. Rock Against Racism,* 1989).

Track Two owes its origins to *United States v. O'Brien* (1968), in which defense counsel took the position that O'Brien's burning of his draft card during a protest against the Vietnam War was pure speech, while counsel for the government took the position that it was pure conduct, so that no First Amendment issue was presented at all.

16. Compare, for example, Tribe (1988, pp. 928-944—generally disapproving of the development) and Kraut (1995—same) with Schauer (1982), generally approving and Shiffrin (1983-same).

REFERENCES

Abrams, F. (1992). Hate speech: The present implications of a historical dilemma. *Villanova Law Review, 37,* 743, 752.

Alexander, L.A. (1993). Trouble on track two: Incidental regulations of speech and free speech theory. *Hastings Law Journal, 44,* 921, 957-60.

Arcara v. Cloud Books, 478 U.S. 697 (1986), *on remand* 503 N.E. 2d 492 (N.Y. 1986).

Berman, J., & Weitzner, D. J. (1994). Abundance and user control: Renewing the democratic heart of the First Amendment in the age of interactive media. *Yale Law Journal, 104,* 1619, 1623-1624.

BeVier, L.R. (1978). The First Amendment and political speech: An inquiry into the substance and limits of principle. *Stanford Law Review, 30,* 299, 300.

Joseph Burstyn, Inc. v. Wilson, 343 U.S. 495, 502 (1952).

Butler v. Michigan, 352 U.S. 380, 383-4 (1957).

Cleary, E.J. (1994). *Beyond the burning cross: The First Amendment and the landmark R.A.V. case.* New York: Random House.

Collins, R. K., & Skover, D. (1993). Commerce & communication. *Texas Law Review, 71,* 697.

Collins, R.K.L., & Skover, D.M. (1994). The pornographic state. *Harvard Law Review, 107,* 1374, 1377.

Cordes, M. (1995). Sign regulation after Ladue: Examining the evolving limits of First Amendment protection. *Nebraska Law Review, 74,* 36.

Cornelius v. NAACP Legal Defense and Educ. Fund, 473 U.S. 788, 812-14 (1985).

Degan, M.S. (1993). Note, "Adding the First Amendment to the fire": Cross burning and hate crime laws. *Creighton Law Review, 26,* 1109, 1135.

de Grazia, E. (1992). *Girls lean back everywhere: The law of obscenity and the assault on genius.* New York: Random House.

Edwards v. Aquillard, 482 U.S. 578, 586-87 (1987).

Farber, D.A., & Nowak, J.E. (1984). The misleading nature of public forum analysis: Content and contest in First Amendment adjudication. *Virginia Law Review, 70,* 1219, 1226-1229.

FCC v. Pacifica Foundation, 438 U.S. 726 (1978).

Freedman, E. M. (1996). A lot more comes into focus when you remove the lens cap: Why proliferating new communications technologies make it particularly urgent for the Supreme Court to abandon its inside-out approach to freedom of speech and bring obscenity, fighting words, and group libel within the First Amendment. *Iowa Law Review, 81,* 883-968.

Fried, C. (1992). The new first amendment jurisprudence: A threat to liberty. *Chicago Law Review, 59*, 225, 231.

Gey, S.G. (1988). The apologetics of suppression: The regulation of pornography as act and idea. *Michigan Law Review, 86*, 1564, 1596.

Goldsamt, S. (1995). Crucified by the FCC? Howard Stern, the FCC, and selective prosecution. *Columbia Journal of Law and Social Problems, 28*, 203, 250-252.

Greenfield, K. (1994). Our conflicting judgments about pornography. *American University Law Review, 43*, 1197, 1216-1217.

Haggerty, J.T. (1993). Begging and public forum doctrine in the First Amendment. *B.C. Law Review, 34*, 1121, 1123-1130.

Heinemann, M. (1993). Drama and opinion in the 1620s: Middleton and Massinger. In J.R. Mulryne & M. Shewring (Eds.), *Theatre and government under the early Stuarts* (p. 237). Cambridge: Cambridge University Press.

Hill, T. (1991). The enemy within: Censorship in rock music in the 1950's. *South Atlantic Quarterly, 90*, 675.

Human Rights Watch. (1996). *Silencing the net.* gopher://gopher. ic.apc.org.5000/oo/int/hrw/expression/7.

Jamison v. Texas, 318 U.S. 413, 416 (1943).

Johnston, G. (1994). It's all in the cards: Serial killers, trading cards, and the First Amendment. *New York Law School Law Review, 39*, 549, 552-553, 555-557.

Kalven, H., Jr. (1960). The metaphysics of the law of obscenity, 1960. *Supreme Court Review 1960*, 25-26.

Keynes, J. M. (1923). *A tract on monetary reform.* London: MacMillan..

Kim, J. H. (1995). Cyber-porn obscenity: The viability of local community standards and the federal venue rules in the computer network age. *Loyola Law and Entertainment Law Journal, 15*, 415, 435-38.

Kingsley International Picture Corp. v. Board of Regents, 360 U.S. 684, 688-89 (1957).

Klapper, J. T. (1960). *The effects of mass communications.* Glencoe, IL: Free Press.

Knoll, A. (1996). Any which way but loose: Nations regulate the Internet. *Tulane Journal of International & Comparative Law, 4*, 275.

Konigsberg v. State Bar of California, 366 U.S. 36, 50-51 (1961).

Kraut, N. (1995). Speech: A freedom in search of one rule. *Cooley Law Review, 12*, 177, 178.

Ladue v. Gilleo, 512 U.S. 43 (1994).

Lewis, P. H. (1996, March 1). Microsoft backs ratings system for the Internet. *New York Times*, Section D-5.

Lovell v. Griffin, 303 U.S. 444, 451-52 (1938).

Markoff, J. (1996, July 3). New Internet features will make voluntary ratings possible. *The New York Times*, p. A1.

Marshall, T. R., & Ignagni, J. (1994). Supreme Court and public support for rights claims. *Judicature, 78*, 146, 151.

Martin v. Struthers, 319 U.S. 141, 145-49 (1943).

Meyer, C. (1994). Sex, sin, and women's liberation: Against porn-suppression. *Texas Law Review, 72*, 1097, 1189-90.

Mincberg, E. (1993). A look at recent Supreme Court decisions: Judicial prior restraint and the First Amendment, *Hastings Law Journal, 44*, 871, 872.

Mutual Film Corp. v. Industrial Commission of Ohio, 236 U.S. 230 (1915).

National Bank of Boston v. Bellotti, 435 U.S. 765, 786 (1978).

New York v. Ferber, 458 U.S. 747, 754, 763-65 (1982).

New York Times v. Sullivan, 376 U.S. 254, 268-69 (1964).

Phelan, T. (1995). Selective hearing: A challenge to the FCC's indecency policy. *New York Law School Journal on Human Rights, 12*, 347, 390-392.

Post, R.C. (1990). The constitutional concept of public discourse: Outrageous opinion, democratic deliberation, and *Hustler Magazine* v. Falwell. *Harvard Law Review, 103*, 603, 683.

Post, R. C. (1991). Racist speech, democracy, and the First Amendment. *William & Mary Law Review, 32*, 267, 278-279.

Price, M. E. (1994). The market for loyalties: Electronic media and the global competition for allegiances. *Yale Law Journal, 104*, 667, 691-694.

R.A.V. v. City of St. Paul, 505 U.S. 377, 382-383 (1992).

Rigdon, J. E. (1996, January 25). For some, the web is just a slow crawl to a splattered cat. *Wall Street Journal*, p. A1.

Ringel, W. E. (1970). *Obscenity law today*. Jamaica, NY: Gould Publications.

Roberts, S. (1995, January 19). Giving poverty and hardship a human face. *The New York Times*, Section 2-1.

Rubin v. Coors Brewing Co., 115 S.Ct. 1585, 1592 (1995).

Sable Communications v. FCC, 492 U.S. 115, 126 (1989).

Safire, W. (1991, May 26). "Explicit" is not a dirty word, *New York Times Magazine*, p. 8.

Schad v. Mount Ephraim, 452, U.S. 61, 75-76 (1981).

Schauer, F. (1976). *The law of obscenity*. Washington, DC: Bureau of National Affairs.

Schauer, F. (1978-79). Response: Pornography and the First Amendment, *U. Pitt. Law Review, 40*, 605, 607-08.

Schauer, F. (1982). Codifying the First Amendment: New York v. Ferber. *Supreme Court Review, 1982*, 285.

Schauer, F. (1989). The aim and the target in free speech methodology. *Northwest University Law Review, 83,* 562, 562-64.

Schneider v. State, 308 U.S. 147, 164-65 (1939).

Senate Report. (1996). No. 104-358, 104th Cong., 2d Sess., pt. I, p. 7.

Shackleton, R.. (1975). *Censure and censorship: Impediments to free publication in the age of enlightment.* Austin Humanities Research Center, University of Texas.

Shiffrin, S. (1978). Defamatory non-media speech and First Amendment methodology. *U.C.L.A. Law Review, 25,* 915, 955.

Shiffrin, S. H. (1983). The First Amendment and economic regulation: Away from a general theory of the First Amendment. *Northwestern University Law Review, 78,* 1212.

Shiffrin, S.H. (1994). Racist speech, outsider jurisprudence, and the meaning of America. *Cornell Law Review, 80,* 43, 46.

Simpson, S.M. (1994). Note, The commercial speech doctrine: An analysis of the consequences of basing First Amendment protections on the "public interest." *New York Law School Law Review, 39,* 575, 605-606.

Tribe, L.H. (1988). *American constitutional law* (2d ed.). Mineola, NY: Foundation Press.

Trollinger, T. (1994). Reconceptualizing the free speech clause: From a refuse of dualism to the reason of holism. *George Mason Independent Law Review, 3,* 137, 172-173.

United States v. Juvenile Male, 22 F.3d 821 (8th Cir. 1994).

United States v. O'Brian, 391 U.S. 367, 377 (1968).

Virginia v. American Booksellers Association, 484 U.S. 383, 389 (1988).

Virginia State Bd. of Pharmacy v. Virginia Citizens Consumer Council, 425 U.S. 748, 775-81 (1976) (Steward, J., concurring).

Volokh, E. (1996). Freedom of speech, permissible tailoring and transcending strict scrutiny. *University of Pennsylvania Law Review, 144,* 2417.

Ward v. Rock Against Racism, 491 U.S. 781, 796-98 (1989).

Wilson, J.L. (1993, December 27). Commercial speech approaches full protected status, *New York Law Journal,* p. 1

Wolfson, N. (1994). Eroticism, obscenity, pornography and free speech. *Brook. Law Review, 60,* 1037.

Woolfall, B. D. (1994). Comment, implications of a bond requirement for 900-number dial-a-porn providers: Exploring the need for tighter restrictions on obscenity and indecency. *California Western Law Review, 30,* 297, 310-311.

Zito, T. (1993, December 17). Senate demagoguery; Leave my company's video game alone. *Washington Post,* Section A-25.

9

REGULATION OF INDECENCY IN ELECTRONIC COMMUNICATION

SHARON DOCTER

Whether or not indecency may be regulated when communicated over a given medium depends on the unique characteristics of the communication technology employed. Sharon Docter critiques the rationale for regulating indecent speech across various media and offers policy alternatives by comparing electronic communications to the broadcasting, the cable television, and the common carrier models of regulation.

The advent of new communication technologies presents policymakers and the courts with increasing challenges concerning the ways in which these new technologies should be regulated. Electronic bulletin board systems are one such new innovation. The term *electronic bulletin board systems* refers generally to two-way information services that provide electronic information to the home (Tydeman, Lipinski, Adler, Nyhan, & Zwimpfer, 1982). Using a modem and a personal computer, the end-user may post and receive messages, obtain information from databases, retrieve software, or perform other activities (Schlacter, 1993). By 1993, there were at least 60,000 public and commercially accessible bulletin board systems in the United States (Rafaeli & LaRose, 1993; Schlacter, 1993). The rapid of growth of the Internet in recent years, with its 40 million users and over 38,000 networks, has most assuredly increased access to electronic bulletin board systems.

Because electronic bulletin board systems are a speech medium, policy themes have arisen concerning the regulation of that medium and how that regulation implicates the First Amendment.[1] The establishment of electronic bulletin board systems and electronic communications will place new challenges on the courts and policymakers as they seek to apply existing legal metaphors to new technologies. Electronic communications are particularly interesting because, as Ithiel de Sola Pool (1983) predicted over 10 years ago, they represent a convergence of communications technologies. This convergence of communications technologies— broadcasting, the telephone and the print media—has tended to blur traditional legal categories.

One important policy theme that has arisen as electronic information services penetrate more homes concerns the regulation of indecent messages. Systems such as Prodigy allow large numbers of persons, including minors, to access unedited electronic mail and bulletin board messages that might contain indecent words or pictures. *Penthouse* magazine, for example, offers an online service that allows subscribers to "download beautiful color images of Penthouse Pets" and "receive revealing electronic mail from other members" through a service called "Petline." Rimm (1995) recently conducted a content analysis of pornography on the Internet and concluded that three of the five most popular Usenet newsgroups worldwide contained pornographic images, stories, or discussions

The proliferation of indecent messages has become a concern of both policymakers and information service providers. In late 1995, CompuServe, the second largest information service provider, suspended access to at least 200 Internet newsgroups worldwide in response to an order by German authorities who had deemed the newsgroups indecent and in violation of German law. The order affected all 4 million users in 147 countries, including the United States (Kaplan, 1995). Similarly, the regulation of indecent content in electronic communications also appears inevitable in the United States, as antipornography amendments to the Telecommunications Act impose criminal penalties for the communication of indecent messages on the Internet.

The proliferation of indecency on the Internet and the subsequent concern of policymakers is not surprising, as speech pertaining to sex has accounted for the early use of many new technologies. Many initial sales of videocassette recorders, for example, were attributable to consumers' desires to view pornography in the privacy of their home. Similarly, sexually-related speech accounted for the early adoption of pay-per-view TV, laser discs, and 976 calling (Harmon, 1993). Historically, as new media have developed, the courts have allowed the government to regulate indecent speech transmitted via these media. However, the courts have emphasized that policies that completely ban indecent speech from a particular medium are unconstitutional. As issues concerning the regulation of indecent speech communicated over other new technologies have arisen, the courts have generally attempted to fashion unusual remedies that accommodate the interests of both those who would like to receive indecent messages and those who would like to prevent indecent messages from entering their home.

The FCC defined "indecent speech" as "language that describes, in terms patently offensive as measured by contemporary community standards, . . . sexual or excretory activities or organs" (In the Matter of Enforcement Prohibitions Against Broadcast Indecency in 18 U.S.C. 1464, 1990, p. 5300). Obscene speech, however, is patently offensive speech that lacks "serious, literary, artistic, political or scientific value" and that appeals to a prurient interest in sex, as measured by contemporary community standards (*Miller v. California*, 1973). Whereas indecent speech is protected by the First Amendment, obscene speech constitutes a category of speech that falls outside the scope of First Amendment protection. Because obscenity is not protected by the Constitution, obscenity may be prohibited uniformly across all media. Indecent speech, however, is not uniformly prohibited. Instead, whether or not indecency is regulated when communicated over a given medium depends on the unique characteristics of the communication technology. The regulations concerning indecent speech, for example, differ when the indecency is transmitted via the broadcasting medium, cable television, the telephone, or a newspaper.

In this chapter, I examine policy alternatives concerning the regulation of indecent speech communicated electronically. This chapter examines possibilities for the regulation of indecent speech by comparing electronic information services to the broadcasting model, the cable television model, and the common carrier model. In order to effectively understand these comparisons, however, it is important first to examine and critique the rationale for regulating indecent speech.

JUSTIFICATIONS FOR THE REGULATION OF INDECENT SPEECH

Because indecent speech is protected by the First Amendment, the government may regulate indecent speech only to promote a "compelling interest" and only if the regulation is the least restrictive means of achieving the government's interest (*Sable Communications of California, Inc. v. FCC*, 1989).

Protecting Children From Harm

One compelling interest that the government has identified and that the courts have accepted as a rationale for regulating indecent speech broadcast over the public airwaves is the interest in protecting the psychological welfare of children (In the Matter of Enforcement, 1990). Similarly, the U.S. Supreme Court's most recent holding on the regulation of indecent speech in the context of indecent telephone messages identified the protection of the "physical and psychological well-being of minors" as a compelling government interest (*Action for Children's Television v. FCC*, 1991; *Sable Communications v. FCC*, 1989).

Embedded in this justification for the regulation of indecent speech is the assumption that indecent speech, whether broadcast via radio or television or communicated over telephone lines, causes harm to children. However, there is no empirical evidence that supports the proposition that indecent messages harm children. In a recent assessment of all of the available social scientific literature concerning the effects of indecent speech on children, Donnerstein, Wilson, and Linz (1992) concluded that "relevant empirical research provides no reasonable evidence to suggest harmful effects result from exposure to such [indecent] content" (p. 111). The dissent in *Action for Children's Television v. FCC* (1995) recognized that this lack of evidence undermined the protection of minors from harm as a compelling interest:

> There is not one iota of evidence in the record to support the claim that exposure to indecency is harmful—indeed the nature of the alleged "harm" is never explained. There is significant evidence suggesting a causal connection between viewing violence on television and antisocial behavior; but . . . the FCC has pointed to no such evidence addressing the effects of *indecent* programming. (p. 671, Edwards dissenting; emphasis in original)

The lack of empirical evidence concerning a relationship between indecent speech and harmful effects on children suggests that this justification for regulating indecent speech is not appropriate. The government can hardly claim a "compelling" interest in protecting children from indecent messages when no record of harm to children can be established.

However, the court in *Action for Children's Television v. FCC* (1995) has held that a showing of harm is not necessary to justify the protection of minors from harm as a compelling interest. The court noted that "a scientific demonstration of psychological harm is [not] required in order to establish the constitutionality of measures protecting minors from exposure to indecent speech" (pp. 661-662). The court instead rests its justification on normative considerations concerning children's moral and ethical development. However, even though a clear scientific demonstration of harm should not be required to justify a compelling interest, it appears that at least some demonstration of harm is necessary. Otherwise, the distinction between a "reasonable basis" for regulation, a "substantial interest," and a "compelling interest" become blurred. Moreover, the need for at least some demonstration of harm is particularly important when Congress seeks to suppress constitutionally protected expression. Without at least some demonstration of evidence, it would become increasingly easy for Congress to ban marginalized speech based on a claim that such speech undermines the moral and ethical standards of society. This principle is counter to the bedrock of the First Amendment.

The lack of evidence linking indecency and harm to children is of particular concern when one considers that the reason for denying individuals a right to express constitutionally protected speech has been based on a tenuous assumption. Unlike regulations of media that are designed to enhance speech by promoting diversity (such as the Fairness Doctrine), the curtailment of indecent speech in this context abridges speech by narrowing the diversity of messages and by directly burdening the free speech rights of those who seek to express and those who seek access to indecent speech. Thus, the assumption that indecent speech will harm children should *not* be used as a justification for regulating indecent electronic messages.

Protecting Unsuspecting Adults

In *FCC v. Pacifica Foundation* (1978), the Court justified regulating indecent speech by identifying an interest in protecting unsuspecting adults from receiving shocking messages in "the privacy of the home, where the individual's right to be left alone plainly outweighs the First Amendment rights of an intruder" (p. 748). The Court, in a plurality opinion, noted that the broadcast medium is uniquely pervasive and, therefore, "unconsenting viewers may tune into a station without any warning that offensive language is being or will be broadcast" (p. 732, n. 2). Viewers, then, are considered a captive audience who lack the ability to control and monitor the messages they see and hear. Neustadt, Skall, and Hammer (1981) noted, "the fact that broadcasting is a 'pervasive medium' not under the recipient's control was central to the Supreme Court's decision upholding the FCC's reprimand of a radio station for broadcasting indecent language" (p. 349, n. 66).

The justification that indecent speech may be regulated because it might shock unsuspecting adults also runs contrary to the principles of the First Amendment. In *Cohen v. California* (1971), the Court held that speech cannot be banned simply because it is offensive to some people. In the Cohen case, a young man was criminally prosecuted for wearing a jacket that said "Fuck the Draft" in a courthouse. In reversing the conviction, the Court held that it is *not* the function of government to maintain what it regards as a suitable level of discourse within society. The free speech rights of individuals cannot be abridged simply because exercising those rights might create a danger that some will be offended: "The ability of government, consonant with the Constitution, to shut off discourse solely to protect others from hearing it is . . . dependent upon a showing that substantial privacy interests are being invaded in an essentially intolerable manner. Any broader view of this authority would effectively empower a majority to silence dissidents simply as a matter of personal predilections" (p. 18).[2]

Moreover, the Court noted that if individuals were offended by Cohen's message, they could simply avert their eyes to avoid further exposure to the message because they were not a captive audience. Similarly, the viewers and listeners of indecent messages via broadcast media hardly can be considered a captive audience; to the extent that viewers are offended by indecent messages, they possess the ability to simply turn the channel.[3] Users of electronic bulletin boards and electronic mail and publishing services also cannot be considered a captive audience as they possess even greater control over which pages and images they wish to display or ignore than can viewers and listeners of radio and television (Neustadt et al., 1981). To the extent that users come across offensive messages, they can electronically and instantaneously "avert their eyes" by proceeding to the next message.

In balancing the First Amendment rights of those who wish to disseminate and receive indecent messages versus those who are offended by indecent messages, the balance should tip in favor of the free dissemination of ideas, especially given the power of those offended by the messages to choose to ignore them. The justification, then, that indecent speech should be regulated because it offends unsuspecting adults is not a valid rationale for regulating indecent speech communicated via *any* media, but it is particularly inappropriate when applied to the delivery of electronic information services when one considers the amount of control available to users of electronic information services to avoid unwanted messages.

Protecting Parents' Rights to Direct the Rearing of Their Children

A final justification for regulating indecent speech recognizes the interests of *parents* to raise their children in a manner as they see fit. In this regard, the government does not seek to regulate indecent speech because it assumes that indecent speech will harm children or offend adults; rather, the government regulates indecent speech only during times of the day when unsupervised children are likely to be in the audience. The goal is to protect the decision of some parents to prevent their children's exposure to indecent speech. The government, in this view, has a "compelling interest" in facilitating parents' choices about the kinds of programs they will allow their children to view (*Action for Children's Television v. FCC*, 1988).

The government interest in protecting parents' rights to direct the rearing of their children was initially recognized in the context of the broadcast of indecent messages in the *FCC v. Pacifica* (1978) case. More recently, the D.C. Court of Appeals relied specifically on the government's interest in facilitating parents' programming choices in its initial decision concerning the constitutionality of the FCC's 24-hour ban on indecent speech (*Action for Children's Television v. FCC*, 1988). The court repeatedly stressed that the government had an interest in "*assist[ing] parents* in controlling the material young children will hear" (p. 1334; emphasis in original). Relying primarily on testimony from the FCC General Counsel, the court held that the government may regulate the broadcast of indecent speech *not* because the government has made an independent determination that a child's exposure to indecent material is morally wrong or harmful, but because the government has an interest in protecting parents' rights to control the material that their children may view. As the court noted, "the government does not propose to act *in loco parentis* to deny children access *contrary* to parents' wishes" (p. 1343; emphasis in original). Instead, the court held that the government may regulate indecent speech broadcast over the airwaves only to the extent that the regulation will promote parental control of viewing choices and will balance the interests of those parents who object to their children viewing indecent programming versus those parents who allow it.

To the extent that the government continues to identify an interest in assisting parents in controlling their children's exposure to indecent messages, it finds a valid justification for regulating indecent speech, at least for those media that are accessible to unsupervised children. Importantly, this justification is independent of any harmful effects of indecent speech on minors as well as any offensive effects of indecent speech on unsuspecting adults. In comparing the regulation of indecent speech communicated electronically to other media, only this justification is considered.

THE BROADCASTING MODEL

Unlike the print medium, the broadcast medium has historically been regulated by the government. The classic justification for allowing the government to intrude into areas traditionally protected by the First Amendment and regulate the speech of its citizens is that there exists a scarcity of the electronic magnetic spectrum (*Red Lion v. FCC*, 1969). Although theoretically anyone can have access to the print medium to disseminate views, the nature of the broadcast medium requires that only a limited number of voices can communicate over the airwaves at one time. Thus, the government must act as a "traffic cop," granting licenses to a limited number of individuals and guaranteeing limited rights of access in certain instances. In addition, the scarce nature of the broadcasting medium has been used as a justification for enacting regulations designed to ensure that a diversity of viewpoints are heard over the airwaves.

The scarcity rationale for regulation of the broadcast medium has come under increasing criticism in recent years (see Pool, 1983), and there have been signs from the Court that it will no longer accept scarcity as a valid justification for regulating broadcasting (*FCC v. League of Women Voters*, 1984). Scarcity of the electromagnetic spectrum, however, only justifies regulations that are designed to enhance speech by *increasing* the diversity of voices. The Fairness Doctrine and the limited rights of access for federal political candidates are examples of such speech-enhancing regulations. In contrast, regulations that *curtail* indecent speech cannot be justified through the scarcity argument, for regulations that abridge speech inevitably limit the range of viewpoints. As noted previously, the curtailment of indecent speech communicated over the broadcast medium has been permitted because radio and television are "uniquely pervasive" and "uniquely accessible to children" (*FCC v. Pacifica*, 1978, p. 748).

Relying on the rationale that broadcasting is uniquely accessible to children, the FCC during the late 1980s, pursuant to a directive from Congress, promulgated regulations that completely banned indecent speech from the broadcast medium. The D.C. Court of Appeals then issued a stay on enforcement of the ban; the court then voided such 24-hour bans as unconstitutional because the 24-hour ban impermissibly infringed on the First Amendment rights of those who wanted access to indecent messages (*Action for Children's Television v. FCC*, 1988, 1991). The court held that "the FCC may regulate such [indecent] material only with due respect for the high value our Constitution places on freedom and choice in what the people say and hear" (*Action for Children's Television v. FCC*, 1988, p. 1344; cf. *Action for Children's Television v. FCC*, 1991, p. 1508). Implicit in the court's opinions is the assumption that the government cannot reduce public debate to a level that is only appropriate for children (see *Ginsberg v. New York*, 1968). However, given that "the power of the state to control the conduct of children reaches beyond the scope of its authority over adults" (*Action for Children's Television v. FCC*, 1988, p. 1340), the court permitted some regulation of indecent messages such as a requirement that indecent speech be broadcast during the late evening hours when children are not likely to be in the audience (*Action for Children's Television v. FCC*, 1991). The court has currently set the hours of 10:00 p.m. to 6:00 a.m. as the hours when indecent material may be broadcast (*Action for Children's Television v. FCC*, 1995). If the broadcasting model were applied to the regulation of electronic information services, this would suggest a model in which indecent messages only would be allowed to be posted during the late evening hours when children are not likely to be using the service. This option, however, cannot be applied to electronic communications because of the asynchronous nature of the technology.

Other differences between broadcasting and the delivery of electronic information suggest that the broadcasting regulatory model should *not* be applied to electronic communications. Electronic information services are not as accessible to children as broadcasting. There can be no doubt that television is accessible to children. Turning on a television or radio requires only that children turn on one switch. Children as young as 3 years old, for example, can generally understand how to turn on a television. One can argue that accessing electronic bulletin boards and electronic publishing and mail services requires a much more sophisticated understanding of the technology. In the case of electronic mail services, for example, one must have an understanding of how to call up particular programs as well as knowledge of specific commands.

On the contrary, the argument that electronic information services are not accessible to children can be undercut by two factors that should be tested empirically. First, there appears to be a growing trend in the creation of computer programs to make use of such programs more user-friendly. Features such as pull-down menus and initiating commands by merely touching a screen have made computer technologies much more accessible. It is almost inevitable that these increasingly user-friendly features will be incorporated into electronic publishing and electronic bulletin board services. It is easy to imagine, for example, computer programs designed so that the user need not even be able to read in order to use the technology. Second, it appears that children are becoming increasingly sophisticated about their use of computer technologies. Many schools, for example, have programs designed to teach children about the use of computers at a very young age. Whether or not the trends identified here are supported by empirical evidence may have important public policy consequences concerning the regulation of indecent material. To the extent that electronic information services become accessible to children to the same degree that television is accessible to children, policymakers may use this similarity to apply the broadcasting model to the regulation of indecent material communicated electronically.

However, as a matter of policy, the broadcasting model for the regulation of indecent material still seems inappropriate in the context of electronic communications. As noted earlier, in order to justify the regulation of indecent material, the government must show *both* a compelling interest and must use the least speech-restrictive means of achieving its interest (*Sable Communications v. FCC*, 1989). In the broadcasting context, the least-restrictive means of protecting parents' viewing choices is to allow indecent programming only during the late evening hours. However, in the context of electronic information services, other less speech-restrictive options are available, such as requiring distributors of indecent materials to provide special passwords to parents who would like to curtail their children's access to such materials. Although the risk still exists that children will be exposed to indecent messages when using services such as electronic bulletin boards with many subscribers, the flexibility of the technology allows for less speech-restrictive alternatives to be developed. For example, designers and distributors of electronic bulletin board software could request that those who wish to disseminate indecent messages input a special "indecency" code when posting a message; the code would activate a blocking device for those parents who do not want such messages entering their home (although this alternative would only be acceptable if inputting the "indecency" code could be done with relative ease and at no cost to the user). Another less speech-restrictive alternative would be to build a program into the electronic messaging system that recognized indecent language and put the language into a special category that could be blocked by the end-user.

Because less speech-restrictive alternatives are available, the application of the broadcasting model to the regulation of electronic information services, so that indecent speech could only be communicated during the late evening hours, infringes on the free speech rights of those who would like to disseminate and receive indecent messages and would be difficult to enforce, given the asynchronous nature of electronic communications.

THE CABLE TELEVISION MODEL

Unlike the broadcasting model, the courts have held that indecent material may not be restricted to the late evening hours on cable television (Community Television of Utah, Inc. v. Roy City, 1982; Jones v. Wilkinson, 1986). In reaching this holding, the courts have noted that the fundamental differences between cable and broadcast television require that cable television be treated differently with regard to indecent material than the traditional broadcast model. One of the most important distinctions between cable and broadcast television is the viewer's choice over programming content. According to the courts, subscribers to cable television have a greater degree of choice than do viewers of broadcast television. First, viewers may choose to subscribe or not, and "a similar choice is not available with broadcast television" (Community Television v. Roy City, 1982, p. 1166).[4] In addition, subscribers to cable television may select from varying tiers of service. There is the sense, then, that viewers of cable television are aware that programs on the higher tiers of service (such as Home Box Office) may contain more indecent material. By actively selecting tiers of service in which indecent material is likely to be present, the viewer implicitly consents to allowing the material into his or her home: "Cable signals travel over wires, not in the air. Such signals do not travel except upon request. They are asked for. They are invited" (p. 1166). Finally, the subscriber to cable television may choose to terminate this service. A viewer of broadcast television, however, "cannot terminate his subscription to a publicly allocated broadcast channel" (p. 1166).

Similarly, when a subscriber to electronic information services requests specific kinds of electronic publishing and bulletin board services, the subscriber "invites" the material into his or her home. In fact, the subscriber to electronic information services has much greater choice over the kinds of content he or she wishes to receive than does the subscriber to cable television. The subscriber to cable television must choose from the limited programming packages offered by the cable companies and generally has only three tiers of service from which to choose. On the contrary, subscribers to electronic information services can pick and choose among the types of material they would like to access in their homes. In this sense, electronic information services are more analogous to a bookstore or magazine rack, in which subscribers can choose from a wide range of material, from the electronic *Penthouse* noted earlier, to children's books and magazines. If parents are concerned about their children gaining access to indecent messages through a bulletin board service, parents can simply choose not to subscribe to such services. Thus, to the extent that the court has relied on the degree of viewer choice over programming or information content as a rationale for allowing indecent speech to be cablecast during all times of the day, the greater degree of viewer choice available to subscribers of electronic information services suggests that indecent speech in this context also may not be restricted to hours when children are unlikely to be in the audience.

Given that the government cannot restrict the hours that indecent material may be cablecast, Congress used other means to accommodate the interests of parents who would like to ensure that their children not be exposed to indecent material. The Cable Communications Policy Act of 1984 provides that cable companies must make lock boxes available to subscribers at a reasonable price (47 U.S.C. section 624 (d)(2)(A) (1984)). Lock boxes are devices that are installed on the cable box, which allow parents to lock out their access to cable television.[5]

Like the cable model, electronic information services offer the possibility of creating electronic lock boxes. Parents can block access to objectionable material by requiring that the user input a special code in order to access certain kinds of material. Distributors of electronic information services should make this option available to the subscriber, but the cost should be borne by those who want to block access, as is the case with cable. The advantage of electronic information services is that the characteristics of the technology offer great flexibility; features such as access codes can be incorporated into the software programs at a relatively low cost. The technology, then, allows for an efficient means to protect the interests of all parties (parents, disseminators of information, and receivers of information) without in any way jeopardizing constitutional values.

THE COMMON CARRIER MODEL

In 1988, Congress amended the Communications Act to impose a ban on indecent interstate commercial telephone messages, known as dial-a-porn messages. Then, in *Sable Communications v. FCC* (1989) the Court held that indecent speech is protected by the First

Amendment and that dial-a-porn services could not be banned. Congress responded to the Sable decision by amending the Communications Act to implement a scheme that would prevent children from accessing dial-a-porn messages. The Communications Act now provides that carriers and providers of indecent messages communicated over the phone lines may be held liable for those messages unless the carrier and provider have adopted a reverse blocking scheme. Congress ordered the FCC to implement the reverse blocking scheme.

According to FCC regulations, reverse blocking requires subscribers to request access to indecent message services, such as dial-a-porn, in writing. This scheme presumes that people do not want access to indecent material unless specifically requested. The FCC also considered and ultimately rejected a voluntary blocking scheme, in which parents who wanted to block access to the service would have to request the blocking in writing. The FCC rejected the voluntary blocking scheme because it maintained that parents would not recognize the need to block their access to dial-a-porn messages until after they had received expensive bills for services which they did not request. As the FCC noted, "a voluntary blocking scheme would be far less effective in protecting children from exposure to indecent material because it is likely that most parents would not realize the need for blocking until their children had already obtained access to indecent messages" (Regulations Concerning Indecent Communications By Telephone, Report and Order, 1990).

The amendments to the Communications Act require the carriers (the telephone companies) to implement the reverse blocking scheme and requires the message providers (the dial-a-porn services) to notify the carriers that they are transmitting indecent messages (Communications Act of 1934, as amended, 47 U.S.C. section 223). Both the carrier and the message provider are subject to criminal penalties, including fines and/or imprisonment if they violate section 223 of the Communications Act. However, the carrier may not be prosecuted if, in carrying the indecent messages, the carrier has relied on the lack of notification by the message provider that the material is indecent. In addition, the carrier can avoid prosecution if the message provider (the dial-a-porn service) utilized credit cards, access codes, or scrambling in providing access to indecent messages.

The common carrier model for the regulation of indecent messages should not be applied to electronic information services for a variety of reasons. First, implicit in Congress's and the FCC's rationale for requiring the telephone companies to implement reverse blocking is the assumption that children can and will gain access to indecent messages communicated over the telephone. Like television, the telephone is easily accessible to children. Although accessing dial-a-porn messages is somewhat sophisticated because users must have knowledge of the special prefixes (such as "976" numbers), once a child has knowledge of the dial-a-porn prefixes, accessing such messages is quite simple. In fact, many children have accessed dial-a-porn messages without their parents' consent; it was the widespread accessing of indecent messages by minors that eventually led Congress to ban indecent telephone services. However, as noted earlier, the use of electronic information services probably requires more sophistication than using a telephone and requires some degree of computer literacy. The risk that children will gain access to indecent material electronically, therefore, is probably less than the risk that children will gain access to indecent material via the telephone (although this assumption should be tested empirically). If electronic information services are less accessible to children than the telephone, a reverse blocking scheme, in which those seeking indecent electronic information services would have to request access to such services in writing, should not be used.

In implementing the reverse blocking scheme in the context of indecent telephone messages, the FCC also seemed concerned that parents should not have to pay for services that they have not requested. It is important to note that this rationale for reverse blocking does not arise out of a concern that children will be harmed if they receive indecent telephone messages; instead, the justification centers around a concern that people must consent in order to have indecent material enter their homes. Requiring users to explicitly consent in writing to receive indecent telephone messages should not be required for access to electronic information services. Unlike the telephone, when one purchases electronic information services, one does not in a single purchase automatically gain access to services that might carry indecent speech. Instead, the purchaser must pick and choose among the wide variety of software available to determine what types of content to access. By allowing particular kinds of software into the home, the purchaser already has explicitly consented to the access of such material. Because the subscriber to electronic information services has explicitly consented to having indecent material in the home, the user should assume the risk that children might be exposed to such material, just as a parent who purchases a pornographic magazine assumes the risk that his or her child might be exposed to such material. It is up to the parent, then, to take precautionary measures to shield the child from exposure to such material if he or she so chooses.

The final justification for requiring reverse blocking to access indecent telephone messages centers around a concern that children must be protected from potential harm. In this regard, the FCC has determined that it is better to put a heavier burden on those who would like to gain access to indecent messages rather than on those who would like to block indecent messages. As the FCC noted, "a reverse blocking approach puts the burden on those who want access to messages, rather than on those who wish to protect their children. The burden is not great in either case—it requires merely writing to the telephone company to request access or blocking. Balancing all the interests, it is apparent that reverse blocking is an effective, not unduly restrictive means of protecting children" (Regulations Concerning Indecent Communications By Telephone, reprinted in Brenner, 1992, p. 65). In balancing the interests and placing the greater burden on those who would like access to indecent material, the FCC advocates a policy of restricting the constitutionally protected rights of some in order to protect children from a harm that has never been empirically supported.

Such a balancing burdens the exercise of constitutional rights because of the FCC's normative determination that indecent material might harm children. This policy certainly should not be extended to the delivery of electronic information services. It allows the government too much latitude to censor or burden free speech interests in favor of interests that may in fact be illusory. Any balancing of interests, therefore, should tip in favor of the free dissemination of and access to ideas, even ideas that the majority of the citizenry may find objectionable. Finally, the common carrier model should not be extended to the delivery of electronic information services because, as a matter of policy, carriers should not be involved in monitoring the content of communication.

The job of the carrier is simply to carry; carriers should not be threatened with possible criminal prosecution because of the content of information disseminated by others. Similarly, providers of electronic information services should not be required to be concerned about the content of the messages they provide. The advantage of electronic communication is that it allows for the rapid dissemination of massive amounts of information. Electronic publishers will have potentially volumes of information that they can provide daily to subscribers. It would be extremely costly to require the operators or the providers of the message services to review the information in advance in order to determine if the material is indecent. Threatening message providers or operators of electronic information services with indecency prosecutions could serve to undercut the advantages of the service—its speed and breadth in providing information. The amount of pages that would have to be reviewed as well as the legal fees, therefore, could be tremendous and could thwart the development of the industry. Moreover, because they will fear criminal prosecutions, electronic information service providers may be overly cautious and categorize speech that is *not* indecent as such. This tendency to err on the side of caution by categorizing any speech that is questionable as indecent will have the effect of chilling speech that is entitled to the maximum amount of constitutional protection. For all the reasons stated here, the common carrier model for the regulation of indecency should not be applied to electronic information services.

THE COMMUNICATIONS DECENCY ACT

On the one hand, the Communications Decency Act appears aimed at restricting access to indecent messages by children, a constitutionally permissible goal. On the other hand, the Communications Decency Act goes much further than the regulation of indecency over any other medium of expression. With the possible exception of one-to-one e-mail communication, it is impossible for Internet users to discern the age of those individuals who are likely recipients of messages (*ACLU v. Reno*, 1996). The CDA, then, constitutes a virtual 24-hour ban on indecency in electronic communications. Given the Supreme Court's and lower court's rejection of 24-hour bans in the broadcasting and telecommunications contexts (*Action for Children's Television v. FCC*, 1988; *Sable Communications v. FCC*, 1989), such a ban in the context of electronic communications cannot withstand constitutional scrutiny. The net effect of the CDA would be to reduce communication to a level appropriate to children. Two lower courts then have already stayed enforcement of the CDA because it is overbroad and reaches speech protected by the First Amendment (*ACLU v. Reno*, 1996; *Shea v. Reno*, 1996). In December 1996, the U.S. Supreme Court agreed to review the constitutionality of the CDA.

Thus, whereas the goal of preventing children's access to electronic indecent material is permissible, the means of achieving that goal are constitutionally suspect. The Supreme Court in *Sable Communications v. FCC* (1989) was very clear that indecency may be regulated only if the regulation constitutes the least-restrictive means of achieving the government's interest. In this case, many other alternatives are available that are less speech restrictive. As noted earlier, blocking devices and filtering mechanisms are available that parents could load, so that sexually explicit material could be limited to adults.[6] As discussed previously, when balancing between the interests of those who would like access to constitutionally protected speech and those who would like to block access, the balance should always tip in favor of protecting constitutional values.

In addition, the Communications Decency Act may chill constitutionally protected expression. Users and information service providers, fearing criminal prosecution because of minors' access to such material, may avoid exercising their First Amendment rights by receiving or initiating indecent communications. The chilling effect is even more likely when communication takes place over a medium like electronic bulletin board systems because such communication is many to many instead of one to one. Because users are not aware of the number of individuals who will receive their communications, the risk and fear that minors will receive such material and the likely chilling effect is exacerbated.

The Communications Decency Act does offer some affirmative defenses. If content providers, for example, require credit card access and adult verification for use, or if content providers tag indecent messages with a special code for easy screening, then such content providers cannot be held liable. However, as the court noted in *ACLU v. Reno* (1996), "these defenses are not technologically or economically feasible for most providers." Given the wide access to information via electronic communication, credit card companies are still seeking an effective means for credit card authorization. Moreover, requiring nonprofit entities with little resources to review content and tag indecent speech would impermissibly burden free speech.

Finally, the Communications Decency Act should be rejected as an approach to regulating indecent messages because it will not necessarily achieve its goal of protecting children from indecent messages. The Internet represents a vast array of networks, with communications initiating both within the United States and internationally. A system that imposes criminal penalties for making available indecent communication to a minor does not preclude those outside the United States from making indecent communication available to minors. Although the language of the Communications Decency Act applies to "foreign communications," there is no jurisdiction for enforcing this Act beyond the borders of the United States. Thus, a system allowing the end-user to block indecent messages would be much more effective at achieving the legislation's goal. The Communications Decency Act, therefore, is an unconstitutional and impractical method for protecting the interests of parents who seek to block access to indecent material.

CONCLUSIONS

In determining the appropriate regulatory model for a new communication technology, it is important to select a model that will not hinder the development of the industry and that will place little or no burden on constitutional values. The cable television model for regulating indecent speech appears to be the most appropriate model to apply to electronic information services for both economic and constitutional reasons. The cable television model operates on the presumption that cable companies may *not* be held liable for allowing indecent messages into the home. It is important that this presumption also be extended to electronic information services, for new communications industries should not be saddled with excessive regulations that require companies to review and possibly edit information content. Such a policy would place too great an economic burden on new industries because compliance could be costly. Moreover, a policy that would require electronic information service providers either to review and edit indecent material discourages the candid and free flow of ideas that is contrary to First Amendment values.

Finally, the cable television model offers advantages if applied to electronic information services because the cable television model takes into account the legitimate interests of parents to raise their children in the manner they see fit, while at the same time placing no burden on those who would like to disseminate and receive indecent messages. The burden is placed on those who would like to block access to speech, and those parties are required to bear any costs. Thus, the value of allowing free access to information content is preserved.

ENDNOTES

1. Some of these policy themes include the degree of content regulation that is permissible, copyright issues, liability for defamation, guarantees of access, and privacy and security.
2. Interestingly, when considering indecency regulations in the broadcasting context, the court declined to address whether the "protection of the home against intrusion by offensive broadcasts" constituted a compelling interest justifying the regulation of indecency (*Action for Children's Television v. FCC* (1995, pp. 660-661) because other justifications were sufficiently compelling.
3. *FCC v. Pacifica* (1978) can be distinguished from *Cohen v. California* (1971). In Pacifica, the Court distinguished Cohen by noting that there was no evidence any person was in fact offended by Cohen's jacket. In Pacifica, however, there was evidence that at least one person was offended by the indecent radio broadcast. Moreover, the offensive speech communicated in Cohen and Pacifica did occur in different contexts. Cohen concerned indecent speech communicated in a public place. Pacifica concerned indecent speech communicated over the public airwaves and brought into people's homes and car radios. One important justification for regulating indecent speech in Pacifica, then, concerned protecting unconsenting adults from being shocked in the privacy of their homes.

4. See also *Action for Children's Television v. FCC* (1995), in which the court noted that "unlike cable subscribers who are offered such options as 'pay-per-view channels'" broadcast audiences have no choice but to 'subscribe' to the entire output of traditional broadcasters" (p. 660).

5. In 1992, Congress amended the Communications Act to provide that indecent programming on leased access channels must be carried on a single channel and will be blocked unless the customer requests access in writing. The number of leased access channels vary depending on the total number of cable channels available. However, leased access channels represent a relatively small percentage of the total number of channels. Moreover, the Senate has passed a bill requiring that cable operators scramble programming that is unsuitable for children. Passage of such legislation by the House appears likely.

6. Microsystems Software, for example, already has made such a filtering mechanism available to parents. The software, called "Cyber Patrol," allows parents to screen sexual and violent content. Microsystems Software staff conduct extensive searches of the Internet each week to update the content included in the filtering software. Cyber Patrol is already available free of charge to subscribers of CompuServe and Prodigy (*ACLU v. Reno*, 1996).

REFERENCES

Action for Children's Television et al. v. FCC, 58 F.3d 654 (D.C. Cir. 1995).

Action for Children's Television et al. v. FCC, 932 F.2d 1504 (D.C. Cir. 1991).

Action for Children's Television et al. v. FCC, 852 F.2d 1332 (D.C. Cir. 1988).

American Civil Liberties Union (ACLU) v. Reno, 929 F. Supp. 824 (E.D. Pa. 1996), cert. granted, 65 U.S.L.W. 3411 (1996).

Brenner, D. (1992). *Law and regulation of common carriers in the communications industry*. Unpublished manuscript. University of California, Los Angeles School of Law.

Cohen v. California, 403 U.S. 15 (1971).

Community Television of Utah, Inc. v. Roy City, 555 F. Supp. 1164 (D. Utah, 1982).

Donnerstein, E., Wilson, B., & Linz, D. (1992). On the regulation of broadcast indecency to protect children. *Journal of Broadcast & Electronic Media, 36*, 111-117.

FCC v. League of Women Voters, 468 U.S. 364 (1984).

FCC v. Pacifica Foundation, 438 U.S. 726 (1978).

Ginsburg v. New York, 390 U.S. 629 (1968).

Harmon, A. (1993, December 29). The "seedy" side of CD-ROMs. *Los Angeles Times*, p. A26.

In the Matter of Enforcement of Prohibitions Against Broadcast Indecency in 18 U.S.C. 1464, 5 F.C.C.2d 5297 (1990).

Jones v. Wilkinson, 300 F.2d 989 (10th Cir. 1986).

Kaplan, K. (1995, December 29). Germany forces online service to censor Internet. *Los Angeles Times*, p.A1.

Miller v. California, 413 U.S. 15 (1973).

Neustadt, R.M., Skall, G.P., & Hammer, M. (1981). The regulation of electronic publishing. *Federal Communications Law Journal, 33*, 331-402.

Pool, I. (1983). *Technologies of freedom.* Cambridge, MA: Harvard University Press.

Rafaeli, S., & LaRose, R.J. (1993). Electronic bulletin boards and "public goods" explanations of collaborative mass media. *Communication Research, 20*, 277-297.

Regulations Concerning Indecent Communications By Telephone, Report and Order 5 F.C.C. Rcd. 4926 (1990).

Red Lion v. FCC, 395 U.S. 367 (1969).

Rimm, M. (1995). Marketing pornography on the information superhighway: A survey of 917,410 images, descriptions, short stories, and animations downloaded 8.5 million times by consumers in over 2000 cities in forty countries, provinces and territories. *Georgetown Law Journal, 83*, 1849-1934.

Sable Communications of California, Inc. v. Federal Communications Commission (FCC), 492 U.S. 115 (1989).

Schlacter, E. (1993). Cyberspace, the free market and the free market of ideas: Recognizing legal differences in computer bulletin board function. *Hastings Comm/Ent L.J., 16*, 87-150.

Shea v. Reno, 930 F. Supp. 916 (S.D.N.Y 1996), petition for cert. filed 65 U.S.L.W. 3323 (1996).

Tydeman, J., Lipinski, H., Adler, R., Nyhan, M., & Zwimpfer, L. (1982). *Teletext and videotex in the United States: Market potential, technology, public policy issues.* New York: McGraw-Hill.

PART 3

PROPERTY INTERESTS

10

Copyright in a Digital World: Intellectual Property Rights in Cyberspace

Donald Fishman

When approaching electronic reproduction the legal implication that emerges most prominently is that of intellectual property, most significantly, copyright interests in the object to be digitalized. Although much in this realm is undecided, the principle that copyrights apply to cyberspace (i.e., electronic digitalized media) has been clearly established. Donald Fishman identifies the troubling areas confronted with the application of copyright law to digitalized images. The author identifies policy considerations and the need to rearticulate fundamental concepts of copyright law including what constitutes unauthorized "copying" and "display." Unsettled too is the issue of what is to be deemed "fixation" into a tangible medium of expression, thus triggering possible copyright claims.

Copyright has increasingly become a focal point of attention as the United States moves into an information-oriented economy. As we approach the new millennium, a large and growing number of professions and occupations play important roles as information producers. They may either create the original information, or they may acquire the initial information, add to it, and then redistribute a new version of the data. This value-adding process is an especially important characteristic of the information-oriented economy.

Moreover, as we move from analog to digital technology, the role of being an information producer becomes increasingly easier to enact. The convergence of data, voice, and video into one digitally designed medium allows individuals and organizations to store, edit, format, and combine data in ways unimagined a generation ago. As more information becomes digital, the information becomes easier to copy, reformat, and redistribute. As Katsh (1995) observes, value in this new digital environment will lie not only in "owning and possessing the information," but rather in the "opportunities presented to use and exploit the information" (p. 224). Katsh contends that secondary users of this information play a vital role by enhancing the original information so that there is an "evolutionary" quality in the transfer of the information from the first producer to the now second user-producer. Ginsburg (1995) argues that there is a "collaborative" process to the authorship of this new data that did not exist in an analog world. But this newly found capacity to create, reconfigure, and redistribute information, while adding value to the original work, raises issues that go to the heart of the traditional meaning of copyright law.

The concept of a vast network of linked computers providing access to an unlimited amount of information and also the means to redistribute this information directly challenges what has been the traditional relationship of author as producer and reader as user. Ginsburg (1995) identifies three major components of this newly emerging system: "Pervasive audience access" to information, the ability to copy easily and on a large scale, and the ability to distribute and redistribute.

Copyright, as we know it, is at a crossroads in its development. As Goldstein (1994) notes, "The digital revolution promises both new strains and new opportunities for copyright law" (p. 197). Samuelson (1990) depicts the digital revolution in terms of six characteristics: the ease of copying, the ease of transmitting works, the ease with which information can be "modified and manipulated" and thus customized and resold to targeted customers, the interchangeability of works in digital forms as opposed to the medium-specific constraints that limit analog works, the compactness of digitized information, and the capacity for creating "new methods of searching digital space and linking works together" (pp. 324, 330). Overall, these six features characterize a high-capacity information system composed of multiple networks and that makes information transfers convenient, inexpensive, and widely accessible.

This digital revolution challenges two underlying assumptions of the copyright systems. First, the older view held that an information producer was granted a copyright that provided the right to exclude others from unauthorized copying. The ambiguous terms in this formulation are "exclude" and "unauthorized copying." In our new environment, copying already has become a frequent, necessary, and even inevitable component of using electronic information. Saving or using a file requires making a copy of what is in memory. Downloading a file also requires making a copy. Reading a file involves not only making a copy but displaying previously copyrighted information on a screen. Katsh (1995) observes that "as we interact with the new media, our work experience inevitably changes since copying is an act that inevitably takes place on a new scale as one works with information in electronic form" (p. 216).

A second assumption rendered problematic by the digital revolution is the centrality of the "fixation standard" in copyright law. The "fixation standard" is a relatively new test. Reacting to the tedious process that the 1909 Act required in order to determine the eligibility of works for copyright protection, Congress in the 1976 Copyright Act set forth a resourceful, even forward-looking, approach to define the eligibility of new works for copyright.

To receive copyright protection, a work has to be an "original work of authorship fixed in a tangible medium of expression, now known or later developed, from which they can be perceived, reproduced, or otherwise communicated, either directly or with the aid of a machine or device" (17 U.S.C.§ 102). The Act further defines fixation as a condition that is "sufficiently permanent or stable to permit it to be perceived, reproduce, or otherwise communicated for a period of more than transitory duration" (17 U.S. C. § 101). Yet, in an electronic format, a work can be fixed for a "transitory" moment, edited, reformatted, and then reconfigured in a way that the second work no longer resembles the original. The question then arises: Is this information that is temporarily used "fixed" or "unfixed"? And, if we conclude that the information is not fixed, or that fixation is a complex and nuanced procedure, then are we forced to reassess the meaning of the concept of "fixation" that during the past two decades has become, along with the originality test, the threshold element of modern copyright law?

Less than a generation ago, terms like the *World Wide Web*, *Information Superhighway*, *Digital Age*, *Electronic Marketplace*, and the *Internet* were either nonexistent or confined to use by a small subculture. In 1984, William Gibson in his book the *Neuromancer* coined the term *cyberspace* to explain the paradigmatic shift from a print- and broadcast-based society to the electronic era.

A year earlier, Ithiel de Sola Pool (1983) wrote his now-classic book *Technologies of Freedom*, which explained the digital revolution in broad but useful generalizations. Pool argued that electronic modes of communication would displace print and broadcast technologies and that the computers would "become the printing presses of the twenty-first century" (p. 189). Pool's first chapter was entitled "A Shadow Darkens" because he envisioned confusion arising about the new technologies, and he predicted the emergence of newly discovered difficulties with the "norms that govern communication" (p. 10). As to the persistence of copyright, Pool was equally pessimistic:

> Established notions about copyright become obsolete, rooted as they are in the technology of print. The recognition of a copyright and the practice of paying royalties emerged with the printing press. With the arrival of electronic reproduction, these practices become unworkable. Electronic publishing is analogous, not so much to the print shop of the eighteenth century as to word-of-mouth communication, to which copyright was never applied. (p. 214)

Pool insisted that "totally new concepts will have to be invented to compensate creative works in this new environment. The print-based notion of copyright simply will not work" (p. 215). Rose (1994) reaffirmed Pool's basic question when he inquired: "What can 'copyright' possibly mean when millions of people can download the information they find on the Internet?" (p. 112). There also is a growing literature that questions the role and efficacy of the Copyright Office in the context of the information superhighway (Samuelson, 1994; Schwartz, 1994; Weisgrau, 1994).

The rapid growth of the Internet has intensified the pressure to clarify the scope of copyright law. In 1994, an estimated 2.3 million U.S. citizens purchased personal computers for their home, and the number of computer in use currently is estimated at 33.9 million (Stuckey, 1996). Most of these computers come equipped with high-speed modems making electronic communication one of their more popular uses. Information also is available through a plethora of networks and online services. The emergence of HTML, or Hypertext Markup Language, when coupled with the creation of HTTP (Hypertext Transfer Protocol), a standard protocol that links thousands of servers or host computers, has prompted the explosive growth of the Internet. Equally important, the Internet now reaches 37 million browsers in 180 counties, and the number of Internet users is expected to double in the near future (Sandberg, 1995). This expanding system of interlinked and distributed servers has led to the creation of numerous new computer applications, more total users, and more control and manipulation of data by information users. It is a scenario that frightens owners and creators of copyright materials. They fear that the electronic marketplace will displace the traditional owner-user relationship and undermine the meaning of copyright because of the largely unforeseen contexts in which the original information may be applied.

The purposes of this chapter are twofold. First, I discuss the reasons that a copyright system is needed even in a digital world to sustain creative works. Second, I identify several problems that occur in regulating intellectual property in cyberspace and that create strong pressure to reconfigure the relationship between owners and users of copyrighted materials.

A RATIONALE FOR A COPYRIGHT SYSTEM

Article I, Section 8, Clause 8 of the Constitution of the United States empowers Congress "to promote the Progress of Science and the useful Arts, by securing for Limited Times to Authors and Investors the exclusive Right to their respective Writings and Discoveries". This clause is one of the few instances in which the term *right* is explicitly used in the Constitution. The premise underlying the copyright clause is that an economic incentive should be provided to encourage authors and inventors to produce, and that society as a whole will benefit because the writings and inventions will create new ideas and new products. The emphasis is placed on providing incentives to individuals that will lead to producing a public benefit. In *Mazer v. Stein* (1954), the Court wrote that "encouragement of individual effort by personal gain is the best way to advance public welfare through the talents of authors" (p. 201).

The notion that the copyright system should provide incentives to innovators sanctioned the legitimacy of proprietary rights for data, and this assumption allows information to be both privately owned and selectively distributed. The rationale for excluding others from copying, distributing, or displaying information is based on the need to foster attractive incentives for individuals to produce creative works and to allow them to reap the benefits of their labors. But these proprietary rights did not exist in perpetuity, and they were limited by the Constitution.

In fact, the actual language of the Constitution provides a framework for the copyright statutes that subsequently were enacted. One key phrase in the Constitution that guided statutory construction was "limited times." An individual was granted a monopoly, whether it be a copyright or a patent, for a limited amount of time. The first copyright statute used two terms of 14 years. The more widely known 1909 Copyright Act used two terms of 28 years. The current 1976 Copyright Act extends the duration to the life of an author plus 50 years. The concept of a monopoly usually carries with it a pejorative status in U.S. law. In copyright law, however, the author or creator is given a monopoly for a limited period in order to encourage him or her to produce. According to the Constitution, authors and creators are thus guaranteed a period when they have an "exclusive right" to control the product in order to reap a profit. The Constitution probably would not permit a "perpetual right" to copyrighted materials, but it does allow Congress the latitude to develop a time frame in order to optimize the benefits of copyright protection. The word *writings* in the Constitution has been interpreted by Congress and the courts in an expansive way to include sculpture, videotapes, graphics, maps, paintings, and even computer software programs.

A copyright thus provides a monopoly to authors, artists, and creators for their respective writings and works. The author has the exclusive right to control the work and can deny authorization to use, reproduce, perform, or display the work for the statutory life of the copyright. This is the tradeoff that Congress makes in order to promote intellectual, artistic, and creative work. The monopoly privileges have predetermined goals:

> The monopoly privileges that Congress may authorize are neither unlimited nor primarily designed to provide a special private benefit. Rather, the limited grant is a means by which an important public purpose may be achieved. It is intended to motivate the creative activity of authors and inventors by the provision of a special reward, and to allow the public access to the products of their genius after the limited period of exclusive control has expired. (*Sony Corporation v. Universal City Studio*, 1984, p. 774)

The 1976 Copyright Act provided a solution to disentangle copyright law from a difficult and recurrent problem. Prior to the 1976 Act, copyright relied on a categorical approach to subject matter. The Copyright Act of 1790 limited copyright to "books, maps, and charts." Later copyright acts added photography, movies, phonograph records, and cable television to the list of protected works. The categorical approach meant that the courts were compelled to examine each new communication format or technology to determine whether it could be interpreted as a "writing" within the constitutional scope of the copyright clause. Understandably, there was much judicial diffidence in approaching this difficult task. The courts believed it was the express responsibility of Congress to legislate whether a new technology should be covered under copyright protection. In the 1976 Act, Congress defined a copyright as an "original work of authorship fixed in a tangible medium of expression." The "fixation standard" was designed to cover existing and yet-to-be discovered technologies (Brandriss, 1996).

In theory, the fixation standard was a choice based on sound policy decisions. Congress could have selected various other points along a continuum as the place to begin the copyright protection for a work. For instance, Congress could have offered copyright protection at the point of creation, at the point of publication, at the point of registration, at the point of placing notice on a work, or at the point of depositing a work at the Library of Congress. The point of creation was problematic because it presented evidentiary problems and left no record for the innovator whose creation was still in his or her head. The points of registration, notice, and deposit were formalities that our European counterparts already had rejected. Because the United States was attempting to move closer in philosophy and administrative procedures to the countries that were signatories of the Berne Agreement, Congress decided not to make copyright dependent on fulfilling any one of these mechanical steps. Thus, the fixation standard that goes into effect when a work is "fixed in a tangible medium of expression" became the new definition of copyright.

There were two unforeseen problems with this definition. First, the fixation standard, which initially seemed far superior to the older categorical approach, encountered difficulties in the electronic age. Imagine a Web browser that picks up an image and places it on a computer screen. When the image is placed on the screen, is it actually fixed? Can an individual use information that appears on the screen on the grounds that it is not fixed and therefore not copyrightable information? There were no clear-cut answers available to resolve this issue, but there is sufficient reason to believe that fixation will be a problem in a digital environment.

Second, the problem of judicial diffidence persisted. In the widely celebrated 1984 *Sony v. Universal Studios* case, Justice Stevens's majority opinion upheld home videotaping, but it also contained a strong protest that this was not the type of decision that the courts should be making. This complaint was more than a feigned sigh of anguish on the part of the Court in making a difficult decision. The Court felt ill equipped to make such a decision in which Congress has been silent on its intentions. Moreover, because Congress has the ability to conduct hearings, investigate industry policies, and legislate new initiatives, the Court understandably wanted to defer the decision making to an institutional setting that had more expertise. But the Court was forced to act as Congress defaulted on making a decision. In the Sony case, the Court ruled that commercial copying was presumptively unfair, but that copying in the privacy of one's home was permissible. For the digital age, this holding opened the door for massive copying so long as it occurred in one's domicile. In *Campbell v. Acuff Rose* (1994), the Court sought to narrow this holding, retreating from the expansive nature of allowing home reproduction. Home reproduction that looked benign in the eyes of the Sony court was highly troublesome for the Acuff-Rose court. Among the changes that had occurred in the decade between the two decisions were the increasing reliance on a home office, the widespread use of personal computers, and the growth of the Internet, which gave a vastly different coloration to "working at home."

The 1976 Copyright Act clarified the exclusive rights of owners of copyrighted materials, but the meaning of these rights becomes increasingly more difficult to ascertain as the digital age unfolds. Section 106 of the Act sets forth the five exclusive rights of owners: (a) the right to make copies, (b) the right to prepare derivative works, (c) the right to publicly display, (d) the right to publicly perform, and (e) the right to distribute publicly. These five rights constitute the "bundle of rights" (Ginsburg, 1995, p. 1475), and under copyright law, no one may exercise these rights without expressed authorization from the owner. The word public, which seemed more straightforward in a predigital age, now assumes an ambiguous meaning when one talks about downloading materials in the privacy of one's home. In addition, the term *electronic transmission* is not addressed anywhere in the 1976 Act, and whether electronic transmission is an extension of "distribution" or itself a new medium with special "rights" is unclear and subject to widespread debate (Gailey, 1996; Kravis, 1993). Under traditional copyright law, rights not established by contract or developed under a work-for-hire situation are reserved for owners. This tradition, although occasionally modified by judge-made exceptions, serves as an formidable obstacle for users successfully to assert "new" or "unclaimed" rights in digitized information.

The chief exception to the "exclusive rights of owners" in Section 106 of the 1976 Copyright Act is the "fair use doctrine" in Section 107, which grants privileges to users of copyrighted works. The fair use doctrine is a device employed to minimize the conflict between owners and users of copyrighted materials (Crews, 1996). The 1976 Act gave statutory recognition to what had been a long-standing judicial doctrine. The doctrine has four criteria, and the courts attempt to apply all four when considering a given case.

Purpose of the Use

Courts are willing to grant wider latitude for some purposes. Section 107 mentions six purposes that receive special attention: (a) criticism, (b) comment, (c) newsreporting, (d) teaching—classroom, (e) scholarship, and (f) research. In addition, courts have been willing to grant special breathing room to nonprofit activities. In the Sony case (1984), the Court stated that a "for-profit" enterprise should be treated as "presumptively unfair" (p. 774). The Court has been willing to read into the objectives of the "purpose category" activities that recast, transform, or constitute a creative use of the original work toward a desirable social objective. In the Sony case, the dissent argued vigorously that a distinction should be drawn between a productive and nonproductive use. A productive use involved something that was creative and required the user to add an element to what previously existed. A nonproductive use merely took the item and used it passively for entertainment.

The dissent viewed videotaping off the air as nonproductive use and contended it should never be treated as fair use (*Sony v. Universal*, 1984). This distinction between productive and nonproductive uses has appeared elsewhere in recent court decisions, making it a key ingredient in interpreting the "purpose of the work" provision of the fair use doctrine (Stuckey, 1996). Moreover, the productive/nonproductive dichotomy increasingly will become an important boundary-drawing test as commentators and courts focus on the value-added dimension of the second user-producer.

Nature of the Work

Some works are treated differently than others in the eye of the courts. News is treated with more leeway for the copier than a work of entertainment. A factual and nonfiction work receives less weight than a creative work. Items such as music sheets and work books are regarded as consumable items, and there is a presumption against using materials from them, whereas nonconsumable work may be treated with greater leeway. It is likely that items such as electronic mail, bulletin board postings, electronic journals, and online, fact-based databases will warrant different treatment, despite being common elements of the digital revolution.

Amount Taken

The courts examine the amount of materials taken and weigh it against the work as a whole. Different ratios have been applied to different types of work. It is possible, for example, for a classroom teacher to take a chapter in a prose book if only one copy is handed out to each student and the copying is regarded as spontaneous. At the same time, even taking a limited number of words of poetry or music may trigger the claim of an unfair appropriation of another's work.

Market Effect

When the economic injury to the copyright holder can be demonstrated, making even a single copy or taking a limited appropriation, no matter how small the money involved in the case, may result in an infringement action. If the unauthorized use damages the market for the original work, then the courts have been reluctant to extend protection against infringement to the copyright users. Among the four criteria, the market variable has usually been given the greatest weight by the courts.

The fair use doctrine has been used in the past to make accommodations when new technologies have arisen. At present, it has become an important benchmark for determining attitudes toward regulation of information in an electronic age. A debate between copyright optimists and pessimists has raged in books, journals, convention papers, and industry-user conferences, but the discussion has produced mixed results. As Goldstein (1994) explains, copyright optimists believe that the fair use doctrine once again will be employed to accommodate the need of owners and users, granting reasonable compensation and use to each side. Copyright pessimists, however, demur. They argue the digital revolution is not just a new mechanism to acquire information, but a completely new set of procedures that have far-reaching implications for most types of copyrighted materials. They acknowledge that the flexibility of the fair use doctrine has allowed it to serve as a useful device to resolve past difficulties. But they argue that the scale of the digital revolution goes well beyond the dislocations made by any one single innovation. First, the technological innovations now allow for value-added interactions, with additional links that permit users to pursue a subject at a depth and scope that the users, not the initiating author, establish. The user therefore "becomes a director, or creator, a driver or navigator perhaps even an author, and much less of a subject or recipient of an author's message" (Katsh, 1995, p. 202). Second, cyberspace is not medium-specific as were the analog formats. Instead, digitized information covers several media and allows the user to interact simultaneously with multiple formats.

There are many blue-sky predictions of what changes will likely occur because of the digital revolution and why the label "information age" represents an astute depiction of an economy that is now the legitimate successor to the "agrarian" and "manufacturing" era (Straubhaar & LaRose, 1997). Despite the controversy about the nature and scope of the digital revolution, there is a growing consensus that Pool's (1983) earlier assessment is correct: that the development of digital technology represents a paradigmatic shift on a scale that is difficult to imagine.

However, the rationale behind the copyright system will continue to be important even in an information-oriented economy. Copyright exists to provide incentives to authors and creators so that they will undertake the labor to create new works. Without a system of incentives and a means to reap the benefits of their own labor, authors and creators will have less desire to provide society with intellectual property. Litman (1994) and Samuelson (1996) are correct in warning that the bargain society strikes with authors and innovators in cyberspace should not unduly "privilege" owners of copyrights materials. They contend that care must be taken to protect the rights of the public against the many stakeholders and their accompanying attorneys who represent vested intellectual property interests at odds with providing access to information users. At the same time, there is a widespread belief among commentators within the intellectual property community that attention should be devoted to protecting the rights of creators because "without authors, there are no works to use," and authors remain the primary vehicle for creating intellectual and artistic innovations and thus serving the public interest at large (Ginsburg, 1995). Copyright policy traditionally has been designed to maintain an equitable balance between encouraging authorship and providing reasonable access for users of copyrighted materials. Despite the novel problems posed by cyberspace, the long-standing rationale of balancing incentives for authors with reasonable access for users should be maintained.

PROBLEMS WITH ELECTRONIC MATERIALS

David Nimmer (1996) refers to the "familiar specter of technology leapfrogging legislative intent" (p. 11) as he considers the special problems posed by cyberspace. Despite the widely acclaimed flexibility of the fair use doctrine, new technologies have emerged that pose problems unanticipated by Congress or the existing stakeholders in the copyright arena. Beginning in the 1960s, the new technologies have altered the traditional relationship between owners and users of copyrighted materials.

The first major battle with the new technologies was fought over the photocopier. Handcopying was labor-intensive, time-consuming, and ultimately created a copy that was inferior to the original printed work (Samuelson, 1990). However, the photocopier made copying easy, inexpensive, and accessible to a large proportion of the population who otherwise would have purchased a book, a journal, back issues, or reprints from the copyright owner. As photocopying became more widespread, publishers vigorously protested what they perceived as the infringement on their exclusive rights to make copies. They also bitterly assailed the magnitude of the copying, claiming unquantifiable sums of lost potential revenue. But the courts, not wanting to stifle technological innovations, reluctantly affirmed the right of an individual to photocopy under the fair use doctrine, subject only to minor restrictions. In *William and Wilkins* (1973), the Court of Appeals held that photocopying by individuals constituted a fair use, and the Supreme Court allowed that decision to stand because of the 4-4 split among the justices on how to assess the photocopying process (Justice Blackmun did not participate in the voting because of his prior association with medical publishers while serving as counsel at the Mayo Clinic in Rochester, MN).

Twenty years later, the market and submarket for photocopying had crystallized. The courts, therefore, began to identify particular segments of the photocopying industry that infringed on the legitimate rights belonging to authors and publisher. In *Basic Books v. Kinko's* (1991), *American Geophysical Union v. Texaco* (1994), and *Princeton University Press v. Michigan Documents Service* (1996), different courts set forth substantially narrower and more restrictive interpretations of fair use. These decisions, in turn, stimulated the creation and widespread use of a clearinghouse system for permissions for printed materials. Ironically, the clearinghouse for print permissions has been aided by other new technologies—the computer and fax machines—that allow permissions typically to be obtained within a three-week period.

The second major battle with the new technologies was fought over the videocassette recorder (VCR). Videotape has existed for a long time, but the introduction of VCR in 1976 made copying complete television programs easy and inexpensive (Lardner, 1987). In a controversial 5-4 decision, the Supreme Court interpreted videotaping in the home as a noncommercial use permitted by the fair use doctrine. The Court contended that because the VCR had substantial noninfringing purposes, the manufacturer of the technology, Sony, could not be held liable as a contributory infringement. But the courts have been vigilant in regulating videotaping when done in a commercial context or outside the privacy of an individual's house. In *Pacific & Southern v. Duncan* (1984), the court held that a videographer who taped newscasts and then contacted individuals mentioned in the news stories, offering to sell them a video copy of their appearance on a particular news broadcast, infringed on the rights for owners of the television station.

The court assailed not only the commercial nature of that entrepreneurial venture but stated that the "public" distribution of the videotapes from the company called "TV News Clips" militated against a finding of fair use for the defendant. Thus, the early videotape decisions strongly reinforced a private-public distinction in using copyright materials.

Understandably, the copyright decisions in a limited number of cases concerning the new technologies do not allow us to infer a "typical" pattern. Nonetheless, it is evident the courts have adopted one strategy for the formative period of a new technology and another strategy for the technology when the market begins to mature, and it is easier to identify which parties are benefitting or being harmed by the application of the technology. Gordon (1982) believes that "markets are a system for consensual exchange of owned good" (p. 1605), and that a market system will mature over time as the ability to handle problems such as transactions costs diminish.

To the extent that the history of regulating the photocopier and VCR provides any guidance, the Internet in 20 years will look vastly different than its current configuration. Yet there are several similarities in the use of the new technologies that are worth noting. Cyberspace continues the technological trend of making copying easier and less expensive for users. In addition, it allows items to be copied, adapted, and distributed to other users in vastly changed formats (Samuelson, 1990). However, it is still too early to identify either the scope of this emerging system, or the nature of the eventual relationship between owners and users of copyrighted materials, or even the types of online service providers that will emerge as intermediaries between creators and end-users of materials. Like the photocopier and VCR, it will take time for a market structure and entrepreneurial context in cyberspace to mature. Gordon (1982) is correct in her assessment that a "market failure" may only be a temporary condition, and a market system for a given technological use may unfold with the passage of time.

With new technologies, both Congress and the courts have followed what William James (1912) has termed Kierkegaard's paradox: "We live forwards but we understand backwards" (p. 238). The literature on cyberspace devotes a disproportionate amount of space to discussing the photocopier, the VCR, and the regulation of the cable industry because these are concrete instances in which the courts were forced to grapple with market failure, new technologies, and in which new rules eventually emerged. They have become the templates to understanding the information superhighway.

Yet, several of the issues raised by cyberspace are truly novel. First, the ease of technological copying substantially outstrips any notion of copying currently in the 1976 Copyright Act or reflected in the development of previous technologies. Second, users are not only extremely numerous, but they are working from widely diverse locations, often in their homes, which makes enforcement of any particular right more problematic (Ginsburg, 1995). Third, the concept of a user must be reformulated to reach a conception that there are *multiple types of users*, several of whom will add value to the information. The "simple end-users" (SEU) who do not transform the original data may become only a minor part of a market structure. But, in what sense, if any, will end-users exist, or will we all be user-producers and thus step on the derivative rights of copyright owners under Section 106? At this stage in the development of the information superhighway, the answer to this question is unclear.

The following is a list of four major issues that deal with copyright and cyberspace. This is not an exhaustive list because new developments consistently force us to reconfigure the central questions underlying the creation, development, and protection of intellectual property in light of the maturity of technologies in cyberspace. Yet this discussion attempts to address several vexing copyright issues that may require a new legislative or judicial approach. As O'Rourke (1994) astutely observes, "the law is a moving target" (p. 511), but some pivotal issues, nevertheless, may be identified.

The right to browse should be reconsidered in light of the widespread confusion concerning the treatment of Random Access Memory (RAM).

Certain parts of the Internet, such as Web pages and bulletin boards, invite people to browse. If the browsing is defined as glancing, browsing might be the functional equivalent to reading. Yet, in order to browse, computer users are required to download information onto the RAM of their own computer. This process, and whether it constitutes making an illegal copy, is open to dispute. The key questions are: (a) does downloading information into RAM constitute fixation?; and (b) at what point should downloading trigger copyright infringement?

In *Advanced Computers Services of Michigan v. MAI Systems* (1994), the district court of Virginia ruled that transferring a program or information into the RAM of a computer constitutes making a copy, thus representing a copyright infringement. Plaintiffs had argued that "the nature of RAM is so ephemeral, so transitory, as to preclude a finding that a 'copy' of the program is made when it is transferred from a permanent memory source to the computer's

RAM" (p. 362). Moreover, the plaintiffs contended that the threshold for fixation had not been actually reached because once the computer is turned off, the information in RAM disappears.

In rejecting the plaintiffs' arguments, the court concluded that the Copyright Act "does not require absolute permanence for the creation of a copy" (p. 363). Rather, the court stated that the test for copying should be whether the information is "sufficiently permanent or stable to permit it to be perceived, reproduced, or otherwise communicated for a period of more than a transitory duration" (p. 363). The court therefore concluded that such a work was indeed "fixed" as defined by the Copyright Act, and the court openly refused to consider where along a time continuum—a millisecond, a second, a minute—that fixation should be said to have occurred.

A year earlier, the Ninth Circuit Court, in *MAI System Corp. v. Peak Computer, Inc.* (1993), ruled that a MAI software license did not allow the loading of software into one of MAI's computers by Peak, a third-party computer maintenance company. The court similarly upheld a finding that the loading of copyrighted computer software from a storage medium, such as a hard disk, floppy disk, or read-only-memory, into the "memory of a central processing unit ('CPU') causes a copy to be made" (p. 518). The defendant Peak Computer contended that a copy created in RAM is not fixed, but the court insisted that there were no material facts or precedent to support such a conclusion. Instead, the court held that a "copy made in RAM is 'fixed' and qualifies as a copy under the Copyright Act" (p. 519).

The decisions reached in the courts on "the fixation issue" have found support elsewhere. In September 1995, a report issued from the Commerce Department entitled "Intellectual Property and the National Information Infrastructure" (commonly referred to as the White Paper) set forth the view of the Clinton administration that material in RAM does constitute a fixation (Stuckey, 1996). A year later, in his introductory address to the Harvard Conference on the Internet and Society, David Nimmer (1996) insisted that this policy was "eminently defensible" on the grounds that 100 separate users may tap into a computer and make copies of the RAM-only text, and this overall pattern directly implicates "the copyright owner's reproduction right" (p. 11).

Despite a seemingly strong consensus of opinion, the debate over fixation is far from settled. Brandriss (1996) regards "fixation" as a pivotal issue because of its far-reaching implications for multiple activity on the Internet. As a result, he perceives that the issues actually being debated transcend the technical questions about the stability of RAM in a computer. "The real question," writes Brandriss, "is whether, in the digital age, the very demand of fixation as a condition of reproduction has the same meaning as it has as far as creation, or indeed, whether it has any at all" (p. 240). For Brandriss, the more significant question that follows from the current controversy about fixation is whether "the view that *browsing on-line*—accessing documents into say, a home computer's RAM and viewing screen—could also be considered reproductive fixation and copyright infringement" (p. 252; emphasis in original).

The status of browsing may one day be reconsidered. The court's decision reached in Peak and its progeny about the status of online browsing has generated widespread concern. Several commentators claim that the interpretation of "browsing as reproduction" seemingly amounts to a right to control reading, which was not the intention of Congress in enacting the copyright statute (Brandriss, 1996; Litman, 1994). Thus, the controversy about the treatment of RAM is a topic in which digital technology may compel a legislative revamping of the copyright law and ultimately may require Congress to draw clearer boundaries between online browsing and online transmissions. This is not an issue of "market failure" per se, in which Congress must intervene to restore market equality as much as a novel problem created by the existence of communication on various servers in cyberspace. At present, there is no such entity as a "right to browse." Moreover, the Clinton administration's White Paper openly opposes establishing a "right to browse" that would apply to cyberspace (Samuelson, 1996).

Fair use should be expanded in cyberspace so long as it does not damage or supplant a market where an initiating author or creator would enter.

Based on previous experience, the application of the fair use doctrine to cyberspace should be a useful approach to accommodating the competing interests of owners and users of copyrighted materials. The Clinton administration's White Paper opposes applying the fair use doctrine in cyberspace, where a possible licensing agreement could occur. As Samuelson observes, the White Paper's position is "neither historically accurate nor good public policy" (Samuelson, 1996, p. 138). Unfortunately, the White Paper's position on fair use privileges authors and publishers and dismisses the needs of users.

The rationale for developing and even expanding the fair use doctrine to cyberspace issues is to promote "reasonable" access to information. In theory, fair use has been a device designed to aid users of copyrighted materials without undermining the livelihood of creators and innovators. For users and distributors of information, including online providers, the fair use doctrine represents a sensible approach to balance competing interests. The four criteria of

Section 107—purpose of the use, nature of the work, amount and substantiality taken, and market effect—serve as lenses from which courts may approach a particular contested use. Moreover, the six enumerated factors in the preface of Section 107 should permit scholars, teachers, and journalists reasonable leeway in using data off the Internet. The key factors will be the noncommercial use of the material and the lack of profit-making activities by the users. This is the central meaning of the *Basic Book v. Kinko's* (1991) and *Princeton University Press v. Michigan Document Services* (1996). O'Rourke (1994) views applying the fair use approach to cyberspace as sound policy, especially in its applications to e-mail and bulletin board postings, the latter of which alternately also could be perceived as a dedication to the public domain. O'Rourke maintains that these views incorporate acceptable standards of "netiquette" currently in vogue.

Yet, the one major extant bulletin board case openly rejects a fair use defense. In *Playboy Enterprises Inc. v. Frena* (1993), the U.S. District Court for the Middle District of Florida concluded that the operator of a bulletin board service had violated *Playboy*'s exclusive right to display and distribute material when a picture from the magazine, uploaded by a subscriber, was made available through the bulletin board. The court reached this conclusion partially because membership on the bulletin board was preconditioned on the payment of a subscriber's fee. The court also found that the contested work was entertainment, and not of a factual nature, and thereby ruled that the future market harm could be detrimental to *Playboy* if such postings became widespread.

However, the effective application of fair use analysis to cyberspace issues will not occur if courts mechanically check off the four factors of the doctrine. Rather, a greater emphasis should be placed on what the "initiating author" intended to do with the work: Was it an e-mail letter that was expected to be forwarded, or was it an e-mail that should be treated similarly to a regular letter? If it is the latter, then the rights to the expression in the letter still belong to the initiating author. Similarly, is the bulletin board service open and free of charge, or is there a commercial nature to the service? In essence, there is no inherent barrier to applying fair use inquiries in cyberspace, but the analysis should be retooled to fit the nature and function of information in a digital era. A case-by-case approach will provide a slow, but sure-footed, orientation to developing an effective set of cyberspace guidelines.

Transaction costs in cyberspace may be easier to monitor than traditional materials allow.

Computer technology will aid users of copyrighted materials to obtain works quickly and easily, but owners also will benefit from the technology. Goldstein (1994) maintains that transaction costs in cyberspace can be more easily monitored and billed, thus setting up a system that will continue to provide an incentive for individuals to produce works.

Copyrighted works downloaded in the home or in a place of business will be subjected to fees. The very technology that poses challenges to a system of copyright may be used to sustain and simplify the difficult tasks of billing and fee collection. The use of passwords, PIN numbers, and other identifying mechanisms will minimize the transaction costs so that the copyright system is not spending dollars to collect nickels and dimes. In this respect, the new technologies will aid authors and creators overcome the formidable obstacles of billing and collection of payment that existed in a pre-cyberspace era. In fact, because of the ability to monitor transaction costs, a market system in cyberspace may develop more rapidly in a digitally designed network than occurred in earlier instances of the new technologies such as the photocopier and videotape.

The private-public distinction that has strongly influenced copyright principles should be abandoned in light of the characteristics of the digital revolution.

The current copyright law places a heavy reliance on distinguishing between activities that occur within the home and those that occur in public places. In *Sony v. Universal Studios* (1984), the court determined that videotaping at home constituted fair use. In another instance, the "public display" of five consecutive hours of videotapes of ABC's popular soap opera "General Hospital" in a bar on a Saturday afternoon in Quincy, MA, as opposed to viewing the videos at home, was a key factor in determining that copyrighted infringement had occurred.

In fact, the newly emerging digital environment places a strain on this public-private distinction. The home office, which once was a typewriter, a pencil, and some file cabinets, changes dramatically with the addition of a computer and a modem. It now becomes an individual's entry point to the information superhighway. Goldstein (1994) observes that many uses in the new digital environment "will take place in the privacy of the home, a trend that began in the mid-1960s when home audio taping and then videotaping started to displace revenues earned in the retail marketplace of movie theaters, videocassette stores, and record outlets. But copyright has primarily been a doctrine of public places" (p. 201).

Section 106 of the 1976 Copyright Act reinforces the heavy reliance of a finding of copyright infringement on the notion of detecting a "public" use. The exclusive rights extended to the copyright owners include "public" distribution, "public" display, and "public" performance. The usage of this term in the copyright statute is premised on the ability to draw a clear and meaningful line between the public and private spheres. However, in the 20 years since the enactment of this statute, the Internet has radically changed our conception of the home office and what constitutes the private sphere. In a digital environment, the terms *private* and *public* have become blurred and thus provide less meaning for making distinctions to guide individual conduct. A reassessment of the terms *private* and *public* in light of the emerging environment is warranted.

CONCLUSION

The new digital technologies promise to alter the relationship between owners and users of copyrighted materials. These new technologies will compel us to reconceptualize our notion of proprietary rights in information. The relationship between owners and users of copyrighted materials increasingly will become more collaborative as the conception of an "end-user" becomes more complicated. Furthermore, as the information economy matures, the value-adding activities of users will become more important, and it will place intense strains on the traditional relationship between creators and users of information.

Technological developments in cyberspace will continue the trend of making copying easier, more inexpensive, and more frequent. The combination of these trends will force a reassessment of the major component of our current copyright system, such as the fixation test, the applicability of the fair use doctrine, the changing nature of transactions costs, and the heavy reliance that has been placed on a public-private distinction in constructing copyright policy.

Unfortunately, there is no grand intellectual property scheme that can be superimposed on cyberspace at the present time. As the contours of cyberspace materialize, policymakers will acquire a better idea about the market structure and the infrastructure that support the system. In addition, policymakers need to have a better vantage point to determine to what extent the information superhighway should be a "toll road" or a "freeway." The fair use doctrine has never meant "free use," and some equitable scheme must be devised to satisfy the widely divergent needs of owners and users. In a digital environment, this balancing act will require a major reassessment of our principles of intellectual property.

Finally, there is some controversy in the literature on how proactive policymakers should be in addressing the problems of a digital environment. Goldstein (1994) believes that Congress must act quickly because once a technology or process becomes widespread, and when its uses occur in the privacy of one's own home, it creates an attitudinal presumption against enacting legislation to regulate it—"making it virtually impossible to get Congress to prohibit its use" (p. 216). Goldstein implies that if Congress and the courts continue to hesitate about extending copyright regulations to the Internet, then the pervasiveness of the uses of the new technologies will create a standard by default and unwittingly serve as a threat to the "integrity of copyright law" (p. 30). Yet Nimmer (1996) believes that "biding our time may be the most prudent course" (pp. 11-12), and he urges temporary restraint to allow some of the critical issues to simmer before seeking a legislative or private clearinghouse solution. Given the multiple dimensions of the problem, this may be the more prudent and productive course of action to follow.

REFERENCES

Advanced Computer Services of Michigan v. MAI Systems, 845 F. Supp. 356 (E.D., VA, 1994).

American Geophysical Union v. Texaco Incl, 60 F. 3d 913 (1994).

Basic Books, Inc. v. Kinko's Graphic Corp., 758 F. Supp. 1522 (S.D. N.Y., 1991).

Brandriss, I. (1996). Writing in frost on a window pane: E-mail and chatting on Ram and copyright fixation. *Journal of the Copyright Society of the USA, 43*, 237-278.

Campbell v. Acuff Rose, 114 S.Ct. Reporter, 1170 (1994).

Crews, K.D. (1996, May 17). What qualifies as "fair use." *The Chronicle of Higher Education*, pp. B1-2.

Gailey, E.A. (1996). Who owns digital rights? Examining the scope of copyright protection for electronically distributed works. *Communication and Law, 18*, 3-28.

Gibson, W. (1984). *Neuromancer.* New York: Berkeley Publishing Co.

Ginsburg, J. (1995). Putting cars on the "information superhighway": Authors, exploiters, and copyright in cyberspace. *Columbia Law Review, 95*, 1466-1499.

Goldstein, P. (1995). *Copyright's highway*. New York: Hill and Wang.

Gordon, W. (1982). Fair use as market failure. A structural and economic analysis of the Betamax case and its predecessors. *Columbia Law Review, 82*, 1600-1657.

James, W. (1912). *Essays in radical empiricism*. London: Longmans, Green.

Katsh, M.E. (1995). *Law in a digital world*. New York: Oxford University Press.

Kravis, R. (1993). Does a song by any other name still sound as sweet?: Digital sampling and its copyright implications. *The American University Law Review, 43*, 231-276.

Lardner, J. (1987). *Fast forward*. New York: W.W. Norton.

Litman, J. (1994). The exclusive right to read. *Cardozo Arts & Entertainment Law Journal, 13*, 29-54.

MAI System Corp. v. Peak Computer, 991 F. 2d 511 (ninth Circuit, 1993).

Mazer v. Stein, 347 U.S. 201 (1954).

Nimmer, D. (1996). Brains and other paraphernalia of the digital age. *Harvard Journal of Law & Technology, 10*, 1-46.

O'Rourke, M. (1994). Proprietary rights in digital data. *Federal Bar News and Journal, 41*, 511- 517.

Pacific & Southern Co. V. Duncan, 744 F. 2d 1490 (11th Circuit, 1984).

Playboy Enterprises, Inc. v. Frena, 839 F. Supp. (M.D. FL, 1993).

Pool, I. (1983). *Technologies of freedom*. Cambridge, MA: Belknap Press.

Princeton University Press v. Michigan Document Services (1996). U.S. App. Lexis 29132; 1996 Federal Appeals 0357 (6th Circuit).

Rose, L. (1994). Is copyright dead on the net? *Wired*, pp. 112-113.

Samuelson, P. (1990). Digital media and the changing face of intellectual property. *Rutgers Computer and Technology Law Journal, 16*, 323-340.

Samuelson, P. (1994). Will the copyright office be obsolete in the twenty-first century. *Cardozo Arts & Entertainment Law Journal, 13*, 55-68.

Samuelson, P. (1996, January). The copyright grab. *Wired*, pp. 134-138.

Sandberg, J. (1995, July 5). Regulator try to tame the untamable on-line world. *The Wall Street Journal*, p. B1.

Schwartz, E. (1994). The role of the copyright office in the age of information. *Cardozo Arts & Entertainment Law Journal, 13*, 69-79.

Sony Corporation of America v. University City Studios, 464 U.S. 414 (1984).

Straubhaar, J., & LaRose, R. (1997). *Communication media in the information age.* Belmont, MA: Wadsworth Publishing Company.

Stuckey, K.D. (1996). *Internet online law.* New York: Law Journal Seminar Press.

Weisgrau, R. (1994). The copyright office: A proposed direction. *Cardozo Arts & Entertainment Law Journal, 13,* 81-87.

White Paper (1995). *Information infrastructure task force, intellectual property group and the national information infrastructure: The report of the working group on intellectual property rights.* Washington, DC.

Williams & Wilkins Co. v. the United States, 487 F. 2d. 1345 (1973).

11

MUSEUMS WITHOUT WALLS: PROPERTY RIGHTS AND REPRODUCTION IN THE WORLD OF CYBERSPACE*

SUSAN J. DRUCKER AND GARY GUMPERT

The extension and creation of legal rules applicable to new means of distribution and interaction raise questions as to whether technological advances require rethinking legal principles that have existed for previous modalities. In isolating key legal concerns raised by multimedia productions such as the virtual museum, there is a need to isolate the "work," to reference it as a physical entity situated in a particular place and time. This chapter provides a survey of issues introduced by the creation of virtual museums, focusing on issues of copyright and licensing, derivative rights, and jurisdiction.

There has always been something special about visiting the museum. It usually involved a stroll into the unexpected—a nonprogrammed gambol into a room that you had not visited before. Do you remember

*An earlier version of this chapter was presented at the Law and the Arts Symposium, Hofstra University, October 30, 1996, and is reprinted with permission.

your first encounter with Degas? Or that sudden realization that you have stumbled into a Monet, Renoir, or a Chagall? Do you remember the place as well as the experience? The museum has always been something special because it was the venue for the aesthetic moment and the place where loneliness could be transcended because every beautiful person next to you was a potential lover. Every visit to the museum was punctuated by the purchase of postcard or poster reproduction of some new discovery. Relatively cheap reproductions of art substituted for expensive interior designers.

Instead of a train, plane, bus, or car trip, the computer and the virtual museum beckon. How different is that finger tapping, mouse pointing, sojourn into the virtual realm? What an extraordinary experience! On to the Internet, and the AltaVista search engine reveals a listing of the virtual museums around the world. The decision is difficult—whether to visit the Pompidou in Paris, the National Archaeological Museum of Athens, or the Hungarian National Museum in Budapest. Eventually we choose the Diego Rivera Virtual Museum, located somewhere in Mexico (the URL address does not reveal the actual address). Metaphorically wandering through the gallery we see an unfamiliar work, "Los Viejos" (The Old Ones), painted by him in 1912. It is lovely, and the subject and treatment appeal to us. "Los Viejos" is downloaded and printed through a colorless laser jet printer and then enlarged on the photocopy machine so that a slide can be taken of it to be used in an upcoming lecture on "communication and public space."

Time on the Internet is measured not by the price of admission, but by the cost of the telephone connection. Besides that, the fax machine is being tied up and so one of two new CD-ROM discs is slipped into the computer tower of magic in order to visit the Louvre and the Orsay in Paris. The interactive visit is advertised as the "plus grand musée du monde" and accompanied by a baroque fanfare and the disembodied voice of an electronic docent as we enter the Richelieu wing. A floor plan of the Richelieu is chosen rather than an index of available works. Using the mouse one can select where in the wing the virtual visitor would like to go. Each room in the Louvre is generally devoted to a theme, artist, or period. Room 21, devoted to the work of Rubens, is selected, and we eventually we click on a small frame of La Bohémienne by Frans Hals, who painted the lusty individual some time sometime between 1628 and 1630. A number of options are available. We are given the choice of enlarging details of the particular work and can examine about 25% of the frame at a time. We can also place that work on a comparative scale, which provides an idea of its actual size (measured in meters and centimeters) and juxtaposes it along other works and human figures.

This new experience is phenomenal and initially exiting, but it raises complex issues of qualitative and legal dimensions. On a qualitative level, the nature of the museum and its intrinsic aesthetic experience and relationship to the public becomes a matter of importance. From the moment that museums became public institutions of import, economic and legal factors played an important role. It is somewhat easy to get side-tracked in examining the implication of the virtual museum because a number of other factors need to be considered, particularly, the early development of the museum concept and later the impact of technology on the nature of art.

Museums began as private collections formed for reasons of prestige or out of genuine interest (Hudson, 1987), but some time during the 18th century they evolved into institutions whose works would be accessible to the public. Thus, in 1793, the Louvre was opened as the national showcase of France: "The fact that it existed was the consequence of the Revolution, which had nationalized the property of the Church and religious establishments, and of Napoleon's campaigns, which swept the artistic treasures of Europe into the booty-waggons of the conquerors" (Hudson, 1987, p. 41). The nature of the museum, originally derived from the Greek temple of the Muses (Partridge, 1958), would be altered by the access of individuals to works of art. The shift from the private to the public collection becomes a fundamental factor in changing the economic identity of the museum. The second factor that would alter and transform the relationship of art and public would be the reproducibility of the work. The technologies of duplication, including printing, the casting of molds, etching, lithography, photography, and now digitalized multimedia transmission would potentially transform the artistic experience—once based on the economics of scarcity. In *The Work of Art in the Age of Mechanical Reproduction* (1977), Walter Benjamin noted that works of art were always "reproducible," and the "artifacts could always be imitated," but mechanical reproductions of a work of art represent a new development because before copies were restricted by efforts to repeat the same process of creation as that which was originally used and each copy contained unavoidable variation, with each copy being somewhat unique (Gumpert, 1987). Such variations could now be avoidable.

The questions raised by a jaunt through a virtual museum concern the relationship between a physical object and the experience that is derived from it. A communication perspective accounts for the influence of the medium utilized, the sensory engagement, and the qualitative relationship of art and audience in context. Corporeal communication is now but one option with many of our communicative experiences shifting into more controllable, safe confines of electronic landscapes in which information and potential contacts abound. But do not confuse quality and function. Viewing and listening on the Internet or on CD-ROM may be functionally equivalent but quite distinct experientially. Although the possibilities of museums without walls are dizzying, they must also raise the specter of an element of personal loss of connection, of sensory displacement, of the loss of civic engagement in the physical public space in which that work is situated.[1]

At times communication and legal perspectives coalesce providing a more complete and realistic understanding and approach to the legal implications.[2] In isolating key *legal* concerns raised by multimedia productions such as the virtual museum, there is a need to isolate the "work," to reference it as a physical entity situated in a particular place and time. We refer to that entity as the "primary base point." Rights and liabilities are then derived from the nature of the physical "primary base point" with economic/property rights of paramount importance.

The extension and creation of legal rules applicable to new means of distribution and interaction raise questions as to whether technological advances require rethinking legal principles that have existed for previous modalities (*Daniel v. Dow Jones & Co.*, 1987). The one consistency found in the evolutionary development of media law is that technologies develop more rapidly than legal approaches, which often results in falling back on first preexisting principles and analogies to other media (Stuckey, Rose, & Stele, 1994). This chapter provides a survey of issues introduced by the creation of virtual museums, while suggesting an approach that can meld the communication and legal perspectives.

COPYRIGHTS AND LICENSING AGREEMENTS

When approaching electronic reproduction the legal implication that emerges most prominently is that of intellectual property, most significantly, copyright interests in the object to be digitalized (Goldstein, 1994).[3] Museums acquire materials for their collections in a variety of ways ranging from purchase or loan to gift or bequest, but title does not determine copyright, trademark rights, or the interests reserved to the creator or seller (Milone, 1995). Most copyright systems in the world sever ownership of an object and copyright so that completeness of title held by the museum cannot be assumed.[4] Copyright may be held by museums, individual artists, or their estates, but museums do hold the copyright to photographic images of many works of art in their collections as well as to those works in the public domain. Even the use of works in the public domain are not automatically free from proprietary rights because these works may be covered by trademark protections so that publishers would have to negotiate and pay a fee for the use of the title alone (Nimmer, 1980; Smegal, 1994).[5]

The traditional method of acquiring rights for reproduction has been a one-time use license for a fee payable to the holder of the copyright (Grogen, 1993).[6] Compliance with licensing agreements comes through contract theory backed by international copyright protections and U.S. copyright law (Raysman & Brown, 1993). Exclusive and nonexclusive licensing agreements are each options. In one of the earliest attempts to enter into an exclusive licensing agreement in order to furnish images to be digitalized, Corbis, the publishing subsidiary of Microsoft, negotiated digital rights licenses with the Seattle Art Museum, the Barnes Foundation, and the National Gallery in London, but failed in its efforts to purchase an exclusive agreement (Hoffman, 1996).[7] Presently there are several ongoing projects to launch a licensing organization for collective administration of licenses that would ensure full benefit to owners of copyrighted artworks similar to those organizations created for composers and lyricists (Ibbotson & Shah, 1993.)[8,9] In *The Indiana International & Comparative Law Review* (1995), Kim Milone argued that standard language used in licensing agreements may require some revision within the context of the "intersection of international copyright and contract in multimedia licensing agreements" (p. 417), a position that clearly recognizes that the acquisition of images from museums raises complex questions for museums and artists.[10]

For multimedia producers of both online and CD-ROM products the initial challenge is the acquisition of images. New media publishers faced with acquiring massive numbers of images as content for one compilation realize the limits of traditional one-time use licenses and favor dealing with museums because they are single entities holding the reproduction rights to thousands of items (Milone, 1995).

Museums also possess works in the public domain that are valuable sources of content for a publisher providing the publisher with a less expensive option in gathering material for new media products. Some museums use on-site computer workstations, others provide material to online networks, and some develop CD-ROMS that may be sold to off-site users (Milone, 1995). Another variation occurs when museums themselves establish an Internet presence, an approach gaining in popularity among museums large and small all over the world. The Smithsonian, The Louvre, The Whitney, Vatican Museums, the Peggy Guggenheim collection in Venice, the National Museum of Modern Art in Tokyo, Carillo Gil Museum of

Contemporary Art in Mexico City, the Warhol, Dallas Art Museum, Montreal's Museum of Fine Arts, and the National Gallery of Australia, to name but a few, have taken this approach (Bowen, 1996). Not only are actual museums going digital, but collections gathered together only in electronic form without physical counterparts are springing up such as the interactive people's museum on the Internet from Austria, the Tina Modotti Museum from Mexico, the Auckland Web Museum, and *Le Web Museum*, from Paris which collected images from galleries around the world and sends out over three million pages of electronic information weekly (Hoffman, 1996). The relationship between museums going online and the creation of virtual museums that exist nowhere but online or in disk form is problematic. *Le Web* was originally called *Le Web Louvre* but had to change its name based on action taken by lawyers for the Louvre, in which the equivalent of U.S. trademark law was invoked.[11]

Although the lure of electronic public access (and potential profits) may be great, digital reproduction imposes a dilemma of conflicting duties on a museum. Both public and private museums share a mission to preserve and display the artworks they hold, which is accompanied by fiduciary duties to the public and to the artists they represent (Milone, 1995). Electronic technology will allow the display of the fine arts to a greater number of people in what may be asserted to be a more educationally rewarding manner, creating an obligation on the part of the museum to explore this new technology. The museum functions as educational forum, making works accessible to the public in *appropriate* displays. A spokesperson for the Louvre states:

> We think that electronic reproductions are just the next step in the history of reproducing art works which started in the 18th century with the engravings of famous paintings, then photography etc. We think that we should take part in this evolution in the same way as we did with other "more traditional" reproductions. (M. Naber, October 1, 1996, personal communication)

What is significant here is the distinction that is made between the work itself and electronic copies of such a work. The position taken by Louvre is that what is seen on the Web are not works of art but reproductions of works of art (M. Naber, October 1, 1996, personal communication). But if the technology that will allow for greater public exposure to artwork will put the integrity of the artwork at risk, then the path to follow in fulfilling that duty is uncertain.[12]

Although much in this realm is undecided, the principle that copyrights apply to cyberspace (i.e., electronic digitalized media) was established in a United States District Court in Florida's ruling in

Playboy Enterprises Inc. v. Frena (1993). In a case in which the magazine brought suit against the operator of a subscription computer billboard's use of copyrighted photographs, the court found "display right" of copyrighted material includes unauthorized transmission of display from one place to another, for example, by computer system.[13] However, the application of copyright law to digitalized images is complex.

Copying

The complexity of copyright in virtual museums reveals itself with a very elementary question with regard to a fundamental right of copyright holders, the right to control copying. But what constitutes copying in the digital realm?

> The language in a typical license specifies that the artwork is furnished for the purpose of one time reproduction but must not be loaned, syndicated or used for advertising or other purpose without prior written permission from the artists . . . but once a piece of art becomes part of a new media compilation however, neither the grantor nor the licensee can guarantee that unauthorized duplication or alteration will not occur in the hands of home, library, or museum users. (Milone, 1995, p. 398)

In her four-part series entitled, "From Virtual Gallery to the Legal Web," which appeared in the *New York Law Journal,* Barbara Hoffman (1996a) raised the following questions with regard to what constitutes copying.

> Is the mere display of an image on a video monitor a technical violation of the copyright law? Is the transitory storage of an image in a computer memory a copy? What rights of adaptation and reproduction exist for users who download images? Does the right to display accompany transmission of a digital image? (p. 11)

One answer to when digitalized artwork has been copied was offered by the authors of the recent White Paper issued by The Working Group on Intellectual Property Rights in the National Information Infrastructure (NII), chaired by Bruce A. Lehman, assistant secretary of Commerce and Commissioner of Patents and Trademarks. Their conclusion is that temporary storage of a computer file in memory constitutes copying for the purposes of copyright, as does "browsing," "scanning," "uploading," and "downloading." The proposed amendment to Sec. 106(3) of the U.S. copyright law, which creates a right of distribution by transmission, blurs the distinction between the right of display, reproduction, and performance. Thus, the copyright owner's exclusive rights to reproduce the work, to display a work publicly, and to distribute the work by transmission are implicated on the basis of NII interpretation (Hoffman, 1996).

Alteration, Adaptation, and Moral Rights

Alteration of the art is a special consideration with multimedia works, simply because the digital nature of the work lends itself to modification: "The computer's ability to break a work down into digital fragments and to recombine these fragments with bits and pieces from other works and databases means that an author who commits his work to a digital database exposes it irretrievably to a potentially indeterminate degree of sampling, rearrangement, and recombination" (Goldstein, 1994, p. 31).

> Terms like "interactivity" and "non-linearity" which mean that the end user may determine the sequence, timing and repetitions of the work . . . to complicate this factor further, concepts such as "scalability" or "manipulability" suggest how images can [be] changed in size and modified by the end user or consumer who is interacting with the work. (Crawford, 1995, p. 8)

Some museums are reticent to grant a publisher a license to use copyrighted images because of the ease with which they can be reproduced, with and without alterations, thereby creating a conflict with their fiduciary duty to the artwork and the artists or their estates (Milone, 1995).

Various technological responses to a technologically created dilemma have been explored in response to copying and modifications. A watermark can be encoded on the image to provide copyright information during home printing (Choe, 1994). Printing of an image could be prevented entirely, or prevention of printing only those images that have been distorted is another option. Yet another approach is that of using audit trail devices with data on the exact number of copies of each individual work reported back to the producer. One suggestion with regard to such an audit device would establish a per use charge for each copyrighted image downloaded, tracking and billing for each copy printed (Ibbotson & Shah, 1996). However, it should be kept in mind that each technological attempt at protection may prove unreliable or surmountable (Hoffman, 1996).

Moral rights have been recognized as a means by which an artist may guarantee the integrity of their work after it has been sold and provide protection so that artists will be accurately identified with their works. Countries belonging to the Berne Convention for the Protection of Literary and Artistic Works are required to protect artists' "moral rights"[14] in their work.[15] These rights include the right to be known as the creator of one's work and to withdraw the work from distribution and the right to allow the creator of works to prevent others from deforming a work or using it in a way that reflects poorly on the creator. In the United States 11 states have enacted moral rights legislation in recent years.[16] On the federal level the Visual Artists Rights Act (VARA) constitutes landmark legislation creating moral rights for artists in the United States, which was enacted on December 1, 1990 as an amendment to the copyright law (taking effect on June 1, 1991). This law is analogous to the moral rights protection in the Berne Convention by protecting artists' rights of attribution and integrity in paintings, drawings, photographs produced for exhibition, prints, and sculpture. Remedies for an artist whose work is violated include suit to stop the violation as well as monetary damages.[17] The law prohibits intentional distortion, mutilation, or other modification of an artist's work if changes "would be prejudicial to his or her honor or reputation" (Crawford, 1995, p. 62),but it is not a violation of the Visual Artist's Rights Act to modify a work of art in an effort to preserve it. The term of protection for works created after the effective date of VARA is the artist's life,[18] which suggests that the inability to bring an action for copyright infringement might lead to seeking a remedy under VARA. The enactment of VARA at a time when digital technologies are rapidly evolving reflects concern for potential abuses created by the technology.

Fair Use and the Public/Private Dilemma

The fair use doctrine has been said to provide a safety valve (Goldstein, 1994) allowing copying of copyrighted materials if done for commendable purposes such as new reports, education, criticism, and comment.[19] According to Nimmer (1980), for copying to be of fair use, the copier should be "engaged in creating a work of authorship whereby he adds his own original contribution to that which is copied."[20] The design of a virtual museum involves the selection and placement of images, choices as to which works receive commentary and which may be scrutinized through successive points and clicks of the mouse. Although most CD-ROMs are produced for commercial purposes, many Internet sites are created for informational or public relations purposes rather than as profit-seeking enterprises[21] so that these sites may well fall within the fair use privilege with regard to its creators. Users of portions of both CD-ROM and Internet virtual museums may also fall under the fair use privilege if they make use of the images for teaching, criticism, comment, or noncommercial research.

The fair use doctrine is at the heart of the issue as to whether private use of copyrighted materials is fair use. Museums are public places, environments in which public display and contact with others (both wanted and unwanted) are essential components of the experience: "Copyright has been primarily a doctrine of *public places*" (Goldstein, 1994, p. 201; emphasis added).

> Every American copyright act since 1790 has clung to the idea that copyright is a law of public places and commercial interest. . . . [T]his idea has dominated some of copyright law's central doctrines: only public, not private, performances infringe copyright, noncommercial uses are more likely to be held fair use than commercial ones; to prevail against a fair use defense, a copyright owner must often show that it has suffered economic harm. (p. 131)

> Historically, Congress has declined to extend copyright to protect against private uses because transaction costs—the costs to copyright owners and users of locating and negotiating with each other as a practical matter prevent them from entering into a copyright license. (p. 217)[22]

Although the European approach to copyright has tended to extend rights in any direction that might have economic value, the U.S. approach has been reticent to extend copyright into private use situations. Enjoying the beauty of the Mona Lisa from one's bedroom, or wherever a laptop is taken, may not only serve teaching and noncommercial research functions that fall under the fair use doctrine, but may also be used for personal entertainment. Private (personal entertainment) was at the very heart of *Sony Corporation of America v. Universal City Studios, Inc.* (1984), in which the U.S. Supreme Court ruled that homeowners may record complete copyrighted television shows off the air for their personal, noncommercial use.[23] Although efforts were made in Congress to impose a statutory royalty on recording equipment and blank tapes, this measure was never passed into law. The Sony decision did not deal with other forms of home electronic copying such as audiotape recording.[24]

Current developments and the quest for privacy have been inextricably linked to the swift evolution of media technology. From the 1970s onward there has been a consistent increase in the value placed on privacy by U.S. citizens (Regan, 1995).[25] Public life, time spent in public places, and public amusements and cultural activities has declined as the ability to transcend place alters the importance we attributed to the nature of privacy and publicness. Evidence of the decline of public social life is revealed in "time budget" studies (Putnam, 1996).[26] Laws protecting rights and creating liability reflect changing societal values and the relationship between private life (and uses) and copyright is no exception, with Congress continuing to refrain from extending liability against private uses of copyrighted materials.

The private use of copies made by downloading or printing images from a virtual museum appear to avoid copyright liability. However, one of the justifications for this approach protecting private use may be eroding. Congress and courts have excused the otherwise infringing use of copyrighted material, in large part due to pragmatic considerations when it would be too cumbersome or costly for each private user to negotiate a license. But just as technology has made private use more accessible and attractive, technological advances could reopen the issue of private use of virtual museums. In ©opyright's Highway: The Law and Lore of Copyright from Gutenberg to the Celestial Jukebox, Paul Goldstein (1994) notes:

> Technologies exist today to enable copyright owners and users to negotiate individual licenses for electronically stored works at a cost lower even than the cost of administering a blanket license. When a copyright owner deposits its works into some electronic retrieval system, it will be able to attach a price tag to each work, listing its rates for different uses of the work. If the user decides to make a copy at the posted rate, the system will print it out and charge. (p. 223)

THE VIRTUAL MUSEUM AS A DISTINCT ENTITY

As one surfs the Net entering virtual museum after virtual museum or replaces one CD-ROM from a disk drive with another, the uniqueness of packaging, marketing, and selections become apparent. Virtual museums gather, organize, adapt, reconfigure, and yield a whole that may be quite distinct from the sum of the parts alone. Intellectual property rights issues may belong not only to those holding rights to the physical works but to the creators of virtual museums themselves.[27] Thus, the Musée d'Orsay and Éditions Assouline package Livre d'ARt & CD-ROM. What constitutes the work in question, the primary base point, is something other than the work found within the Musée d'Orsay and includes a gestalt of music, narration, and treatment found within the CD and the rendering of a print volume inexorably linked to the CD.

Is the treatment given to create the new product, the virtual museum, copyrightable? Copyrights can be placed on compilations formed by collecting and assembling preexisting materials that are "selected, coordinated, or arranged in such a way" (see 17 USCAS 101) as to create an original work.[28] The original authorship that the law protects in compilations[29] is the selection, coordination, or arrangement of items, which is copyrightable as distinct from any of the materials in the collection. Virtual museums often include biographical text and commentary along with the digitalized images of works of art: "Technically, the copyright in the editorial text is separate from the copyright in the collective work, although they are rarely separated in practice" (Strong, 1993). In the creation of a compilation of digitalized artworks there is a good deal of editorial judgment exercised in the selection and organization of collected works. Trademark issues concerning a CD-ROM or name of a web site may also become a relevant issue (Smegel, 1994).

Virtual museums raise a rather unique question with regard to their distinct copyrightability. The nomenclature of space and architecture have been transformed into metaphors of cyberspace. Thus, the user is linked to bulletin boards, malls, rooms through ports, highways, exits, gateways, bridges, and routers. The vocabulary surrounding these new technologies and multimedia creations shapes the perception of the reality being named. In the creation of a virtual museum, some tours are linked directly to the arrangement of rooms in physical museums, others create their own aspatial rooms. Floor plans may be provided so that, to access an image, the electronic visitor to the museum clicks on the desired "room." If one were to create a CD-ROM version of a collection of Monets, would there be a copyright infringement for a digital "room" in which all of the works gathered in one room of the Marmottan Museum were also placed together in similar digital arrangement? Should virtual spatial arrangement of artworks be treated like physical spatial arrangements and some architectural designs and receive copyright protection, or may they fall under fair use? The issue would be settled by the degree of creativity or originality in terms of selection and arrangement in order for the spatial arrangement of display to be copyrightable.[30] The Copyright Act defines compilation as a work in which separate elements are selected, coordinated, or arranged in a way that meets the standard of originality. The Court has not established any guidelines as to what specific type of coordination or arrangement is required.[31]

Beyond the issues of what constitutes a copyright infringement and what is fair use, beyond the queries as to who retains intellectual property rights for a work of art and the nature and duration of those rights lies a fundamental question as to who may infringe on those rights. Although attention has been focused on the producer of a virtual museum or the end-user there lies another potential candidate for liability in an area of law not settled. When dealing with online virtual museums, what is the responsibility of information service providers? Service providers have argued that they function like common carriers and do not make "individualized decisions" that determine what is transmitted or carried, thereby avoiding liability (Johnson & Marks, 1993).[32] Common carriers avoid liability when they merely make equipment available (Ramos & Hempe, 1996; Restatement of Torts, 1976).[33] In the United States, Congress is taking steps toward passing legislation that attempts to preserve existing theories of copyright liability for online infringements but would limit copyright-owner recovery against "service providers." The broadest exemption from copyright liability would be provided for "mere conduit services and private or real-time electronic communication" that would cover online service providers as well as Internet access providers.[34] The resolution of this issue will be in large part determined by how courts view the nature of the medium and the expectations and experiences of those utilizing that medium.

JURISDICTION WITHIN THE BORDERS OF CYBERSPACE

Virtual museum in online or CD-ROM formats are made available by delivery systems that can easily flow across nation boundaries thereby requiring a reexamination of fundamental legal issues including jurisdiction and conflict of laws. In an age when signals are beamed and borders crossed via keyboard strokes, geography becomes irrelevant. "Global Information Infrastructures rely on disintegrating concepts of territory and sector while ignoring the new network and technological borders that transcend national boundaries" (Reidenberg, 1996, p. 45). Although copyright is intrinsically a creature of national law, there are now few countries that do not have treaty arrangements for the international protection of copyrights with most of these countries being members of either or both of the two great conventions: the Berne Convention for the Protection of Literary and Artistic Works and the Universal Copyright (UCC).[35] These conventions are essentially multilateral agreements to give certain recognition to copyrights that arise in other member countries.[36] The treaties require that nations conform their laws to international standards, but there is little to none effective enforcement mechanisms to compel compliance, although other member states could pursue a claim in the International[37] Court of Justice for infringement on the agreement (Milone, 1995). There is clearly potential for conflict of laws, a situation foreseen by the European Community, which has tried to establish a rule of interpretation to prevent incompatibility of convention law with European law such that member states of the European Community signed revised convention agreements with the knowledge of community law and member states should seek to balance the convention requirements with Community law (Milone, 1995).[38]

The United States was a founding member of the UCC in the early 1950s but did not join the Berne Convention until 1989. Both Berne and the UCC deal with "national treatment" and the setting of minimum standards of protection by which all treaty members must abide. National treatment mandates that each member nation extend the protection of its laws to works that originate in other member nations. Most nations impose their own rules on the validity of copyright transfers that allocate rights within their borders. The setting of standards is also addressed by these two conventions. Berne requires longer terms of protection than the UCC.

The clear trend has been toward the internationalization of copyright, but computer-mediated communication complicates the situation because its electronic nature need not recognize borders. As technical obstacles are disappearing, regulatory barriers are easily circumvented. In December 1996, 160 countries reached agreement in Geneva on "the most sweeping extension of international copyright law in 25 years" (Schisel, 1996, p. 1). Negotiators met under the auspices of the World Intellectual Property Organization of the United Nations and agreed on two treaties. These treaties, on ratification, will cover two distinct types of works——one covering literary and artistic works including films and computer software, the other covering recorded music. These treaties would grant copyright owners protection for distributing their work in digital form.[39]

In the *Emory Law Journal* article "Governing Networks and Cyberspace Rule-making," Joel Reidenberg (1996) explores the challenges of redefining jurisdiction in a borderless, aspatial realm stating:

> With the Global Information Infrastructure, however, territorial borders and substantive borders as key paradigms for regulatory governance disintegrate. . . . International law grants legitimacy to a governing authority if it exercises sovereignty over a physical territory and its people. Constitutional governance predicates sovereignty on the existence of geographically distinct political and social units. Regulatory power has always been defined in terms of national borders . . . restricted. Transnational information flows on the GII undermine these foundational borders and erode state sovereignty over regulatory policy and enforcement. Geographic limits have diminishing value. Physical borders become transparent and foreign legal systems have local relevance. (p. 913)

Over time, changes in social and business practices revealed that jurisdiction limited to geography required reevaluation.

Before cyberspace challenged notions of jurisdiction, it was decided that jurisdiction over nonresidents would lie wherever minimum contacts could be established such that the maintenance of the suit does not offend traditional notions of fair play and substantial justice. In fact, courts have found jurisdictional authority in contacts by telephone and mail alone (*Quill Corp. v. North Dakota*, 1992). Most recently, jurisdiction by computer-mediated contact has been asserted by several states including New York and Minnesota.[40] Whose law applies, and how does one define the scope of jurisdiction that has become increasingly murky. One approach to the jurisdictional chaos that is emerging is a move toward entering into enforcement treaties of interstate and international scope.

CONCLUSIONS

"The technological de-monopolization of the arts requires a distinction between object and experience" (Gumpert, 1987, p. 37). Clearly, aesthetic responses, environmental contexts, and economic worth require reevaluation of what Walter Benjamin might have called "The Work of Art in the Age of Digital Reproduction and Aspatial Environments":

> Copyright was technology's child from the start. There was no need for copyrights before the printing press. But as movable type brought literature within the reach of everyone, and as the preferences of a few royal, aristocratic, or simply wealthy patrons were supplanted by the accumulated demands of mass consumers, a legal mechanism was needed to connect consumers to authors and commercial publishers. Copyright was the answer. Centuries later, photographs, sound recordings, motion pictures, videocassette recorders, compact disc, and digital computers have dramatically expanded the markets for mechanically reproduced entertainment and information , and increased copyright's function in ordering these markets. (Goldstein, 1994, pp. 27-28)

The language of the law, particularly the use of metaphors, has been of concern (Bosmajian, 1982). It has been argued that the metaphors found within judicial opinions have shaped the substance of laws themselves. Cyberspace, in general, and museums without walls, more specifically, reflect the adoption of spatial terminology and introduce the economics of a newly emerging commercial realm. These metaphors are useful mechanisms for dealing with the revolutionary changes of the information age making the new territory more familiar, less intimidating, and more manageable within existing legal frames of reference. However, such metaphors are based on the economics of place rather than on the economics of the digital electronic realm. So, for example, the entrance fee at a museum is quite different than the purchase price of a CD-ROM, access fee to an online service, or the cost of a telephone connection.

The technology of communications challenge developments in applicable laws governing rights of privacy, free expression, liability in such areas as libel,[41] hate speech,[42] and obscenity,[43] as well as sexual harassment, jurisdictional issues, as well as copyright. In an effort to keep pace with technological developments in "cyberlaw," the legal perspective should be joined with the communication perspective to adequately address changing conceptions of space, control, the significance of nation status, economic valuation, and the ever-changing relationship between publicness and privateness. A museum without walls is also an environment posing issues of significance without end.

ENDNOTES

1.   The loss of an opportunity to directly experience a work of art and the public place in which it is located along with eliminating the experience of being with others on a fully sensory level are significant dimensions to be considered in the examination of the virtual museum.

2.   This may be illustrated by privacy issues. Privacy rights and the nature of communication experiences are among those areas particularly intertwined with psychological and functional anticipation in using a given medium or instrument forming the basis of legal standards such as the "reasonable expectation of privacy." Dating back to 1967, the Supreme Court enunciated this point, in *Katz v. United States*, 389 U.S. 347 (1967). At that time the Court stated that expectations of privacy in the use of particular media technologies in specific locations was the issue. Constitutional protections of the Fourth Amendment were found to protect people from unwarranted government use of electronic devices as in this case in which FBI agents bugged a public telephone without a warrant.

3.   Paul Goldstein (1994) notes widespread confusion even from within the legal profession as to the distinctions and nature of intellectual property rights. He notes that copyright is the law of authorship, patent the law of invention, and technology and trademark the law of consumer marketing and the protection of names.

4.   Ownership of an object must be conceived of as separate from ownership of copyrights, "even if the museum owns a painting, bought at great expense, it does not hold the copyright on the painting unless it is specifically transferred by the artists" (Berkowitz

& Leaffer, 1984, p. 258). However, if an object was acquired before January 1, 1978, without mention of copyright interests, the U.S. Copyright Code presumes that the copyright was transferred along with the object (see Burr, 1995).

5. According to Nimmer (1980), copyright owners control a bundle of rights, including the right to distribute their work; create derivative works; and perform, display, and copy their work. Works enter the public domain in one of two ways: (a) copyright has expired; and (b) under the 1909 U.S. Copyright statute, the artist failed to copyright the object, and with first public showing the work entered the public domain (Milone, 1995).

6. Many such agreements do not adequately define the rights of each party with respect to new technologies emerging today (Grogen, 1994).

7. Bill Gates and Microsoft aim to compile a massive archive of images including fine art. In October 1995, publishing subsidiary Corbis purchased the Bettmann photo archive, which included purchase of the archive's proprietary rights including copyrights (Hoffman, 1996).

8. Several projects are underway, including the Getty Museum Site Licensing Project and the DACS licensing scheme in England (Ibbotson & Shah, 1993).

9. Many concerns that should be addressed in license agreements apply in traditional as well as multimedia contexts. Addressing issues such as the guarantee that the grantor of the license is a rightful holder of the rights and that the work does not infringe on the copyrights of others, indemnification clauses, and terms limits of the license may include a reversion clause for the return of the rights to the grantor if the licensee does not produce the product within a set time period (Raysman & Brown, 1993).

10. Milone (1995) notes five key rights that could be addressed in multimedia licensing: (a) initialization; (b) multiplication; (c) public display; (d) printout; and (e) online access.

11. Most of the images used by Le Web were in the public domain (Hoffman, 1996).

12. Interestingly, the position taken by the Louvre assumes personal use of reproductions. It has been noted that there have been requests for links to the Louvre site on the Web but not for use of separate electronic artifacts.

13. In *Playboy Enterprise, Inc. v. Freana* the court noted that in the United States, The Copyright Act of 1976 gives copyright owners control over most, if not all, activities of conceivable commercial value, including public distribution and display. Furthermore, the concept of display was considered to be broad and would cover the projection of an image on a screen or other surface by any method, the transmission of an image by electronic or other means, and the showing of an image on a cathode ray tube or similar viewing apparatus connected with any sort of information storage and retrieval system.

14. Moral rights derive from codes of civil law countries where they have been recognized, including *droit d'auteur* in France and the *derecho*

de autor in Spain and Mexico. This approach recognizes an artist's work as an extension of personality and the personal act of creation. These moral rights are perpetual (Crawford, 1995).

15.   The Berne Convention for the Protection of Literary and Artistic Works of September 9, 1886, completed in Paris, revised in Berlin, November 1908; complete at Berne in March 1914; revised in Rome, June 1928; Brussels, June 1948; Stockholm, July 1967; Paris, July 1971; and amended October 1979.

16.   The 11 states with moral rights laws in force are California, Connecticut, Massachusetts, Louisiana, Maine, Nevada, New Jersey, New Mexico, New York, Pennsylvania, and Rhode Island. Utah enacted a law dealing with commissioned works (Crawford, 1995).

17.   VARA covers unique works and consecutively numbered limited editions of 200 or fewer copies of either prints or sculptures, as long as the artist has done the numbering and signed the edition. The limited edition provision also applies to still photographic images (must also be an edition of 200 copies or less consecutively numbered and signed by the artists. This is a narrow definition eluding from protection posters, applied art, motion pictures, databases, election information services, electronic publication, merchandising items, packaging materials, and any work made for hire and any work not copyrightable (see 17 U.S.C.A.§ 106A).

18.   VARA allows an artist to waive these rights in a written, signed instrument, but the waiver does not transfer any right of ownership, nor does the sale or transfer of ownership of a work or of a copyright transfer the artist's moral rights (17 U.S.C.A.§ 106A).

19.   The fair use doctrine has been said to be a significant buffer for copyright from charges that copyright violate First Amendment guarantees of free speech and press.

20.   The factors considered by a court determining if copying is to be regarded as fair use are: (a) the purpose and character of the use, including whether such use is of a commercial nature or is for nonprofit educational purposes; (b) the nature of the copyrighted work; (c) the amount and substantiality of the portion used in relating to the copyrighted work as a whole; and (d) the effect of the use on the potential market for, or value of, the copyrighted work (17 U.S.C.A. § 107).

21.   Commercial copying is not a fair use. When considering the issue of commercial copying in broadcast media, the U.S. Circuit Court of Appeals for the Eleventh Circuit ruled that "clipping services" such as those that copy portions of broadcasts for profit by selling segments of broadcasts was not a fair use (see *Pacific & Southern Co. v. Duncan*, 1984).

22.   Goldstein points out that television and radio broadcasts come within the U.S. Copyright's definition of public performance. but the question unanswered by courts to date is whether broadcasting on demand in which a broadcast is not simultaneous but transmitted one performance at a time will be considered a public or private event for purposes of copyright.

23.   Justice Stevens addressed the issue of private copies as a matter of statutory interpretation rather than fair use. "Quite remarkably, in the detailed revision of the entire law, Congress studiously avoided any direct comment on the single-copy private-use question, " Stevens observed, and he argued for statutory exemption of private copying: "(1) the privacy interests implicated whenever the law seeks to control conduct within the home; (2) the principle of fair warning that should counsel hesitation in branding literally millions of person as lawbreakers; and (3) the economic interest in not imposing a substantial retroactive penalty on an entrepreneur who has successfully developed and marketed a new and useful product, particularly when there is not evidence of actual harm" (quoted in Goldstein, 1994, p. 150).

24.   The Audio Home Recording Act of 1992 signed into law by President Bush in October of that year required the incorporation of Serial Copy Management System (SCMS) controls in digital audio equipment sold in the United States. SCMS allows copying from an original prerecorded work but blocks making a copy of a copy. This was agreed on as a standard sought in legislatures around the world. The Audio Home Recording Act of 1992 is also a statutory levy to be paid by the producers of blank digital audiotapes and digital audiotape equipment (3% of the sales price for tapes and 2% of the sales price of equipment). These sums were to be deposited in the Copyright Office and divided into two funds distributed annually, with two thirds going to the Sound Recordings Fund and one third to the Musical Works Funds (Goldstein, 1994).

25.   During the past several decades public opinion polls indicate that U.S. citizens consider privacy a genuine value "not as a means of concealing improper activities or avoiding punishment or detection" (Regan, 1995, p. 48). Furthermore, there has been an increase in the concern for privacy protection.

26.   Time budget studies indicate that since 1965, time spent on informal socializing and visiting has gone down by as much as 25%, and time devoted to organizations and clubs has dropped by 50%. Surveys show sharp declines in collective participation and sites of civic engagement from political parties to bowling leagues (Putnam, 1996).

27.   For purpose of this discussion property interests are being confined to the substance of the digitalized work rather than underlying computer software required in the creation of the virtual museum online or in CD-ROM form.

28.   *Eckes v. Card Prices Update,* 736 F.2d 859 (2d Cir. 1984). Compilations such as data bases and stocklists have been copyrightable compilations, even though the individual items in them are not copyright able (see *Dow Jones & Co. v. Board of Trade of Chicago* (1982).

29.   Compilations are distinct from derivative works that are created when copyright owners or licensees recast, transform, or adapt a work. The potential for derivative works in the realm of digitalized art is clear but outside the scope of this treatment. For more on derivative works see 17 U.S.C.A. § 101.

30. In *Feist Publications, Inc. v. Rural telephone Service Co.* (1991), the issue of arrangement of a compilation, in this case, the organization of the "white pages" of a telephone book, was addressed by the U.S. Supreme Court, which held that industrious labor alone would not create copyrightable work, but "some spark of creativity" is needed for arrangement of a compilation to be copyrightable. However, shortly after Feist was decided, a lower court upheld copyright in telephone yellow pages noting whoever compiles a yellow pages directory exercises some arbitrary selection process and categorization requiring some degree of originality (see *Bellsouth Advertising and Publishing Corp. v. Donnelley Information Publishing, Inc.*, 1991).

31. A compilation that includes all the facts, and arranges them by a principle as obvious as the alphabet, is not going to qualify for copyright protection (Strong, 1993).

32. Johnson and Marks (1993) explore the approach to regulating cyberspace, which seeks to find the "best fit" between existing law and a new medium as reflected by looking to see if actions in cyberspace are most similar to publishing, common carrier status, or distribution.

33. H.R. 2441/S.1284, 104th Cong., 1st Sess. (1995 clarifies when royalties are due for books and videos transmitted over the Internet. In 1995, Congress began to address issues of digital transmissions by enacting legislation to clarify that the Copyright Act does cover digital as well as physical distribution of phono records (see The Digital Performance Right in Sound Recordings Act of 1995, 1995).

34. Online service providers argue they cannot and should not be required to police millions of transmissions, whereas copyright owners counter that online service providers would only encounter copyright liability in cases of contributory infringement or vicarious liability, both of which requires either the ability to control the infringement or knowledge of the infringement. The Intellectual Property Subcommittee of the House Judiciary Committee responded by proposing an exemption for service providers from copyright liability when they "(i) provided local exchange, trunk line, or backbone services; (ii) carried material over their systems on behalf of another user, did not generate or alter the content carried, and the user committed an act of infringement; (iii) provided material contained in private electronic communications which an OSP/IAP [online service provider/Internet access providers] lacked either the technical ability, or authority under law, to access or to disclose to any third party in the normal course of business; or (iv) provided real-time conversation formats, including voice messaging or electronic mail services" (Ramos & Hempe, 1996, p. S8).

35. The People's Republic of China is one of the few remaining nations that does not belong to one of the two international copyright conventions.

36. These conventions do not protect copyright in sound recordings that are the subject of a separate treaty, the Convention for the Protection of Producers of Phonograms Against Unauthorized Duplication of Their Phonograms (Strong, 1993).

37. The Berne Convention was established to further uniformity of copyright protection. Under Berne, copyright protect extends over the life of the author plus 50 years, unlike U.S. copyright protection of 56 years until 1976 and the revisions of U.S. Copyright Code, which harmonized the two standards. Protection applies to nationals of Berne Convention signatory countries and to authors who either publish their works first in a Berne nation (see Burr, 1995).

38. Many conflicts of law between convention and country's domestic regulation arise, but contracting nations must adopt domestic law. In the case of conflicts, if domestic law differs from subsequent convention law, the later statue removes the effect of the prior one, but the subsequent statute must expressly repeal the earlier one. More recent domestic law, however, that differs from prior convention law may lead to the domestic law being interpreted in light of convention law, or different law may apply to nationals or convention law could be interpreted in light of domestic law.

39. A third proposal, which would have extended copyright protection to computerized databases that provide sports scores, telephone listings, and so on was abandoned over objections from other countries. Additionally, wording was deleted that treated even temporary computer copies automatically created to view graphics from the Internet as possible violations of international copyright law.

40. In New York State, on Sept. 4, 1996, Governor George Pataki signed into law Senate Bill S. 210-E/ Assembly Bill A. 3967-C, known as the Cybersex Law or the Pedophile Law. The law amends the Penal code to create Class D and Class E felonies for attempting to lure minors to contact with adults who knowingly and intentionally use any computer communication system allowing input and output. Section 235 of the Penal law was amended to address long-distance, high-tech sexual abuse (see New York State Senate Introducer's Memorandum in Support of Senate Bill #: S. 210-E. Sponsored by Senator William R. Sears). Other states have claimed jurisdiction based on Internet contact. The Attorney General of Minnesota, for example, has asserted Internet jurisdiction over "persons outside of Minnesota who transmit information via the Internet knowing that information will be disseminated in Minnesota." The question of what constitutes "knowing" that information posted on a home page will be accessed in a jurisdiction has not been addressed.

41. *Cubby v. CompuServe Incorporated* (1991) is the sole case to date in which a libel action was reportedly brought against an information service provider. In this case a plaintiff sued CompuServe on the basis of allegedly false and defamatory statements contained in an electronic newsletter available in CompuServe's Journalism Forum. The newsletter was published by a third party (not CompuServe). The court granted CompuServe's motion for summary judgment relying upon CompuServe's actions as distributor, exercising no editorial control and acting as an electronic library.

42. Hate speech has become an issue faced by information providers. The Anti-Defamation League of B'nai B'rith cited anti-Semitic notes sent

via e-mail but rejected for public posting by Prodigy as an example of electronically networked hate speech (see Leroux, 1991; Miller, 1991).

43.   Obscenity has received a good deal of attention within the context of cyberspace (see Jackson, 1994). In a prominent case the operators of "Amateur Action" electronic bulletin board service were convicted under the federal law criminalizing transmitting obscene images electronically from California to Tennessee (see Landis, 1994).

REFERENCES

Bellsouth Advertising and Publishing Corp. v. Donnelley Information Publishing, Inc. 933 F. 2d 952 (11th Cir. 1991).

Berkowitz, R. L., & Leaffer, M.A. (1984). Copyright and the art museum. *Columbia Journal of Art, 8*(1), 249, 258.

Benjamin W. (1977). The work of art in the age of mechanical reproduction. In J. Curan et al. (Eds.), *Mass communication and society* (pp. 384-408). London: Edward Arnold.

Bosmajian, H. (1982). Fire, snakes and poisons: Metaphors and analogues in some landmark free speech cases *Free Speech Yearbook, 20,* 16-22.

Bowen, J.P. (1996, September 25). Museums around the world, http://www.comlab.ox.a...eumus/world.html.

Burr, S.I. (1995, February). Introducing art law. *Copyright World*, p. 22.

Choe, J.D. (1994). Note. Interactive multimedia: A new technology tests the limits of copyright law. *Rutgers Law Review, 46,* 929-1001.

Crawford, T. (1995). *Legal guide for the visual artists: The professional handbook* (rev. 3rd ed.). New York: Allworth Press.

Cubby v. CompuServe Incorporated, 776 F. Supp. 135 (S.D.N.Y 1991) .

Daniel v. Dow Jones & Co., 520 N.Y.S. 2d 334 (N.Y.C. Civ. Ct., 1987).

Digital performance right in sound recording act of 1995. 109 Stat. 336 (1995).

Dow Jones & Co. v. Board of Trade of Chicago, 546 F. Supp. 113 (S.D.N.Y. 1982).

Eckes v. Card Prices Update, 736 F.2d 859 (2d Cir. 1984).

Feist Publications, Inc. v. Rural telephone Service Co.,111 S.Ct. 1282 (1991) .

Goldstein, P. (1994). ©opyright's highway: The law and lore of copyright from Gutenberg to the celestial jukebox. New York: Hill and Wang.

Grogen, A. R. (1994, November). Licensing for the next generation new media technology. *The Computer Law*, p. 4.

Gumpert, G. (1987). *Talking tombstones and other tales of the media age.* New York: Oxford University Press.

Hoffman, B. (1996, March 15). From virtual gallery to the legal web. *The New York Law Journal,* p. 11.

Hudson, K. (1987). *Museums of influence.* Cambridge, UK: Cambridge University Press.

Ibbotson, J., & Shah, N. (1993, October). Interactive multimedia and electronic publishing. *Copyright World,* p. 31.

Jackson, D.S. (1994, July 25). Battle for the soul of internet. *Time,* pp. 50, 56.

Johnson, D.R., & Marks, K. (1993). Mapping electronic data communication onto existing legal metaphors: Should we let our conscience (our contracts) be our guide? *Villanova Law Review, 81,* 482-516.

Katz v. United States, 389 U.S. 347 (1967).

Landis, C. (1994, August 9). Regulating porn: Does it compute? *USA Today,* p. D1.

Leroux, C. (1991, 27 October). *Speech enters computer age.* Chicago Tribune, p. C4.

Miller, M.W. (1991, October 22). Prodigy network defends display of anti-semitic notes. *Wall Street Journal,* p. B.

Milone, K.L. (1995). Dithering over digitization: International copyright and licensing agreements between museums, artists, and new media publishers. *Indiana International & Comparative Law Review, 5,* 393.

Nimmer, M.B. (1980). *Nimmer on copyright.* New York: Matthew Bender.

Pacific & Southern Co. v. Duncan, 744 F. 2d 1490 (11th Cir. 1984).

Partridge, E. (1958). *Origins: A short etymological dictionary of modern English.* New York: Macmillian.

Playboy Enterprises, Inc. v. Frena, 839 F. Supp. 1552 (1993).

Putnam, R. (1996, March 11). The strange death of civic America. *The Independent,* p 13.

Quill Corp. v. North Dakota, 112 S.Ct. 1904 (1992).

Ramos, C.R., & Hempe, C.W. (1996, September 30). "Mere conduit" exemption stirs debate. *New York Law Journal,* pp. S1, S-9.

Raysman, R., & Brown, P. (1993, July 13). Multimedia licensing. *New York Law Journal,* p. 3.

Regan, P.M. (1995). *Legislating privacy: Technology, social values, and public policy.* Chapel Hill: The University of North Carolina.

Reidenberg, J. (1996). Governing networks and cyberspace rule-making. *Emory Law Journal,* pp. 911-930.

Restatement of Torts (2nd ed.). (1976). St Paul, MN: West Publishing.

Schisel, S. (1996, December 21). Global agreement reached to widen copyright law. *The New York Times,* p. 1.

Smegal, T. F., Jr. (1994, July 4). By taking precautions, sellers of CD-ROMs and multimedia products can minimize the liability risks involved in using public-domain works. *The National Law Journal*, pp. B5, B8.

Sony Corporation of America v. Universal City Studios, Inc., 464 U.S. 417 (1984).

Strong, W. (1993). *The copyright book: A practical guide* (4th ed.). Cambridge, MA: MIT Press.

Stuckey, K.D., Rose, L., & Stele, S. (Eds.). (1994). *Business and legal aspects of the Internet and online services.* New York: Law Journal Seminars Press.

White Paper. (1995). *The report on the working group on intellectual property rights.* Washington, DC.

12

RIGHTS OF ATTRIBUTION AND INTEGRITY IN ONLINE COMMUNICATION*

MARK A. LEMLEY

Is there a right of attribution in cyberspace? A right to have others credit your statements to you or to the personality you present to others? Mark Lemley explores the interrelated rights of attribution, integrity of identity, and anonymity as they apply to electronic communications. These issues emerge as particularly complex in an electronic realm in which anonymity is possible and pseudonymity is generally an option. The author concludes that Net users may be able to protect their rights to attribution and the integrity of their electronic personalities only by imperiling their anonymity.

In his powerful novel *Ender's Game*, science fiction author Orson Scott Card (1977) conceives of a near-future world in which all

*© Mark A. Lemley. An earlier version of this chapter originally appeared as an article in the *Journal of Online Law* in 1995. The author thanks Rose Hagan, Trotter Hardy, Jim Treece, and participants at a faculty workshop at the University of Texas School of Law for helpful comments and discussion of these issues.

political discussion and decision making occurs by means of a computer network. An important attribute of this network is pseudonymity: Any citizen of the republic is entitled to post his or her views into the worldwide marketplace of ideas using a pseudonym. In the novel, two children (Peter and Valentine) take advantage of this fact to sway public opinion by using the pseudonymous names Locke and Demosthenes, respectively. The fact that they are not known is critical to their success: No one would pay the slightest attention to their opinions if they realized the authors were less than 13 years old. In the end, they are successful and are (pseudonymously) lauded for their efforts.

Reality, alas, is more complex than even the very best science fiction. Consider the fate of Card's heroes were they to venture onto the Internet in the present day.

Peter and Valentine begin to publish their arguments on Usenet as Locke and Demosthenes. Their words are rapidly swept into the torrent of dispute on Usenet. Someone responds, quoting part of Locke's posting. Someone else jumps in, quoting the same posting but without attributing it to Locke. Soon, while the debate rages, Locke is forgotten as the source of the initial posting. Meanwhile, a Usenet reader—who has joined this debate late—takes some choice words and reposts them as part of her own argument on a different part of the Net. The words are Locke's (well, Peter's), but the new reader has no way of knowing that, and neither does anyone at the new posting site. They assume that the words are those of the new reader. In turn, the new reader's "authorship" is rapidly lost in the course of the new discussion. Over time, not only the authorship but the textual integrity of the argument is likely to be degraded as well. What survives, if anything, may be a "meme" that is replicated across the network, but that has scant resemblance to the original posting.

Another user, "Machiavelli," upset by the implications of Demosthenes' argument, decides to prove his point by the time-honored method of reductio ad absurdium. To accomplish this, Machiavelli begins posting arguments under the name of Demosthenes that take more and more extreme positions, until finally "Demosthenes" is advocating controlled genocide. Valentine—still operating as Demosthenes—attempts to distance herself from these new arguments, and confusion reigns. Because readers cannot easily tell which opinions come from the "real" Demosthenes and which from the imposter, Valentine's arguments are ignored by most people.

Lawyers are mercifully absent from *Ender's Game*. But in the real world, those who live, work, and play in cyberspace cannot afford to ignore the problems that surround issues of attribution, integrity, and identity. The problems just listed present several different legal issues—the existence and scope of rights to attribution, the integrity of authorship, and the integrity of "electronic personality" (Karnow, 1994), respectively.

ATTRIBUTION

There is no explicit right of attribution for written works in the United States. Put another way, plagiarism is not itself illegal. This may be surprising to some. Certainly, the basic layperson's view of copyright law is the idea "thou shalt not copy." And what is plagiarism, if not a particularly egregious form of copying—egregious because you don't even admit that your ideas aren't your own?

The reason plagiarism is not necessarily copyright infringement has to do with the fact that copyright law does not condemn all copying—only the copying of certain things, under certain circumstances. There are several important limitations on the scope of copyright protection. One is the idea-expression dichotomy, arguably the most fundamental rule in all of copyright law. The short version of the story is that it is permissible (indeed, even encouraged) to copy the ideas of another, but illegal to copy the original expression of those ideas. A second significant limitation on copyright is the fair use doctrine, which makes it permissible to copy even the original expression from a copyrighted work under certain circumstances. Finally, some works may be copied because they fall into the public domain and are "free for the taking" by subsequent authors.

To be sure, much plagiarism is also copyright infringement. If you take a chapter from my book and copy it verbatim, you are guilty of copyright infringement. But that is merely because you copied; in theory, nothing hinges on whether you attributed my work to me or claimed it for yourself. If you are careful with what you copy, so that you stay within the boundaries set by the copyright law, you are free to take the ideas at the heart of this or any other article and use them in your own work. There is nothing I can do about it.

For many authors, the absence of attribution right in United States copyright law is not very important. If authorship is primarily a commercial venture, very little may hinge on attribution—the author is more likely to be concerned about getting paid (Gleick, 1996). The fact that someone else sells your concept for a screenplay for $3 million will not bother you any less because the "playwright" acknowledges you in a footnote. What you wanted was the $3 million.[1] But for other authors, particularly those in the academic community, attribution may be more important than the right to commercial control. Certainly, I do not get paid by law reviews for the articles I publish; my return comes (if at all) in the form of peer recognition of my ideas.[2] From my perspective, the *Harvard Law Review* is more than welcome to copy this article in its entirety, as long as they put my name at the top. However, I am likely to be very upset if Harvard publishes my article with *someone else's* name on it.

How is this relevant to the Internet? Basically, the answer is that the Internet makes it dramatically easier to republish another author's works. Academic discourse between multiple participants used to take place in the rather stilted environment of academic journals, in which months and even years would elapse between argument and rejoinder. In this environment, attribution was a practical necessity—before you made your argument, you usually had to remind your audience what you were responding to, often summarizing the prior paper at length. By contrast, Internet discussions are typically characterized by rapid responses from a host of people, by the dissecting and excerpting of original components for discussion purposes, and by the cross-posting of ideas and discussions to other lists.

In all of this confusion, it is a relatively common occurrence for people's words (and certainly their ideas) to be reproduced without attribution. Indeed, even Card's (1977) heroes in *Ender's Game* suffered such a fate. Their early postings as Locke and Demosthenes were replicated in other areas of the Net, but were not attributed to the authors. And in the context of discussions on Usenet or on a listserv, such reproduction may not be actionable— either legally because posting a message implies a license for others to copy or repost it, or practically because the provable economic gain or loss from such copying is nonexistent. If authors want to be identified with their ideas, they need something more than what copyright law will give them. That "something more" may be a right of attribution—a right to be identified as the author of your writings.

Does the Law Compel Attribution?

A couple of recent cases suggest that the federal courts are well on their way to creating a de facto right of attribution in the federal intellectual property laws. The first case suggests a cause of action not for copyright infringement, but for "false designation of origin" under section 43(a) of the Lanham Act. In *Waldman Publishing v. Landoll* (1994), both Waldman and Landoll published adaptations of classic, public domain books and marketed them for children. Waldman claimed that it had put substantial work into creating its children's versions of the classic books, and that Landoll merely copied Waldman's chapter arrangement and a large portion of its text. Because the underlying works were in the public domain and could be freely copied, however, Waldman apparently decided that it could not make out a case of copyright infringement. Instead, it claimed that Landoll's sales of books based on Waldman's adaptations constituted a "false designation of origin" in violation of the Lanham Act. The Second Circuit agreed, finding that because Waldman had indeed contributed original expression to the public domain works, Landoll was required to credit Waldman as the originator of the children's edition: "It would constitute a false designation of origin to publish without attribution to its author a work that is original enough to deserve copyright protection" (*Waldman Publishing v. Landoll*, 1994, p. 782; but see *Cleary v. News Corp.*, 1994, in which the Ninth Circuit required "bodily appropriation" of a work unchanged in order to violate the Lanham Act).

In the second case, *Robinson v. Random House* (1995), Random House represented Daley, an author who wrote a book about Pan AM airlines. Random House sued Robinson, who published a competing book that included approximately 25% of Daley's text verbatim. After finding that Robinson had infringed on Daley's protectable expression, the district court proceeded to consider Robinson's claim of fair use. The court found Robinson's failure to give attribution for the material taken from Daley's book doomed his fair use claim:

> In this case, although a significant portion of 9 out of 14 chapters in Robinson's book was taken directly from the Daley Book, Robinson fails to quote the Daley book, to cite to the Daley Book, or even to acknowledge the Daley Book. This reprehensible conduct places Robinson far closer to the scissor-wielding cut-and-paste plagiarist than to the scholar building on others' past works. Second, confusion between the original and the infringing work is also an issue to consider. . . . In this case, a reader would have absolutely no way of knowing that thousands upon thousands of the words used in the Robinson Book actually were penned by Daley.

Based largely on this reasoning, the court found that Robinson's use of Daley's language was commercial rather than academic, and so rejected his fair use claim.

Both of these cases suggest that a right of attribution has a commercial effect (see *Semco Inc. v. Amcast Inc.*, 1995, requiring commercial effect to invoke the Lanham Act). If you copy material without identifying it as copied, that fact may hurt you in a copyright infringement suit. Even if you cannot be sued for copyright infringement, your failure to attribute copied material may be actionable under the Lanham Act if it confuses consumers as to the source of the copied material (Kelly & Paine-Powell, 1995). Taken together, these cases suggest that the worse cases of nonattribution will be taken care of by the existing law.

Other cases, however, are likely to fall between the cracks of copyright and trademark law, either because they have no obvious commercial consequence or because the nature of the Net makes application of existing laws difficult. E-mail conversations are prominent in the former group. Excerpts taken from someone else's e-mail message may be sufficiently short or unoriginal that they do not constitute copyright infringement. Alternatively, the taking may be considered "fair" because it is for the purpose of criticism or comment, is not for financial gain, and does not impose a market loss on the original author. Finally, the nature of many e-mail conversations is clearly noncommercial, a fact that both precludes a finding of trademark infringement and makes a finding of "fair use" more likely in copyright cases.

As an example of the latter, consider the automatic "inlining" of images when a normally configured Web browser visits a Web page. The page can be set up so that the browser automatically travels to a second site and grabs an image from that site, portraying it in the middle of the first Web page. The owner of the first Web page is not copying anything herself—the Web browser does that (albeit at the direction of the first Web page).[3] But depending on the circumstance, the page owner may well be misattributing the image because to the casual browser the image appears to be part of the first Web page. The Lanham Act may offer some sort of limited attribution right in such a case, at least to the extent of preventing deceptive commercial inlining of images from another site.

Is a Stronger Right of Attribution Desirable?

Do we need an explicit right of attribution in online communication that applies regardless of commercial effect? The answer may depend on what the right encompasses and what, if anything, it replaces. For instance, many on the Net are skeptical of any enhancement of intellectual property rights, but view a right of attribution as a suitable *replacement* for the more powerful protections of copyright law (see Schlachter, 1995). Others see a right of attribution as a natural application of the "moral rights" given to authors in most of the world (see Berne Convention, 1971). On this latter view, a right of attribution ought to exist over and above the rights granted to authors or their assignees by copyright law.

The formulation of any right of attribution is complicated by the ease with which works can be *altered* online. Because it is possible not just to edit but also to change the content of someone else's posting, a right of attribution to be effective might also have to include a right of integrity. Indeed, the Berne Convention provides for authors in signatory countries (with the de facto exception of the

United States, which has signed the Berne Convention but has not altered its intellectual property laws to comply in this respect), "the right to claim authorship of the work and to object to any distortion, mutilation or modification of, or other derogatory action in relation to, the said work, which would be prejudicial to his honor or reputation."

The United States has a similar provision protecting the integrity of works of visual art, but does not extend such protection to other types of copyrighted works (17 U.S.C. §106A). Once again, however, U.S. courts have stepped into the breach, at least in some cases. In *Gilliam v. ABC* (1976), the producers of "Monty Python's Flying Circus" sued ABC for "mutilating" their work by editing it substantially before broadcasting it. The court found that ABC's substantial editing violated the Lanham Act because it created the false impression that the edited work was the product of Monty Python. This Lanham Act protection, coupled with the copyright owner's strong rights to control the creation of adaptations or "derivative works" (Lemley, 1997), may mean that in practice authors already have a right to preserve the integrity of their works against at least some forms of alteration.

Rights of attribution and integrity, however, need not be so strong as to prevent the unauthorized modification of a prior work. A more limited right, suggested by the Lanham Act cases, might focus on how the altered work is presented to the public. Under this approach, the question in any case of copying begins with "did you attribute the work to the original author?" If you have not only copied but also changed the work, it should be up to the reviser to make clear what belongs to the original author and what he or she has added, changed, or deleted. This is not very difficult in many contexts. We have a number of conventions from print media— quotation marks, ellipses—that identify preexisting material taken from others. Similar conventions are developing online. For example, if I want to incorporate a preexisting message into my e-mail, I may begin the excerpt by typing "T.S. Eliot writes: . . ." If I edit Eliot's comments, I can indicate that by writing "[snip]" where material has been elided.

Of course, in other contexts identifying the work of the original author will not be so easy. Musicians and visual artists obviously cannot use quotation marks to identify the authors whose work they appropriate (Harris, 1994). They may be able to credit the original artist in a side note, but even in that circumstance it may be impossible to distinguish effectively between original and derivative elements in the work. What do we do in those instances? If it is impossible to distinguish the parts of the two works, so that audiences will be likely to misattribute authorship, a right of integrity can take one of two tacks. First, it might give the original artist the right to disavow any connection with the adapted work and require the adapter to disclose that fact. (On this view, it would be the adapter's responsibility to contact the original artist to seek permission or disavowal before publishing derivative work.) Alternatively, the legal rule could be that if you cannot create an adaptation without engendering confusion as to authorship, the original author has the right to prevent his or her work from being used at all.

Other problems with a right of attribution generally parallel the difficulties the United States and other countries have faced in giving protection to "moral rights." The moral rights protection that the Berne Convention compels is personal to the author and cannot be transferred under any circumstances (except to the author's heirs when he or she dies). Although designed to benefit authors, a nontransferable right may end up hurting them in some circumstances. If publishers are unable to buy the moral rights from authors whose works they want to acquire, they may be willing to pay less for the work than they otherwise would. Certainly, the existence of moral rights makes it more difficult to create new works based on the works of others because the number and nature of permissions that must be obtained increases significantly. Thus, it may have a devastating impact on the field of "appropriation art," particularly to the extent that the artists engage in a parody of the appropriated works (see generally, *Campbell v. Acuff-Rose*, 1994). Furthermore, because the right of attribution contemplated in the Berne Convention is not subject to a "fair use" or private use exception, the effect of a full right of attribution will be to limit the use the public can make of copyrighted works.

Whether a right of attribution makes sense online depends in large part on what we think is at stake. On the one hand, as information is increasingly the currency of the modern economy, proper attribution takes on increasing commercial importance. On the other hand, if rights of attribution and integrity are read broadly to prevent alteration and adaptation of works, much of the valuable flexibility of the Net will be lost. If copyright and trademark law will protect against willful or commercial nonattribution, perhaps the informal customs of the Internet ("netiquette") and common courtesy can be relied on to do the rest—without the need for a new statute assigning attribution rights to authors.

INTEGRITY OF IDENTITY

In the introduction, we posited that an unknown third party "impersonates" Demosthenes by circulating messages under her name. This scenario is not particularly hypothetical: Joshua Quittner reported in Wired magazine on an automated "bot" (slang for "electronic robot") that posted messages to Internet Relay Chat using his identity (Quittner, 1995; see also Rheingold, 1993). The implications of online impersonation are quite troubling. In a context in which communication is still largely verbal, readers have very few cues to the identity or intention of the author of the message except what the author actually posts. If authorial claims of identity are readily hackable and thus untrustworthy, all the social and legal rules that depend on identity—liability for defamation or copyright infringement, the effectiveness of flaming or other forms of social sanctions, and so on—are thrown into doubt.

Perhaps there is a legal solution to this problem. If using Joshua Quittner's electronic mail address involved improper access to his computer system, charges could be pressed under various federal and state criminal "computer trespass" laws. But Quittner identifies in the article ways in which his identity might be forged on the Net itself, without the forger having improper access to his computer (Quittner, 1995). Alternatively, representing oneself falsely as Joshua Quittner might constitute trademark infringement, depending on the purpose for which one did it and the effect it had. Because the trademark laws are designed to protect only against the confusion of consumers regarding goods or services sold in commerce, however, most citizens could not avail themselves of such protection if their online identities were hijacked by noncommercial messages.

A more promising area for legal liability involves the communications torts. In particular, taking over someone's online personal might in various circumstances constitute fraud or misrepresentation, defamation, or invasion of privacy. But fraud and misrepresentation, like trademark infringement, require some sort of commercial or other injurious effect. The fake Joshua Quittner must have induced others to act to their detriment on the basis of this false identity. That may well be the case in certain circumstances, but many intrusions on online identity lack that element and so would not be actionable. Defamation is a better claim; the fake Joshua Quittner has arguably published a false statement (the assertion that he is in fact Joshua Quittner). But defamation requires that the plaintiff be "defamed," that is, be cast in disrepute or held up to mockery or ridicule. Moreover, depending on the nature of the defamatory statements, the plaintiff may have to provide some actual damage. Both of these may be difficult to show, meaning that defamation provides only uncertain protection against impersonation.

Invasion of privacy appears to provide the strongest cause of action for someone whose online identity was appropriated by another. Two separate torts for invasion of privacy are relevant here. The first is the tort of "appropriation of name or likeness." This sounds promising—certainly the "appropriation" of Joshua Quittner's name is precisely what has occurred here. As Prosser and Keeton (1984) put it, "the effect of the appropriation decisions is to recognize or create an exclusive right in the individual plaintiff to a species of trade name, his own, and a kind of trade mark in his likeness" (p. 854). Unfortunately for our purposes, the common law tort of appropriation of name or likeness—and the state right of publicity that has evolved from it in the past 50 years—are limited to circumstances in which the name of the plaintiff has been appropriated for commercial purposes (*Waits v. Frito-Lay* 1992; *White v. Samsung Electronics*, 1993). This makes the "appropriation" privacy tort even less useful for impersonation plaintiffs than trademark infringement or defamation: Not only must one prove that the defendant made money from using the plaintiff's name, but that it was the "commercial value" of the plaintiff's name itself that was taken.

That leaves us with the second prong of the privacy tort, governing "publicity which places the plaintiff in a false light in the public eye" (or "false light" privacy; Prosser & Keeton, 1984, p. 863). It is here that the impersonation tort must rest. False light privacy originated in the English case of *Byron v. Johnston* (1816), in which the poet Lord Byron convinced the English equity courts to enjoin Johnston from circulating a "bad poem" that Johnston had falsely attributed to Byron. Since then, it has been used to protect plaintiffs from having their name linked to books, articles, political statements, or legal documents that they did not in fact author (Keeton, 1994). So if Mr. Quittner can identify the person (or "bot") using his identity online, he ought to have a cause of action for invasion of privacy, regardless of what is said using his name (*Time v. Hill*, 1967; but see *Cain v. Hearst Corp.*, 1994, in which Texas abolished the tort of false light privacy).

But we are not concerned only with Joshua Quittner. What about Valentine in our example? Here, the difficulty is that no one has published articles using the name "Valentine"—instead, both the original author and the "impersonator" used the pseudonym "Demosthenes." Can Valentine prevent a third party from "impersonating" her pseudonym? Is it realistic to say that Valentine has been "placed in a false light in the public eye"—or alternatively, that "Demosthenes" has?

It is here that I believe the law fails to take account of the realities of Internet discourse. Both defamation and invasion of privacy are bound tightly to the concept of the person. Just as it is impossible to defame the dead (Prosser & Keeton, 1984), it appears to be impossible to defame (or portray in a false light) a fictional entity. Thus, in circumstances in which objectionable publications use a pseudonym, courts generally require that the plaintiff prove that the public know that the objectionable meaning attached to him or her personally, not just to the pseudonym (*Carlisle v. Fawcett Publications,* 1962). As a result, "Demosthenes" could be defamed or placed in a false light only if the public knows who she really is. Similarly, corporations can be defamed, but only because it is a known collection of persons that is assumed to have prestige and standing in the community (Prosser & Keeton, 1984). This helps those who are easily identified with their pseudonyms, but it does nothing to aid those who truly wish to remain pseudonymous.

The failure of the law to protect pseudonymous personalities online ("electronic personalities" or "epers," in the words of Karnow, 1994) can do serious damage to what Howard Rheingold (1993) calls "virtual community." It is one of the virtues of electronic interaction that individuals may in a large sense design their own personality, freed from the boundaries of physical appearance and social convention. Men can (and do) become women online; the old become young; lawyers and business people become artists and poets (Rheingold, 1993). But for a community to develop online, these new electronic personalities must be able to interact, share experiences, and confront adversity together on a consistent basis. This takes time, during which a particular electronic personality (which generally means a particular person) becomes a member of the community. Impersonation of electronic personalities—in Rheingold's (1993) words, "violating the sanctity of nicknames" (p. 181)—prevents the development of that community. The result is damaging whether or not the impersonation is discovered. If it is revealed, people are less likely to trust messages from that particular electronic personality because they cannot be sure of the authenticity of the message. If it is not revealed, the electronic personality is harmed because the community attributes to it messages it did not author.

Protecting the integrity of electronic personalities explicitly would solve these problems. There are a number of informal social norms that make electronic impersonation "taboo" (Rheingold, 1993), but informal social norms are effective only to the extent that the transgressors are members of the community. Some form of legal protection seems appropriate in those circumstance in which a painstakingly developed electronic personality is hijacked by an outsider for his or her own ends. The obvious legal analogy to the physical world is the false light privacy tort. That tort protects "real" persons against impersonation, and it does not need much alteration to be retrofitted for the online world. All that is required to apply the false light privacy doctrine in the electronic context is for us to accept the electronic personality as "real." Indeed, Georgia has recently passed a law that bans the use of someone else's name or identifying symbol in computer communication "to falsely identify the person . . . transmitting such data" (Ga. H.B. 1630, section 1(a)). Statues protecting such rights may serve a valuable purpose, provided they are narrowly tailored.[4]

It is possible, however, that we do not need to rely on the law at all to protect electronic personalities. In his article in the *Journal of Online Law*, Michael Froomkin (1995a) suggests that by combining cryptography and anonymous remailers, individuals can create verifiable but unforgeable "digital signatures" for their pseudonyms. Using this technology, it should be possible to create a pseudonym that cannot be hijacked without access to the actual author's private encryption "key."

Creating unforgeable digital signatures is only possible, however, if robust encryption remains legal. The issue of pseudonymity is bound up with the more troubling one of anonymity because all electronic personalities are at least potentially anonymous, and both truly anonymous and truly pseudonymous individuals are not accountable to society.[5] This simple fact is both the greatest virtue and the greatest problem with anonymity. Revolutionaries and others who fear political repression have historically expressed their views anonymously, as they did during the American Revolution. On a less dramatic but no less important note, early women writers often used pseudonyms that disguised their gender so that their books would be read. The historical accomplishments of anonymity are laudable, and should not be disregarded lightly. At the same time, anonymity is the key to the successful commission of crimes and torts against others. Anonymous Internet users can commit copyright infringement, fraud, and defamation with impunity online, and they can conspire with others in the virtual world to commit physical crimes.

There is no easy way out of this conundrum, particularly because it seems extremely unlikely that any one government has the technical ability to prevent the private use of encryption devices and anonymous remailers.[6] Various people have proposed different solutions, ranging from complete anonymity to proposals to give the government a limited right to determine identity (Long, 1994; Karnow, 1994; see also Branscomb, 1995) to banning anonymity entirely (Hardy, 1994; see also *Anderson v. Nidorf*, 1994). How you come down on the issue of anonymity probably depends in large measure on how you weigh the danger of these competing scenarios—in short, whether you fear anarchy more or less than an all-powerful government.

Perhaps surprisingly, the U.S. Supreme Court came down rather strongly in favor of a right to anonymity in the recent case of *McIntyre v. Ohio Elections Commission* (1995). In that case, the court held that a state statute that prohibited the distribution of anonymous political campaign literature violated the First Amendment. The Court extolled the virtues of anonymity in literature and politics throughout U.S. history, commenting that "an author generally is free to decide whether or not to disclose her true identity," and that "at least in the field of literary endeavor, the interest in having anonymous works enter the marketplace of ideas unquestionably outweighs any public interest in requiring disclosure as a condition of entry" (*McIntyre v. Ohio Elections Commission*, 1995).

I do not propose to enter the debate over anonymity here because I do not believe that rights of attribution and integrity of electronic personality necessarily depend on the status of a "right" to anonymity. The reason is simple: Invocation of a legal rule based on misuse of identity necessarily requires proof of identity. If Locke and Demosthenes want to avail themselves of a legal right to have their words attributed to them, or if Peter and Valentine want to claim the exclusive right to hold themselves out as Locke and Demosthenes, they will have to be able to prove that they "are" in fact Locke and Demosthenes! Truly anonymous postings will therefore not be eligible for legal protection of identity in the sense discussed in this chapter. This is true not because of any legal rule disfavoring anonymity, but by the very nature of anonymity itself.[7]

To be sure, there are so-called "anonymous" remailers that strip the identity from messages, but log that identity in a file from which it can be obtained if need be. The notorious "anon.penet.fi" remailer in Finland worked on this model. If Peter and Valentine use such a pseudo-anonymous mailer, they will be able to prove authorship (and nonauthorship) in court if necessary. But, by the same token, governments and private litigants will be able to find the same information, and so it is wrong to call their messages "anonymous" in a pure sense.

In short, Peter and Valentine will need to protect their putative rights to attribution and integrity under the legal regime I propose here only if they are not truly untraceably anonymous or pseudonymous. If true pseudonymity remains legal, there may be no need for legal protection of identity because technical protections will suffice.

CONCLUSION

The Internet presents, if not completely new legal issues, at least new spins on some very old issues. But new legal issues do not necessarily require new laws. It is well to heed the suggestion of several commentators that government tread carefully in regulating a system that has to date worked fairly well on its own (Branscomb, 1995; see also Hardy, 1994, who recommends a presumption in favor of flexible, decentralized rule making).

Each of the issues discussed in this chapter could be resolved by the legislative or judicial creation of a new right—a right to attribution, integrity of creation, and integrity of personality, respectively. But I am not convinced that we need to go that far. Many cases of mis- or nonattribution can be resolved satisfactorily under the existing copyright and trademark laws. Other cases can be resolved by the use of informal social norms against plagiarism, particularly in the academic communities in which attribution is of great importance. Although society may eventually conclude that authors should have an unfettered right to attribution or authorial integrity online, we should at least be cognizant of the problems such a right has engendered in other contexts.

Similarly, it is tempting to create a personal right to maintain the integrity of one's online personality. Changing the law to account for cyberspace poses less risk in this context because we have various tort theories that seem readymade for protecting integrity of personality. A minor modification to the right of privacy is less troubling than the creation of an entirely new right. Nonetheless, this new right may be unnecessary, particularly if encrypted pseudonyms that can be both verifiable and untraceable remain legal and are put into widespread use.

ENDNOTES

1. This overstates the case, of course. Attribution may still be important to commercially motivated authors because it may affect their reputation (and hence the size of their compensation for future works).
2. Of course, I can afford to publish for "free" only because my work is generously subsidized by the academic institution where I work.
3. Under such circumstances, it is possible that the first Web page owner is liable for contributory copyright infringement, if the copying by the browser is itself a direct infringement.
4. Online activists complained that H.B. 1630 swept too broadly, threatening the right to post messages pseudonymously. A review of the language of the statute, however, belies that fear.
5. Michael Froomkin (1995a) distinguishes usefully between "traceable" and "untraceable" pseudonyms and anonyms.
6. A government could, however, make it illegal to use such devices, thus reducing their use by law-abiding citizens and raising the costs of such a use (Froomkin, 1995a).

7.   It is possible that legal recognition of electronic personalities will grant them rights in court, much as corporations are fictitious entities with legal rights (Perry, 1995; Post, 1996). Perry postulates a world in which the actions of an individual with an electronic personality will be both benefited and constrained by the reputational capital the individual invests in that personality.

REFERENCES

Anderson v. Nidorf, 26 F. 3d 100 (9th Cir. 1994).

Berne Convention for the Protection of Literary and Artistic Works (1971).

Branscomb, A. W. (1995). Anonymity, autonomy, and accountability: Challenges to the First Amendment in cyberspace. *Yale Law Journal, 104,* 1639-1679.

Byron (Lord) v. Johnston, 35 Eng. Rep. 851 (1816).

Cain v. Hearst Corp. 878 S.W. 2d 577 (Tex. 1994).

Campbell v. Acuff-Rose Music, Inc., 114 S.Ct. 1164 (1994).

Carlisle v. Fawcett Publications, Inc. 20 Cal. Rptr. 405, 410-11 (Ct. App. 1962).

Card, O.S. (1977). *Ender's game.* New York: Tor Publishers.

Cleary v. News Corp., 30 F. 3d 1255 (9th Cir. 1994).

Froomkin, A. M. (1995). Anonymity and its enmities. *Journal of Online Law,* Art. 1

Gleick, J. (1996, August 4). I'll take the money, thanks. *The New York Times Magazine,* p. 16.

Gilliam v. American Broadcasting Companies, 538 F. 2d 14 (2d Cir. 1976).

Hardy, I.T. (1994). The peoper legal regime for "cyberspace." *University of Pittsburgh Law Review, 55,* 993-1055.

Harris, C.R. (1994). Manipulation of photographs and the Lanham Act. *Communication & Law, 16,* 29-43.

Karnow, C.E.A. (1994). The encrypted self: Fleshing out the rights of electronic personalities. *John Marshall Journal of Computer & Information Law, 13,* 1.

Prosser, W. L., & Keeton, W. P. (1984). *Prosser & Keeton on torts* (5th ed.). St. Paul, MN: West Publishing.

Kelly, D. M., & Paine-Powell, L.S. (1995). Developments in American unfair competition law: Implications for the computer industry. *European Intellectual Property Review, 4,* 184-194.

Lemley, M.A. (1997). The economics of improvement in intellectual property law. *Texas Law Review, 75,* 989.

Long, G. P. III (1994). Who are you? Identity and anonymity in cyberspace. *University of Pittsburgh Law Review, 55,* 1177-1213.

McIntyre v. Ohio Elections Commission, 115 S.Ct. 1511 (1995).

Perry the Cynic. (1995, August 17). *Virtual personas.* Message to cyberia-1 listserv.

Post, D. (1996). Pooling intellectual capital: Anonymity, pseudonymity, and contingent identity in cyberspace. *University of Chicago Law Forum,* 139-170.

Quittner, J. (1995, April). Automata non grata. *Wired,* p. 119.

Rheingold, H. (1993). *The virtual community: Homesteading on the electronic frontier.* Reading, MA: Addision Wesley.

Robinson v. Random House Inc. 877 F. Supp 830 (S.D. N.Y. 1995).

Schlachter, E. (1995, March 20). *IP issues on the net.* Electronic mail to cni-copyright listserv.

Semco Inc. v. Amcast Inc. 52 F. 3d 108 (6th Cir. 1995).

Time v. Hill, 385 U.S. 374 (1967).

Waits v. Frito-Lay, Inc., 978 F. 2d 1093 (9th Cir. 1992).

Waldman Publishing Corp. v. Landoll Inc., 43 F. 3d 775 (2d Cir. 1994).

White v. Samsung Electronics, 989 F. 2d 1512 (9th Cir. 1993) (dissent from denial of rehearing en banc).

13

IDENTITIES, COMMODITIES, AND INFORMATION FLOWS: INTELLECTUAL PROPERTY RIGHTS AND THE CONSTRUCTION OF EMERGENT ELECTRONIC SOCIAL SPACES

JOHN MONBERG

The central argument of this chapter is that the privacy implications of the information society need to be reconceptualized. As troubling as the release of sensitive or embarrassing information may be for individuals, at a more profound level, privacy violations are a social problem. In order to make this argument, the author begins with an exploration of the media landscape of the information society, noting the enhanced significance of commercial images for social ties, values, and identity. In the following section the author shows how the legal definition of intellectual property allows nearly unfettered collection of information that marks and characterizes individuals. The impact of this data collection requires an understanding of how personal data is collected, analyzed, and mobilized, reshaping the social terrain and affecting long-held expectations of identity, power, and intimacy. He concludes with an argument in favor of legal reforms that would make the marketing webs open and accountable; reforms that are requirements for a more democratic social order.

> Blockbuster Video claims the right to collect customer rental data for the creation of marketing databases, databases that will be sold to third parties. (Miller, 1990, p. 9)

> A *cookie* is a mechanism by which a server can both store and retrieve information on client (of service provider's) connections. A simple yet powerful new tool allows shopping applications to be stored about selected items, sites can store per-user preferences on the client on file, all generally without the client's knowledge. (Client Side State-HTTP Cookies, 1997)

"Information Wants to Be Free"—first coined by Stewart Brand, is a slogan that has been taken up as a rallying cry against market intervention by techno-optimists as diverse as former Grateful Dead songwriter John Perry Barlow, Time-Warner C.E.O. Gerald Levin, and conservative futurist George Gilder. This chapter shows that information is not and cannot be free, in two senses of the term. Information is plainly not free from cost, nor, more importantly, is information freed from the legal, economic, and technical structures that define, constitute, and give meaning to it. Although traditionally privacy law has been relied on to protect the personality of individuals, the law of intellectual property has been the province of protections for the creative works of personalities. Trademark law provides control over the commercial use of one's name or other identifying symbol. But captured data flows allow the construction of a powerful representational technology—customer purchasing profiles that generate statistically determined predictions about consumer behavior. This use of information regarding personality is increasing in significance during this age of computerization, which seemingly falls through the legal cracks.

Marketing data flows are especially pernicious because the mechanisms, categories, and contacts are hidden and opaque, removed from public deliberation and critique, a quality likely to intensify as more social and commercial interactions take place in a cyberspace of electronic envelopes, intelligent agents, and automated contracting. The privacy implications of the information society need to be reconceptualized because as troubling as the release of sensitive or embarrassing information may be for individuals, at a more profound level, privacy violations are a social problem. The vast amount of collected electronic data that characterizes individuals enables a new form of redlining, a redlining that excludes social groups from participating fully in the social dialog. This is both unjust to excluded groups and detrimental to society as a whole. Political philosophers from John Stuart Mill to John Dewey, Jurgen Habermas (1987), and Richard Rorty have stressed that when the range of debate, points of contact, and variety of positions within the social conversation are diminished, the social conversation as a whole is diminished.

The general thrust of the computer/communication policies now in place creates a climate in which information functions essentially as a commodity, and citizens function essentially as consumers. The values implicit in these policies mean that only information that is commercially viable should be created, and distribution of this information should be limited to only those who can afford it. These values imply that no harm would be done by removing all limits on the kind and amount of information gathered to describe and classify individuals, and that no limits, beyond economic feasibility, should be placed on how this information is used.

This argument is made by exploring the media landscape of the information society, noting the enhanced significance of commercial images for social ties, values, and identity. The legal definition of intellectual property allows nearly unfettered collection of information that marks and characterizes individuals. The impact of this data collection requires an understanding of how personal data is collected, analyzed, and mobilized, reshaping the social terrain and affecting long-held expectations of identity, power, and intimacy. This chapter concludes with an argument in favor of legal reforms that would make the marketing webs open and accountable, reforms that are requirements for a more democratic social order.

Intellectual property exists at an intersection of law, economics, technology, and culture. This complex, shifting, negotiated terrain calls for analysis from a cultural studies perspective. Traditional definitions of intellectual property assume that a copyrightable work is fixed in a material object, and that identifiable distinctions can be made among categories, including "first sale," "publication," and "public performance"—categories undermined by the new spaces and possibilities created by digital technologies. A cultural studies analysis is needed to explore the situatedness of technological consumption that constitute publics as audiences, mixing desires, resistances, and subject positions. Given the importance of the connections among media, advertising, and commodities in shaping our understanding of our place in the world, these linkages form a rich site for tracing through important fields, networks, and strategies.

"Reach Out and Touch Someone," "What's on Your Powerbook Is You," "What Information targeting has come to.

Introducing the Segment of Bob"—these phrases have become commonplace and as such exemplify a distinguishing characteristic of our era—the extent to which we inhabit an environment of mediated experience, our sense of self tied into complex interlinkages of machines, advertisements, commodities, and commandments spread across time and space. It is impossible to draw a line placing attitudes, hopes, fears, passions, and normative injunctions on one side and commodities, screens, and databases on the other. The strategies and processes of consumer capitalism suffuse local experience with distant and multiple connections, eroding fixed distinctions between subject and object.

POSTMODERN MEDIA LANDSCAPE—IMAGE FLOWS AND SOCIAL IDENTITY

Perhaps the dominant chord struck by the term *postmodernism* is that society has become, in the words of Gianni Vattimo (1992), a "society of generalized communication" (p. 1). Jean-Francois Lyotard's (1984) important work on postmodernity emphasized that the change from modernity was engendered by new possibilities of knowledge production, analysis, and transfer. These possibilities have been opened by long-term economic processes that have multiplied both the number of specialists engaged in symbolic production, dissemination, and reproduction, as well as their valorization as compared with other social groups (Hennion & Meadel, 1994). No previous society has ever been as saturated with signs and images. To pick merely one example—neglecting film, video, and other media— Sygma, a single stock photo agency, by itself produces 6,000 images per day (Tomlinson & Harris, 1994). The economic value associated with intellectual property rights accounted for $326 billion and 5.5 million jobs in the United States in 1991.

These images are not merely prevalent in all our lives, they are integrated deeply into the fabric of everyday experience. The frequency, availability, regularity, and interactivity of emerging media technologies are seen by many as increasingly popular, time-efficient substitutes for personal contact with friends, family, and neighbors. At times supplementing and at times supplanting the traditional contexts of identity formation such as families, neighborhoods, and churches, the mass media have become a new source of primary group ties, generating strong and enduring emotional bonds (Cerulo, Ruane, & Chayko, 1992).

People lacking direct interpersonal relations with each other are led by political symbols to imagine themselves as members of communities defined by common ascriptive characteristics, personal tastes, habits, or concerns. These phenomena highlight the need for an analytical focus sensitive to the dynamics of the coordination of action through indirect relationships and the formation of individuals' identity as members of imagined communities. Stimulus-response models attempting to identify the "impact" of specific advertisements miss the most significant aspects of these transmissions. The devices that Jody Berland (1992) terms "cultural technologies" mediate social and spatial relationships and produce not only texts, but also material practices that situate and place individuals as listeners, consumers, citizens, structuring the social roles that can be taken up by individuals. For example, television creates a sense of place to the extent that physical, social, and ideological systems are integrated (Adams, 1992).

Television locates both a bounded system in which symbolic interactions among people occur and a nucleus around which shared experiences are constructed, a center of meaning. Television positions viewers by presenting a "window on the world." This window, like any perspective, is value-laden—foregrounding certain features and making invisible others. As Frederic Jameson (1991) stresses, television is a product of late capitalism and must be seen in the context of the culture of consumerism, directing attention to the production of needs and wants and the mobilization of desire and fantasy (Kellner, 1990; Sack, 1992).

PROTECTED FICTIONS, FICTIONAL PROTECTIONS: LEGAL FRAMEWORK OF INTELLECTUAL PROPERTY RIGHTS

Given the prevalence of words, images, and data flows, it is crucial how these symbols are controlled, how the issues of ownership are framed, and to what uses and under what conditions these circuits are constructed. This fruitful field of inquiry for cultural studies is formed at the intersection of law, economics, technology, and culture, as intellectual property is constituted by a hodgepodge of evolving common law, corporate tactics, ad hoc legislative remedies, novel distribution channels, negotiated contractual agreements, and international treaties. The understandings surrounding property rights are under pressure as technological change prompts unforeseen uses of old intellectual products and additional venues for new forms of intellectual property. Digital colorization of black-and-white movies clashes with the "moral right" of the artist not to have his or her product defaced, a right codified by the Berne Convention. Music distributors persuade hardware companies to incorporate restrictive circuitry in mechanical devices so as to maintain control over intellectual property, in machines in lieu of legal penalties or moral commandments. The adoption of digital technologies and the convergence of hitherto relatively disjunct specialties generate many avenues and sites worth pursuing. Among the interesting possibilities are the use of digital sampling in rap music; the altered position of freelance photographers in an era of photojournalism marked by digital production, distribution, and alteration; shifting conceptions of "freedom of inquiry" and "fair use" in academic publishing; the postmodern aesthetic and the use of appropriated images; digital libraries and the privatization of public information; and the creation of space as laws are crafted both to forbid computer invasion and to carve up ownership of the broadcast spectrum.

Intellectual property, the mosaic of personal information, categorizes and situates discrete individuals. The current status of the legal definition of intellectual property in the United States may be succinctly described as fictional protections, protected fictions. Statutory and common law in general do not recognize individuals as having a definable interest in the personal data that describe them and provide scant recourse for privacy violations. Privacy protection is illusory. In contrast, courts have clearly defined the intellectual property rights of commercial creations through copyrights, software laws, and other regulatory mechanisms. Real people do not have privacy rights, but cartoon characters do.

These laws allow Barney, our friend the purple dinosaur, to enlist the services of five lawyers to control under what circumstances his image can be used; protect Little Debbie, the cake-selling snack girl, from mockery; and grant Disney the power to forbid 5- and 6- year-old children at Florida day-care centers from decorating their playground walls with images of Mickey Mouse, Donald Duck, and Goofy (Buskirk, 1993).

A redefinition of intellectual property could provide individuals with control over the data used to mark and describe them, but U.S. privacy protection is notoriously lax, applying in general only to government use of data. Legislation of this type includes the Federal Credit Reporting Act, the Family Education Rights and the Privacy Act of 1974, and the Computer Matching and Privacy Act of 1988 (Wilson, 1988). Furthermore, these laws only protect certain kinds of information and include "routine use" loopholes that allow even government agencies to use information as they see fit. The medical records, credit histories, and purchase information that classify millions of U.S. citizens are routinely collected and made available from centralized commercial repositories. Unlike Sweden and European Community initiatives, the United States has no clearly defined privacy right, no central privacy commission, and no enforcement mechanisms.

Common law holds that the name, phone number, and likeness of an individual are without value and is thus not the intellectual property of the individual. In cases such as *Shibley v. Time, Inc.* (1974) courts have explicitly ruled that individuals do not have the right to stop corporations from selling personal data to any third party as well as the right to approve uses of such data.

The situation is much different for celebrities, whether real or fictional. The "right of publicity" holds that a celebrity's likeness is protected and cannot be used without compensation. Image is transformed into intellectual property—a commodity, with all that that implies, including the ability to be defined, produced, and consumed. A large body of case law affirms this transformation; for example, *Gracey v. Maddin* (1989) grants the famous a general marketability in their personality in the form of goodwill. This right is extensive and prevents anyone from using any identifying characteristics of the famous, including the pitch, tone, accent, inflection, comic delivery of voice, or any of the recognizably identifying style of movement. Celebrities are protected from possible infringements that need not even be human representations, as Vanna White successfully prevented Samsung from using a blond-wigged, letter-turning robot in its television commercials.

However, protection is only granted to those who have a commercial stake in their identities. The multiple rulings of judges in *Martin Luther King Jr. Center for Social Change, Inc. v. American Heritage Products* (1982) and *Rosemont Enters., Inc. v. Random House, Inc.* (1968) refused to extend intellectual property right protection to or recognize the privacy rights ordinary individuals might have in controlling their appropriated identities. In both the limitation of privacy rights and the creation of intellectual property rights, the ground is set for a more intensive penetration of market criteria into social experience. This process of commodification allows mass audiences and publics to be transformed into carefully measured, graded, and detailed products.

Moving from an online world in which individuals use menus, screens, and indexes to navigate and place themselves to an electronic universe of software envelops, intelligent agents, and automated contracting will greatly expand potentially commodifiable social spaces. The delimitation of intellectual property rights enables organizations to renegotiate the boundaries of inside/outside across the producer/product/consumer conjunction. Much as Enlightenment surveys of time and space vastly expanded the ability of European mercantile and military interests to project their power, control over information flows allow corporate interests to construct and mobilize representations, to create laboratories, and to generate a new form of power, the power to map the terrain of the social.

INTELLECTUAL PROPERTY MOBILIZED IN ADVANCED MARKETING CIRCUITS

The modernist era of mass production and Fordist managerial phalanxes is over, given way to the flexible production strategies of the lean corporation. With capital mobility has come corporate malleability, as relatively fixed bureaucracies decompose and recompose into complex networks, renegotiating boundaries between system and environment, goals and strategies, the global and the local. Corporations no longer understand themselves to be static entities defined by fixed mission statements and organization charts. Strategists attempt to create profitable networks of technical competencies, regulatory opportunities, and market opportunities. David Collis (1993), associate professor at the Harvard Business School, advises, "We should never consider the company's value chain in isolation but should instead treat it as part of a value system, as a link in a chain of value chains" (p.46). Corporate actors strive to translate operational and logistical efficiencies into strategic leverage vis-à-vis competitors. Investments in technical capabilities may be used to raise the stakes for competing firms, create economies of scale, or alter the balance of power between large firms and small firms, retailers, and manufacturers.

Target marketing technologies are among the most important initiatives of this kind. These technologies—arrays and assemblages of laser scanners, universal product codes, demographic databases, expert systems, television advertisements, and a host of others—are utilized in concert, enabling a subtle, hidden, but nonetheless profound operation of power. Neodata is a quintessential example of a virtual corporation (Wilson, 1993). Neodata sells no product and owns no data, but it has created a $200 million market, processing the orders and subscription information of other corporate partners and creating a terabyte-sized database holding detailed profiles of 22 million consumers. Aexiom, a corporation with an equally opaque name, has constructed a database containing some or all of the following facts on 195 million U.S. citizens: age, estimated income, home ownership, cars owned, occupation, children, education, buying habits, types of credit cars used, height, and weight. This information was used to construct mailing lists totaling 3.7 billion names in 1996.

MARKETING DATA AS REPRESENTATIONAL TECHNOLOGY

Because personal data are not considered to be intellectual property, these are outside the control of the individuals it describes, legally free to be collected by corporations and transformed into detailed descriptions of targeted consumers. These data take many forms. Some of the data have been collected by the government and are thus public information. Demographic data collected by the Census Bureau and other government agencies are refined by a method referred to as psychographic analysis. Firms such as SRI International, Yankelovich Clancy Shulman, Donnelley, Acorn, and others collect data on tens of thousands of individuals through telephone surveys, mail surveys, focus groups, and personal interviews to create descriptions of how "consumers feel about themselves and the world around them." Surveys measure respondents' levels of self-esteem, leadership ability, need for group inclusion, and cosmopolitanism, attitudes at the core of personality. Customer purchasing profiles offer descriptions that can be increasingly detailed, "Fingerhut captures as many as 1,400 pieces of information about a household. These include typical demographic items like income and home ownership, appliance ownership, and purchasing histories for various products" (Bessen, 1993, p. 156).

Alternating lines encode universal product code (UPC) information on a wide variety of consumer products. Stores use UPC information to track inventory and sales information more quickly and cheaply. When customers use identification cards entitling them to automatic discounts, stores can determine exactly what purchases were made by each specific customer. This allows marketers to decompose the mass market into an audience of potentially addressable individuals. UPC information can be used to identify purchasers' of drugs, books and periodicals, personal hygiene products, beverages, condoms, diapers, tobacco, home pregnancy-testing kits, and any number of other products that provide tell-tale traces of lifestyle choices.

Advertisers also require accurate and detailed information about media use to determine their targeting decisions. Up to now, this data collection has required the active participation of viewers and is therefore subject to error. Massachusetts Institute of Technology (MIT) technologists have developed a "passive people meter" that digitizes and stores an image of every individual in a home. Rooms are scanned every two seconds allowing statistics to be gathered on everyone who is facing the television. This intrusive technology seems the stuff of science fiction, but commercial pressures are likely to prompt the widespread adoption of this technology within three years. Interactive cable television would allow an arbitrarily high level of data categorizing customers' precise viewing habits to be captured automatically. Arbitron, casting an even wider net, is developing a "pocket people meter" device that would be worn by viewers and record their exposure to commercials watched in bars, bowling alleys, or college dormitories by tracking inaudible sounds etched into television programs. Large swaths of social experience formerly laying outside the mechanisms of corporate surveillance are thus incorporated into representations suitable for managerial decision making. The volume of data collected by scanners, passive television monitors, credit card transactions, the telephone system, and the myriad other collection technologies far outstrips the capacity of human beings to make sense of it.

Marketing corporations combine individuals' patterns of purchases with their patterns of media usage to create an *automated* representational technology. The information is mobilized and made useful through the creation of computer environments that can effectively utilize the output of statistical relationship software, forming geo-demo-psycho-graphic, single-source media-exposure and purchasing-behavior expert systems: "Artificial intelligence systems, based on the emerging technology of neural networks, can sift through mountains of data and identify shopping trends and product opportunities" (Bessen, 1993, p. 153).

Product, corporation, customer, advertisement—these terms no longer remain stable. Employing customer purchasing profiles, managers and strategists enhance their power to interpret and define reality, to shift definitions, and to create new actors when it is in their interests to do so. For example, "the high-profit customer is not always a pre-existing category defined by volume, transaction size, price sensitivity and the like. A company can manage customers to high profitability" (Slywotski & Shapiro, 1993, p. 103) and distinguish between the masses and "customers worthy of long-term attention" (p. 102), no doubt providing them with the attention they "need."

THE SOCIAL RECONFIGURED AS MARKETING LABORATORY

With the right combination of information, instruments, practices, and allies, corporations construct laboratories in the field, correlating an exposure to media stimuli with subsequent purchasing responses. "Single-source" data combine media usage and product consumption data with the array of demographic and "psycho-dynamic" information that categorizes individuals by income, neighborhood, and lifestyle. These data are now available from Nielsen, Equifax, Mediamark Research, and other clearinghouses. Given the prevalence of images, the importance of mediated social interactions, and the ability of commodities to engender a consumer world of fine-grained imagined communities—

points outlined earlier in this chapter—control over these laboratories of data flows implies not merely the control over numerous stimulus/response cycles, but indeed the power to reshape social terrain.

MARKETING SYSTEMS RECONFIGURE SOCIAL RELATIONSHIPS AND EXPECTATIONS

The system for the collection, analysis, and use of personal data in a sense stands behind the face-to-face interactions that an individual has with representatives of public and private institutions. Tapping into electronic dossiers, sales clerks possess information about newly encountered customers, information such as customer's birthdays, their favorite designers, their spouse's interests, even their hobbies or leisure activities—information perhaps collected and distributed without the consent or even knowledge of the individual. These codified data allow the clerk to project a level of familiarity with the customer that in the past served to mark a relationship as close or even intimate.

Corporations strive to create commercial relationships that have the impact of familial relationships, but without the context of reciprocal interests, responsibilities, and concerns that familial relationships are embedded within. The Fingerhut company utilizes "magic moment" marketing, producing a monthly series of birthday flyers tailored to specific age groups and sex of those in a household, which include selections of toys and gifts (Bessen, 1993). Taking an interest in children, vendors turn a celebratory ritual into an opportunity to socialize children with the attitudes and values required by consumer capitalism.

The complex interlinkages of computer/communication technologies inscribe subjects within a discourse shaped by the requirements of a consumer society. Advanced cable television shopping will provide advertisers with a new level of presence in the home. Already, interactive media architect Barry Diller has assembled the QVC network—a merchandiser of cubic zirconium jewelry, electronic gadgets, and "collectibles"—by coordinating telephone connections, credit card transactions, customer profiles, real-time inventory controls, and host personalities carefully crafted to create the illusion of intimacy. This supple, responsive, highly articulated chain utilizes second-by-second sales graphs that allow host personalities—hucksters—to alter their sales pitches for maximum effectiveness. QVC aims not simply to sell as much as possible, but strives to position viewers as members of their corporate "family." Television is transformed from a passive receptacle into the interactive electronic hub of every household in the United States.

Given control over the tide of information flows that pervades and structures social interactions, strategists proclaim, "They'll be able to *probe almost continuously and test for new product opportunities*" (Bessen, 1993, p. 139; emphasis added). Marketers explicitly recognize that "this complex of programs serves as a kind of marketing laboratory" (p. 157). These webs of information flow and intellectual property should not be understood as neutral media, as frictionless transfers of information; they are implicated in the transfer and construction of values and power. Marie-Christine Leps (1990) warned of a social discourse in which "a purchasing subject is inscribed in the circulation of information . . . information allowing production and distribution modes to be customized and capitalized, transforming existing relations of economic and political power: the knowing subject is automatically a known object" (p. 208). In a search for a stable identity, Citibank vice president Catherine Allen looks to cutting-edge technologies for a solution, "The smart card allows me to identify myself securely" (quoted in Hansell, 1994, p. D5). It seems though that these identities will be neither stable nor secure.

These data flows and feedback circuits erase traditional distinctions between presence and absence, intimacy and strangeness, public and private, voluntary and imposed. The worldview of high-tech marketers is illustrated by a selection of phrases culled from the recent literature:

> The phrase "getting close to the customer" now has a definite high-tech ring. (Bessen, 1993, p.150)

> Romancing the segment of one, "database marketing" allows companies to get to know their customers intimately. (Betts, 1993, p. 63)

> Form long-term relationships with customers. (Bessen, 1993, p. 154)

> The marketing war gets automated. (Free, 1988, p. 154)

> The Great Atlantic and Pacific Tea Company are using technology, such as point-of-sale scanning and frequent shopper programs, *to own the customer*. (Bessen, 1993, p. 154)

The structure of relationships among marketers, products, and consumers has now become of the kind Anthony Giddens (1990) describes as a "structure of domination"—a form of space-time distanciation in which aspects of a relationship that up to now have been fleeting, temporary, and tacit are transformed into quantifiable, permanent, and transferable information resources. These dense connections change the terrain of social interaction, increasing the ability of corporations to prescribe, structure, and assign capacities and options to the roles of participants. Large corporate entities, in an increasing number of senses, can be "present" and "close" to prospective customers without incurring the high financial cost or the traditional expectations required by the physical presence of their representatives.

WIRING AND MAPPING THE SOCIAL: DATA DISTINCTIONS AS CULTURAL REDLINING

If reality is lived social relations, then as Donna Haraway (1990) has emphasized, access to the power to signify, access to the technologies that write the world, access to the instruments for enforcing meanings is a crucial battleground. Information technologies map the social when they inscribe fine-grained, overlapping differences of age, gender, income, occupation, and race, determining what experiences are shared, who is connected to whom, who is excluded, and on what basis. Predictive models are used to devise series of tests, defining their target customers not just by demographic characteristics but also by complex clusters of actual purchasing behavior, inscribing social differences into the models that direct consumer behavior and shape the meanings attributed to the imagined communities that center around consumer products. Capitalism carves up society, atomizing and splintering the social world in order to unify, individualizing differences in order to totalize a global logic (Gandy, 1993). How is the responsibility in constructing these boundaries to be assigned?

Dick Hebdige (1979) analyzed intensive forms of "lifestyle research" designed to offer a "social map of desire" that cut across traditional socioeconomic polarities to constitute in their place a new version of "the social." The topography of consumption is increasingly identified as (and thus expands to stand in for) the map of the social. Complex, individualized, capital- and expertise-intensive communication technologies are fundamental to the eradication of public life for everyone. The chance to engage freely, openly, and equally in the dialogue that shapes our understanding of ourself, our values, and our world is circumvented and replaced by new circuits of discourse. When our social roles are formed not through a process of dialogue and negotiation, but instead are imposed through prestructured, hierarchical, bureaucratic mechanisms, this is manipulation in a deep sense.

Specialization in the design, manufacture, and distribution of goods and services serves to diminish the knowledge held in common across individuals within a society. Consumers have limited contact with intermediaries in financial, administrative, insurance, and testing personnel of corporations. Individuals possess neither a thorough understanding of these roles, nor the ability to judge their performance; indeed they may be unaware of the very existence of these intermediaries. Important aspects shaping our lives are opaque, outside the exercise of our control or consent.

We can no longer look back on a nostalgic golden age or a community untouched by "progress." Information capitalism, the specialized global division of labor, and a highly mediated environment collapse traditional distinctions between public and private, product and image, intimate and strange, mass and personal, voluntary and imposed. It is the purpose of this chapter to track down, explore, and examine some of the linkages, interconnections, and data flows that constitute the web of relations in an era of flexible production and information capitalism. Jonathon Crary (1994) argues that by eliding the distinction between "interactivity" and "shopping," it becomes impossible to distinguish effective resistance from alternate fashions of consumption. It is only by making the representations and laboratories constructed by concentrated powers less opaque and more open to joint creation that such distinctions may retain any sense of relevance.

TOWARD A REVITALIZED PUBLIC SPHERE: DECODING THE WIRING DIAGRAM

I have identified some of the ways that computer/communication technologies serve as mechanisms and conduits through which the prerogatives of money and power come to shape individuals, limit autonomy, and dominate societal conceptions of the good society. A society that allows the free reign of market imperatives to shape the public debate is confusing the means to an end with the end itself. In many circumstances, markets foster the efficient allocation of resources and the satisfaction of preferences; however, like the ends and goals that determine what a society is about, preferences are assumed to be given, fixed, and outside the scope of the market mechanism.

If these values are allowed to shape the future development of computer/communication industries, there will be no public discussion as such. Large capital requirements, the economies of scale that exist in the media industry, and limited distribution channels are reducing the number of media conglomerates to a handful. These few media outlets could narrowly focus the information that is made available. Feedback cycles are being put in place. Individuals' responses, in terms of political attitudes, preferences, and purchasing behavior, are closely and automatically monitored, and the media content made available to them is refined and modified so that it is more likely to influence their behavior in ways useful to marketers and corporations.

MEANINGFUL PRIVACY POLICIES

Privacy policies are required not merely to control the release of sensitive or embarrassing personal information but because control over personal information is required for individual agency and control over social relationships. Computer/communication technologies create new webs of social relationships. Relationships are increasingly guided by the prerogatives of money and power. Unless an individual is aware of these relationships, and has control over the personal data that circulate within these webs, a one-sided, administered, instrumental rationality oriented toward the expansion of corporate imperatives will predominate.

In the United States, little regulatory protection is available for an individual attempting to maintain a level of control over the collection and dissemination of personal data. The Privacy Protection Act of 1974 controls only government access and use of personal information. The Federal Fair Credit Reporting Act regulates only credit information and is deeply flawed in several respects. This law allows credit agencies to share information with anyone it believes has a legitimate business need, which includes the creation of mailing lists and demographic databases marketed by these firms. Lack of funding over the past decade at the Federal Trade Commission, which enforces the law, has lead to a "regulatory meltdown." Albert Foer, an agency staffer, testified that "the agency can hardly survive" (quoted in Rothfelder, 1989, p. 76). In general, the U.S. government has relied on voluntary industry codes to prevent privacy abuses (Wilson, 1988). These codes require individuals to initiate enforcement proceedings and offer little in the way of civil penalties and criminal fines to deter violations.

Marketers face increasing economic pressure to identify and influence high-income consumers. The use of new technologies to create, analyze, and employ a torrent of personal data is one consequence of this pressure. The use of these data is presently constrained by two factors. The first is an economic calculation; is the benefit gained by the use of this technology greater than the investment required to implement it? The second is the sense on the part of consumers that some uses of these technologies are illegitimate and should be stopped. This diffuse sense is expressed on occasion in grass roots efforts of the kind mounted against Lotus and Equifax, which was successful in preventing the sale of Lotus Marketplace, a $695 CD-ROM containing credit and demographic information on 160 million U.S. citizens (Winner, 1991). Although such efforts are valuable, they offer individuals little control over the almost constant, day-to-day collection and exchange of personal data. The existing regulatory framework allows routine collection of data without the consent of the individual.

Although the Supreme Court recognizes that technology may prove increasingly intrusive, when it ruled that helicopter surveillance of property is acceptable, it signaled that a correspondingly reduced expectation of privacy was in order, not expanded set of legal protections. Without a general privacy protection in place, technological change can render laws tailored to specific cases obsolete. In such an environment an individual may know very little about the information that is collected. Even if concern does exist, no market or legal mechanisms are in place to allow individuals to retain effective control over personal information.

An adequate privacy protection safeguard requires adopting and enforcing the principle of informed consent. Gary Marx (1991) outlined five elements needed to embody this principle: (a) the existence of the data-collecting system itself should never be kept secret, (b) individuals must have a way of discovering what information about them is collected and how it is used, (c) information can be transferred between companies only on consent of the individual, and (d) a process must be put in place to correct/amend invalid data, and (e) organizations must be held responsible and accountable for the accuracy and distribution of the information they collect. These principles would adequately inform individuals about the particular data that is collected to mark and categorize them.

An extension of these principles is needed. Informed consent requires not merely the knowledge of the existence of data collection and the uses to which it is put, but also an understanding of the power of these uses. From the time the field began, communication theorists have debated the degree to which the media influence the behavior of individuals. The controversy continues in part because empirical tests of their theories require many control groups, given the large number of variables that must be controlled for and the expensive collection of massive amounts of data. The same technologies used by marketers hold the answers to some of these questions. The expert systems and single-source databases described in this chapter allow advertisers to determine the relative effectiveness that different marketing approaches have in modifying consumers' behavior. Access to this information would allow consumers' informed consent to be meaningful. Consumers would not only be aware of the collection of personal data, they would also be aware of the extent to which uses of these data are shaping their behavior.

CONCLUSIONS

To establish a truly reciprocal relationship between individuals and corporations, the data collected by corporations should be considered a social good. The use of standard access protocols and cheaper and more widely available communication technologies would allow individuals to have as much exposure to corporations as corporations have exposure to individuals. Countries such as Austria, Sweden, and Germany are already expanding the concept of civil rights so that they apply to corporations that have evolved a public role and character (Warren, 1989). This reinterpretation is required to achieve Jurgen Habermas's (1987) call for an extension of "the order of publicity" from the "organs of government to every active, state-related organization" (p. 256).

A federal data review board would be required to implement and enforce effective privacy legislation. Despite the existence of regulations, they would merely serve to legitimate privacy violations if enforcement mechanisms are not put in place. Such experiences demonstrate the need for strong agency enforcement efforts, including adequate funding, elimination of routine use loopholes, consumer access to files that are collected, and statutory damages sufficient to deter abuses. Corporations have argued that these restrictions would be impractical, and that the notification of individuals would be overburdensome. This is an odd way of looking at the problem; if notification is burdensome for the corporations that collect personal data, it must be nearly impossible for individuals to establish control over this data collection, given that they may be unaware of even the existence of data collection. In fact, there are practical solutions. Information system developers should follow design principles that would limit the amount of personal data collected to the minimum required for billing. Stung by public pressure, and concerned about the direction of future legislation, Equifax is already developing consensual databases, containing only information gathered about individuals who have been notified and have consented to the collection of information.

Most European countries already have in place much stricter privacy protection, and the European Economic Commission is developing privacy regulations that would regulate Europe as a whole. The Digital Services Data Protection Directive most likely will require that all marketing databases be registered with the commission, that consumers be notified specifically about what data are to be collected and how they are to be used, and that consumers be renotified if the uses are changed or expanded. The European initiative could create an incentive for the United States to adopt an equivalent standard. Under the European directive, countries without privacy protection in place are considered data havens, and individual data cannot be transferred to these countries. Given the rise of foreign trade, and the difficulties involved in separating the data and complying with two sets of restrictions, tighter U.S. privacy protection may become more palatable to multinational corporations.

The most threatening uses of computer/communication technologies are still only potential uses. These technologies are not yet entrenched, although we are quickly moving toward a society in which more interaction is electronically mediated, hence, potentially more selected, monitored, and targeted. Experience with grass roots activism, the pressure put on TRW, the elimination of Lotus Marketplace, and polling data all demonstrate that public concerns about the uses of personal information are felt and widespread. Now is the time to begin a rich, participatory public debate about the norms and values that shape and direct these technologies. Perhaps policies may be put in place to enhance openness, autonomy, and freedom before these technologies are further designed, implemented, and entrenched in our society.

REFERENCES

Adams, P.C. (1992). Television as gathering place. *Annals of American Geographers, 82*(1), 117-135

Berland, J. (1992). Angels dancing: Cultural technologies and the production of space. In L. Grossberg, C. Nelson, & P. Treichler (Eds.), *Cultural studies* (pp. 38-50). New York: Routledge.

Bessen, J. (1993, September-October). Riding the marketing wave. *Harvard Business Review*, 150-160.

Betts, M. (1990, March). Romancing the segment of one. *Computer World*, pp. 63-64.

Buskirk, M. (1992). Commodification as censor: Copyrights and fair use. *October*, 83-109.

Cerulo, K.A., Ruane, J.M., & Chayko, M. (1992, February). Technological ties that bind: Media-generated primary groups. *Communication Research*, pp. 109-129.

Client side state-HTTP cookies. (1977, February 1). http://home.netscape.com/newsref/std/cookie_spec.html.

Collis, D.J. (1993, September/October). Corporate strategy. *Harvard Business Review*, 46-47.

Crary, J. (1994, February). Critical reflections. *Artforum*, pp. 58-103.

Free, V. (1988, June). The marketing war gets automated. *Marketing Communications*, pp. 40-45.

Gandy, O.H. (1993). *The panoptic sort: A political economy of personal information.* Boulder, CO: Westview Press.

Giddens, A. (1990). *Consequences of modernity.* Stanford: Stanford University Press.

Gracey v. Maddin. (1989). 769 SW 2nd 477.

Habermas, J. (1987). *The theory of communicative action: Vol. Two. Lifeworld and system: A critique of functionalist reason* (T. McCarthy, trans.). Boston: Beacon Press.

Hansell, S. (1994, September 4). *An end to nightmare of cash.* The *New York Times*, p. D5.

Haraway, D. (1990). A manifesto for cyborgs: Science technology and socialist feminism in the 1980s. In L.J. Nicholson (Ed.), *Feminism/postmodernism* (pp. 190-223). New York: Routledge.

Hebdige, D. (1979). *Subculture: The meaning of style.* New York: Routledge.

Hennion, A., & Meadel, C. (1994). The artisans of desire: The mediation of advertising between product and consumer. *Sociological Theory*, 191-223.

Jameson, F. (1991). *Postmodernism.* Durham, NC: Duke University Press.

Kellner, D. (1990). *Television and the crisis of democracy.* Boulder, CO: Westview Press.

Leps, M-C. (1990). Crossdisciplinary inquiry in the information age. *Social Epistemology*, 4(3), 281-291.

Lyotard, J-F. (1984). *The postmodern condition: A report on knowledge.* Minneapolis: University of Minnesota Press.

The Martin Luther King, Jr. Center for Social Change, Inc.; Mrs. Coretta Scott King, Administratrix of the Estate of Dr. Martin Luther King, Jr., Deceased; and Motown Record Corp. v American Heritage Products, Inc.; B & S Sales, Inc., a/k/a B & S Sales; and James E. Bolen and James F. Bolen, 508 F. Supp. 854; 1981 U.S. DIst. LEXIS 12147; 213 U.S.P.Q. (BNA) 540 (1981).

Marx, G. (1991, Winter). Privacy and technology. *Whole Earth Review*, 78-84.

Miller, M.W. (1990, December 26). Coming soon to your local video store: Big brother. *Wall Street Journal*, p. 9.

Rosemont Enters., Inc. v. Random House, Inc. (1968). 58 Mis. 2d.

Rothfelder, J. (1989, September 4). Is nothing private? *Business Week*, p. 76.

Sack, R.D. (1992). *Place, modernity and the consumer's world.* Baltimore: Johns Hopkins Press.

Shibley v. Time Inc. (1974). 40 Ohio Misc. 51.

Slywotzky, A.J., & Shapiro, B.P. (1993, September-October). Leveraging to beat the odds: The new marketing mind-set. *Harvard Business Review*, pp. 97-107.

Tomlinson, D.E., & Harris, C.R. (1994). Free-lance photojournalism in a digital world: Copyright, Lanham Act and Droit moral considerations plus a sui generis solution. *Federal Communications Law Journal, 45*(1), 1-61.

Vattimo, G. (1992). *The transparent society* (D. Webb, Trans.). Baltimore: Johns Hopkins University Press.

Warren, M. (1989, November). Liberal constitutionalism as ideology: Marx v. Haberman. *Political Theory*, 31-60.

Wilson, K. (1988). *Technologies of control.* Madison: University of Wisconsin Press.

Wilson, L. (1993, May 3). Getting a read on the customer. *Informationweek*, pp. 22-26.

Winner, L. (1991, May/June). A victory for computer populism. *Technology Review*, 31-60.

14

SELLING ON, NOT OUT, THE INTERNET

DAVID F. DONNELLY

David Donnelly examines the commercialization of the Internet and considers the implications of the advertising applications of the Net. After noting the history of advertising on other media and the unique attributes of the Internet context, the chapter examines new marketing and promotion techniques available on the Net. The author suggests a set of safeguards that may avoid negative consequences of increased commercialization of the Net.

> It is inconceivable that we should allow so great a possibility for service, for news, for entertainment, for education, to be drowned in advertising chatter.

So spoke Secretary of Commerce Herbert Hoover in 1922, commenting on the uses to which the new broadcasting medium radio might be put. Today computer-mediated communication similarly is in its early stages of development, and much the same thing is being said by early users of the Internet—that global interconnection of networks offers great promise for the future.

The onslaught of commercial activity threatens the vitality and nature of this new mode of communication. Given the momentum behind such commercialization, and the enormous public benefits at risk, the implications of current and future commercialization demand immediate exploration.

The way a new communication medium develops and evolves is a complex process that includes technological, social, economic, and regulatory forces. These forces interact, pushing and pulling an innovation into obsolescence or maturity. In the United States, this interaction is strongly influenced by a media philosophy that favors private ownership and commercial exploitation. The development of U.S. media, therefore, is not completely unpredictable, as the process is controlled by profit-driven entities with predictable objectives and desires. Although individual media are unique and their fate not ultimately predetermined, this reliance on commercialization and privatization helps direct U.S. media down a very specific path. Computer-mediated communication is the latest communication medium to enter this process of development.

In the United States, the Internet is no longer the sole domain of an elite group of researchers and scientists. The Internet has attracted great interest in the private sector. It is now widely employed by profit-driven organizations as yet another tool of commerce. The commercial applications of the Internet continue to multiply as corporations and individuals in the pursuit of profits have found new ways to sell, market, promote, and advertise goods and services via the Internet. Given the rapid expansion and significance of this recent commercialization, there are some important issues that require immediate exploration:

1. What might be the effect of this growing commercialization?
2. How will it impact the development and direction of the Internet?
3. Can the Internet be protected against the possible negative effects of excessive commercialization?
4. Will computer-mediated communication follow the well-traveled path of previous media, or is it somehow inherently or fundamentally different?
5. If overcommercialization refers to a situation in which the primary usage of a medium heavily favors the private interests of profit-driven corporations, to what degree will that situation obtain for the Internet?

This chapter addresses these questions and finds both reason for concern and cause for action. If proactive measures are taken fairly soon, many of the negative consequences of overcommercialization may be avoided. This essay concludes with a set of suggested policies and safeguards that would alleviate some of the negative impacts. These safeguards would serve to protect the integrity of the online communications and help ensure that unprofitable yet important and beneficial uses of this new form of communication do not get "drowned in advertising chatter."

AND NOW "U.S. MASS MEDIA" BROUGHT TO YOU BY . . .

Unlike many nations, the media philosophy in the United States reflects a long-standing belief that "the media" and "the government" should remain distinct. Moreover, private ownership of media outlets is reflective of an economic philosophy favoring free enterprise. Although there exists a system of public broadcasting, it is fragile, constantly under attack, and increasingly dependent on private-sector funding. Thus, media in the United States are almost exclusively privately owned and controlled.

This reliance on private ownership and free enterprise is also based on a belief that competition in the media industries will produce a diversity of resources and information—a marketplace of ideas. This objective is frequently compromised, however, as media organizations tend to eliminate competition through consolidation and mergers to achieve greater economic efficiency. When a medium is young, there are many small, independent players. As it matures, there is increasing consolidation. Historically, such concentration has been followed by government antitrust action aimed at stemming such monopolization or oligopolization (for example: the Motion Pictures Patent Corporation or "the Trust" case, the Paramount decision, the splitting up of NBC and of the creation of ABC, the Modified Final Judgment and the split up of AT&T).

Recently, concentration of ownership has increased with considerable consolidation within and across media industries. Through horizontal and vertical integration, mergers, joint ventures, and buyouts, media behemoths are growing to unprecedented proportions, not merely in the United States but worldwide. Ironically, while consolidation has been on the rise, antitrust intervention has receded. There has been a shift to encouraging competition on a global rather than a national scale and to promoting large, strong, and secure U.S.-based companies. As the Internet represents new unconquered territory for these expanding entities, corporate consolidation and government deregulation are important contextual factors that promise to have a major influence on the development of the Internet within the United States and elsewhere.

Big or small, owners of U.S. media for the most part are permitted to employ whatever strategy they choose to generate revenue. The sale of "space and time" to other companies for advertising purposes has proven to be an effective means of generating generous profit margins for owners. Although not all U.S. media are supported by advertising, many are. Indeed, the line between those few media that are and those that are not has become blurred. Even the book publishing industry has sometimes resorted to an occasional advertising insert. The motion picture industry has also turned to nontraditional ways of supplementing the revenue generated by individual ticket sales. Commercials have made their way into U.S. theaters; on occasion they precede a feature released on a videotape. Indirectly, they appear in the subtle guise of take-home toys accompanying children's fast food.

The history of U.S. media illustrates a parallel growth and increasing interdependence of the media and advertising industries. Newspapers in early colonial America were produced by printers, not journalists, and many even acknowledged the predominance of advertising by including the word in their names (Hiebert, Ungurait, & Bohn, 1991). Even the text of the Declaration of Independence, published in the July 6, 1776 edition of the *Pennsylvania Evening Post*, appeared alongside advertisements (Hiebert et al., 1991). The Penny Press in the 1830s, an idea that made newspapers an affordable mass medium, was driven by the then innovative strategy to increase circulation to attract sufficient advertising dollars to replace the money lost through the lower individual sales costs.

In the early days of broadcasting, the radio industry relied on sales of radio receivers as a primary source of revenue. As receiver penetration levels increased, this source of revenue began to dissipate. At the same time, audiences became more discerning, leading to increased production costs. The debate over radio advertising alluded to in the opening passage was short-lived. Advertising quickly became the accepted means of financial support for radio stations and networks. By the time television arrived, broadcasting had been heavily commercialized, and the same organizations that had profited handsomely in radio quickly moved into television, bringing with them their established system of commercial support. The pervasive commercial interruption became a staple of broadcasting content.

The rhetoric that surrounded the expansion of cable television in the 1970s promised a transformation of television and was based on the belief that it would provide an electronic forum that was both diverse and open to the public. Such optimism proved to be unwarranted. Public access channels have sat underfunded, underutilized, and generally unwatched, and the new channel capacity did more to increase the quantity of television than it did to improve the quality. From an advertising perspective, however, cable offered a clear advantage: It delivered targeted and prepackaged audiences.

How has this reliance on advertising revenue affected the direction, development, and uses of existing media? Although it would be impossible to answer this question precisely, several broad generalizations can be offered. It should be conceded that advertising has affected U.S. media in several positive ways. For example, the sale of advertising time and space has helped to lower or eliminate the direct cost of information and entertainment to the consumer. By subsidizing costs, advertising has helped make the media more accessible. For example, "free" (advertiser-supported) television is universally available to all who own a television set. The U.S. system of advertising also supports an economic system based upon the promotion of competing goods in a marketplace.

The money generated by advertising revenues has also benefited the media by enabling the production of high-quality content. Ironically, it can also be argued that the increasing reliance on advertising has lowered the quality of media-delivered information and entertainment in several ways. In a hierarchy of artistic value, media that are dependent on advertising are placed several notches below those that are not advertising-dependent, that is, film and literature. With most advertiser-supported media, the emphasis traditionally has been placed on quantity of audience rather than quality of product, and these two do not always go hand in hand.

In serving two sets of masters—advertisers and consumers— media organizations often have placed their own interest in profits over the public interest. By providing a supportive environment conducive to the insertion of sales pitches, owners repeatedly have compromised the quality of media content. Perhaps the most concise and compelling summation was offered by Gloria Steinem (1990) in explaining the decision to hike the individual copy costs of *Ms.* magazine and publish sans advertisements. In sum, the optimism that has surrounded the early years of all U.S. media has been quashed by the negative influence of commercialism.

CYBERBUCKS AND ELECTRONIC ADVERTISING

The origins of the Internet have been recorded in many places by many people (see, e.g., gopher://gopher.isoc.org/11/internet/history). These historical treatises tell of a technology that began as a system designed by and for a select group of somewhat homogeneous early users. Developed originally as a vehicle to communicate and exchange information for noncommercial purposes—primarily defense-oriented, scientific, and research data—it was not long before additional applications were found for this new "network of networks."

It is hard to document the very first time the Internet was used to sell a good or service. However, one particularly offensive commercial message stands out as mobilizing opposition of Internet users. In 1994, two Arizona-based lawyers, Lawrence Canter and Martha Siegel, posted a message advertising their legal services aiding applicants for the U.S. government green card lottery throughout the Usenet. The Usenet is basically a giant collection of electronic discussion groups. It is available through the Internet, sometimes confused with the Internet, but merely an application riding on the Internet.[1] Though this commercial activity was not illegal, it came as a surprise to many Usenet users and violated an unwritten consensual community code.

Although others followed Canter and Siegel,[2] there was no immediate onslaught of commercial pitches on the Internet. The text-only format of the Net had limited appeal for advertisers, and the early Net population was not terribly alluring demographically. Recently, however, the growth of the World Wide Web has prompted an enormous increase in commercial traffic. The Web provides companies with a glitzy multimedia format, and it has also attracted countless new users to the Internet. Because of the popularity of the Web, the Internet population has grown considerably. As of January 12, 1996, there were an estimated 46,523,158 people on the Internet (for a more up-to-date estimate, see http://www.netree. com/netbin/internetstats). Many different commercial applications of the Net have appeared. Advertising, both blatant and disguised, marketing, product promotion, and direct sales are but a few of the more prevalent forms of commercial activity. Many businesses exploiting the commercial applications of the Net have found the experience to be worthwhile and financially rewarding (see, e.g., ActivMedia's report summarized at http://www.activmedia.com/ Trends.html).

THE NET AND OVERCOMMERCIALIZATION: THREATENED OR IMMUNE?

To determine the future impact of this growing commercialization, one needs to understand the nature of the Internet itself. Such an examination will help determine the degree to which it is immune from or threatened by overcommercialization.

The "lexicon of cyberspace" offered by Steven Klines offers a set of descriptors defining the Internet as free, egalitarian, decentralized, peer-to-peer, experimental, autonomous, and anarchic. To assess the accuracy of this characterization, each descriptor is addressed individually.

"The Internet is Free"

The word *free* has several connotations. The most common are "cost-free" and "free from regulations and controls." Anyone who characterizes the Net as cost-free must have their access subsidized. For example, many academics can surf cyberspace from their offices, unaware of the source of funds used to compensate for their use. Residential users, surfing cyberspace from their homes, are reminded when they pay their bills every month that it is not an entirely free service. Posting of information, even advertising, is comparatively inexpensive, but with indirect costs; it is not totally free either. Most of the information itself is currently available for free, but this will likely change as copyright holders seek compensation for their work. In terms of regulations and controls, the Internet has been relatively unencumbered, but this is changing, especially in the area of content regulation. The Communication Decency Act provides perhaps the most flagrant example of such attempted regulation.

"The Internet is Egalitarian"

For some, life on the Internet seems blissfully democratic and egalitarian. For others, many of the same sort of inequities that exist in real life are mirrored in cyberspace. Doubters might like to consult with women who experience the same sort of discriminatory harassment and inequities online as they do in face-to-face interaction (see, e.g., http://www.voyagerco.com/gg/internetposter.html). Access to the Net world is not available in any sort of equal or egalitarian fashion. The largest gaps are socioeconomic and are even more glaring on the international level (see http://info.isoc.org:80/images/mapv14.gif; see also http://www.hfac.uh.edu/Media Futures/Gap.html).

"The Internet is Decentralized"

Computer networking generally facilitates decentralization. For example, networks have helped to decentralize work (i.e., telecommuting) and education (distance education). In terms of organizational structure, many firms now favor horizontal arrangements over vertical hierarchies. Networks do not indiscriminately and universally decentralize; they do centralize certain activities. This is one of the paradoxes of technology that explains why people can look at the same thing but arrive at differing conclusions (see Donnelly, 1995).

"The Internet is a Peer-to-Peer Means of Communicating"

Despite the intent of the designers that the Internet be used to access mainframe computers for professional and research purposes, the initial popularity became more personal in nature, primarily in the form of mail, discussion groups, and home-grown Web pages. Such material is now being supplemented by a flood of nonpersonal information. An enormous amount of material is posted by large, impersonal organizations and is accessed by a heterogeneous group of browsers. The Net still serves as a one-on-one form of communication, but it is also a one-to-many and many-to-many medium. Characterizing it solely as a peer-to-peer vehicle is inadequate.

"The Internet is Experimental"

The Internet, like all young media, is indeed experimental. Early Net users even bear a strong resemblance to pioneering radio amateurs. Several characteristics of the current experimental work on the technology of the Internet, however, are worth noting. A great deal of this experimentation is being driven by private interests that expect commercial returns on their investment. This experimentation will also make the Net more like other media in terms of the material it can handle (audio, moving video, etc.) and, therefore, a more attractive vehicle for commercial applications.

"The Net is Autonomous"

At the present time, there is no centralized control of the Internet. One does not need permission to post information on the Internet, and there is no single controlling government agency overseeing it. One does, however, need an access provider who establishes rules and regulations for users employing its technical capabilities. However, as public concern mounts over such freedom of expression and as corporations begin to battle over this new media territory, the autonomous nature of the Internet will certainly be partially compromised.

"The Net is an Anarchy"

Although the Internet does resemble a wild and free frontier in many respects, even those who use the word *anarchy* contradict themselves by also insisting on adherence to netiquette—a form of self imposed regulation. As more users and more money becomes involved, the anarchy will likely disappear as civilization in cyberspace arrives online (see, e.g., the paper by Spar & Bussgang, 1996, "Ruling Commerce in the Networld").

In summary, these descriptors offer a questionable and incomplete characterization of the Internet in its present form and an even less accurate characterization of what the Internet will look like in the near future. Other terms have been offered to distinguish the Internet from other media. Many people have pointed out that the Internet is unique because it is a highly interactive medium. Many applications of, or places on, the Net are highly interactive. This sense of participation has helped popularize the metaphor "cybercommunity." Reading or sending e-mail, for example, is a personal and interactive activity. Discussion groups are a forum for dialogue, though there are often more lurkers than posters. In other applications, interactivity is limited to locating specific information. Net browsing is akin to channel grazing via the remote control, and most of the future activity on the Net will consist of this clicking around. The Internet is fast becoming, like other media, a place where most of the information exchanged is provided by producers and consumed by consumers.

The Internet is also characterized as unique because it is global in nature. The Internet does connect different national infrastructures, providing a somewhat seamless network enabling users to transmit and exchange material easily and cheaply across national boundaries. This phenomenon is unique and the basis for some "jurisdictional quandaries" for the legal community (see Branscomb, 1994). Legal jurisdictional differences aside, however, it should be noted that a great deal of other media material (i.e., television programs, recordings, films) is provided by and consumed by people separated by vast geographic distances. Hence, many media are built around global distribution infrastructures.

The feeling that the Internet is seamless and ubiquitous, unrestricted by geography, has prompted the overuse of another descriptor: cyberspace. Such a term posits online communication not as a thing, but as an intangible gathering place. What gets lost in the overuse of this metaphor is that such transactions take place within a specific context, be it the school room, the office, the bedroom, and within a specific nation.

Public concern over the distribution of questionable material illustrates that online transactions are not entirely removed from the real world. When compared to other media, the Internet is an interesting phenomenon because it is both like and unlike existing communication technologies. It is part telephone, computer, printing press, bulletin board, brochure, mail order catalog. Soon it will possess many of the qualities of radios and televisions. Although such a hybrid is truly unprecedented, such overlap also makes it difficult to distinguish it as a radically new phenomenon.

The metaphors shape the way the users see the Internet. Much of the Internet community sees this medium as truly unique. In misunderstanding the nature of online communication, many users of the Internet have become complacent about the threat of commercialization.

For a more complete understanding of what online communication offers, it is helpful to reexamine the electronic environment from the perspective of advertisers. From their perspective, the Internet, and especially the World Wide Web, offers a new and different means of reaching potential consumers. Compared to other media, it has numerous advantages. It is cheaper. It can provide a direct link between a company and a consumer in ways that the media cannot. A wealth of information can be supplied. Audiences often come prepackaged around specific interests, or they come directly to the advertisers. The World Wide Web is not the perfect vehicle for marketing and advertising, but it is extremely well suited to some applications. In the end, the advantages make it an alluring and highly attractive vehicle for advertisers and commercial applications.

Given the antipathy of pioneer users of the Internet to advertising and the potential for exploitation by commercial interests now turning to online communications in great numbers, there is a potential for conflict that needs to be resolved so that the values of the pioneers might be preserved while still accommodating the needs of the new arrivals.

PROTECTING ONLINE COMMUNICATIONS FROM OVERCOMMERCIALIZATION

Identifying a potential problem is relatively easy compared to reaching consensus concerning its resolution. Typically problems are resolved though a group process of debate based on proposals articulated and offered by individuals, who best serve as discussion prodders. Thus qualified, there follows some specific problem areas along with solutions offered for debate.

There are numerous potential dangers that need to be monitored and protected by establishing formal safeguards. The following addresses two of the most pressing dangers: the possibility that commercial traffic will drown out public speech and limit the prosocial benefits of a much needed public forum, and the possibility that commercialization will contribute to an erosion of the privacy rights of Net users.

It would be futile to attempt to stop advertising and commercial activity on the Internet. Advertising and commercialization should not be allowed to run rampant, however, to the detriment of noncommercial applications. The Net world offers vast areas, not just one cyberspace. Technically, it may be divided into different cyberspaces—some areas in which advertising and commercial traffic is acceptable and some areas in which it is not.

In the "real world" we have attempted to set aside areas in which advertising is taboo or discouraged, but our attempts have been ineffectual, and we have become increasingly tolerant of the encroachment of advertising into many public and private spaces.[3] We must try and ensure that the demarcations drawn in the networld are more resilient. For starters, we must ensure that our electronic mailboxes do not become the overstuffed repositories of unsolicited junk mail that our sidewalk mailboxes have become.

Although few people seem to like junk mail, advertisers argue that it is an inexpensive and proven means of effectively relaying a message to potential consumers. In areas in which people pay to have their trash removed by the pound, however, it is more than a mere nuisance; people are paying for something that they did not seek and do not want. There is little legal control over the nature or the amount of commercial material that may be delivered into mailboxes. To prevent a similar loss of control over online communication, clear and enforceable lines need to be established placing electronic mailboxes off limits to unsolicited commercial solicitation. From a legal perspective, this issue is complicated as it involves privacy issues as well as First Amendment issues, both extremely murky legal areas. Nonetheless, an individual's rights to the sanctity of this private space should be preserved. A total ban on junk e-mail is unnecessary, for some might opt to receive it. Such an option might in fact help subsidize online access for individuals so inclined. For example, those who make their e-mail boxes available to commercial traffic could do so in exchange for reduced rates. Recipients, however, should not have to pay extra to stop unsolicited commercial e-mail, nor be required to take action to opt not to receive it.[4]

The informal delineation of cyberspaces has already begun by users conveying the attitude that the Usenet is off limits to sales pitches. Guidelines have been set by netizens who have devised their own methods of enforcement and punishment. These techniques include boycotts, placement on an actual blacklist of Internet advertisers, engaging in fake e-mail dialogs, and cancelbots (for more information, see the Blacklist of Internet Advertisers at

http://www.cco.caltech.edu/~cbrown/BL/#what). The effectiveness
of such harassment and self-enforcement is not clear. Although
violators like Siegel and Canter dismiss such efforts as ineffective
"objections from the same tired few" (see their interview with .Net
magazine at http://www.futurenet.co.uk/netmag/Features/
CnS/CnS.html [registration is required]), such comments could be a
ploy to discourage further harassment. Such threats of retaliation
have likely deterred some potential advertisers. Advertisers will not
find it good business to alienate potential customers. The real test of
such enforcement powers is fast approaching as a greater number of
potential violators come online, and the pioneers who have
established the informal rule may be overwhelmed by new users.

In the end, clever cyberpranks and technoterrorism targeted
at violators may prove counterproductive, because they might be
interpreted as violations of the rights of the advertisers. Influencing
public opinion will be critical in establishing the broad-based
support necessary to civilize cyberspace. Software designers as well
as lawyers need to join forces with concerned users to establish
consensual protocols for acceptable practices. In determining such
practices, legal scholars would be especially useful as allies and
"could engage in a useful public service if they would concentrate on
defining these emerging legal boundaries rather than criticizing and
rejecting the meager legal structures that currently exist"
(Branscomb, 1995, p. 1673).

Establishing ad-free zones in the Net world and presentation of
advertisements in an unobtrusive manner may accommodate the
needs of users for autonomy over their own cyberspaces while
facilitating online advertising. The prevalent mode of advertising on the
Web, the clickable logo/link, provides a relatively benign means of
conveying a commercial message. The information is physically
unobtrusive, empowering consumers by giving them the option to click
if they so desire.

Advertising may soon appear before the selected page loads,
thus interrupting the content flow a lá the broadcasting model. Aural
sales pitches may appear during browsing. With more live events
appearing on the web, users may be inundated with commercial
interruptions (i.e., "We'll be right back after this brief download from
Netscape . . . "). The possibilities are alluring for advertisers, and
disturbing for many users. Influencing how advertisements appear is
an even more challenging task than trying to regulate where they will
be permitted. Curbing unacceptable practices will depend on
cultivating an ethos and ultimately a cyberlaw derived through a
consensual process involving both users and advertisers.

As advertisers begin investing greater resources in online
advertising as a vehicle to reach potential buyers, they will want

more information about who is seeing or reading what. The medium is built around an interactive terminal designed for entering data, a means of readily transmitting information, and a built-in computerized method of storing and interpreting data and could potentially provide the most effective and reliable audience measurement tool ever devised. What would be a tremendous gain for advertisers, however, would entail a considerable loss for consumers. Such a quest for information threatens both autonomy and anonymity and needs to be kept in check. It is important to reserve the option to not give away personal information without being informed how it will be used. Perhaps some will wish to cash in on the economic value of personal information and trade it for desired and expensive online content.

Whatever rules and laws are established, they will only be effective if they are enforceable. Without a manageable enforcement strategy, commercialization of online communication will run rampant. Such enforcement needs to be a shared responsibility. Although pioneer netizens are wary of any sort of government intervention, only the government has the clout to threaten legal enforcement. As many government agencies are undergoing budget cuts and downsizing, additional responsibilities are unwelcome. Moreover, the sheer volume of traffic and the privacy issues surrounding the monitoring of messages would make it impossible and inappropriate for a government agency to handle all the enforcement duties. Besides, not all the rules would be legally enforceable laws and under government jurisdiction.

Enforcement and monitoring duties need to be shared. An organization maintained in a cooperative effort involving private and nonprofit entities could be established online as a place where violations could be reported initially. Such a self-regulatory body, with a narrowly defined but widely agreed on charter addressing inappropriate commercial speech, would help police the Net world and empower cybercommunities by sharing the responsibility of control. Such empowerment will help to preserve the sense of community spirit or obligation that will make such enforcement manageable. Warnings to cease and desist a reported inappropriate activity could be issued by this group, and if applicable, repeat offenders could be reported to the federal government for legal action. Such filtering will help make the government's enforcement duties more manageable. The online enforcement activities need not be centralized. There can be numerous mirror sites. However, a tendency to decentralize may dissipate the effectiveness of the system. Some netizens would argue that widespread decentralization is preferable because it is more in keeping with the sort of decentralized anarchy they would like to encourage. However, it would undermine the strength of the rules, leave the impression that there is no single agreed on policy regarding commercialization, and weaken compliance by advertisers.

Informing all users of what is and is not acceptable with regard to commercial speech will make potential advertisers aware of the rules restricting their behavior, and it would help them realize that posting inappropriate commercial speech is not just violating the sensitivities of a few but disregarding the values of many.

Informing everyone of the rules governing commercial speech and how they will be enforced will be tricky, and we will need to solicit the support of access providers. Presently, there is a great deal of competition in the provider area. Inevitably, we will see a shakeout and consolidation in this business that will make it easier to elicit widespread cooperation from these critical players. Some sort of consensual agreement and uniformity should be sought in contracts signed by users seeking access to the Internet. This will also help to publicize established rules.

Publicizing established rules is an extremely important part of the enforcement process. It will be especially challenging as U.S. mass media, the major vehicle for information dissemination in U.S. society, are owned by private companies who have a future stake in the Net world, and who have traditionally disliked obligations, especially those that affect commercial speech. On the Internet, it is easy to relay information, but the glut that exists makes it almost impossible to convey a small body of important information to the majority of users. (Who ever reads the READ ME FIRST files anyway?) Hopefully, the debate over the establishment of such rules would be public enough to generate awareness of both the specific rules as well as the logic behind them.

Ultimately, what a democratic society requires is an information agora. The word agora comes to us from the Greek and refers to an open square or community gathering place where merchants gather to sell their goods and citizens come to exchange ideas. Although the existing media are effective at providing a place for advertisers to gather, they are less effective as open and vital public forums. Advertising dollars are finite. As some of this money is allocated to online communication, the traditional media may be even more willing to make concessions to attract those lost dollars back or they may place more of the economic burden on individual consumers by increasing their direct costs.

Add to this the fragile status of public broadcasting and the lax enforcement and possible elimination of the public interest, convenience and necessity broadcasting obligations, as well as the tendency to allow the marketplace to solve problems, and the situation appears to be deterioriating. More than ever an effective public forum is needed, not just within the United States, but worldwide. The Net world appears to be poised to provide such a global agora.

In sum, computer-mediated communication is not just a new technology. It is a collection of technologies as well as a new and important means of communicating. As a global medium, however, it still develops within different national contexts and is shaped by differing cultural values and varying media and economic philosophies. One can, therefore, think of its evolution both within specific national contexts, as well as on a global level. This chapter focused on the Internet as it is evolving within the United States.

The strength of a democratic society is based upon a vital and diverse communication system that ensures equitable access. Some netizens have seen the potential of the Internet as filling a huge public void left by market forces. These cyberleaders have spoken eloquently about the benefits of universal access, but less effectively about how such an objective could be achieved. Although providing equitable access to the infrastructure has remained elusive, that is only one step toward parity. There will always be some free information available on the Net, but its utility may be limited. The more useful and desirable information will be costly to collect, package, and post. The providers will undoubtedly and justifiably seek compensation. Some will be content paying for material, but others might prefer to see part of the burden shifted to advertisers. The beauty of online communication is its flexibility. Several varieties of presentations could appear; for example, "click here to pay for content sans advertisements," "click here for the advertisement supported version." Advertising, if unobtrusive and optional, could improve the accessibility, affordability, and utility of the content.

Advertising could become an ally in promoting the prosocial and democratic development of the Net world, but its potential to drown out beneficial uses and damage democratic governance must be recognized and curbed before its effects become irreversible. Users must recognize that they are not only consumers of online information but also netizens with responsibilities for self-government. How the new Net world will evolve will depend on how seriously netizens answer the call to action to mold the future in their collective public interest.

ACKNOWLEDGMENT

The author is indebted to the late Anne Branscomb for her comments on an earlier version.

ENDNOTES

1. For a lengthy clarification of the distinction, see http://www.fas. sfu.ca/cs/people/ResearchStaff/jamie/personal/use-inter.
2. For other examples, see the Blacklist of Internet Advertisers at http://www.cco.caltech.edu/~cbrown/BL/#list. The activity is prevalent enough to have earned a label "spamming." For more information on spamming and the related phenomenon velveeta, see http//www.cco.caltech.edu/~cbrown/BL/#spam.
3. For example, Whittle Communication's Channel One has brought advertising into U.S. public classrooms; public sporting and concert events frequently bear the name of a sponsor; the Empire State Building was recently illuminated in blue to advertise new blue M & Ms. Advertisements appear inside and outside U.S. public buses, and they appear inside some public bathroom stalls as well. On PBS, sponsorship acknowledgments have essentially turned into short commercials.
4. Such control might be based on the ability to block commercial messages that would depend on a clear scheme of coding messages. Such a coding system also can be a major asset in searching for information. In searching for specific information, individuals would be better equipped to block out commercial hits and cites if they so choose.

REFERENCES

Branscomb, A. (1995). Anonymity, autonomy, and accountability: Challenges to the First Amendment in cyberspaces. *The Yale Law Journal, 104*(7), 1639-1679.

Branscomb, A. (1994). Jurisdictional quandaries for global networks. In L. Harasim (Ed.), *Global networks: Computers and international communication* (pp. 83-103). Cambridge, MA: MIT Press.

Donnelly, D. (1995). *Studying communication technologies.* Unpublished manuscript.

Donnelly, D. (1996, June). Selling on, not out, the Internet. *Journal of Computer Mediated Communication, 2*(1). http:/www.usc. edu/dept/annenberg/vol2/issue1/

Hiebert, R., Ungurait, D., & Bohn, T. (1991). *Mass media VI.* New York: Longman.

Spar D., & Bussgang. J. (1996, June). Ruling commerce in the Networld. *Journal of Computer Mediated Communication, 2*(1). http:/www.usc. edu/dept/annenberg/vol2/issue1/

Steinem, G. (1990, July/August). Sex, lies & advertising. *Ms.,* pp. 18-28.

PART 4

PERSONAL LIABILITIES

15

CUBBY OR *STRATTON OAKMONT?*: DEFAMATORY SPEECH ON COMPUTER BULLETIN BOARDS

DALE A. HERBECK

There are more than 100,000 computer bulletin board systems currently operating in the United States. Referred to as "BBSs," these high-tech forums facilitate instantaneous communication by enabling anyone with a personal computer and a modem to "post" messages, read replies, engage in debates, chat casually, and share graphic images about topics ranging from politics, religion, and sex to recipes and sports. But just as the popularity of computer bulletin board systems is proliferating, so is the controversy surrounding their use. Increasingly, BBS operators are prescreening and censoring "controversial" speech posted on their boards. Such censorship has triggered a heated debate about the extent to which the First Amendment protects speech on BBSs. Dale Herbeck examines the extent to which the First Amendment should protect speech on computer bulletin board systems. This is done within the context of the controversy surrounding their use in Cubby v. Compuserve and Stratton Oakmont v. Prodigy. He argues that BBS users deserve the greatest level of free speech protection, thereby fostering free expression over this increasingly important medium of communication.

Early on the morning of Sunday, October 24, 1994, an anonymous message appeared on the "Money Talk" bulletin board of Prodigy Services Company. Referring to a Long Island-based broker, the posting said "THANK GOD! THE END OF STRATTON OAKMONT WILL FINALLY COME THIS WEEK!" The message continued, "This brokerage firm headed by president and soon to be proven criminal—Daniel Porush—will close this week." To document this claim, the posting offered the following circumstantial evidence: On Thursday, October 20, Stratton Oakmont had underwritten an initial public offering by the Solomon-Page Group, a recruiting and placement company. After the close of trading on Friday, October 21, Stratton Oakmont and Solomon-Page had jointly announced that Solomon-Page's biggest customer was leaving the company. The posting concluded, "THIS IS FRAUD, FRAUD, FRAUD, AND CRIMINAL!!!!!!!" (Frankel, 1995, p. 58).

The anonymous user posted additional messages over the weekend, and these postings remained on "Money Talk" for two weeks. Although Daniel Porush was not a Prodigy subscriber, he eventually learned of the postings and immediately brought a defamation action. Subsequent research by Prodigy revealed that the messages in question were posted from an account issued to David Lusby, a former employee of Prodigy. Lusby, who had departed from Prodigy in 1991, denied authorship of the postings. Because the messages were posted anonymously through a valid account, Prodigy found itself party to one of the first legal actions brought against a provider for defamatory speech posted on a computer bulletin board.

In an effort to expedite settlement on a $200 million claim for damages, counsel for Stratton Oakmont hastily moved for partial summary judgment on the question of whether Prodigy was a publisher, and thus liable for defamatory speech. If Prodigy was a publisher, Stratton Oakmont reasoned it would have a strong claim for damages. At the same time, if Prodigy was merely a distributor, Stratton Oakmont knew it would have a weak case as Prodigy could persuasively argue that it was not liable for the defamatory postings. Much to the surprise of many legal commentators (Haddad, 1995; Walker, 1995; Zitner, 1995), acting New York State Supreme Court Justice Stuart Ain decided that Prodigy was not a distributor. Because Prodigy used software to prescreen postings for obscenities and racial slurs, and because Prodigy had previously claimed to be a "family-oriented computer network," Ain held that Prodigy was exercising editorial control and could therefore be sued as the publisher of a defamatory posting.

In the months following Ain's ruling, Prodigy successfully negotiated a settlement with Stratton Oakmont based largely on the following public apology: "Prodigy is sorry if the offensive statements concerning Stratton and Mr. Porush, which were posted on Prodigy's

Money Talk bulletin board by an unauthorized and unidentified individual, in any way caused injury to their reputation" (Lewis, 1995, p. D1). As part of the settlement that produced the apology, Stratton Oakmont did not contest Prodigy's appeal of Judge Ain's earlier decision. Having resolved the defamation action, Prodigy asked Judge Ain to reconsider his holding that service providers were publishers. The judge refused, citing *Paramount Communications v. Gibraltar Casualty Co.* (1995), which held that "while we appreciate the desirability of settlement, we do not believe it would be advisable to allow private parties to demand that the Court eradicate precedent which they personally find unacceptable on threat of burdensome litigation should the Court refuse." The court found the reasoning in the original holding especially compelling as "this is a developing area of the law (in which it appears that the law has thus far not kept pace with the technology) so that there is a real need for some precedent" (*Stratton Oakmont v. Prodigy Services*, 1995).

Although *Stratton Oakmont v. Prodigy* has been resolved, the holding raises difficult First Amendment issues. Even if the precedent is narrowly limited to New York State, "its effect could reach far beyond the Empire State. For example, if a Prodigy customer in Memphis or Phoenix writes a libelous message about a person in New York, the New Yorker could sue Prodigy, and win" (Bray, 1995, p. 51). Moreover, the precedent creates the possibility that online services might be held responsible when subscribers use their bulletin boards to violate the rights of third parties. Furthermore, the opinion in Stratton Oakmont seems to contradict the leading case, *Cubby v. CompuServe* (1991). In that case, a federal court analogized CompuServe to a library or bookstore rather than a publisher. Accordingly, the court found that CompuServe could not be held legally responsible for defamatory speech an independent contractor had placed on "Rumorville, USA."

Given the conflict between these cases, and the seemingly limitless potential for defamation actions arising from speech on the Internet (Shields & Bowles, 1996), it seems both necessary and prudent to consider the extent to which the First Amendment should protect speech on computer bulletin boards. The first section of this chapter describes the general nature of computer bulletin board systems, and the second section outlines the controversy surrounding their use. The final section, in a very preliminary way, argues that the holding in Cubby is preferable to Stratton Oakmont. This essay concludes that commercial service providers are best conceived as distributors, and not publishers, and claims that such a view would protect freedom of speech on this increasingly important medium of communication.

COMPUTER BULLETIN BOARDS

In the "Findings of Fact" in the *ACLU v. Reno* (1996) decision, the court claimed "the Internet is not a physical or tangible entity, but rather a giant network which interconnects innumerable smaller groups of linked computer networks. It is thus a network of networks" (p. 830). Some of the computers and computer networks that comprise the Internet are owned by governmental institutions, others by nonprofit organizations, and others by business or private entities.

The Internet is able to support a variety of different methods of communication. Although the methods are constantly evolving, at present the most common forms include: one-to-one messaging (e-mail), one-to-many messaging (listservers), distributed message databases (bulletin boards), real time communication (Internet Relay Chat), real-time remote computer utilization (telnet), and remote information retrieval (World-Wide Web) (*ACLU v. Reno*, 1996, p. 834). Each form, it should be noted, raises its own set of issues. The courts are already considering questions involving indecency and obscenity, copyright and intellectual property, and fraudulent and unsolicited advertising. Even though all of these areas demand critical scrutiny, one of the most fundamental questions that must be addressed is whether commercial online services can be held liable for defamatory postings made by their subscribers (Sideritis, 1996). Before attempting to respond to this query, it is necessary to briefly characterize bulletin boards as a method of computer-mediated communication.

Distributed message databases, or computer bulletin boards, have been likened to backyard fences (Oldenburg, 1991), 18th century French salons (Barringer, 1990), convention centers (Oldenberg, 1991), college dormitory message boards (Silver, 1991), and electronic soapboxes (Jensen, 1987). "The advantage of a bulletin board is the rapid availability of information among those sharing a common interest" (Miranda, 1996, p. 232). Not surprisingly, "computer bulletin boards are rapidly becoming the forum in which society conducts debates on a variety of matters" (Weber, 1995, p. 239).

At a basic level, setting up a bulletin board system is a relatively simple and inexpensive endeavor. Establishing a bulletin board requires at least one computer with a capacity to store information, a "host" program that controls the computer, and a means through which to access and receive information via telephone or other communication lines. The baseline cost for establishing a useful board is approximately $1000, although the establishment of a large commercial service requires a considerably more substantial investment.

Using a computer bulletin board is even simpler than setting one up. To communicate on a computer bulletin board, a user merely needs a terminal connected to a modem and the information necessary to "log on" to the service—such as a phone number, a user name, and a private access code. Because most bulletin boards are designed to accommodate the general public, the procedure for gaining access has been simplified. A user simply turns on his or her computer and "calls" the bulletin board. The bulletin board automatically responds, thereby connecting the user's computer to the system's central computer. Once the two computers are linked, the user must affirmatively select and access a particular board on the system, from which the user can scan and read "posted" messages left by others, or "post" messages for other board users to read. Generally, users "post" messages for the entire community of board users, although it is possible to respond to a particular user.

The process of selecting which "posted" messages to read is very user directed. A typical bulletin board system is divided into major subject groupings, or individual boards, known as "newsgroups." In turn, depending on the system, each newsgroup may be divided by topic. Oftentimes postings have a subject line that allows users to discern which postings might be of special interest. To read a message, a user has to first select the newsgroup and then each note within the newsgroup that the user wishes to read. Typically, a user chooses a particular note by tabbing to a check box and typing an "X" next to the selected note heading.

Individuals may connect to computer bulletin boards through terminals that are directly linked to the computer network, or via a personal computer and a modem. Many individuals affiliated with colleges and universities gain access through their institution, and some corporations provide access for their employees. A limited number of local communities have established access to the Internet, and it is also possible to arrange for access through noncommercial Internet service providers. Individuals not otherwise able to obtain access to the Internet, or those wishing to have access to additional propriety resources, can easily arrange access through a commercial provider like America Online, CompuServe, Prodigy, Microsoft Network, or ZD Net. *The Electronic Information Report* ("EIR Monthly," 1996) observed that these services, the five largest, provided access to nearly 13.5 million subscribers in mid-June 1996, and the number of subscribers is increasing by more than 20% annually. Although the costs vary with the type of service, an account with any of the commercial providers offers relatively inexpensive Internet access for someone who owns a personal computer and a modem (Venditto, 1996).

THE CENSORSHIP CONTROVERSY

The instantaneous nature of communication on bulletin boards, coupled with low startup costs, ease of use, and minimal membership fees have all contributed to the increasing popularity of these systems. By one conservative estimate (Miller, 1996), there are approximately 60,000 bulletin boards in operation worldwide. "User-sponsored newsgroups," the court noted in *ACLU v. Reno* (1996), "are among the most popular and widespread applications of Internet services, and cover all imaginable topics of interest to users" (p. 834). There are newsgroups on more than thousands of different subjects including boards for political candidates, U.F.O. enthusiasts, Civil War buffs, those with alternative lifestyles, Fortune 500 executives, and even people who hate Barney the dinosaur. Given the diversity of boards available, it is not difficult to understand why tens of thousands of messages are posted daily.

Speech on computer bulletin boards is often rather raucous. In the relative anonymity of the home or office, many of the traditional inhibitions quickly disappear. The absence of a receiver sending instantaneous feedback to questionable or obnoxious expression eliminates cues that may encourage moderation. The sterility of the word on the computer screen makes it difficult to indicate satire or attempts at humor. So too, the absence of immediate rebuttal and the lack of reprisal empowers many normally well-mannered speakers to rhetorical excess. Finally, many bulletin boards allow users to use pseudonyms instead of their full names, offering the protection of anonymity. Even when names are used, the absence of addresses and the distance between speakers makes an actual physical confrontation extremely unlikely. The combination of these factors, coupled with the general absence of government regulation, has made computer bulletin boards a lively forum.

Not surprisingly, there is a growing amount of speech that might be considered defamatory on computer bulletin boards. In a case that has received national attention, a college student posted a message that accused a Maryland woman of mistreating her daughter and urged readers to call the family (Shields & Bowles, 1996). Although the family has not brought a defamation action, lawsuits have already been initiated based on speech posted on computer bulletin boards. In *Medphone v. DeNigris* (1992), a medical equipment company sued for defamatory statements on "Money Talk," the same bulletin board involved in Stratton Oakmont. Along the same lines, *Suarez Corp. v. Meeks* (1994) was the result of a particularly unflattering posting about the marketing practices of a direct mail company. In *It's in the Cards v. Meneau* (1995), a user of the SportsNet bulletin board sued another user for posting defamatory messages about a canceled business trip.

Although each of these instances involved an action brought against the speaker, Post (1995) noted that the possibility of anonymous or pseudo-anonymous postings makes it "easier to target the entities that provide access to the medium itself" (p. 116). The Carib Inn in the Antilles, for example, filed suit against America Online after an unknown subscriber reported that she had a scary experience on vacation when she arranged for a scuba lesson from an instructor who was "on drugs" (*Bowker v. America Online*, 1995). Similarly, a Connecticut woman recently initiated a defamation action against America Online because someone had posted a malicious biography that claimed she was a sex phone operator who also made lesbian pornographic films (Rosenkrantz, 1996).

Understandably, commercial online services are troubled by ·the possibility of being held responsible for someone else's defamatory speech. "One of the hottest topics in US corporate boardrooms is the liability of on-line service providers for the actions of their subscribers" (Band, 1996, p. 35). Although some operators have decided to leave their boards alone, others have responded by actively reviewing messages. One of the large commercial service providers, Prodigy, won a dubious reputation in the early 1990s for engaging in the most extensive screening and censoring of messages. To this end, Prodigy established guidelines to prohibit what it determines is, in its sole discretion, "offensive" material. Prodigy defined *offensive* as "grossly repugnant to community standards," and including "blatant expressions of bigotry, racism and hate." According to Prodigy, such standards preserve its "family-oriented" service by ensuring parents that their children can read anything posted on its boards.

Through a membership agreement, all Prodigy users were notified of these standards. To guard against abuses, however, Prodigy's central computer was programmed to enforce the standards and screen out certain "offensive" words. In addition, Prodigy employed "systems operators," or "SYSOPS," to review each message sent to a Prodigy board before posting the message for the public. These SYSOPS were empowered to return any objectionable posting to the sender with a comment stating why the note was rejected.

The examples of speech censored by Prodigy SYSOPS are varied; some are arguably curious in light of the "offensive" speech standard. Messages seeking the least painful methods of suicide, requesting pornographic contacts, and providing instructions for illegally hot-wiring a cable connection represent a few examples of transmissions thwarted by Prodigy SYSOPS. In 1989, Prodigy went so far as to shut down an entire newsgroup called "Health Spa." This newsgroup included frank discussions of gay sexual practices and featured a debate between homosexuals and fundamentalist Christians. Additionally, in 1991, Prodigy censored and ultimately terminated a group of subscribers for using Prodigy's boards to protest a planned rate increase. According to Prodigy, these users were "harassing" other members with protest mail. Later that year, after complaints about postings defending Hitler, Prodigy prohibited expressions of bigotry on its bulletin boards, although it promised to allow discussion about historical events such as the Holocaust.

Although Prodigy strenuously defended prescreening, the commercial success of the service ultimately made this practice impossible. By the end of 1993, Prodigy had more than 2 million subscribers, and its bulletin boards were handling 75,000 postings a day (Frankel, 1995). Because prescreening this volume of messages by monitors was no longer practicable, Prodigy began using a software program that would detect messages containing offensive language or racial epithets (Benkleman, 1995). Although the program can identify and delete specified words, it cannot evaluate the content of a posting. As with the more obtrusive practice of reading postings for content, objectionable messages identified by the language screen were returned to the sender along with an appropriate warning.

In contrast to Prodigy, CompuServe takes a less intrusive approach with respect to managing its boards. It permits all messages to be posted and intervenes only when other users complain. After receiving a complaint, CompuServe immediately evaluates a posting. If the posting is potentially defamatory, the message is removed and the sender admonished. America Online and other providers seem to follow a similar policy, and some services offer a right to respond to individuals who believe that they may have been defamed (Frankel, 1995). It is important to note that Prodigy's competitors do not attempt to identify and delete objectionable messages before they are posted, instead they relied on readers to identify which postings are problematic.

These policies will be tested as bulletin board operators find themselves under increasing pressure to censor speech on computer bulletin boards. The potential for defamatory postings, and the decision in *Stratton Oakmont v. Prodigy* (1995), will undoubtedly cause many providers to reassess their legal responsibility for postings. One result might be a conscious decision to adopt a policy of "benign neglect" (Silvergate, 1995). This response seems unlikely, however, as citizens' groups are actively arguing that providers should censor nondefamatory speech using offensive language or addressing objectionable topics. When access to computer bulletin boards becomes more commonplace, and as people grow more innovative in their use, more voices will surely be calling for greater efforts to regulate messages posted on computer bulletin boards. The potential for any computer user to commit "libel instantly in front of one and a half million people without anyone having the opportunity to take the message out or screen it" (Zamsky, quoted in Lewis, 1994, p. D1), virtually guarantees that service providers and the courts will be forced to seriously consider defamatory expression on the information.

DISTRIBUTOR OR PUBLISHER?

Given the growing popularity of computer bulletin boards and the potential for defamatory postings, the precedents that courts set will have tremendous implications for the future of freedom of expression on the Internet. If commercial online services are held responsible for the content of postings, there is reason for great concern; instead of establishing a speech-expanding precedent, such a rule would severely limit speech on computer bulletin boards and infringe on users' First Amendment rights.

The importance of computer bulletin board systems as a medium of communication cannot be overstated. In many ways, computer bulletin boards have become the common person's printing press. As a practical matter of cost, mediums such as television and radio are unavailable to the average person seeking to disseminate a message. Yet, for the low cost of a subscription fee, computer bulletin board systems provide millions of potential speakers with a cheap, effective, and instantaneous way to get their message across to a targeted audience that might include thousands of people. "It is no exaggeration to conclude that the Internet has achieved, and continues to achieve, the most participatory marketplace of mass speech that this country—and indeed the world—has yet seen," Judge Dalzell wrote in *ACLU v. Reno* (1996), concluding that "due to the 'democratizing' effects of Internet communication . . . individual citizens of limited means can speak to a worldwide audience on issues of concern to them" (p. 881).

What is more, the future promise of computer bulletin boards as a method of communication cannot be ignored. Visionaries like Mitchell Kapor (1991) see bulletin boards as a way to facilitate a new type of participatory democracy. Others see them as New Age village greens, where people can air their gripes or voice their opinions in public or semi-public forums. Still others predict that before the next century, bulletin boards will serve as the main conduit for commerce, education, and entertainment in the United States. In short, computer bulletin board systems have the potential to play a vital role in the dissemination of political and social speech in this country.

Holding providers responsible for the acts of users would force providers to actively censor speech on computer bulletin boards. "If carriers are to be held responsible for the content of all information and communication on their systems they will be forced to attempt to screen all content—every e-mail message, text file, word processing document, or image—before it is allowed to enter the system" (Berman & Weitzner, 1995, p. 1634). For fear of precisely such a result, the U.S. Supreme Court in *Smith v. California* (1959) wisely struck down a Los Angeles ordinance imposing liability on a bookseller for obscenity by reasoning that "every bookseller would be placed under an obligation to make himself aware of the contents of every book in his shop" (p. 153). Stratton Oakmont strays from the holding in Smith, with three significant consequences for freedom of expression.

First, such a practice of censorship permits the conformist impulses of service providers to establish and enforce the societal standard of what is, and is not, "offensive." Such an imposition of majoritarian values runs the risk of suppressing the ideas and feelings of those who wish to express themselves in nonconformist ways. Thus, the First Amendment cannot allow the determination of what is offensive or defamatory to be made by a powerful few. As the Supreme Court stated in *Erznoznik v. Jacksonville* (1975), "much that we encounter offends our esthetic, if not our political and moral sensibilities. Nevertheless, the Constitution does not permit the government to decide which types of otherwise protected speech are sufficiently offensive to require protection for the unwilling . . . viewer" (pp. 210-211).

Second, and more importantly, allowing service providers to screen speech is tantamount to a prior restraint on the users' freedom of expression. In the United States, there has long been a constitutional tradition against measures that prevent the free dissemination of ideas (*New York Times Co. v. U.S.*, 1971). In 1931, in the landmark decision of *Near v. Minnesota* (1931), the U.S. Supreme Court made concrete this general principle of First Amendment law prohibiting the use of previous restraints on speech. As a result of Near and its progeny, any system of prior restraints on expression comes to the Court with a heavy presumption against its constitutional validity.

Of course, suggesting that bulletin board users have the right to say whatever they want does not mean that they can do so with immunity. Clearly, freedom of speech principles do not protect all electronic speech any more than they protect all speech in other forms. Beginning with *Chaplinsky v. New Hampshire* (1942), the U.S. Supreme Court has recognized several categories of speech that are deserving of reduced protection under the First Amendment. To date, some examples of these categories include "fighting words" (*Chaplinsky v. New Hampshire*, 1942), defamatory speech (*New York Times v. Sullivan*, 1964), advocacy of imminent lawless behavior (*Brandenburg v. Ohio*, 1969), commercial speech (*Virginia State Board of Pharmacy v. Virginia Citizens Consumer Council*, 1976), obscenity (*Roth v. U.S.*, 1957; *Miller v. California*, 1973), and child pornography (*New York v. Ferber*, 1982). Because of their lesser status under the First Amendment, the Supreme Court has held these categories to be proscribable, actionable, or subject to post facto penalty under certain circumstances. "Though there are circumstances in which restrictions on expression are permissible, in general First Amendment values are best served when such restrictions are kept to an absolute minimum" (Berman & Weitzner, 1995, p. 1620).

Finally, actively monitoring bulletin boards and censoring objectionable postings moves away from the principle that more speech is the best response to bad speech. Justice Brandeis articulated this view of the First Amendment in *Whitney v. California* (1927):

> If there be time to expose through discussion the falsehood and fallacies, to avert the evil by the processes of education, the remedy to be applied is more speech, not enforced silence. Only an emergency can justify repression. Such must be the rule if authority is to be reconciled with freedom. Such, in my opinion, is the command of the Constitution. (p. 377)

This idea that more speech is the best solution to harmful speech holds especially true on computer bulletin board systems. Because of their low costs, ease of use, and capacity to accommodate an almost infinite number of speakers at once, computer bulletin boards provide the perfect environment for counteractive speech.

This line of reasoning was embraced by a federal court in *Cubby v. CompuServe* (1991). In Cubby, the court considered CompuServe's culpability for a series of false and defamatory statements posted on its "Journalism Forum" bulletin board. One part of the "Journalism Forum," which was managed for CompuServe by Cameron Communication, was a publication prepared by Don Fitzpatrick Associates (DFA) entitled "Rumorville, USA." Cubby's suit alleged that when it attempted to market a competing database called "Skuttlebut," postings on Rumorville had defamed Cubby by characterizing the effort as a "new start-up scam," among other things.

In issuing a summary judgment for CompuServe, the court held that "First Amendment guarantees have long been recognized as protecting distribuors of publications. . . . Obviously, the national distributor of hundreds of periodicals has no duty to monitor each issue of every periodical it distributes" (p. 140). Because CompuServe had no opportunity to review Rumorville's contents before DFA uploaded it into CompuServe's computer banks, CompuServe could not be "held liable on the libel claim because it neither knew nor had reason to know of the allegedly defamatory statements" (p. 139). By way of analogy, the court reasoned, "CompuServe has no more editorial control over . . . publication than does a public library, book store, or newsstand, and it would be no more feasible for CompuServe to examine every publication it carries for potentially defamatory statements than it would be for any other distributor to do so" (p. 140). To hold otherwise, the Cubby court concluded, "would impose an undue burden on the free flow of information" (p. 140).

The holding in Cubby clearly suggests that "a distributor must have knowledge of the contents of a publication before liability can be imposed for distributing that publication" (p. 139). However, Conner (1993) has attempted to narrow the Cubby decision, arguing that it is limited to situations in which the service provider delegated responsibility for the contents of a bulletin board. "Since the court's reasoning in Cubby emphasizes CompuServe's lack of knowledge about the alleged defamation," Conner reasons, "the application of a similar analysis may be inappropriate when a BBS does minimal or insignificant screening of its messages" (p. 238). The Stratton Oakmont (1995) decision, for example, relied on the fact that Prodigy had previously claimed the right to screen messages to distinguish away the holding in Cubby. By exerting control over content, the court reasoned that Prodigy had transformed itself from a distributor into a publisher. In the words of Judge Ain:

> The key distinction between CompuServe and Prodigy is two fold. First, Prodigy held itself out to the public and its members as controlling the content of its computer bulletin boards. Second, Prodigy implemented this control through its automatic screening program, and the Guidelines which Board Leaders are required to enforce. By actively utilizing technology and manpower to delete notes from its computer bulletin boards on the basis of offensiveness and "bad taste," for example, Prodigy is clearly making decisions as to content, and such decisions constitute editorial control. (p. 1797)

Thus, the court concluded, "Prodigy's conscious choice, to gain the benefits of editorial control, has opened it up to a greater liability than CompuServe and other computer networks that make no such choice" (p. 1798).

The court's conclusion that Prodigy is a publisher is problematic on several counts. First, the court errs in the factual claim that Prodigy was attempting to enforce a preferred perspective. Although Prodigy had once claimed the right to regulate content, and although Prodigy was screening messages for offensive language and racial epithets, Prodigy was not exercising editorial control in any meaningful sense when the defamatory posting occurred. Although the "emotive function" of the language used by the speaker clearly contributes to content (*Cohen v. California*, 1971), Prodigy's motivation was clearly a narrow set of swear words and racial slurs. Prodigy had publicly renounced the practice of assessing content before posting messages 18 months earlier, and there is no evidence in the record available to the court that demonstrates any subsequent attempt to exercise meaningful editorial control. The record does not prove that Prodigy "knew or had reason to know of the allegedly defamatory" statements that the court set as the standard in Cubby (1991, p. 141).

Furthermore, the presence of a language screen and the designation of a Board Leader does not prove that Prodigy was exerting editorial control over the "Money Talk" bulletin board. The language screen software that systematically identifies and deletes particular words, irrespective of meaning or context, is an automatic process executed by a computer program and not a discretionary editorial act performed by an editor. In this sense, the screen employed by Prodigy is no different than the tape delay system routinely used by radio stations to monitor incoming phone calls for offensive language. The availability and use of such screening technology, in and of itself, does not make the disk jockey an editor, nor is the radio station responsible for defamatory statements made by callers. By the same reasoning, the presence of the language screen should not be construed to imply editorial control by Prodigy for the contents of its bulletin boards.

The Board Leader, an agent employed by Prodigy who initiates dialogue, periodically revises the bulletin board's opening screen, and coordinates guests and promotional efforts, is not analogous to an editor. In this instance, it is impossible to believe that a single individual could be responsible for reviewing the 40,000 postings made each month to "Money Talk." Even if leaders occasionally delete objectionable messages, their primary objective is to facilitate discussion and encourage participation on a bulletin board. In many senses, Prodigy's decision to employ leaders is analogous to designating a moderator to facilitate and manage speech in a public forum. The fact that speech may occasionally be limited does not mean that the moderator suddenly becomes an editor responsible for the content of all utterances.

On this point, the Cubby (1991) court properly concludes that CompuServe's decision to enforce "editorial and technical standards and conventions of style" (p. 140) did not transform it into an editor. Nor did the decision to remove postings that violated the standards mean that CompuServe was no longer a distributor. This characterization is decisive, for it explains how CompuServe can remain a distributor while simultaneously enforcing minimum standards for postings on its bulletin boards. The Stratton Oakmont court incorrectly distinguished the service provided by Prodigy from CompuServe, erroneously implying that there is a significant difference in the scrutiny provided by the competing providers.

Second, the holding in Stratton Oakmont seems to place commercial service providers in an impossible dilemma "of having to abandon their basic subscriber guidelines against obscene or offensive materials, or investigate the truth of every message before it appears on the providers' bulletin boards" (Miranda, 1996, p. 232). To the extent that the service provider attempts any regulation of content, the Stratton Oakmont reasoning forces the conclusion that the provider is a publisher, and hence responsible for all speech. At the same time, to qualify as a distributor, a service provider would have to renounce any and all interest in reviewing content. The resulting system would be composed of two types of bulletin boards: "distributor" boards that are totally devoid of rules and "publisher" boards that are rigidly controlled by the provider for fear of litigation.

It may prove difficult for providers to avoid responsibility, as the Telecommunications Act of 1996 and leading copyright infringement cases may eventually compel providers to scrutinize content. Recognizing this possibility, Congress added "Good Samaritan" language to the Communications Decency Act, a key element of the Telecommunications Act, stating that a provider would not incur any liability on account of scrutiny required to police for indecent or otherwise objectionable material. Regrettably, Counts and Martin (1996) conclude, "there is no guarantee that the[se] Good Samaritan protections will apply to libel cases" (p. 1112). Although there is some evidence in the legislative record suggesting that the Congress was responding to Stratton Oakmont, it is also true that the focus of the Act was screening aimed at sexually explicit material. Indeed, it is impossible to predict with any confidence how the courts might respond to a defamation action based on the claim that the service provider was an editor because software was used to detect and delete sexually explicit material. The very presence of such a screen, it should be remembered, was a significant distinction used by the Stratton Oakmont court to distinguish away the Cubby precedent and hold that Prodigy was a publisher.

Finally, "it is preposterous to require Prodigy to verify the accuracy of the comments that appear on its bulletin boards because the enormous volume of material that appears there makes it impossible to assert the kind of 'editorial control' that would be necessary to prevent even a fraction of the possible libel statements that could be made over a period of time" (Post, 1995, p. 117). Even if it was possible, Post concludes, "the assertion of such control would render these forums useless for the purposes for which they are designed and which people find so attractive—spontaneous, real-time communication" (p. 117).

The idea of reviewing content before dissemination was considered in *Auvil v. CBS "60 Minutes"* (1992). In that case, a federal district court heard an action brought by apple growers for a segment on the use of the chemical Alar. Although CBS had produced the story, the action also named television affiliates in Washington state because they had received the text of the show while it aired on the East Coat. During the three-hour delay, the apple growers claimed the local affiliates had time to exercise editorial control. The court correctly absolved the affiliates, reasoning that they could not be expected to prescreen all network programming prior to its broadcasting. Holding the affiliates responsible, the court concluded, "would force the creation of full time editorial boards . . . which possess sufficient knowledge, legal acumen and access to experts to continually monitor incoming transmissions and exercise on-the-spot discretionary calls or face lawsuits at every turn" (p. 931).

The decision in Auvil is instructive for it suggests that the court must address pragmatic considerations in assessing responsibility for defamatory speech. If affiliates cannot be expected to screen the network or syndicated programming they broadcast each week, it is difficult to expect service providers to screen and assess hundreds of thousands of messages for potentially defamatory language. It would be impossible for even the most zealous provider to read and accurately evaluate thousands of postings, and a system of random checks might fail to detect or deter defamatory speech. Meaningful random checks would also be difficult to complete as many statements are defamatory only in context, and the context may be a message that was removed long before the monitor joined the thread. Even if it was possible to actively monitor a bulletin board for defamation, the economic burden imposed by such a system would make computer bulletin boards cost prohibitive.

If providers were held responsible for defamatory postings, Miranda (1996) concludes, "the floodgates of litigation would burst wide open, and on-line providers would be subject to lawsuits any time an allegedly defamatory statement is transmitted on its service. Such a prohibitive public policy would unduly limit free speech and encourage litigation in already overburdened courts" (p. 246). As a result of such ill-fated efforts to police speech, the content of speech on bulletin boards would become either vacuous or innocuous, and the First Amendment's freedom of expression would be forever diminished.

"Where possible we must avoid legal structures that force those who merely carry messages to screen their content" (Berman & Weitzner, 1995, p. 1635). To avoid such a result, it is necessary to conclude that service providers are not publishers in any meaningful sense of the term. Holding that providers are distributors would absolve them from the necessity of playing the role of the censor so long as they respond to defamatory postings they discover in a timely manner. If the Stratton Oakmont court had concluded Prodigy was a distributor, "it would have sent a message to prospective plaintiffs that if they do not like what is said about them, their solution lies on-line in the form of a rebuttal rather than in the arena of the court system" (Sideritis, 1996, p. 1079). Although this remedy would not necessarily absolve speakers of responsibility, Branscomb (1995) has suggested that the right to reply is "an alternative to strict liability of information services without imposing an obligation to monitor all messages in order to avoid provider liability" (p. 1671).

THE FUTURE OF COMPUTER BULLETIN BOARDS

The potential for defamatory expression, coupled with the conflicting holdings in Cubby and Stratton Oakmont, suggests that the federal courts will eventually be forced to determine whether commercial service providers are distributors or publishers. "The court that next faces this issue should rule that commercial on-line services are distributors entitled to protection from liability for defamatory statements made by users" (Sideritis, 1996, p. 1079). Such an outcome would make both conceptual and practical sense, as providers should be treated as distributors like newsstands or libraries, not like editors who control newspapers or manage publishing houses. Such a conclusion would form a solid platform for speech on computer bulletin boards and offer a framework for addressing the myriad of issues related to defamation on the information superhighway (Friedman, 1995).

Computer bulletin boards must be taken seriously. Even though the ultimate impact of bulletin boards is impossible to project, current trends indicate tremendous and increasing public response to the medium. Already, these "last bastions of free swinging free speech" (Sanger & Quittner, 1991, p. 5) have established themselves as major public forums for political debate and social exchange. It is certainly conceivable that in the next decade computer bulletin board systems may surpass the printing press and the broadcast media in importance.

In the absence of legislation or controlling precedent, policymakers face the daunting task of adapting existing regulatory schemes to new forms of communication technology. If our society hopes to maintain robust communication of all ideas, speech on computer bulletin boards must be protected. "The challenge for courts and will be to recognize and define the rights and responsibilities of both those who own and those who utilize the new 'superhighway'" (Redlich & Lurie, 1995, p. 1459). To this end, the proper response to defamatory expression on bulletin boards is to treat commercial online service providers as distributors that provide access to users who pay for a service. According to this view, providers should be seen as conduits for the distribution of electronic expression, not as publishers who exercise editorial control over speech. At the same time, those who speak on bulletin boards should be aware that electronic expression may be just as defamatory as the printed word. Although this may be unsettling to some speakers, it is necessary to assign responsibility before considering the difficult task of fashioning appropriate remedies for defamatory expression appearing on computer bulletin boards.

REFERENCES

ACLU v. Reno, 929 F.Supp. 824 (E.D. Pa 1996).

Auvil v. CBS "60 Minutes," 800 F. Supp. 928 (E.D.Wash 1992).

Band, J. (1996). Online service provider liability. *International Commercial Litigation, 20*, 35-36.

Barringer, F. (1990, March 11). Electronic bulletin boards need editing. No they don't. *The New York Times*, p. 4.

Benkleman, S. (1995, December 26). Watch your talk, online cops walk thin line in monitoring. *Newsday*, p. A8.

Berman, J., & Weitzner, D. (1995). Abundance and user control: Renewing the democratic heart of the First Amendment in the age of interactive media. *Yale Law Journal, 104*, 1619-1637.

Bowker v. America Online, No. 95L 013509 (Cir. Ct. Cook Cty. Ill, Sept. 1995).

Brandenburg v. Ohio, 395 U.S. 444 (1969).

Branscomb, A. W. (1995). Anonymity, autonomy, and accountability: Challenges to the First amendment in cyberspaces. *Yale Law Journal, 104*, 1639-1679.

Bray, H. (1995, December 14). Prodigy loses appeal in libel case; Ruling finding form liable for material is upheld. *Boston Globe*, p. 51.

Chaplinsky v. New Hampshire, 315 U.S. 568 (1942).

Cohen v. California, 403 U.S. 18 (1971).

Conner, D. J. (1993). Cubby v. CompuServe: Defamation law on the electronic frontier. *George Mason Independent Law Review, 2,* 227-248.

Counts, C. L., & Martin, C. A. (1996). Libel in cyberspace: A framework for addressing liability and jurisdictional issues in this new frontier. *Albany Law Review, 59,* 1083-1133.

Cubby Inc. v. CompuServe, Inc., 776 F. Supp. 135 (S.D.N.Y. 1991).

EIR monthly exclusive: Five leading consumer services exceed 13.9m. (1996, June 28). *Electronic Information Report,* no pages.

Erznoznik v. Jacksonville, 422 U.S. 205 (1975).

Frankel, A. (1995, October). On-line, on the hook. *American Lawyer,* pp. 59-66.

Friedman, J. R. (1995). A lawyer's ramble down the information superhighway: Defamation. *Fordham Law Review, 64,* 794-803.

Haddad, C. (1995, 27 May). Prodigy libel ruling raises questions of on-line services' responsibilities. *Atlanta Journal and Constitution,* p. 3D.

It's in the Cards v. Meneau, 535 N.W. 2d 11 (Wis. Ct. App. 1995).

Jensen, E. C. (1987). An electronic soapbox: Computer bulletin boards and the First Amendment. *Federal Communications Law Journal, 39,* 217-257.

Kapor, M. (1991, September). Civil Liberties in cyberspace: Computers, networks and public policy. *Scientific American,* pp. 158-164.

Lewis, P. H. (1994, 16 November). Libel suit against Prodigy tests on-line speech limits. *The New York Times,* p. D1.

Lewis, P. H. (1995, 25 October). After apology from Prodigy, firm drops suit. *The New York Times,* p. D1.

Medphone Corp. v. DeNigris, Civil Action No. 92-3785 (D.N.J. 1992).

Miller v. California, 413 U.S. 15 (1973).

Miller, G. (1996, July 15). Old electronic watering holes are drying up. *Los Angeles Times,* p. D8.

Miranda, D. P. (1996). Defamation in cyberspace: Stratton Oakmont, Inc. v. Prodigy Services, Co. *Albany Law Journal of Science and Technology, 5,* 229-247.

Near v. Minnesota, 283 U.S. 697 (1931).

New York Times Co. v. Sullivan, 376 U.S. 254 (1964).

New York Times Co. v. U.S., 403 U.S. 713 (1971).

New York v. Ferber, 458 U.S. 747 (1982).

Oldenberg, D. (1991, 1 October). Rights on the line: Defining the limits on the networks. *Washington Post,* p. E5.

Paramount Communications v. Gibraltar Casualty Co., 623 N.Y.S. 2d 850 (1st Dep't 1995).

Post, D. (1995, September). Limiting on-line libel. *American Lawyer,* pp. 116-117.

Redlich, N., & Lurie, D. R. (1995). First Amendment issues presented by the "information superhighway." *Seton Hall Law Review, 25,* 1446-1459.

Rosenkrantz, H. (1996, August 5). Woman sues AOL over false sexual biography. *Fairfield County Business Journal,* p. 1.

Roth v. U.S., 354 U.S. 476 (1957).

Sanger, E., & Quittner, J. (1991, October 23). Prodigy computers: Electronic insults flap. *Newsday,* p. 5.

Shields, T., & Bowles, S. (1996, February 14). Over the line on-line: Family put under siege. *Washington Post,* p. 1.

Sideritis, M.C. (1996). Defamation in cyberspace: Reconciling Cubby, Inc. v. CompuServe, Inc. and Stratton Oakmont v. Prodigy Services Co. *Marquette Law Review, 79,* 1065-1082.

Silver, M. (1991, November 18). Action on the boards. *United States News and World Report,* p. 96.

Silvergate, H. (1995, July 24). Podium. *National Law Journal,* A20.

Smith v. California, 361 U.S. 147 (1959).

Stratton Oakmont, Inc. and Daniel Porush v. Prodigy Services Co., 23 Med. L. Rptr. 1795 (1995).

Stratton Oakmont, Inc. v. Prodigy Services Co., No. 94-03163 (N.Y. Sup. Ct., 11 December 1995)

Suarez Corp. Ind. v. Meeks, No. 267513 (Ct. of Common Pleas, Cuyahoga Co., Ohio 1994).

Venditto, G. (1996, March). Online services: How does their net access stack up? *Internet World,* pp. 55-65.

Virginia State Board of Pharmacy v. Virginia Citizens Consumer Council, 425 U.S. 748 (1976).

Walker, M. (1995, 27 May). Internet rocked by US libel case. *London Guardian,* p. 3.

Weber, J. S. (1995). Defining cyberlibel: A First Amendment limit for libel suits against individuals arising from computer bulletin board speech. *Case Western Law Review, 46,* 235-278.

Whitney v. California, 264 U.S. 357 (1927).

Zitner, A. (1995, May 26). New York judge allows ground-breaking libel suit against Prodigy. *Boston Globe,* p. 68.

16

OF FIREWALLS AND UNLOCKED DOORS: EXPECTATIONS OF PRIVACY

SUSAN J. DRUCKER AND GARY GUMPERT

The onslaught of e-mail, Internet access, chat rooms, intranets and Web sites generate new legal and ethical issues as the technology of communications challenge developments in applicable laws governing privacy rights. The authors ask questions such as: Is this electronic space private? Can one assume no one would open e-mail? Do employees have a privacy right in their electronic mail communications? Can one choose to remain anonymous in their computer-mediated communication? Drucker and Gumpert argue that the 20th century has seen the ascendence of the value placed on privacy and control. This chapter provides an outline of the parameters of privacy in cyberspace.

For a mere $11.95 *Info-revolution* in Lawrenceville, GA offers the following in its advertisement:

> We give you addresses to hundreds of sites that will supply you with DMV records, credit profiles, medical and criminal records, most

anything you would want to know . . . with this information you can
track down phone numbers, social security information, e-mail
addresses, surnames, birth, marriage, divorce and death records. Look
up a long lost relative with sites like Parent-Finders and Birth-Quest,
look for biological parents! . . . You can know EVERYTHING about
EVERYBODY with this information!!! (Searcher@finder.com, 1996)

For law enforcement officers, professional and amateur
detectives, debt collectors, voyeurs, and the just plain curious,
cyberspace, in its various incarnations, offers a wonderland of
surveillance tools. Virtually nothing in cyberspace should be
assumed to be private. As Matthew Hawn (1996) in the *New York
Times* warns, "as the pulse of the Web flows through the network's
veins, it is possible for just about every machine it passes through to
record some of those vital signs—an electrocardiogram of mouse
clicks and keystrokes" (p. D5). From the 1970s onward there has
been a consistent increase in not only the value placed on privacy
but with the concern for threats on personal privacy (Regan, 1995).
It is, therefore, somewhat ironic, but understandable, that privacy
and security are such important issues in the developing world of
computer mediated communication.

The vast amount of potential data and the quest for privacy
and control sets up a complex and perplexing balancing game.
Perhaps the personal right most associated with the conception of
protecting the individual is that of privacy so it is not surprising that
privacy is one of the areas that appears to be of greatest concern to
online users and governments as well. Privacy is often
conceptualized as "the right of individuals" to decide for themselves
how much they wish to share with others in terms of thoughts,
feelings, and facts of personal life. Privacy rights have to be
conceived of as the right to be let alone, therefore encompassing the
protection of individual dignity and integrity by preventing the loss of
individual freedom and independence (Hixson, 1987, p. 55). During
the past several decades public opinion polls have indicated the
importance U.S. citizens place on privacy. In 1990, 79% of
respondents felt that privacy should be added to "life, liberty, and
the pursuit of happiness" as a fundamental right (Louis Harris and
Associates & Westin, 1992). Posed the question—"How concerned
are you about threats to your personal privacy in America today?"—
the response indicated that the percentage of those somewhat
concerned increased from 64% in 1978 to 79% in 1990 (Louis Harris
and Associates & Westin, 1992).[1] An ACLU survey addressed a broad
range of privacy issues ranging from employer monitoring, to
secondary use of information, to gay and lesbian rights (Cantril &
Cantril, 1994)[2] with respondents generally indicating a high level of
concern (Regan, 1995). Yet, at the dawn of cyberlaw, perhaps one of

the stickiest values to be addressed is that of privacy, which has long been the subject of heated debate and inconsistent rulings as well as occupying the status of penumbra right, not enunciated, but recognized, in the U.S. Constitution. Although the value placed on personal privacy has changed over time, so have the media technologies that may protect or invade that privacy.

Privacy has long been seen as crucial to individual liberties. Alan Westin's (1970) seminal works on privacy rests on the significance of it in the individual's relationship to society, arguing that privacy in a democratic system is a critical element in the individual's relationship to government and noting, for instance, the importance of privacy with regard to supporting limits on police power, electoral system integrity and religious tolerance. More recently, Priscilla M. Regan (1995), in *Legislating Privacy: Technology, Social Values and Public Policy*, has argued that this individualistic conception of privacy is insufficient in requiring the re-conceptualization of privacy as having broader social and collective purposes. In distinguishing informational privacy,[3] communication privacy, and psychological privacy, Regan makes the case for the social importance of privacy:

> This social importance derives from the fact that privacy is a common value in that it is shared by individuals, a public value in that it has value to the democratic political system, and a collective value in that technology and market forces make it increasingly difficult for any one person to have privacy unless everyone has a similar minimum level of privacy. (pp. xv-xvi)

Regan's approach when combined with the individual liberties conceptualization of privacy supports the reevaluation of privacy at a time in history in which there is some reconsideration of the value placed on public and private relationships.

Privacy rights and communication freedoms are among those areas particularly intertwined in societal valuation of individual rights. Diverse laws around the world reflect just these competing and often conflicting liberties. Given the global nature of cyberspace then, any discussion of privacy and personal control must take these value differences into account when evaluating the expectation of privacy at points of transmission and reception as well as at all nodes through which information passes through. Therefore, privacy rights may well invoke culturally divergent conceptualization and protection for computer-mediated communication. Privacy rights also invoke psychological and functional anticipation in using that given medium or instrument.

In his comprehensive work, *Internet and Online Law*, Kent Stuckey (1996) outlines the developments in "cyberlaw." He identifies principles that have formed the basis of most privacy protection in the United States and Canada as well as Europe. He isolates the following principles based on fair informational practice principles:

1. Personal data record-keeping practices should not be kept secret.
2. An individual should have the ability to find out what information about him or her is on record and how it is disclosed, as well as have the ability to correct it.
3. An individual should have the ability to correct or amend a record of identifiable information about him or her.
4. An individual should have the ability to limit the disclosure of information about him or her that was obtained for one purpose from being disclosed for other unrelated purposes.
5. An organization creating, maintaining, using, or disseminating records of identifiable personal data must guarantee the reliability of the data for their intended use and must take precautions to prevent misuse of the data (Stuckey, 1996).

Among the many privacy issues floating around and about computer-mediated communication are data confidentiality, law enforcement eavesdropping and/or surveillance, unrestricted access to erotic and pornographic text and images, message encryption, the ability to have secured transactions, source anonymity, and associational privacy.

ASSOCIATIONAL PRIVACY

The first significant dimension of interpersonal electronic privacy is the degree to which a message can be directed and shared with only the intended recipient(s). Is the nearly instantaneous means of delivering written messages and documents via electronic mail (e-mail) a private transaction? Can one assume that no unseen intruder could open e-mail? E-mail conjures up images of letters in sealed envelopes, but "mail messages being routed from computer system to computer system on their journey through the Internet [for example] are more like postcards than letters" (*Netsurfer Digest,* 1995). The nature of e-mail may also lead to behavior in which disclosure of information is fostered. It has been noted that "e-mail is a very informal medium. It is far closer to speech than written communication, and . . . the care given to a written communication. It has evolved into a hybrid of speech and writing by the use of emoticons, those shorthand signs which explain the tones of the e-mail" (Aftab, 1996, p. S2).

Private service providers including Prodigy, CompuServe, and America Online, under contract with customers to deliver service, claim the right to monitor not only publicly posted bulletin board messages but person to person messages (America Online Service Membership, 1995). For example, the America Online Service Agreement stipulates:

> AOL Inc. may elect to electronically monitor the public areas (e.g., chat rooms and public message boards) for adherence to the TOS Agreement and the Rules of the Road and may disclose any content or records to satisfy any law, regulation or other governmental request or to properly operate the AOL Service and protect its members. AOL Inc. reserves the right at its sole discretion to review, edit, or refuse to post any material or information submitted for display or posted on the AOL Service. *Notwithstanding the foregoing, AOL will not intentionally monitor or disclose any private E-mail message unless permitted or required by law.*[4] (emphasis in original)

Despite the assurance of e-mail privacy, in the fall of 1995, America Online gave law enforcement agents access to the private electronic mailboxes of an unknown number of subscribers leading to the arrest of a dozen people suspected of being among the most active traders of online child pornography. The Justice department indicated more arrests were planned (Lewis, 1995). In another fray, America Online recently blocked all e-mail messages sent from five domains (Internet addresses), including three used by CyberPromotions, which sent unsolicited e-mail or "spam." AOL argues that spamming violates the Electronic Privacy Act and the Computer Fraud and Abuse Act.[5] Inherent in this case is not only the right of AOL to monitor but to also block transmissions implicating the rights of not only those who would send the messages but limiting what subscribers receive.[6] AOL maintains that AOL is a private, proprietary system, and that the spammers are not "leafleting" the public square (Leibowitz, 1996b). Lawyers for CyberPromotions claimed a First Amendment right to send junk e-mail to America Online users over AOL's objections, noting that messages were sent over the public Internet rather than the private AOL pipeline.[7] This distinction they argued leads to applying laws of privately owned public places like the shopping mall by analogy.[8]

The Electronic Communication Privacy Act and similar state statues prohibit service providers from reviewing transmitted communications. The providers have no editorial control, acting like a bookseller or news vendor in the analogy used to determine liability and responsibility (Stuckey, 1994). However, several providers have attempted to exercise editorial control over the content of their services, as in the case of Prodigy, which censors messages that directly attack other subscribers and uses what it calls "George Carlin" software that searches and deletes messages containing objectionable words (Lewis, 1994).

Kent Stukey (1994) identifies a dozen key privacy laws in the United States governing personal privacy related to issues arising in cyberspace. Most of these laws concern the relationship between government and the individual. For example, in the United States, the Fourth Amendment, which guarantees the right of the people to be secure in their persons, houses, papers, and effects against unreasonable searches and seizures, has been recognized as "creating a zone of privacy which courts have interpreted to mean limits government surveillance, data collection and intrusion. The U.S. Supreme Court has relied on the analysis of 'reasonable expectations of privacy' and have found that there is no reasonable expectation of privacy in numbers dialed on the telephone" (*Smith v. Maryland*, 1979), bank records (*United States v. Miller*, 1976), and even in secured areas such as the curtilage (area around) a home (*California v. Ciraolo*, 1986).[9]

The Fifth Amendment of the U.S. constitution which protects a person from being compelled to bear witness against him or herself in a criminal case, limits how the government may gather incriminating information from an individual so that the government may be limited in using business records and encrypted records.[10] "It is unclear that compelling a person to furnish the key to encrypted electronic records or communications is a means available to the government for collecting evidence of a crime" (Stuckey, 1994, Section 2). Law enforcement agents with a warrant may decrypt and encrypted file themselves, but it is unclear whether the government can coerce a person to provide the code for decrypting the file (Stuckey, 1994). Stuckey goes on to note the mail privacy statute, which prohibits the opening of mail without a search warrant or addressee consent (39 U.S.C. §3623),[11] and federal wiretap statutes (18 U.S.C. §§ 2510 *et seq.*), which prohibits the use of eavesdropping technology and the interception of radio communications, data transmission, and telephone calls without consent of at least one party to the communication. The Computer Fraud and Abuse Act (18 U.S. C. §1030) focuses on computer crime and security. The Act addresses six offenses designed to protect the federal interest in computers and protects private computers connected to an interstate network. Personal information that is secure is a "by-product" of the protection of the system (Stuckey, 1994).[12]

The Privacy Act (5 U.S.C. §552a) protects the privacy of personally identifiable information held by the federal government and applies primarily to records maintained in an agency's "system of records" (Stuckey, 1994). The act restricts federal agencies from disclosing personal data and requires agencies to publish detailed notices of records kept on the system and procedures for individuals to obtain access to records about themselves. The Fair Credit Reporting Act (15 U.S.C. §§ 1681 et seq.) regulates the collection and use of personal data by credit reporting agencies and prohibits agency reports on people from disclosing information about an individual without consent. But beyond the governmental setting, many privacy issues emerge.

On the federal level the prime statutory law in this area is the Electronic Communications Privacy Act of 1986 (ECPA), which generally protects e-mail from illegal monitoring and makes it a federal crime to intercept and disclose electronic communications, punishable by imprisonment for up to five years for a fine of up to $250,000 for an individual and $500,000 for an organization (18 USC 2510).[13,14] The ECPA addresses the problem of unauthorized access or access by persons exceeding their authorization for items such as personal and business correspondence that were intended to be kept confidential. The ECPA includes a stored communication provision (18 U.S.C. § 2701), which prohibits the unauthorized access to or use of stored electronic communication, including voice and electronic mail, and prohibits providers of electronic communication services from disclosing the contents of stored communication. The rules against disclosure apply only to e-mail systems offered to the public (Stuckey, 1994). The law makes it a crime and also creates a civil cause of action against any party committing a "knowing or intentional" violation of the provisions (18 U.S.C. § 2707).[15]

Issues that are addressed by the ECPA become more complex when raised in the university or business setting. Employers often monitor employee's job performance, but should employers have access to their employee's e-mail? Employers say yes and claim they do this for reasons ranging from system maintenance, message routing, troubleshooting, protection of trade secrets, and quality control (Kelly, 1994).[16] Do employees have a privacy right in their electronic mail communications? Under what circumstances can managers lawfully monitor employees' electronic mail? Is employee consent necessary? What facts are necessary to show consent? Answers? The ECPA does *not* protect privacy of messages sent on internal company electronic mail systems. The laws treats such messages as interoffice memos that can be read by authorized employees, supervisors, or systems managers—without violating the law. The prime exceptions to the ECPA allow employers broad rights to monitor employees if monitoring occurs in the ordinary course of business or with the employee's implied consent.

One party to the communication must consent to the monitoring but the employees' consent can be implied from the circumstances of employment. Employees claim this violates their privacy rights, particularly if the intercepted communication is of a personal nature. However, to date, the courts have not addressed the right of privacy in the context of employer's monitoring of employee e-mail for legitimate business reasons. Under the Fourth Amendment courts have even upheld an employer's right to engage in workplace surveillance for legitimate business reasons (O'Connor v. Ortega 1987).[17] The ECPA contains a "business exclusion exemption" that excepts interceptions that are made by equipment furnished to the subscriber or users by a communications carrier in the ordinary course of its business and that are being used by the subscriber or user in the ordinary course of its business so that under this exception an employer may monitor phone calls in an employer supplied telephone system by attaching a device supplied by the employer.[18] At this point, unless legislation or judicial decisions recognize a new employee's privacy right, employers have the right to monitor and read workers' e-mail correspondence.

A state law in Illinois, signed in December 1995, provides greater freedom for employers to monitor employee communication (720 ILCS 5/14-3 (j)). Critics of the Illinois Eavesdropping Act allege the measure inserts Big Brother into the workplace, creating "electronic sweatshops" (Smolowe, 1996). The Illinois law allows employers to use any monitoring system to intercept "communications" relating to "quality control or educational purposes," as long as one party consents meaning that even personal communication may be intercepted (Van Duch, 1996, pp. B1-B2). This measure differs from the federal law in a number of ways, including removing the requirement that instructs listeners to hang up if they recognize the communication to be of a personal nature (Smolowe, 1996). Critics argue the Illinois law[19] is so broad that it may allow an employer to eavesdrop on an employee from the time they come in the door as well as read their e-mail.[20] Leaders of unions such as the AFL-CIO and the ACLU's National Task Force on Civil Liberties are fighting this law, fearing it will be followed by other states. Forty-four other states have statutes requiring employers to obtain consent of one party to a conversation (usually assumed as a condition of employment), and the surveillance must relate to legitimate business purposes. Given the lack of protection afforded by the ECPA and state action, many employees are seeking recourse under common law rights action typically for invasions of privacy but most often the cases are decided on the key condition of "reasonable expectation of privacy" which courts across the country are finding with such frequency that there is reasonable expectation with regard to employee e-mail (Smith v. The Pillsbury Company, 1996).[21]

Ad hoc business policies are developing about employee expectations of privacy. These policies seem to reflect the position that privacy is not a reasonable expectation with regard to company files and business correspondence generated by employees during work time, using company equipment. This extends from physical files to e-mail and computer files. Increasingly businesses and universities are dealing with the controversies generated by e-mail privacy by formulating and disseminating e-mail policies as a means of clarifying expectations and averting possible legal action. In formulating these policies the organizational culture is generally addressed along with issues such as whether any messages are considered private, under what circumstances e-mail will be monitored and by whom, and whether personal communication will be permitted (and kept private).

A limited common law tort of invasion of privacy has been judicially recognized, a right generally left to each state. This tort is based on distinct categories: intrusion, false light, and appropriation.[22] In attempting to codify what can and cannot be done in the private sector, Representative Bruce Vento (D-Minn.) proposed the Consumer Internet Privacy Protection Act of 1997 (see Rep. Vento's Consumer Internet Privacy Protection Act, http://www.epic.org/privacy/internet/hr_98. html). This legislation would keep subscriber information from being misused by online service providers (Brier, 1997).

ENCRYPTION

There are many "privacy" sites on the Web, and many have links to places where one may download encryption software. Encryption or cryptographic software to protect identity and the integrity of a message are quite well developed but pose a problem for law enforcement officials who cannot monitor the messages and transactions of those under surveillance. Increasingly, the community is seeking security of electronic proprietary information and commercial information, thus creating a tension between law enforcement and businesses and individuals. Companies are turning to both hardware and software that have the ability to protect data that are being transmitted and stored both in the United States and abroad.

There are many encryption programs available online, including the Electronic Privacy Information Center (http://www.epic.org), Anonymity and Privacy on the Internet (http://www.stack.nl/-galactus/remailers/index.html), anonymizer (http://www.anonymizer.com), and Pretty Good Privacy (http://

www.pgp.com), which sparked a great deal of controversy and led to the articulation of competiting privacy and public policy concerns.

Banning cryptography or mandating weak software open to legitimate government surveillance is problematic. Legal sanctions imposed on those making use of computer-mediated communication for criminal activities such as bribery, extortion and trading in banned software will have little practical effect ("Privacy, Security," 1995). There have been several attempts by governments to stop cryptography. Most recently, the U.S. government has classified cryptographic software as "munitions" (along with nuclear, biological, and chemical weapons). U.S. and Canadian citizens and holders of American permanent residency cards (green cards) are able to obtain all cryptographic software under the stipulation that they not "export" such software.[23] Among the encryption programs available is Pretty Good Privacy (PGP), software written by Phil Zimmerman,[24] an individual at the center of a legal storm.

In 1993, Zimmerman, a nationally known cryptographer, was informed that he was the subject of a grand jury investigation being conducted by the U.S. Customs Office in San Jose, CA, which was looking into the international distribution of that software over the Internet. Zimmerman's culpability would arise from having written the original program, made freely available to U.S. citizens (a legal act), yet exporting it when another individual posted it on the Internet in violation of the exportation law. (Possible felony charges would fall under 22 USC 2778 of the U.S. Code governing "Control of arms exports and imports.") This case garnered press attention in *The Wall Street Journal, Time, The New York Times, Scientific America, Wired,* and *US News and World Reports* (Woolley, 1997). Zimmerman was never formally charged with any offense but it was not until January 1996 that the investigation was dropped ("A victory for online privacy," 1996). The implications of the investigation have important civil liberties implications.[25]

This case raises serious questions beyond the realm of privacy as the inadequacy of traditional lines of jurisdiction become clear. Laws permitting the use of such software packages on domestic computers while prohibiting the transmission of such packages overseas are unenforceable, and policing them when millions of computers are connected to the thousands of networks comprising the NII (National Information Infrastructure) is unrealistic. "As the Internet becomes a global entity, U.S. laws become mere local ordinances" (Wallich, 1994, p. 92).[26]

The Clinton administration has attempted to reevaluate and articulate a policy toward encryption. In October 1996, the administration announced a plan toward liberalizing export laws on encryption programs. It was announced that the administration planned to make it easier for U.S. citizens to use more powerful encryption products both at home and abroad to protect privacy, intellectual property, and other information:

> The plan comprises a comprehensive set of actions to promote the development of key recovery products and an encryption key management infrastructure. Specifically, it allows the export of 56-bit key length encryption products under a general license contingent upon industry commitment to build and market future products that support key recovery. . . . Key recovery presumes that a trusted party (such as a bank or, in cases, a party internal to the user's organization) could recover confidentiality key to the encrypted data for the user or for law enforcement officials acting under proper court authority. ("Vice President announces," 1996)

In November 1996, Vice President Gore announced the appointment of a special envoy for cryptography "with the responsibility to promote the growth of international electronic commerce and robust, secure global communications in a manner that protects the public safety and national security" ("Vice President announces," 1996). The Vice President designated the first such special envoy for cryptography, David L. Aaron.[27] This special envoy will be responsible for coordinating international cooperation on encryption matters. Furthermore, by executive order "Administration of Export Control on Encryption Products," President Clinton directed the transfer of jurisdiction for matters of export control of commercial encryption products from the State Department to the Department of Commerce, an administrative path reminiscent of the development of regulation of radio licenses.[28] The Secretary of Commerce is empowered to use his or her discretion to consider the foreign availability of comparable encryption products in determining whether to issue a license in a particular case or to remove controls on particular products. But it is not required to issue licenses in particular cases or to remove controls on particular products based on such consideration ("Executive Order," 1996).

The revised U.S. encryption export policy articulates the concern that encryption programs may jeopardize our foreign policy and national security interests and may be used by international criminal organizations that may threaten the safety of U.S. citizens both domestically and abroad. The exportation of encryption products is thus controlled " to further U.S. foreign policy objectives, and promote our national security" ("Executive order," 1996). The regulations specify that the encryption products specified are placed on the Commerce Control list administered by the Department of Commerce, and that when final regulations are issues the Secretary of Defense, the Secretary of State and the Attorney General shall reexamine such regulations to determine that adequate controls on encryption products can be maintained ("Executive Order," 1996). When the Commerce Department issued final rules on the exportation of computer encoding products, portions were criticized by the software industry.[29] Under the policy announced in December 1996, it relies on key recovery features that allow government officials to decode encrypted messages when acting under proper authority. Nonkey recovery software with keys up to 56 bits will be exportable under six month renewable licenses until the end of 1998, if the manufacturer commits to producing software with key recovery by then. Encryption products including the 128-bit software without key recovery features will continue to be treated as munitions. These products include commonplace e-mail programs and even the recently introduced set-top box for surfing the Internet with a television ("U.S. sticks to plan," 1996).

Curbing exports of encryption software has led to a number of lawsuits challenging the constitutionality of these restrictions.[30] In December, 1996, Judge Marilyn Hall Patel of the U.S. District Court in San Francisco handed down a ruling in one such challenge, the case of *Bernstein v. U.S. Department of State* (Markoff, 1996). Dan Bernstein, a cryptographer, sued the Department of State in the Northern District of California to allow him to publish his encryption software called "Snuffle." He argued that the export controls on encryption constitute a prior restraint. Daniel J. Bernstein was a graduate student in mathematics at the University of California at Berkeley in 1993, when the State Department ruled he would have to register as an international weapons dealer if he wanted to publish an encryption program or discuss it at academic conferences that might be attended by foreigners. He filed suit in 1995, arguing a violation of his ability to electronically publish his program. Judge Patel ruled that the Arms Export Control Act is an unconstitutional prior restraint on speech because it required Bernstein to submit his ideas about cryptography to the government for review, to register as an arms dealer, and to get a government license to publish his ideas. Citing the Pentagon Papers case as precedent, she ruled that the government's 'interest of national security alone does not justify a prior restraint'" (Markoff, 1996). The judge took the position that this was an unlawful content-based restriction on speech and further noted that the government's licensing requirement failed to provide adequate procedural safeguards to minimize the chance of illegal government censorship (Markoff, 1996).[31]

AUTHENTICATION, MESSAGE INTEGRITY, AND ANONYMITY

The ease and degree to which a sender can ascertain that the recipients have received the message as sent has become increasingly significant in cyberspace and has generated some of the most heated debate and litigation in the realm of cyberprivacy: "Along the way, a message can be read, and even more, it can be modified. E-mail headers are notoriously easy to forge. Encrypting the message is one technique to prevent tampering. In addition, cryptographic techniques can also be used to securely "sign" a mail message without encrypting the message" (*Netsurfer Digest*, 1995).

An individual's signature is certainly of concern when considering the rights of the individual, and of vital concern to those who wish to conduct business online, a method of authenticating "digital signature" has received increased attention. Beyond the question of whose eyes may see electronic mail is the matter of veracity. Are the senders in fact who they claim to be? What is the assurance that senders are who they claim to be? To what degree can a message be verified as coming from a given source on receipt of transmission? A digital signature authenticates the identity of the person who sent an electronic message and verifies the message has not been altered. Using a standard keyboard the form of the signature requires the use of a unique string of numbers and letters that are encrypted. In order to verify the signature, a system of private and public keys that encrypt and decrypt the signature is used. There is a certification authority functioning as an online notary of sorts issuing a certificate verifying the sender's identity and the integrity of the message (Leibowitz, 1996a). In one recent case that reflects the situations and concerns surrounding online signatures, a student at the University of Michigan is suing her roommate, alleging she sent a false message (i.e., engaged in electronic forgery) by sending a message via a shared e-mail account declining the university's offer of an $18,000 scholarship (Leibowitz, 1996a).

Another option for securing e-mail privacy is the use of a pseudonym. Pseudonymity, the state of being known by another identity (known as a "nym"), allows for continuity of identity to be maintained over a period of time. A person posting under a "nym" can develop an image and reputation just like any other online personality. Most people interacted with online are just a name and an e-mail address, plus whatever impression formed by either of them according to what they say. The same thing can be true of "nyms."

Although telephones offer anonymity, the legal protection for privacy of telephonic communication is limited to the degree that telephone calls leave traceable "addresses." When extending the reasonable zone of privacy in the realm of telephonic communication, the court stepped back from some of the privacy protections noted in *Katz v. U.S.* (1967) finding no legitimate expectation of privacy in the numbers dialed because the digits one dials are routinely recorded by the phone company for billing purposes.[32] It is not a far leap to apply this rationale to the tracking of electronic messages.

Cyberspace offers great opportunity for anonymous or pseudonymous interaction, but the question is unsettled as to whether there are any real legal protections for such types of communication in cyberspace (Stuckey, 1994). The right to engage in anonymous speech was one of the theories advanced by the plaintiffs in *ACLU v. Reno* challenging the constitutionality of the Communications Decency Act (see Section II, Chapters 6-9). The plaintiffs argue that requiring advanced identification for access to pornographic materials online would make it impossible for users to engage in anonymous speech that they argued was constitutionally protected (*ACLU v. Reno*, 1996). There is some precedent outside of the realm of cyberspace indicating some protection of anonymity when dealing with compelled disclosure in political communication situations (*McIntyre v. Ohio Elections Commission*, 1995).[33]

PRIVACY IN PUBLIC "PLACES"

Expectations toward electronic communication privacy used in more public contexts such as computer bulletin boards result in different psychological assumptions as well as expectations with regard to privacy. Electronic bulletin boards and newsgroups allow system users to post messages of their own to a central location and to read messages posted there by others in a form of public electronic space. Many services monitor bulletin boards and may restrict message placement. The WELL, in Sausalito, CA, places all responsibility for words posted on their system with the author, removing only clearly illegal or libelous material. Prodigy scans catchwords and phrases it deems offensive, which are edited out by employees before posting. This type of activity has produced considerable controversy. Strange as it may seem, Prodigy banned messages from members protesting pricing and editorial policies while later permitting anti-semitic messages to be played. Subsequently, they announced a policing policy which distinguished derogatory messages aimed at groups vs. individuals ("Electrifying speech," 1992). They have also been known to terminate service to adults for such violations, even when violators were children using their parent's accounts.

Associational privacy involves the control of information about interpersonal contacts, friendships, memberships, and, some would argue, is a corollary to the guaranteed rights to freedom of association and assembly. One aspect of associational privacy described by Alan F. Westin (1970) is the "voluntary and temporary withdrawal of a person from the general society through physical or psychological means . . . in a condition of anonymity or reserve" (p. 7). Life in cyberspace does not require retiring from society to achieve privacy, but rather opens up new vistas of sociability.

E-mail systems generally persist in recording and reporting information about the message originator. An anonymous remailer or anonymous server is a free computer service that privatizes e-mail by removing the senders e-mail address. Andre Bacard, author of *Computer Privacy Handbook* (1995), notes that a remailer strips away the real name and address in the header at the top of an e-mail and replaces these data with a dummy address, forwarding the message. There are presently approximately 20 active public remailers on the Internet.[34] Remailers take steps to safeguard privacy from civilian or government by forwarding messages in a timely manner, which Bacard (1995) notes should include holding for a random time before forwarding to increase difficulty in tracing messages.[35] How secure these remailers are is debatable since the e-mail could be intercepted by the person running an e-mail service as the message goes to or from the remailer or a hacker can break into the remailer and read the messages. It is not impossible to determine the identity of a message originator if criminal activity may be involved as illustrated by a case in February 1995, in which the Church of Scientology was able to obtain the identity of a remailer service by filing a criminal complaint through Interpol (*Netsurfer Digest*, 1995). The hard-core advocates of privacy do not trust remailers. Bacard (1995) notes that these people write programs that send their messages to several remailers with only the first remailer knowing the true sender's address but not the final destination of the message. However, one is left to consider what suspicions are aroused by the very act of using a remailer within a context in which traceable addresses are the norm.

Privacy in physical space has come into direct contact with privacy in cyberspace. Current developments and our quest for privacy (probably more aptly described as safe isolation) could not have occurred without the swift evolution of media technology. The *CyberTimes* version of *The New York Times* reports on the "UpperWestSide Cam" a "slice of life camera which takes a shot every 2 minutes of the street scene at Columbus Avenue and 73rd Street in Manhattan and transmits that panorama to the potential world-wide Internet audience" (Napoli, 1997). The venture, a hobby of a computer consultant, features a 24-hour vista of neighborhood activity and has become unusually popular throughout the cyberworld: "A French artist living in Munich wrote and called it 'contemporary poetry.' Other e-mail responses suggest that Spector [the person who placed the camera in his apartment window] is providing a therapeutic surveillance tool" (Napoli, 1997). Linked, that is, computer access, to *The New York Times* story are hundreds of other "CAM Sites" ranging from a dormitory room at a university to a view of Berlin's new government buildings, from a private office in Denmark to a street scene in Strommen, Norway. The Internet participants select snapshots of the world and watch others.

The detached observer is a citizen without responsibility, disconnected from community, able to be mobile and free without the restraints and obligations of community, yet taking pleasure in a form of eavesdropping that in part recaptures the experience of human association. It is a form of closeness. It is a private relationship to a public world. Does it merely raise the issues of surveillance and privacy in the physical realm, which assumes consent by virtue of entering a particular location, or are the implications changed in any way by virtue of global electronic access of others not sharing that physical public space?

CONCLUSIONS

Privacy is a historical reality, which different societies have construed in different ways. The division of human activity between public and private spheres is subject to change—its history is first of all the history of definition (Prost & Vincent, 1991) and has long been the subject of heated debate and inconsistent rulings (Regan, 1995). The computer offers conflicting opportunities for connection and privacy. As technology has expanded our ability to protect privacy, there has been a psychological shift from an expectation of privacy to near paranoia about loss of privacy. Simultaneously, social interaction has moved from the public realm into protected and controlled homes, offices, and laptops. Control of the communication environment is at the heart of the incongruous public/private nature of our use of computer technology and forays into cyberspace, but the legal protections of those rights remain at a developmental stage.

ENDNOTES

1. Public opinion polls have measured different domains of privacy, revealing that concern about privacy is very context specific. For example, The ACLU Foundation (1994) and Harris-Equifax (1993) surveys broke down issues of privacy with respect to employment

contexts ranging from employer collection of information to the monitoring of employees such as telephone monitoring with regard to job performance and monitoring of employees' out-of-work activities. Concern for secondary uses of personal information of credit card information, insurance company information, telephone records, and even video rental records were considered significant in the ACLU Foundation survey of 1994 (Cantril & Cantril, 1994).

2. Opinion polls reveal that concerns for personal privacy appear to be situation specific. Albert Cantril and Susan Davis Cantril (1994) having worked on the ACLU Foundation's survey concluded that there is little consistency in concern for privacy from one domain of privacy to another.

3. Regan (1995) deals with information privacy associated with computerized data; communication privacy related to interpersonal communication, eavesdropping and bugging devices, and privacy in telephonic communication in particular; and psychological privacy, which she relates to what individuals are thinking, and honesty, which she associates with "mental wire-tapping" and polygraph testing.

4. The AOL service agreement (Section 4.1) goes on to reserve the right to remove "any content that it deems in its sole discretion to be unacceptable, undesirable or in violation of the Rules of the Road. AOL Inc. May terminate immediately any Member who misuses or fails to abide by the applicable AOL rules. AOL Inc. May terminate without notice Member's access to and use of the AOL Service and America Online Software upon a breach of the AOL rules, including without limitation, misuse of the software libraries, discussion boards, E-mail, or public conference areas" (AOL Service Agreement, 1995).

5. The 1991 Telephone Consumer Protection Act bars the transmission of unsolicited commercial faxes and prerecorded telephone calls, but does not directly address unsolicited e-mail (Leibowitz, 1996b).

6. On September 5, 1996, a U.S. District Court Judge in Philadelphia issued a temporary injunction prohibiting AOL from blocking the messages sent by CyberPromotions with a trial date set for November to expedite the case (Leibowitz, 1996b).

7. The argument set forth by CyberPromotions argues from an analogy stating that sending unsolicited e-mail messages through the Internet is not over AOL's private pipeline, and the Internet has governmental origins, thereby placing such messages under the protections of the First Amendment (Leibowitz, 1996b).

8. CyberPromotions relied on *Marsh v. Alabama* (1946) and *Pruneyard Shopping Center v. Robins* (1980), in which the Supreme Court permitted leafletting in a private shopping mall.

9. Some states have provided greater protections against government searches and seizures for banking records and telephone numbers (see, e.g., New Jersey and Pennsylvania with regard to telephone privacy; *Commonwealth of Pennsylvania v. Melilli*, 1989); and *State of New Jersey v. Hunt* (1982).

10. If a document is made voluntarily, such as a personal record, there is no compulsion present to trigger the Fifth Amendment right.

11. There is a good deal of information that can be gotten via "mail covers," an investigatory technique of recording information from the outside of an envelop that does not require a warrant (39 C.F.R. § 233.3).

12. The Computer Fraud and Abuse Act articulates three felonies and three misdemeanor offenses. So it is a felony to fraudulently obtain anything of value by accessing a federal interest computer without authorization or by exceeding authorization.

13. Individuals who show communications have been intercepted or used in violation of said statute can claim actual and punitive damages of up to $100 per day of violation (18 USC 2510).

14. The ECPA is an amendment to Title III of the Omnibus Crime Control and Safe Streets Act of 1968, commonly known as the "wiretap law." This law was originally created to govern third-party interceptions of electronic communications, rather than to address concerns of employee rights.

15. The Stored Communications Provisions of the Electronic Communication Privacy Act prohibits an entity from obtaining access to, altering, or preventing access to an electronic communication while it is in storage. There are exceptions in §2701 of the act, including Subsection (c)(1), which excuses conduct authorized by the provider of the service, but this is not thought to authorized a system operator to monitor the contents of e-mail messages between subscribers. The ECPA prohibits service providers from disclosing the content of a communication, whether it is in storage or transmission. Disclosures of content pursuant to a third-party subpoena in civil litigation are also prohibited (§2702). But the act does not prohibit the collection, disclosure, or use of transnational information such as electronic mailing addresses and billing information that can provide a good deal of information about subscribers (Stuckey, 1996).

16. According to Joel P. Kelly (1994), writing in *Employment Law Strategist*, "The tremendous rise in the number of employees who now use this technology, and the increasing ability of management to monitor such use, raise novel legal and ethical issues including privacy, defamation, sexual harassment, and copyrights.

17. Most of these cases developed under the ECPA have involved criminal justice and investigatory wiretaps of telephone and e-mail communication. In the civil application of ECPA, most of the case law has focused on telephone communication monitoring (Aftab, 1996).

18. There has been legislative activity in this realm recently. Legislation has been introduced in Congress by Senatory Paul Simon that would require advance notification to both employees and customers of electronic monitoring. On the federal level, this bill, known as "The Privacy for Consumers and Workers Act," would prohibit undisclosed monitoring of rest room, dressing room, and locker room facilities unless an employer suspects illegal activities. The bill never passed, and similar legislation on the state level has been unsuccessful in overruling the employer's right to monitor the workplace actions or intercepting communications (Aftab, 1996).

19. In Illinois, local business such as the telemarketing industry and the Illinois Retail Merchant Association lobbied for the newly enacted

eavesdropping law (Van Duch, 1996). Originally the law was intended to enable supervisors to monitor service calls for courtesy and efficiency, but the measure passed is broader than the original intent of these supporters (Smolowe, 1996).

20. The Illinois law does protect privacy by prohibiting the disclosure of intercepted communications to third parties, including law enforcement officials (Van Duch, 1996).

21. Two cases in which no reasonable expectation of privacy was found was the case of *Smith v. The Pillsbury Company* (No. 95-5712, E.D. Pa 1996), and a case involving Epson America and the California-based subsidiary of Nissan.

22. Willam Prosser (1977), formerly dean of the University of California at Berkeley Law School, has been influential in characterizing privacy. The three distinct tort actions outlined by Dean Prosser are each applicable to cyberspace transmissions and interactions. The private facts tort is defined in the *Restatement of Torts* (1977) as a publication of private information that "(a) would be highly offensive to a reasonable person and (b) is not of legitimate concern to the public," covering disclosure of embarrassing facts of a personal nature not justified by newsworthiness.

Appropriation or commercialization involves the unauthorized commercial use of another's name or picture in an advertisement, promotion, or other commercial context (*Restatement of Torts*, 1977), in which case the injury suffered is either the humiliation similar to the tort of private facts or a commercial property harm. A false light invasion of privacy tort is the knowing dissemination of highly offensive false publicity (*Restatement of Torts*, 1977). The injury is to the plaintiff's peace of mind. The right to publicity involved celebrity plaintiffs suing defendants for damaging their right to control the commercialization of their names and likenesses. In 1994, talk radio "shock jock" Howard Stern was involved in such an action when, after he announced his candidacy for the governorship of New York, Delphi Internet Services Corporation established a bulletin board about the candidacy, and Stern sued Delphi for using his name and image without permission in an ad for its Internet service. In that case, the court ruled that Delphi was entitled to advertise its service related to news dissemination (*Stern v. Delphi Internet Services Corp.*, 1995).

23. There is a good deal of cryptographic software available on the Internet, including the MIT Web site to distribute export-controlled cryptographic software to those who qualify. The most widely used encryption algorithm is DES (Data Encryption Standard), developed by IBM and adopted as the official Federal Information Processing Standard in 1976. IDEA (International Data Encryption Algorithm) is a new DES-like algorithm invented in 1991 in Switzerland ("Privacy, Security," 1995).

24. Phil Zimmerman became upset with government proposals, which, if enacted, would encroach on the privacy of telecommunication users, so he drafted the PGP program, making it available free of charge to computer users in the United States. Sometime in mid-1991, someone else placed it on the Net, and people around the world began to download it.

25. After three years of investigation, the United States district attorney announced not to prosecute for breaking the ban on the exportation of munitions. If successfully prosecuted the penalty is a maximum prison sentence of 51 months.

26. In a related encryption skirmish, the Clinton administration support of the Clipper Chip is of significance. "Incorporated into all telephones and other such devices, this would permit encrypted communications through the use of the 'Skipjack' algorithm and the device is built with a 'Law Enforcement Access Field' (LEAF). Given a court order, the law enforcement agency could go to key centers with the field information and obtain the keys necessary to decrypt the conversation ("Privacy, Security," 1995). This proposal generated great protest and eventually was scratched as Dr. Matt Blaze of Bell Labs discovered a way to create a LEAF and thus thwart the decryption by authorities ("Privacy, Security," 1995). Most recently (October 1995), the administration indicated it would soon propose "son of Clipper," which would involve the use of nongovernment escrow centers.

27. Ambassador Aaron "will promote international cooperation, coordinate U.S. contacts with foreign governments on encryption matters and provide a focal point for identifying and resolving bilateral and multilateral encryption issues" ("Vice President announces," 1996).

28. With the case of radio, regulation of licensing moved from the Department of Commerce to the newly created Federal Communication Commission. One is tempted to ask whether a similar move toward the creation of a separate regulatory body may not eventually be required to address the burgeoning issues of cyberspace.

29. The revised rules of the Commerce Department reflected a reevaluation of the rules dating to the Cold War when the administration severely limited the export of products containing encryption programs that use mathematical formulas to scramble information and render it unreadable without a password or software "key." The revised rules were intended as a compromise to allow some U.S. companies to compete in the encryption market ("U.S. sticks to plan," 1996).

30. Phil Karn has filed suit against the U.S. Department of State as well. He attempted to take the source code for some encryption programs that is printed in a book, *Applied Cryptography*, and place it on a disk to be sent abroad. The book is legal to export, but the disk is classified as a munition. Karn is suing the government to allow him to export the disk ("Encryption lawsuits," 1997).

31. The Patel ruling is somewhat limited in that it is not binding outside the Northern Federal District of California.

32. *Smith v. Maryland* (1979) dealt with privacy expectations as to which numbers are dialed and when. The telephone company making use of a "pen register" may use such information for billing, so the majority opinion noted there was no legitimate expectation of privacy in numbers dialed. Justice Stewart's dissent in the case noted "that observation no more than describes the basic nature of telephone calls" (pp. 646-647).

33. In *McIntyre v. Ohio Elections Commission* (1995), the Supreme Court considered an Ohio election law prohibiting the circulation of written

materials endorsing or opposing a candidate or referendum issue without the author's name and address. The Court struck down the statute noting that anonymous pamphleting like the Bill of Rights itself protects individuals from retaliation and helps prevent the suppression of ideas.

34. Bacard (1995) notes that remailers tend to come and go as they are labor intensive to maintain and produce no revenues. Furthermore, he refers to the existence of private remailers that restrict users.

35. A popular Internet remailer is run by Johan Hesingius, President of a Helsinki, Finland company that helps businesses connect to Internet. His "an@anon.penet.fi" address are common in controversial newsgroups. This remailer notifies you of your anonymous address.

REFERENCES

ACLU v. Reno, No. 96-963 (E.D. Pa 1996).

Aftab, P. (1996, September 30). Monitoring communication on the Internet. *The National Law Journal*, pp. S2, S 10.

America Online Service Membership. (1995).

Bacard, A. (1995, August 5). *Computer privacy handbook, FAQ*. Berkeley: Peachpit Press.

Brier, S. (1997, January 13). There's no guarantee of privacy on the Internet. *The New York Times CyberTimes*. http://www. nytimes.com/library/cyber/sites/011397sites.html.

California v. Ciraolo, 476 U.S. 207 (1986).

Cantril, A.H., & Cantril, S.D. (1994). *Live and let live: American public opinion about privacy at home and at work*. New York: American Civil Liberties Union Foundation.

Commonwealth of Pennsylvania v. Melilli, 555 A. 2d 1254 (Pa 1989).

Electrifying speech. (1992). *New communications technologies and traditional civil liberties*. New York: Human Rights Watch.

Encryption lawsuits. (1997, January 6). http://www.crypto.com/ lawsuits.

Executive Order, Encryption Policy Resource Page. (1996). http://www.crypto.com/show.cgi?file=exo.html.

Hawn, M. (1996, January 6). As the web expands, so do surveillance tools. *The New York Times*, p. D5.

Hixson, R.F. (1987). *Privacy in a public society: Human rights in conflict*. New York: Oxford University Press.

Katz v. U.S., 389 U.S. 347 (1967).

Kelly, J.P. (1994). Whose e-mail is it anyway? In E.M. Kirsh, L. Rose, & S. Steele (Eds.), *Business and legal aspects of the Internet and online services* (pp. 831-834). New York: Law Journal Seminars-Press.

Leibowitz, W. L. (1996a, August 5). Technology and the law meet Online commerce: "Digital signature" guidelines and an upgraded U.C.C. will ease Internet transactions. An L.A. court tries it out. *The National Law Journal*, pp. B1 & B2.

Leibowitz, W. L. (1996b, September 3). Geography isn't destiny: High tech is reshaping legal basics. *The National Law Journal*, pp. A1 & A16.

Lewis, P. (1994, June 29). No more "anything goes": Cyberspace gets censors. *The New York Times*, p. A1.

Lewis, P. (1995, September 15). Company says electronic mail was opened to find pornography. *The New York Times*, p. A16.

Louis Harris and Associates, & Westin, A.F. (1992). *Harris-Equifax Consumer Privacy Survey*. Atlanta: Equifax, Inc.

McIntyre v. Ohio Elections Commission, ___U.S.___ 115 S. Ct. 1511 (1995).

Markoff, J. (1996, December 19). Judge rules against curbs on export of encryption software. *The New York Times CyberTimes*.

Marsh v. Alabama, 326 U.S. 501 (1946).

Napoli, L. (1997, January 9). As camera captures a street scene, a corner becomes an online world. *The New York Times Cybertimes*. http://www.nytimes.com/library/cyber/week/010997.html.

Netsurfer Digest Focus on Cryptography and Privacy. (1995, August 24). http://www.nypc.com/netsurfer/nsd.95.08.24.html.

O'Connor v. Ortega, 480 U.S. 709 (1987).

Privacy, security, reputation, cryptography, and you. (1995, October 25). http://baby.indstate.e...sci-tech/comp/privacy.

Prosser, W.L. (1971). *Handbook of the law of torts* (4th ed.). St. Paul, MN: West Publishing.

Prost, A., & Vincent, G. (Eds.). (1991). *A history of private life: Riddles of identity in modern times*. Cambridge, MA: The Belknap Press.

Pruneyard Shopping Center v. Robins, 447 U.S. 74 (1980).

Regan, P.M. (1995). *Legislating privacy: Technology, social values, and public policy*. Chapel Hill: The University of North Carolina Press.

Restatement of Torts Second. (1977). St. Paul, MN: West Publishing.

Searcher@finder.com. (1996, December 27).

Smith v. Maryland, 442 U.S. 735 (1979).

Smith v. The Pillsbury Company, No. 95-5712 (e.D. Pa. 1996).

Smolowe, J. (1996. January 22). My boss, big brother. *Time*, p. 56.

State of New Jersey v. Hunt, 450 A. 2d 952 (N.J. 1982).

Stern v. Delphi Internet Services Corp. 626 N.Y.S. 2d 694 (N.Y. Sup. 1995).

Stuckey, K. (1994). *Internet and online law*. New York: Law Journal Seminars-Press.

United States v. Miller, 425 U.S. 435 (1976).

U.S sticks to plan for encryption keys. (1996, December 29). http://www.msnbc.com/news/48893 and http://www.msnbc.com/news/48893.asp.

Vice President announces special envoy for cryptography. (1996, November 15).

Encryption Policy Resource Page. http://www.crypto.com/show.cgi?file=c311pr.html.

Van Duch, D. (1996, February 5). Workplace monitoring law: Friend of big brother? *The National Law Journal*, pp. B1-2.

A victory for online privacy: U.S. drops inquiry into Boulderite's encryption program. (1996, January 12). *Daily Camera*, pp. 1 & 2A.

Wallich, P. (1994, March). Wire pirates. *Scientific America*, p. 90.

Westin, A. F. (1970). *Privacy and freedom.* New York: Atheneum.

Woolley S. (1997). Banned in Washington. http://www.forbes.com/forbes/97/0421/5908/62a.htm.

17

COMMERCIAL SPEECH IN CYBERSPACE: THE JUNK E-MAIL ISSUE

ROY V. LEEPER AND PHILLIP HEELER

Marketing in cyberspace includes unsolicited commercial e-mail. In this chapter the process of "spamming" is explored with regard to free speech rights of senders and the right to be protected from speech unwilling recipients claim they receive. The authors explore plausible approaches to the conflicting communicative interests represented and argue that unsolicited commercial e-mails should be treated as analogous to unsolicited commercial fax marketing. This leads to the conclusion that it should be brought under the commercial fax section of the 1991 Telephone Consumer Protection Act.

> The golden age of cyberspace is ending, but the golden age for lawyers is just dawning.
> —Law Professor I. Trotter Hardy (quoted in Mauro, 1994)

Although the numbers are difficult to accurately measure, the growth rate of the Internet is staggering. One recent estimate is that the number of networks linked to the Internet increased from about

200 in 1988 to over 46,000 in 1995; that the number of computers linked to the Internet increased from just over 28,000 in 1987 to almost 5 million in 1995; that the number of World-Wide Web servers increased from about 500 in 1993 to about 10,000 in 1994; and that in early 1995, somewhere between 30 and 40 million people had some sort of access to the Internet (Katsh, 1995). It is estimated that in the United States, as of September 1996, 38.7 million U.S. citizens have ventured into cyberspace at least once (Sandberg, 1996). Roughly 9% of major U.S. corporations currently advertise on the Internet, and some 37% of such corporations have plans for advertising or promotion on the Internet (Boroughs, 1995). Although currently less than 1% of the nation's advertising budget is spent on the Internet (Warner, 1995), "commercial information providers" are the Internet's "fastest growing sector" (Cate, 1994). It is estimated that total sales from online sources will grow to $4.8 billion by 1998 (Press, 1994). Estimates of the number of people who purchased something on the Net in 1995 range from 1.51 million to 1.97 million (Lewis, 1996). These numbers are constantly changing and the change in direction seems to be exponentially upward.

This growing interest of advertisers in the Internet should not be surprising because media in the United States have traditionally been receptive to commercial endeavors (Dizard, 1994). Although the interest of commercial providers in the new media is not surprising, it does fundamentally change the nature of that media that previously had not been inundated by advertising (Cavazos & Morin, 1994). The Internet as a medium is a "whole new legal world" (Denning & Lin, 1994), and the role of commercial speech in that medium is unclear. As a result of technology developing faster than the law (Drucker & Gumpert, 1995; Gordon & McKenzie, 1995), most of the legal issues inherent in that medium have not yet been addressed (Sugawara, 1991). This chapter is an attempt to try to answer one of those issues, specifically the legal implications of unsolicited commercial e-mail. (Advertising on commercial services such as Prodigy and America Online is not addressed here.) First, the problem of commercial e-mail is be explored; second, possible approaches to the problem are examined; and third, it is argued that unsolicited commercial e-mail should be brought under the unsolicited commercial facsimile section of the Telephone Consumer Protection Act of 1991.

THE PROBLEM

The incident that brought national attention to the problem of commercial e-mail was an advertisement by two lawyers, Lawrence

Canter and Martha Siegel, offering their services to people with "green card" problems (Branscomb, 1995; Rose, 1995). Identical copies of this 1994 ad were sent to thousands of Usenet groups. This is a process known as "spamming." The name comes from the, hopefully imagined, effect that would occur when spam is thrown into a fan. The advertisement reached an estimated one million plus people. As people often belong to more than one group, a number of people received multiple copies of the ad. The effect for these consumers was described as "opening a mailbox and finding thousands of junk mail letters with postage due" (Branscomb, 1995, pp. 1657-1658).

The reaction was one of outrage. There were a number of e-mail flames sent to Canter and Siegel's mail box. Automatic calling programs were set up to flood their voice mail system with junk messages (Branscomb, 1995). A "cancelbot" was set up to wipe out any further messages from Canter and Siegel, and their Internet provider, responding to public pressure, shut off their account (Rose, 1995). Death threats were made against the lawyers (Lewis, 1994a). The reaction from Canter and Siegel was just as predictable. First, they threatened to file suit against their Internet provider for denial of their First Amendment access rights. Second, following their success and notoriety, they set up a consulting business and wrote a book advising people how to advertise on the Internet (Branscomb 1995). Third, in February 1995, they repeated their earlier activity by advertising for credit record work on over 10,000 newsgroups. This advertisement contained a statement that their ad had the permission of the newsgroup managers—a statement that apparently was not true (Branscomb, 1995).

The reason for the continued work in this area by Canter and Siegel is clear—it is incredibly successful. As a result of their initial ad, they received "25,000 customer inquiries for one night's work—and $100,000 worth of business for a $20 investment" (Spalter, 1995, p. 21). Given such success stories, it is not surprising that others would follow suit. A New York firm, Consumer Credit Advocates, used Cybersell, Inc. (Canter and Siegel's consulting firm) to post advertisements earlier this year to approximately 3,000 Usenet newsgroups ("Online Advertising," 1995). It has been reported that one organization offered to sell a list of 250,000 e-mail addresses. Due to the protests, that offer was rescinded, but other organizations picked up the offer. One individual offered, for a fee, to send messages to 6 million e-mail accounts. Another person, Sanford Wallace of CyberPromotions Inc., offered to send out advertisements to over 600,000 e-mail addresses. Wallace argues that "he has the right to send junk e-mail to anyone with an e-mail address" (quoted in Hayes, 1996). This includes all of the 6.5 million

America Online (AOL) subscribers. AOL decided to block junk e-mail from three bulk e-mail distributors, including Wallace's CyberPromotions. Wallace went to court, and U.S. District Judge Charles R. Weiner ordered AOL not to block the e-mail until the case goes to trial on the issues in November. (Weiner's injunction was lifted by the Third Circuit Court of Appeals in September pending the outcome of the trial; Weber, 1996). Wallace argued that this is an issue not only of advertising revenue but also of free speech versus regulation (Hayes, 1996). Wallace defends his position by saying he gives individuals the opportunity to take their names off his spamming list. Apparently his approach is successful as Wallace reports that 83% of his advertisers use his service again within a month (Bredenberg, 1996). One source reported to Net researchers Hoffman and Novak (1996b) that they had sold 10 times as many units of their product over the Internet at one tenth the advertising budget of traditional advertising. Hoffman and Novak estimate that marketing in cyberspace is one fourth less expensive than conventional marketing methods. Even chain letters have found their way into e-mail accounts (Burgess, 1994).

In spite of the negative Internet user reaction to unsolicited commercial e-mail, it is predicted that the amount of such e-mail will increase, not decrease. Not only is it profitable, but, given the nature of the electronic media, the ads are more appealing than print ads. They are easier to create, cheaper to utilize, and can be targeted more easily to a specific audience (Volokh, 1995). A key to return customer business is to insure that company messages and products are relevant to customer needs (Pine, Peppers, & Rogers, 1995). Internet advertising enables advertisers to more closely tailor and present their messages. As Miller (1996) explains: "Hundreds of lists can be electronically merged and duplicates eliminated. Data from one list can be matched with data from a totally different list. Formerly separate information sources can be combined, and a very complete portrait of each individual can be compiled" (pp. 382-383). Hoffman and Novak (1996a) write that such advertising research "can determine the variables that relate to a consumer's propensity to enter the flow state and such information can be used to develop marketing efforts designed to maximize the chances of the consumer achieving flow." The result is that cyberspace "may eventually turn out to be the greatest new marketing opportunity in history" (Burstein & Kline, 1995, p. 118), and that "commercial speech is beginning to overshadow its [Internet] academic and research uses" (Branscomb, 1995, p. 1657).

Because of these problems scholars, including some who are wary of governmental regulation, are beginning to call for some kind of action to be taken. When there is no central agency to oversee a problem area, as is the case here, courts often step into the void (Dizard, 1994). A leading advocate of First Amendment protection for speech, Eugene Volokh (1995) recognizes a unique problem with regard to commercial e-mail:

> Likewise, as the economic constraints on sending tidal waves of unsolicited mail are removed, legal restrictions may have to take their place. Today such restrictions might be seen as unconstitutional, at least as to noncommercial speech. But if indeed e-mailing is next to free, then the assumption that the "short, though regular, journey from mail box to trash can" is "an acceptable burden, at least so far as the Constitution is concerned" may stop being reasonable. (p. 1845)

Computer Professionals for Social Responsibility (PSR—1993, p. 12), a group very protective of the rights of computer users, recognizes a problem with commercial e-mail:

> Freedom to communicate, however, does not mean freedom to intrude. The right to free speech must be balanced by the right not to listen. Given that many people now find unsolicited mail and telephone calls intrusive, it is easy to imagine that the NII [National Information Infrastructure] might enable the production of an overwhelming amount of electronic "junk mail." It must not fall as a burden to the individual to sift through all such material to find the nuggets of desired communication. There must be ways for people to choose classes of messages they do and do not wish to receive. (p. 12)

Given the growth of commercial e-mail, the question seems to be: What approach can and should be taken to alleviate the problems that have arisen as a result of that growth?

POSSIBLE APPROACHES

No Regulation

According to Anne Branscomb (1994), "there is as yet no law of cyberspace." Referring specifically to the Canter and Siegel advertising situation, Lance Rose (1995) notes that there is no law preventing their action. This state of "anarchy" is preferred by a number of people who are closely connected to, and knowledgeable about, the Internet. Maggie Cannon (1995) wrote that "the anarchy of the Internet and the relatively uncensored discourse on on-line services is a great part of the on-line world's appeal" (p. 17). Jayne Levin, editor of the Internet Letter, said that "the Internet has been such a collegial gathering of people who do their own thing—the diversity, culture and character. To try to muffle that is very sad" (quoted in Sandberg, 1995). Cliff Figallo, managing director of the Whole Earth 'Lectronic Link ("The Well"), stated that "we have always believed that what goes on our conference bulletin boards is the users' responsibility" (quoted in Feder, 1991). Finally, the Computer Professionals for Social Responsibility (1990) quoted favorably from the Senate Science and Technology Committee: "The networks have ad hoc management and it has created anarchy. It's a good thing; it would be very hard to impose a policy on this community, even if we knew how" (p. 2). Later in the report, the CPSR argues that "this seeming chaos and inefficiency creates conditions not only for a free society but for highly robust technical systems and infrastructures to support it" (p. 3).

Although such anarchy may seem to be desirable, there is increasing recognition that regulation is becoming both more likely and necessary. Branscomb, (1995) wrote that "as more and more computer users arrive in these cyberspaces, they bring expectations that the legal norms of the real world will apply" (p. 1646). Professor Hardy is quoted as having said that "the frontier mentality is giving way to a settler mentality and to increasing pressure for legal controls" (quoted in Mauro, 1994, p. A2).

Support for the possibility of groups being able to resolve disagreements without recourse to legal avenues comes from a study by Robert Ellickson (1991). The study focuses on how neighbors in a California county resolve issues arising from problems caused by "wayward cattle"—fencing issues and trespass damage. Ellickson found that these neighbors tended to rely on "informal norms," even while recognizing that those norms may be inconsistent with the law: "They achieve cooperative outcomes not by bargaining from legally established entitlements . . . but rather by developing and enforcing adaptive norms of neighborliness that trump formal legal entitlements" (p. 4). Enforcement of the norms against deviants tends to follow this progression: "(1) self-help retaliation; (2) reports to county authorities; (3) claims for compensation informally submitted without the help of attorneys; and (4) attorney-assisted claims for compensation" (p. 57).

This approach seems analogous to the concept of *netiquette* defined as "an informal, open-ended set of guidelines for fruitful, legitimate, and socially responsible use of Internet applications" (Pfaffenberger, 1994, p. 292). The initial reaction to the commercial e-mail message from Canter and Siegel was one of spontaneous self-help retaliation—flames reminding them of the informal norms of the Net, flooding their voice mail system, a cancelbot, and so on. Given the reaction by Canter and Siegel, these self-help measures were ineffective. Ellickson (1991) noted that disputants tend to turn to the legal system when "the social distance between them increases, when the magnitude of what is at stake rises, and when the legal system provides an opportunity for the disputants to externalize costs to third parties" (p. 283). The "social distance" has certainly increased among users of the Internet. Denning and Lin (1994) note that the Internet system of controls is eroding because (a) new users often do not understand the norms of the system, (b) the Net brings together people from radically different cultures and value systems, and (c) this interaction takes place without the homogenization that often takes place in a face-to-face community as Ellickson was describing. The stakes have certainly risen also. The commercial gain realized by Canter and Siegel and others is significant. And the responses from the Internet community raised the stakes involved. In discussing self-help on the Net, Burgess (1994) writes that "so many inhabitants [of the Net] have appointed themselves guardians of law and order. In many cases, it works well; in others, suspects get all the due process and compassion shown to cattle rustlers" (p. 19). This lack of due process in the pursuit of self-help remedies suggests a possible need to resort to regulation to prevent harm. It is suggested that anarchy starts breaking down at about 100 people (Lewis, 1994b). Spamming certainly increases the number above 100.

Miller (1996) writes:

> Cyberspace's tradition of noncommercial mutual aid is already being eroded as its growing popularity and accessibility attract people who don't care about its traditions or the cooperative ethics that underlie the online community. . . . It is not clear that the Internet's already-weakened cooperative culture will survive the transition to market-rate 'metered' pricing, which will drive up the cost of altruism. (pp. 324-325)

As a result of the ineffectiveness of self-help and self-regulation, it appears as if some sort of legal regulation will be forthcoming. The question is, what sort of regulation will it be?

Commercial Speech Regulation

Initially, commercial speech was not entitled to First Amendment protection (*Valentine v. Chrestensen* 1942). Beginning with the 1975 case, *Bigelow v. Virginia* (1975), the Supreme Court has given some level of First Amendment protection to commercial speech. Although there is some confusion over the meaning of the term *commercial speech* (Petty 1993), the Court in *Central Hudson Gas and Electric Company v. Public Service Commission of New York* (1980) set out the controlling test for such speech.

Central Hudson involved a PSC ban on all promotional advertising ("advertising intended to stimulate the purchase of utility services") by utilities, but did allow "informational" advertising on shifting consumption from peak to low periods of demand. The utility appealed the ban through the judicial system to the Supreme Court, which held the ban to be in violation of the First Amendment rights of the utility. The Court held that although commercial speech is accorded lesser protection than some other forms of speech, because of the informational function of commercial speech it is entitled to First Amendment protection. The level of that protection is set out in a four-part test: (a) Is the speech protected by the First Amendment (does it concern lawful activity and is not misleading)? (b) Is the governmental interest in regulating the speech substantial? (c) Does that regulation directly advance that governmental interest? and (d) Is the regulation "not more extensive than necessary to serve that interest?" (Central Hudson v. Public Service, 1980, p. 566).

The fourth part of the test has recently been the cause of some confusion. The "least restrictive" analysis in Central Hudson is very protective of commercial speech and, under such an approach, the courts do not have to give much deference to legislative judgment. In Posadas de Puerto Rico Associates v. Tourism Company of Puerto Rico (1986), the Supreme Court seemed to back away from that standard. Although purporting to apply the Central Hudson analysis, Justice Rehnquist, in answering the argument that counterspeech against gambling would be a less restrictive means of meeting the purpose of a ban on gambling advertising in Puerto Rico, wrote, "We think it is up to the legislature to decide whether or not such a 'counterspeech' policy would be as effective in reducing the demand for casino gambling as a restriction on advertising" (p. 344). Such deference to the legislature without going into the "least restrictive" approach is a clear retreat from Central Hudson. This shift in approach became more apparent in Board of Trustees v. Fox (1989) when the Court dropped the "least restrictive" language in favor of "reasonable fit": "What our decisions require is a 'fit' between the legislature's ends and the means chosen to accomplish those ends—a fit that is not necessarily perfect, but reasonable; . . . Within those bounds we leave it to governmental decisionmakers to judge what manner of regulation may best be employed" (p. 480). So it seems clear that, in Fox, the Court backed away from the strong protection for commercial speech set out in Central Hudson. This lack of clarity in the Central Hudson test has led to charges of "unpredictability and subjectivity" and a call for the abandonment of a differing level of protection for commercial speech (Mandel, 1994).

In 1993, the Court in Cincinnati v. Discovery Network (1993) struck down Cincinnati's ban on commercial newsracks on public property. Although the majority for the Court claimed to be applying the Fox variation of the fourth prong of the Central Hudson test, it clearly was providing more protection for commercial speech than did Fox (Cahill, 1994). In Discovery Network, the Court argued that there were other less drastic means that the city could have used to accomplish their goal of increasing public safety, and that because such other means existed, the fit between the regulation and the goal was not reasonable. The majority for the Court also held that "we rejected the mere rational basis review" (p. 1515, note 3). This backs away from the deference given to legislative judgment as to the reasonableness of the fit.

The last word from the Supreme Court, *44 Liquormart Inc. v. Rhode Island* (1996), although a 9-0 decision, does little to clarify the situation. With applying Central Hudson to a Rhode Island ban on advertising the price of liquor, the Court again focused on the fourth part of the test and, again, failed to come to an agreement as to its meaning. Justice Stevens, in the principal opinion for the Court, rejected the concept of courts deferring to legislative judgment. His opinion stressed the need of evidence that the goal of the regulation was achieved to a "material degree" and evidence that the regulation "significantly" reduced the problem of alcoholism. In regard to Posadas, Stevens wrote that the Court "erroneously performed the First Amendment analysis" (p. 1685). Justice O'Connor, joined by three others, argued that the Court did not have to question the holding in Posadas and could have decided the case on the basis that the regulation did not meet the reasonable fit test of Central Hudson. As a result of this series of cases following Central Hudson, the level of protection for commercial speech is unclear.

The test in Central Hudson, in whatever form, applies regardless of the medium in which the commercial speech appears.[1] Under Central Hudson and the following cases, the type of commercial speech regulation that is normally struck down by the Courts is regulation aimed at banning consumer information; otherwise, commercial speech regulations tend to be upheld (Collins & Skover, 1993; Tomlinson & Wiley, 1995). Although the test in Central Hudson is medium invariant, there are other regulations that distinguish among the media in the area of commercial speech—for instance, hard alcohol cannot be advertised on television but can be advertised in the print medium.

Some have argued that speech regulation should be the same across the media—that the focus should be on the First Amendment values at stake rather than on the media and their differing impacts on the receiver (Allard, 1994; Corn-Revere, 1994; Krattenmaker & Powe, 1995; Lively, 1994; "The message is in the medium," 1994; Tribe, 1991). A principal spokesperson for this point of view is

Laurence Tribe (1991) who has proposed a constitutional amendment to the effect that constitutional freedoms "shall be construed as fully applicable without regard to the technological method or medium through which information content is generated, stored, altered, transmitted, or controlled" (p. 39). But, of course, this is not the current policy as evidenced by differing First Amendment protections for the differing media, nor is it likely to gain political favor. Indeed, perhaps such a policy is not desirable. The different media undeniably have differing degrees of intrusiveness and impact on the recipients. In responding to Tribe's argument against a public forum analogy for cyberspace, Edward DiLello (1993) argues that Tribe's approach focuses on the rights of the media at the expense of the rights of the users of that media, and that such an approach is not positive.

Assuming that different media will continue to be regulated differently, the issue here is the type of regulation that will be used for cyberspace. That direction will, in all probability, be set by metaphorical reasoning. It has been claimed that, when it comes to making judgments, "all law is metaphoric" (Henly, 1987, p. 82). When confronted with new material, metaphoric thinking is all that there is to guide one through the problem analysis (CPSR, 1990). In assessing the importance of metaphors in legal thought, Haig Bosmajian (1992) wrote that "at all levels, metaphors, metonymies, personifications, and other tropes appearing in court opinions have attained permanence, have become institutionalized and relied upon as principles, standards, doctrines, and premises in arriving at judicial judgments" (p. 1). The value in such reasoning, according to Bosmajian (1992), is that it "can help us comprehend what may have been incomprehensible, can help us find new 'truths,' clarify and create new realities" (p. 205).

Even though metaphoric reasoning can help guide us through uncharted territory, there are dangers involved in such a process. Bosmajian (1992) continued, saying that "there always remains the danger that through the tropes we can also mislead, conceal, create misunderstanding, and come to rely on cliched thinking" (p. 205). Other dangers of metaphoric thinking include: metaphors are "enslaving" because they limit the scope of the thought process (Johnson, 1994; Katsh, 1995); metaphoric reasoning allows the past to control future debate (Allard, 1994; Price, 1985); metaphors are subjective in nature which presents consistency problems (Corn-Revere, 1994); one metaphor can be called on by the media to gain certain rights, but then be discarded for another metaphor in order to avoid responsibility (Uncapher, 1991); and, specifically in the case of cyberspace, it has been argued that any metaphor will fail because of the uniqueness of the new medium (Byassee, 1995; Johnson & Marks, 1993; McGraw, 1995).

In spite of the dangers of metaphoric reasoning, and perhaps because of the necessity of such reasoning in the legal arena, there have been a number of attempts to suggest the proper metaphor for cyberspace (Denning & Lin, 1994; Miller, 1993). When an argument is made for a particular metaphor, the author of the argument generally argues against other suggested possibilities. Following are some metaphors that have been suggested as appropriate for how cyberspace should be approached in terms of possible regulation: real property (Drucker & Gumpert, 1995), telephone (Ayre & Willmott, 1995; Williams & Pavlik, 1994), public forum (DiLello, 1993; Goldstone, 1995; Taviss, 1992), newspaper (Miller, 1991), common carrier (Kapor, 1991), an information flow model (O'Neill, 1994), property rights and the law of trespass (McGinnis, 1996), and contract law (Johnson & Marks, 1993; Perritt, 1993). It is argued in this chapter that, in dealing with the issue of unsolicited commercial e-mail, the proper metaphor is the regulation of unsolicited commercial faxes under the Telephone Consumer Protection Act (TCPA) of 1991. Cass Sunstein (1995) suggests that the new media do not raise new questions but rather new areas for application. The question of commercial e-mail is the same question as unsolicited commercial faxes—the Internet just presents a new area of application.

PROPOSED SOLUTION

In 1991, the TCPA was signed into law (47 U.S.C. 227). The major problem addressed by the Act is telephone solicitation, but 227 (b) (1) (C) states that it shall be "unlawful for any person within the United States—to use any telephone facsimile machine, computer, or other device to send an unsolicited advertisement to a telephone facsimile machine." Section (b) (3) establishes a private right of action against violators, providing for a penalty of $500 or actual monetary loss, whichever is greater, for each violation. Treble damages are possible if there is a knowing or willful violation. State law is not preempted (section (e) (1)) and injunctions are possible against repeat offenders (section (f) (1)).

The purpose of the Act is to "protect residential telephone subscriber privacy rights by restricting certain commercial solicitation and advertising uses of the telephone and related telecommunication equipment" (U.S. House Committee, 1991; Senate, 1991). Commercial fax was seen as "proliferating" as a result of the ability of the advertiser's machine to "easily deliver tens of thousands of unsolicited messages per week to other facsimile machines across the country" (U.S. House Committee, 1991, pp. 6-7). The problem involved with this capability was (a) the shifting of the "cost of advertising from the sender to the recipient," and (b) the fact that the commercial fax "occupies" the recipient's facsimile machine while it is receiving the fax, thereby preventing it from receiving other messages (U.S. House Committee, 1991). The House Committee distinguished unsolicited commercial fax from regular commercial mail on the basis that, with regular mail, the recipient does not bear any cost. It has been argued that the only way to avoid this cost shifting is an outright ban on unsolicited commercial faxing as is done in the Act (Cain, 1994).

In spite of the passage of the Act, in 1994 the FCC received some 300 complaints from recipients of commercial fax (Gerlin, 1995). The response from a group of 35 Texas businessmen was to sue on the basis of the Act. That case is pending (Gerlin, 1995). There has been a case, however, which upheld, through the appellate court level, the constitutionality of the facsimile portion of the Act against a First Amendment challenge. (For a pre-TCPA analysis of state regulations on unsolicited faxes and an argument that a complete ban on such faxes would be struck down, see Broecker, 1990.) *Destination Ventures v. FCC* (1994) involved a suit brought by a group of small business owners who use facsimile advertising to promote their business and by a businessman who wanted to continue receiving unsolicited faxes, to enjoin the enforcement of the facsimile portion of the TCPA. The basis for the suit was that the Act violated both their free speech and equal protection rights. In rejecting plaintiff's arguments, the District Court cited the commercial speech line of cases and applied the four-part test of Central Hudson.

The first part of the test—whether or not the speech engaged in is protected by the First Amendment—was assumed to be met. The Court spent some time discussing the second part of the test—whether or not there was a substantial governmental interest that is being addressed by the regulation. Plaintiffs argued that there is no historical record of Congressional concern with unsolicited faxes. The Court suggested that the lack of a record was probably due to the newness of the medium and pointed to a history of Congressional "efforts to protect consumers from harm" (p. 635). The Court then turned to the legislative history of the facsimile sections of the TCPA, referring to cost shifting, the tying up of the fax machine while receiving the unsolicited commercial fax message, and the tremendous growth of the use of commercial faxes. The Court concluded this part of their analysis by writing that although there was an absence of detailed studies and statistical data in the hearings, "Congress legitimately relied upon the testimony from authorities, as well as the contemporaneous state laws and media reports" (p. 637). The third part of the test is whether or not the regulation directly advances that interest. The Court held that because a harm was created by unsolicited commercial faxes, "the subsequent banning of those unsolicited faxes directly advances that interest" (p. 637).

The fourth part of the Central Hudson test is the "not more extensive" requirement that has been the subject of some confusion. That confusion is briefly reflected in Destination Ventures. When introducing its discussion of the constitutionality of the Act, the Court wrote that it is doing so "under the Central Hudson and Fox tests," yet when the Court got to the fourth part of the test, it wrote that "it is the government's burden to establish that a reasonable fit exists between the legislation it seeks to enact and the burden the law would place upon constitutional rights" (p. 637). The cite for this position is Fox, but that opinion also contains the statement that "within those bounds we leave it to governmental decisionmakers to judge what manner of regulation may best be employed" (*Board of Trustees v. Fox*, 1989, p. 480). This language from Fox, which qualifies the burden of proof language, is one of deference to the legislature, a lower standard of protection for commercial speech than is found in Discovery Network.

The District Court found that the fourth part of the Central Hudson test is satisfied in the TCPA. Plaintiffs in Destination Ventures argued that the TCPA's distinction between commercial and noncommercial faxes is analogous to Discovery Network's distinction between commercial and noncommercial newsracks, which led the Supreme Court to invalidate Cincinnati's ordinance. The District Court in Destination Ventures responded that although the TCPA distinguished between for-profit and not-for-profit telephone solicitations, it banned *all* unsolicited commercial faxes from whatever source. The District Court went on to distinguish the TCPA from other infirmities found in the Cincinnati ordinance. The Court concluded by holding that the fact that Congress did not choose some other means of regulating unsolicited faxes such as the creation of do-not-fax lists, regulating hours, or limiting the number and frequency of unsolicited faxes, "fail[s] to establish that the legislation Congress did choose is improperly tailored for its targeted goal, protecting consumers from the burdens associated with receiving unsolicited fax advertisements" (p. 639). The District Court held that such legislation is "a reasonable fit," again indicating the tension with the "not more extensive" language of Central Hudson.

The issue on appeal was the "reasonable fit" argument. The Appellate Court rejected plaintiff's analogy to Discovery Network. The Court held that because the Congressional goal was to prevent the shifting of advertising costs, "limiting its regulation to faxes containing advertising was justified. The ban is even-handed in that it applies to commercial solicitation by any organization" (*Destination Ventures v. FCC*, 1995, p. 56). Because the problem addressed in the Act is cost shifting, and since the regulation is a ban on such activity, the evidentiary requirement of 44 Liquormart as to proof of problem solution would seem to be met. In response to plaintiff's argument that the costs were de minimis, the Appellate Court held that they were still significant enough to justify the enactment of the legislation.

This chapter argues that unsolicited commercial e-mail is analogous to unsolicited commercial fax. Recognizing the dangers involved in metaphorical reasoning discussed earlier, it is nonetheless argued that unsolicited commercial e-mail should be brought under the Telephone Consumer Protection Act. The parallels between the two situations are striking and the issues perhaps even more telling when discussing commercial e-mail. First, there is a shifting of advertising costs as with commercial fax (Bredenberg, 1996). The commercial e-mailer is using the computer of the recipient just as the commercial faxer is using the facsimile machine of the recipient. The cost absorbed is in terms of disk space being occupied by the storage of that transmission. Second, each transmission requires a certain amount of time to be sent between sites, which in turn occupies the network and requires additional bandwidth to send all the other transmissions. This cost is usually borne by the site instead of the commercial e-mailer. If graphics are involved, the cost in terms of both disk space and band width are increased dramatically. Third, as noted in the introductory part of this chapter, the number of commercial e-mail messages will increase, not decrease over the coming years. If that happens, the costs to the recipient will increase. Fourth, commercial e-mail is even more intrusive than commercial fax. A fax sits there until the recipient decides to pick it up. With commercial e-mail, the message resides on the user's computer until the user decides to delete the message. This unauthorized use of the owner's computer resources is usurping the storage capacities of the system without the permission or authorization of the computer owner/user. (In fact, if the recipient is out of town, or away from the system for other reasons, the recipient may not even know that space is being taken by the advertisement, and the system may be overloaded so that other e-mail is not received.) It is estimated that one half of the cost of commercial junk e-mail is absorbed by the recipient of the mail (Bredenberg, 1996). Commercial e-mail is also intrusive in the same way that a radio broadcast of a George Carlin record was found to be intrusive in the *FCC v. Pacifica Foundation* (1978) case—the mail system is opened by the user (as the radio is turned on by the listener), and the ad is there without any forewarning. (For an argument that computers are not intrusive in this sense, see Cate, 1995.)

This analogy has been alluded to by other sources (Bredenberg, 1996; Denning & Lin, 1994). An individual sued CompuServe on the basis of the TCPA for allowing unsolicited commercial e-mail to be sent to CompuServe subscribers. The case was settled out of court (Eckenwiler, 1996). Eckenwiler suggests that if the TCPA is amended to include unsolicited commercial e-mail, then it would probably be upheld on the basis of the holding in *Destination Ventures v. FCC* (1994). A commentator wrote that "users will have little control if they are bombarded with unsolicited information, such as the electronic equivalent of junk mail or obscene phone calls. . . . The government can protect users' privacy by regulating the transmission of information over which the recipient has no control, and yet allow other users to obtain such information over the same medium" ("The message," 1994, p. 82). The only way to eliminate the cost shifting of unsolicited commercial e-mail is to, as the TCPA does with unsolicited commercial fax, ban it completely (Cain, 1994).

Other possible less onerous approaches are those suggested by the plaintiffs in *Destination Ventures v. FCC* (1994)—creating internal do-not-e-mail lists such as the TCPA allows for telephone solicitation, regulating the hours when unsolicited commercial e-mail could be sent so as to minimize interference with peak hours of use, and limiting the number of unsolicited commercial e-mail messages that a particular advertiser could send and the number of times that a particular advertiser could send a particular advertisement. Another possibility would be to establish, as the TCPA allows the FCC to do, a national database of names of people who do not wish to receive unsolicited ads. An e-mail advertiser would be required to check that database for user names and eliminate them from the mailing. Such a procedure has been established for regular mail involving obscenity (39 U.S.C. 3008, 3010 1991) and its constitutionality has been upheld (*Rowan v. United States Post Office*, 1970). But such approaches would not seem to be much of a deterrent, especially when the stakes are as high as they seem to be, given the effectiveness and profitability of such advertising.[2]

CONCLUSION

Anytime a regulation is proposed for a new media, care must be taken because that regulation and rationale are very difficult to alter once it has been accepted and applied (Lively, 1994). But even the most ardent advocates for freedom on the Internet recognize that there is a problem with commercial e-mail. For example, I. Trotter Hardy (1994) has argued that in considering regulation of the cyberspace, one should start at the "lowest" possible level that he or she sees as "Pure Self-Help" (as in the Ellickson study referred to earlier). As an example of "unilateral self-help at its best," he refers to the chain letter situation mentioned earlier and the responses made to the letter. According to Hardy (1994):

> Advertising on the Internet may soon become a problem. After this article was completed, the author learned of a controversial advertising message over the Internet from a law firm [Canter and Siegel] indirectly seeking clients with questions about immigration law. The controversy centered on the fact that the message apparently went literally to millions of Internet users. It seems likely that this use of the network as a mass medium will increase in the future. (p. 1027, footnote 80)

As explained earlier, self-help did not work with Canter and Siegel. The Internet is no longer an homogenous community. There is much money to be made, as Canter and Siegel and others have demonstrated, in advertising on the Internet.

If anarchy is no longer feasible, if self-help is not practical given the differing values of the users of the Internet, and if there is a problem that affects millions of people as unsolicited commercial e-mail does, then it seems as if the best approach is to solve that problem as similar problems have been solved before. Regulating unsolicited commercial e-mail in the same way unsolicited commercial fax is regulated seems to be not only practical but also desirable.

ENDNOTES

1. For recent summaries of this line of cases, see, for example, Boedecker, Morgan, and Wright (1995); Cahill (1994); Lavery (1994); and Collins and Skover (1993) and the responses in the volume to their article by Kozinski and Banner, Smolla, Jhally, and Bogart. For a discussion of commercial speech in the context of advocacy advertising, see Cutler and Muehling (1989, 1991), and Middleton (1991).

2. Brian Gilpin (1995) suggested a "Model Code for Advertising and Solicitation in Cyberspace." Among the suggested Code provisions are placing notices at the beginning and end of the message to alert the recipient to the fact that the e-mail is an advertisement, a prohibition on spamming, no forging of a newsgroup permission for the sending of the message, and internal do-not-e-mail lists. The problem with this approach is that it lacks enforcement and depends on the good will of

the e-mailer, good will that the Canter and Siegel incidents suggest may be lacking.

Several other possible solutions, also not directly tied to the TCPA, include requiring that e-mail advertisers use some sort of standard code word in their mailing subject line. Then a recipient could have a filter, similar to the v-chip for example, that would automatically eliminate messages with that code. But this solution still entails a cost on the part of the recipient, a cost that should be borne by the advertiser. Another possibility, but one with significant First Amendment implications, would be to have a central computer clearinghouse for e-mail messages. The clearinghouse computer could check through a list of user names of those who did not wish to receive commercial e-mail and not forward such e-mail to those names.

REFERENCES

Allard, N. W. (1994). Reinventing competition. *Hastings Comm/Ent Law Journal, 17*, 473-493.

Ayre, R., & Willmott D. (1995, May 16). The Internet means business. *PC Magazine*, pp. 195-204.

Bigelow v. Virginia 421 U.S. 809 (1975).

Board of Trustees v. Fox 492 U.S. 469 (1989).

Boedecker, K. A., Morgan, F. W., & Wright, L. B. (1995) The evolution of First Amendment protection for commercial speech. *Journal of Marketing, 59*, 38-47.

Boroughs, D. L. (1995, July 10). New age advertising. *U. S. News and World Report*, pp. 38-39.

Bosmajian, H. (1992). *Metaphor and reason in judicial opinions.* Carbondale: Southern Illinois University Press.

Branscomb, A. W. (1994). *Who owns information? From privacy to public access.* New York: Basic Books.

Branscomb, A. W. (1995). Anonymity, autonomy, and accountability: Challenges to the First Amendment in cyberspaces. *Yale Law Journal, 104*, 1639-1679.

Bredenberg, A. (1996). Caveat spammor. *Internet World, 7*, 69-73.

Broecker, E. J. (1990). FAX unto others . . . : A constitutional analysis of unsolicited facsimile statutes. *Indiana University Law Review, 23*(3), 703-730.

Burgess, J. (1994). On the Internet, frontier justice. *Washington Post, Business Suppl.* 19, 25.

Burstein, D., & Kline, D. (1995). *Road warriors: Dreams and nightmares along the information highway.* New York: Dutton

Byassee, W. S. (1995). Jurisdiction of cyberspace: Applying real world precedent to the virtual community. *Wake Forest Law Review, 30*, 197-220.

Cahill, R. T. (1994). City of Cincinnati V. Discovery Network, Inc.: Towards heightened scrutiny for truthful commercial speech? *University of Richmond Law Review, 28,* 225-254.

Cain, R. M. (1994). Call up someone and just say "buy"— Telemarketing and the regulatory environment. *American Business Law Journal, 31,* 641-665.

Cannon, M. (1995). Life in the big city. *MacUser,* 11, 17.

Cate, F. H. (1994). A law antecedent and paramount. *Federal Communications Law Journal, 47,* 205-211.

Cate, F. H. (1995). The First Amendment and the National Information Infrastructure. *Wake Forest Law Review, 30,* 1-50.

Cavazos, E. A., & Morin, G. (1994). *Cyberspace and the law.* Cambridge, MA: MIT Press.

Central Hudson Gas and Electric Company v. Public Service Commission of New York 447 U.S. 557 (1980).

Cincinnati v. Discovery Network 113 S.Ct. 1505 (1993).

Collins, R. K. L., & Skover, D. M. (1993). Commerce and communication. *Texas Law Review, 71,* 697-746.

Computer Professionals for Social Responsibility (CPSR). (1990). *Civil liberties and the electronic frontier: Mapping the terrain* (R. Civille Ed.). Washington, DC: Author.

Computer Professionals for Social Responsibility (CPSR). (1993) *Serving the community: A public interest vision of the national information infrastructure.* Washington, DC: Author.

Corn-Revere, R. (1994). New technology and the First Amendment: Breaking the cycle of repression. *Hastings Comm/Ent Law Journal, 17,* 247-345.

Cutler, B. D., & Muehling, D. D. (1989). Advocacy advertising and the boundaries of commercial speech. *Journal of Advertising, 18*(3), 40-50.

Cutler, B. D., & Muehling, D. D. (1991). Another look at advocacy advertising and the boundaries of commercial speech. *Journal of Advertising, 20,* 49-52.

Denning, D. E., & Lin, H. S. (Eds.). (1994). *Rights and responsibilities of participants in networked communities.* Washington, DC: National Academy Press.

Destination Ventures v. FCC 632 (D.Or. 1994), aff'd 46 F.3d 54 (9th Cir. 1994).

DiLello, E. V. (1993). Functional equivalency and its application to freedom of speech on computer bulletin boards. *Columbia Journal of Law and Social Problems, 26,* 199-247.

Dizard, W. (1994). *Old media new media.* White Plains, NY: Longman.

Drucker, S. J., & Gumpert, G. (1995). Freedom and liability in cyberspace: Media, metaphors and paths of regulation. *1994 Free Speech Yearbook, 33,* 49-64.

Eckenwiler, M. (1996). Net.Law. *Netguide 3*, 37-38.

Ellickson, R. C. (1991). *Order without law: How neighbors settle disputes.* Cambridge, MA: Harvard University Press.

Feder, B. J. (1991). Toward defining free speech in the computer age. *The New York Times*, p. E5.

FCC v. Pacifica Foundation 438 U.S. 726 (1978).

44 Liquormart Inc. v. Rhode Island 24 Med. L. Reptr. 1673 (1996).

Gerlin, A. (1995). Businesses tired of faxed ads sue the senders. *Wall Street Journal*, pp. B1, 12.

Gilpin, B. G. (1995, Summer). Attorney advertising and solicitation on the Internet: Complying with ethics regulations and netiquette. *Journal of Computer and Information Law*, 697-728.

Goldstone, D. J. (1995). The public forum doctrine in the age of the information superhighway (where are the public forums on the information superhighway?). *Hastings Law Journal, 46*, 335-402.

Gordon, M. L., & McKenzie, D. J. P. (1995). A lawyer's roadmap of the information superhighway. *Journal of Computer and Information Law, 13*, 177-230.

Hayes, D. (1996, September 7). Judge blocks attempt to cut off junk e-mail. *Kansas City Star*, pp. B1, B5.

Hardy, I. T. (1994). The proper legal regime for "cyberspace." *University of Pittsburgh Law Review, 55*, 993-1055.

Henly, B. (1987). "Penumbra": The roots of a legal metaphor. *Hastings Constitutional Law Quarterly, 15*, 81-100.

Hoffman, D. L., & Novak, T. P. (1996a). A new marketing paradigm for electronic commerce. http://www2000.ogsm.vanderbilt.edu.

Hoffman, D. L., & Novak, T. P. (1996b). Building new paradigms for electronic commerce. http://colette.ogsm.vanderbilt.edu.

Johnson, D. R., & Marks, K. A. (1993). Mapping data communications onto existing legal metaphors: Should we let our conscience (and our contracts) be our guide? *Villanova Law Review, 38*(2), 487-515.

Johnson, G. J. (1994). Of metaphor and the difficulty of computer discourse. *Communications of the ACM, 37*, 97-102.

Kapor, M. (1991). Civil liberties in cyberspace. *Scientific American, 265*, 158-164.

Katsh, M. E. (1995). Rights, camera, action: Cyberspatial settings and the First Amendment. *Yale Law Journal, 104*, 1681-1717.

Krattenmaker, T. G., & Powe, L. A. (1995). Converging First Amendment principles for converging communications media. *Yale Law Journal, 104*, 1719-1741.

Lavery, T. L. (1994). Casenote—Commercial speech suffers a First Amendment blow in United States v. Edge Broadcasting Co. *Northern Illinois University Law Review, 14*, 549-584.

Lewis, P. H. (1994a, May 11). Anarchy, a threat on the electronic frontier? *The New York Times*, pp. D1, D7.

Lewis, P. H. (1994b, June 26). No more "anything goes": Cyberspace gets censors. *The New York Times*, pp. A1, D5.

Lewis, P. H. (1996, April 17). In a recount, cyber census still confounds. *The New York Times*, pp. D1, D5.

Lively, D. E. (1994). The information superhighway: A First Amendment roadmap. *Boston College Law Review*, *35*, 1067-1101.

Mandel, R. P. (1994). Regulation of commercial speech: Did the 1993 Supreme Court decisions clarify the scope of First Amendment protection? *Journal of Public Policy and Marketing*, *13*, 159-163.

Mauro, T. (1994, November 15). Legal notions transformed by digital age. *USA Today*, pp. A1, 2.

McGinnis, J. O. (1996). The once and future property-based vision of the First Amendment. *University of Chicago Law Review*, *63*, 49-132.

McGraw, D. K. (1995). Sexual harassment in cyberspace: The problem of unwelcome e-mail. *Rutgers Computer and Technology Law Journal*, *21*(2), 491-518.

The message in the medium: The First Amendment on the information superhighway. (1994). *Harvard Law Review*, *107*, 1062-1098.

Middleton, K. R. (1991). Advocacy advertising, the First Amendment and competitive advantage: A comment on Cutler and Muehling. *Journal of Advertising*, *20*, 77-81.

Miller, M. W. (1991, October 22). Prodigy network defends display of anti-semitic notes. *Wall Street Journal*, pp. B1, 4.

Miller, P. H. (1993). Note—new technology, old problem: Determining the First Amendment status of electronic information services. *Fordham Law Review*, *61*, 1147-1201.

Miller, S. E. (1996), *Civilizing cyberspace: Policy, power and the information superhighway*. New York: Addison-Wesley.

O'Neill, P. (1994). Optimizing and restricting the flow of information: Remodeling the First Amendment for a convergent world. *University of Pittsburgh Law Review*, *55*, 1057-1084.

Online advertising prevails, despite effort to remove "e-mail litter." (1995, March 26). *St. Joseph News-Press*, p. 2E.

Perritt, H. J. (1993). Dispute resolution in electronic network communities. *Villanova Law Review*, *38*(2), 349-401.

Petty, R. D. (1993). Advertising and the First Amendment: A practical test for distinguishing commercial speech from fully protected speech. *Journal of Public Policy and Marketing*, *12*, 170-177.

Pfaffenberger, B. (1994). *Internet in plain English.* New York: MIS Press.

Pine, B. J., II, Peppers, D., & Rogers, M. (1995). Do you want to keep your customers forever? *Harvard Business Review, 73,* 103-114.

Press, L. (1994, November). Commercialization of the Internet. *Communications of the ACM,* 17-21

Posadas de Puerto Rico Associates v. Tourism Company of Puerto Rico 478 U.S. 328 (1986).

Price, M. E. (1985). Redefining the First Amendment: The role of the new technology. In M. Greenberger (Ed.), *Electronic publishing plus* (pp. 257-270). White Plains, NY: Knowledge Industry.

Rose, L. (1995). *NetLaw: Your rights in the online world.* Berkeley: Osborne McGraw-Hill.

Rowan v. United States Post Office 397 U.S. 728 (1970).

Sandberg, J. (1995, July 5). Regulators try to tame the untamable on-line world. *Wall Street Journal,* pp. B1, 6.

Sandberg, J. (1996). Internet access doubled in past year; survey shows gains at direct providers. *Wall Street Journal,* p. 39.

Spalter, M. (1995). Here come the cyberyuppies. *Futurist, 29,* 20-22.

Sugawara, S. (1991, October 24). Computer network to ban "repugnant" comments. *Washington Post,* pp. A1, 4.

Sunstein, C.R. (1995). The First Amendment in cyberspace. *Yale Law Journal, 104,* 1757-1804.

Taviss, M. L. (1992). Dueling forums: The public forum doctrine's failure to protect the electronic forum. *University of Cincinnati Law Review, 60,* 757-795.

Tomlinson, D. E., & Wiley, R. L. (1995). People do read large ads: The law of advertising from outer space. *Federal Communications Law Journal, 47,* 535-569.

Tribe, L. H. (1991). The Constitution in cyberspace. *Humanist, 51,* 15-21, 39.

Uncapher, W. (1991). Trouble in cyberspace. *Humanist, 51,* 5-14, 34.

U. S. House Committee on Energy and Commerce. (1991). Telephone Advertising Consumer Rights Act. 102nd Cong., 1st sess., H. Rept. 102-317.

U. S. House Subcommittee on Telecommunications and Finance of the Committee on Energy and Commerce. (1991). Telemarketing/Privacy Issues. 102nd Cong., 1st sess., H. Rept. 102-109.

U.S. Senate Committee on Commerce, Science, and Transportation. (1991). The Automated Telephone Consumer Protection Act, 102nd Cong., 1st sess., S. Rept. 102-178.

Valentine v. Chrestensen 316 U.S. 52 (1942).

Volokh, E. (1995). Cheap speech and what it will do. *Yale Law Journal, 104,* 1805-1850.

Warner, F. (1995, April 14). FTC mulls need for future checks on cybermarketing. *Wall Street Journal*, p. B5.

Weber, T. E. (1996). America Online wins rounds in suits over junk e-mail and billing practices. *Wall Street Journal*, p. B5.

Williams, F., & Pavlik, J. V. (Eds.). (1994). *The people's right to know: Media, democracy, and the information highway.* Hillsdale, NJ: Lawrence Erlbaum.

18

ETHICAL ISSUES FOR A VIRTUAL SELF

SUSAN B. BARNES

Sue Barnes explores how computer networks introduce a new set of moral alternatives because digital technologies facilitates the separation of our physical self from the communication exchange. She examines the ethical and legal implications of the ability to create a false persona that interacts socially with others or may interact anonymously. She considers how the merger of free speech rights with privacy rights yield "anonymous speech" rights, which is the right to communicate with others without revealing one's identity. The use of remailers, which facilitate e-mail transmissions stripped of an actual originating address, is pivotal to this right. Ultimately, this chapter examines concepts of self and how they relate to community.

Ethics, the study of morals, involves communication choices. By examining and developing an awareness of our own values, we can become more responsible for the consequences of our decisions and actions. Computer networks introduce a new set of moral alternatives because digital technologies enable us to separate our physical self from the communication exchange. Separating the physical body from the human communication process enables individuals to assume roles, create fraudulent personas, and utilize pseudonyms. Using false identities, people can write deceptive messages and behave in ways that would be socially unacceptable in traditional face-to-face situations. As a result, the presentation of self in computer-mediated communications introduces new ethical issues that do not exist in other forms of communication.

For example, computer-mediated communication adds a new twist to the question of how society balances individual rights with protecting social interests because individuals can separate themselves from their actions. Anonymous individuals can make false or harmful statements about others without acknowledging responsibility for their acts. Currently, it is difficult to locate the identity of these individuals without legal intervention. How can people be protected from harmful remarks when the identity of the accuser is unknown? Should the rights of these anonymous individuals be protected? Should legal steps be taken to prevent malicious remarks, or can people reasonably govern their own online behavior?

In *On Liberty*, John Stuart Mill (1989) discusses the rights of individuals and the limitation of individual actions by others. Mills states: "The sole end for which mankind are warranted, individually or collectively, in interfering with the liberty of action of any of their number, is self-protection. That the only purpose for which power can be rightfully exercised over any member of a civilised [sic] community, against his will, is to prevent harm to others" (p. 13). Although computer-mediated communications raises new questions about protecting an individual's rights, creating a balance between autonomy and social control has a long history of debate. Mills (1989) describes this debate as follows:

> There is, in fact, no recognized principle by which the propriety or impropriety of government interference is customarily tested. People decide according to their personal preferences. Some, whenever they see any good to be done, or evil to be remedied, would willingly instigate the government to undertake the business; while others prefer to bear almost any amount of social evil, rather than add one to the departments of human interests amenable to governmental control. (p. 12)

Updating this debate, Habermas's (1996) book, *Between Facts and Norms*, examines the legitimate circumstances for political authorities to exercise power over human beings in today's complex societies. His argument focuses on the legal system. Habermas (1996) states: "A legal order must not only guarantee that the rights of each person are in fact recognized by all other persons; the reciprocal recognition of the rights of each by all must in addition be based on laws that are legitimate insofar as they grant equal liberties to each, so that each's freedom of choice can coexist with the freedom of all" (pp. 31-32). Furthermore, he asserts that the language of law can function as a transformer in societywide communication because "conflicting opinions are settled by apportioning the code values legal/illegal through the exchange of reasons" (p. 51). Habermas contends that through legal discourse we can debate and ultimately balance the relationship between autonomy and social control. Although Habermas does not directly address the Internet, the debate over self-government versus legal restrictions in online communication is a controversial topic.

AUTONOMY AND CYBERSPACE

Computer-mediated communications destabilizes traditional conceptions about the autonomous individual because the ability to create a fictitious persona that socially interacts with others calls into question many of the conventional notions about a stable concept of self. According to Harré (1989), English-speaking heirs of Judaeo-Christian civilization tend to believe the following about themselves:

1. We believe that we are autonomous individuals.
2. We also believe that we are, in despite of being trapped in a web of conventions and an apparently inexorable natural order, agents.
3. We also seem to believe that we have both individually and collectively a past and a future, and so have histories. (p. 23)

Looking at these basic beliefs about the physical self in relationship to computer technology, raises several new questions. First, how does cyberspace alter our traditional concepts of an autonomous self? Second, are individuals agents of change or products of social collectivism? Third, how do traditional concepts of self relate to cyberspace? Are we creating a new digital concept of self that has no relationship to the past? Finally, what implications does the digital self have for the future of self, community, and society in general?

According to Anthony Giddens (1991): "The self is not a passive entity, determined by external influences; in forging their self-identities, no matter how local their specific contexts of action, individuals contribute to and directly promote social influences that are global in their consequences and implications" (p. 2). By participating in society, people transform social structures, and they are agents of social change. But this is a two-way process because "the reality of personhood cannot be grasped either at the extreme pole of individualism—in which the seemingly autonomous individual is the ontological reality and prime mover—or at the pole of mechanical collectivism in which he individual is merely a mechanical copy of the underlying social order" (Sampson, 1989, p. 6). The relationship between the individual and society is a dialectical process: "People can transform themselves by transforming the structures by which they are formed" (p. 6).

In this dialectic process, our individual concepts of self have larger social implications because our concepts of self influence social norms. U.S. society, for instance, tends to perceive people as autonomous individuals. Some argue that respect for autonomy in the United States has gone too far. For example, Gaylin and Jennings (1996) assert :

> Autonomy's success in the struggle for the American moral imagination has made it overbearing and overweening. When obeisance to personal liberty and independence triumphs systematically over a relational, communitarian commonsense morality, then a set of attitudes, unexamined assumptions, and a political and ethical style and rhetoric develop that we shall refer to as the "culture of autonomy." (p. 5)

It is argued that by failing properly to recognize the relationship between the individual and community, "we fall into theoretical confusions that reflect and reinforce a deleterious individualism in our intellectual culture. And this failing is often thought to have political significance, legitimizing views which celebrate individuals' rights to liberty and privacy at the expense of the values of fellowship and community" (Bakhurst & Sypnowich, 1995, p. 1).

Protecting the values of individual rights instead of the community is a topic of social debate. In *Sex, Laws, and Cyberspace*, Jonathan Wallace and Mark Mangan (1996) explore the individual versus social ethical and legal issues surrounding a number of recent Internet incidents. For example, a California couple was tried by Memphis community standards and found guilty of transportation of obscene materials through the Internet. "The journalistic and legal communities immediately criticized the trial. They generally portrayed Tennessee as the most conservative state in the union and commented on the absurdity of it governing the standards of the on-line world" (p. 27). In this case, the rights of the individuals were curtailed as an effort to protect the larger community.

In contrast to protecting the community, advocates of cyberrights are attempting to protect the individual by combining free speech with the right to privacy. Merging these concepts together is called "anonymous speech." Anonymous speech is the right to communicate with others without revealing one's identity. This cyberright's concept became a topic of discussion after the Finnish police served a warrant on Johan Helsingius calling for the search and seizure of his anonymous remailer. An anonymous remailer enables people to send electronic mail messages without revealing their identity. "The police wanted to identify someone who had allegedly stolen confidential information off a Church of Scientology computer and then used the remailer to publish the data anonymously" (Bell, 1995, p. 80). Faced with the alternative of giving up the name of the individual or having the entire user list taken by the authorities, Helsingius gave up the suspect. Right to anonymity covers a wide range of issues, including the right to send and receive anonymous messages and to use a pseudonym to engage in cash transactions. There are numerous personal and social implications that surround this digital concept of individual rights. In addition to raising issues about the balance of online autonomy and social order, computer mediated communication challenges traditional concepts of self.

TRADITIONAL CONCEPTS OF SELF

Harré (1989) asserts that English-speaking heirs of Judaeo-Christian civilization tend to view themselves as autonomous individuals. English is specifically cited in his observation because Harré argues that different languages tend to support different types of belief systems. The referent "I" in English, and the relevant first-person inflection in other languages, is used to perform a moral act, or an act of individual commitment to the content of the utterance. Through the use of English grammar, the individual is recognized as autonomous. Moreover, Bruner (1995) argues that all cultures respect the centrality of self in the meaning-making experience: "All cultures take as the mark of having achieved meaning that the individual says an equivalent of 'I understand,' that achieving meaning is marked by a unique subjective state that will be understood as such by others who share a culture" (p. 27).

In Western culture, an emblem of individualism or "atomism" is Descartes. Cartesian philosophy separates the mind from the body or the subject from the world. Bakhurst and Sypnowich (1995) describe this as follows:

> Descartes set the agenda for epistemological inquiry, even if his
> successors did not all agree with the answers he gave or even the
> questions he put. Henceforth philosophers were intent on
> discovering how, in the maelstrom that is our engagement with the
> world and with others, the individual can come to have knowledge.
> The image of the isolated knower remained intact, particularly in
> Anglo-Saxon philosophy. Other enduring ingredients of the
> Cartesian picture are the idea of the external world, and the related
> presumption that the self can be seen as the spectator of the mind's
> show (see Rorty [1979] and Dennett [1991]). His position
> encapsulates the ideal of transparency in subjectivity, where a
> subject can know itself completely, and reaffirms the disavowal of
> the body central to Western philosophy since Plato, where reason
> and the mind are posited against unreason and the corporeal. (p. 4)

In contrast to the Cartesian perspective of an autonomous self that is established through mental reasoning is the idea of the "social self." The social self recognizes our status as social beings whose identities are intimately bound up in corporeal interactions with the communities and cultures in which we live. Arguments for the social self maintain that we are socially constructed because our identities are shaped by social influences. The work of George Herbert Mead (1959) illustrates this idea. He states: "The others and the self arise in the social act together" (p. 169).

An individual self is established by organizing the attitudes of other individuals towards the self and towards one another through participation in social interaction. For example, a social act is playing the game of baseball. Each team member knows his or her role in the game and also the roles of every other player. Because each player understands the role of the "other" players, each player can socially interact according to the game's rules. Every individual player takes on the roles of others and addresses him- or herself in his or her multiple roles as well as singular role. Simply stated, a person could not play the role of the batter, if he or she did not understand the roles of the pitcher and catcher. Thus, by understanding the role of others, we can develop our own individual roles and consequently a sense of self. Mead (1962) invents the term the *generalized other* to describe "the organized community or social group which gives to the individual his unity of self" (p. 154). Individual concepts of self develop through physical social interaction.

Although proponents of the social self argue that the individual self develops as the result of interacting in social relationships, this perspective does not view individuals as being "stamped out" by society: "We are participants in our own construction and exercise some autonomy in the face of the forces of socialization" (Bakhurst & Sypnowich, 1995, p. 5). As individual agents, our interactions with others shape our self-concepts. In addition to interactions, identity is formed through our social roles.

MODERNITY AND SELF

Different historical periods reflect different attitudes toward concepts of self and social roles. In premodern societies, an individual's identity was fixed, solid, and stable. "Identity was a function of predefined social roles and a traditional system of myths which provided orientation and religious sanctions to one's place in the world, while rigorously circumscribing the realm of thought and behavior" (Kellner, 1992, p. 141). A person was born and died as a member of a fixed social group. Identity was not a problem because it was not subject to reflection or discussion. "Individuals did not undergo identity crises, or radically modify their identity. One was a hunter and a member of the tribe and that was that" (p. 141). Additionally, as Giddens (1991) states: "In pre-modern contexts, tradition has a key role in articulating action and ontological frameworks; tradition offers an organising medium of social life" (p. 48). People could not easily change their social group or their relationship to the group.

In contrast, identity in modern society is mobile, multiple, personal, self-reflexive, and subject to change. People are no longer born into a rigid social structure. We have more flexibility to decide what social roles we play, whether or not we get married, become parents, and work as a doctor, lawyer, teacher, or engineer. Consequently, modern concepts of identity are socially constructed as people assume different roles throughout their lives. Modern identity is established as a result of mutual recognition from others combined with self-validation. In the self-validation process, self-identity is "*reflexively understood by the person in terms of her or his biography*" (Giddens, 1991, p. 53; emphasis in original). Individual biographies are constructed from our various social roles

Although people in modern society have more flexibility in selecting their social roles, the norms of behavior associated with those roles tend to be fixed. In modernity, forms of identity are relatively stable because identity forms from a set of previously established social roles and norms. For example, one is a father, daughter, New Yorker, a professor, a liberal, a Catholic, or a combination of these roles. "In modernity, there is still a structure of interaction with socially defined and available roles, norms, customs, and expectations, among which one must choose appropriate, and reproduce in order to gain identity in a complex process of mutual recognition" (Kellner, 1992, p. 142). Although there is flexibility in modern society to select different roles, the norms associated with those roles have already been set. But as we move into a postmodern society, where technology changes both the norms of roles and the forms of social interaction, identity becomes less and less stable.

THE POSTMODERN SELF

The postmodern perspective views the accelerated pace, extension, and complexity of modern societies as a cause of unstable identity. The proliferation of communication technologies exposes individuals to an increasing vocabulary of being. People no longer live within the boundaries of a single geographically restrained community or culture. Gergen (1996) argues that in postmodern culture: "We have not a single satisfying intelligibility within which to dwell, but through the process of social saturation, we are immersed in a plethora of understandings—the psychological ontologies of varying ethnicities, class strata, geographic sectors, racial and religious groupings, professional enclaves, and nationalities" (p. 132). Coherence and consistency are the staples of everyday life in a face-to-face community. They galvanize group members against extraneous and corrosive influences. New technologies do not tend to support the cohesive nature of traditional geographic-oriented communities. Modern transportation and communication technologies foster a high rate of social mobility. Gergen (1991) asserts: "the technology of social saturation works toward the dissolution of homogeneous, face-to-face communities, and toward the creation of a polymorphous perversity in social pattern" (pp. 211-212). Technological change in the postmodern world transforms both concepts of community and concepts of self.

Postmodern theorists argue "that the autonomous, self-constituting subject that was the achievement of modern individuals, of a culture of individualism, is fragmenting and disappearing, owing to the social processes and the leveling of individuality in a rationalized bureaucratized, mediatized, and consumerized mass society" (Kellner, 1992, p. 143). Bukatman's (1993) book, *Terminal Identity*, illustrates this point. Bukatman describes a cultural crisis that has arisen as a result of a new electronically defined reality: "It has become increasingly difficult to separate the human from the technological" (p. 2). As the human and technological become coextensive, codependent, and mutually defining, a new subject emerges: "one constituted by electronic technologies, but also by the machineries of the text " (p. 22).

Bukatman and other poststructuralists "have launched an attack on the very notions of the subject and identity, claiming that subjective identity is itself a myth, a construct of language and society, an overdetermined illusion that one is really a substantial subject, that one really has a fixed identity" (Kellner, 1992, p. 143). To replace the concept of fixed identity, a theme of a transhuman social order emerges in poststructuralist work. "The referential anchor of the individual recedes in social prominence as global communication networks (Lyotard [1991]) and human/machine combinations (Haraway, [1991]) replace older figures of man versus nature and individual versus society" (Poster, 1995, pp. 52-53).

Electronically mediated communication, what Poster refers to as "the mode of information," alters forms of communication and concepts of the individual. Poster (1995) states: "My general thesis is that the mode of information enacts a radical reconfiguration of language, one which constitutes subjects outside the pattern of the rational, autonomous individual. This familiar modern subject is displaced by the mode of information in favor of one that is multiplied, disseminated and decentered, continuously interpellated as a unstable identity" (p. 57). Poster goes on to argue that the instability of the individual poses both challenges and dangers to modern social institutions and structures.

THE COMPUTER-MEDIATED SELF

"In traditional communities, with their relatively unchanging interconnected cast of characters, coherence of personality was favored. Relationships tended to be reliable and repetitive, supporting consistency of action" (Gergen, 1991, p. 174). Eliminating shared space for human interaction impacts on the concept of a unified self. By replacing physical presence with mediated textual or symbolic representations of self, we create a new way of relating that is no longer grounded in a common overall reality. This fragmentation can lead to conflict and confusion because new mediated environments such as the Internet provide individuals with the opportunity to create their own fragmented subrealities. In cyberspace, "the self is decentered, dispersed, and multiplied in continuous instability" (Poster, 1990, p. 6).

Electronic media call into question the idea that people have a single or "root" identity. It replaces this idea of a single core personality with the concept of floating identities. Howard Gardner (1983) describes two different perspectives on identity or concepts of self. The first describes the individual as an integrated or self-actualized individual: "a self that is highly developed and fully differentiated from others . . . individuals who appear to have understood much about themselves and about their societies and who have come to terms successfully with the frailties of the human condition" (p. 252). In contrast to this concept of an autonomous self is the second notion of a set of selves. "Rather than a central 'core self' which organizes one's thoughts, behavior, and goals, the person is better thought of as a collection of relatively diverse masks, none of which takes precedence over the others, and each of which is simply called into services as needed" (p. 252). Computer-mediated communication tends to encourage this second perspective of self.

As a result, Poster (1990) states when computer-mediated communication replaces face-to-face communication, the subject is affected in the following ways: (a) new possibilities for playing with identities is possible, (b) gender cues are removed, and (c) the subject is dispersed and dislocated in space and time. The most publicized example of a false identity dates back to 1982, when a male New York psychiatrist pretended to be a woman. In "The Strange Case of the Electronic Lover," Van Gelder (1985) describes how Alex created a female persona that established long-term friendships with other women through the online service called CompuServe. There have been numerous accounts of this story. However, all the versions have one detail in common: "The discovery of Alex's deception led to shock and outrage. In some versions of the story, the anger erupts because of the initial deception—that a man had posed as a woman, that a man had won confidences as a woman" (Turkle, 1995, p. 229). Today, virtual gender swapping is quite common in computer-mediated communication. People developing relationships in online role-playing games and commercial networking services that allow aliases expect this to happen.

Gergen (1991) and Poster (1990) argue that computer-mediated communication could be harmful to the development of a concept of a unified self because the individual becomes fragmented in electronic space. In addition to changing identities and gender, fragmentation occurs because "mediated communication enables us to encounter many diverse people representing different social enclaves and ethnic or religious backgrounds" (Grodin & Lindlof, 1996, p. 4). The validity of a singular perspective and a univocal judgment are challenged by this new multivocal medium. "Individuals, then, may find that they no longer have a central core with which to evaluate and act, but instead find themselves 'decentered'" (p. 4). The decentered individual can feel dislocated because he or she is not tied to physical space.

Writing from the opposite perspective, Turkle (1995) argues that computer-mediated communication can be beneficial to developing concepts of self. Her research examines people role-playing in Internet games such as MUDs (Multi User Dungeon). MUDs are text-based virtual worlds where people create characters and assume roles by exchanging typed messages across a computer network. Bennahum (1994) describes MUDs as follows:

> The first MUDs were built around 1978. At the time there was a popular text-based adventure game called, appropriately, Adventure, which ran on a university computer. At first, players played alone, against the machine, going from room to room collecting treasure, killing monsters, until they eventually won the game. After a while it got boring. . . . Then, something unexpected happened. People no long played to win the game; they played to be with other people. A virtual community began to form. (p. 22)

According to Turkle, MUDs can be beneficial for the formation of self because they enable adolescent identity development by creating what Erik Erikson (1950, 1963) calls a psychosocial moratorium. According to Turkle (1995), "the notion of moratorium was a central aspect of Erikson's theories about adolescent identity development. . . . The adolescent moratorium is a time of intense interaction with people and ideas. It is a time of passionate friendships and experimentation" (p. 203). In MUDs, adolescents can experiment with roles, relationships, and virtual sex without the consequences of real-world experiences, such as reckless driving that leads to teenage deaths and careless sex that can lead to pregnancy. Turkle contends that even though the experiences on MUDs are removed from the structured surroundings of one's normal life, the moratorium facilitates the development of a personal sense of self. Thus, game playing can have a positive influence on real life because individuals can use online role playing to act out and experiment with different aspects of their personality. However, Turkle (1995) does not consider online experiences to be the same as actions in the real world. She states that "today what disturbs us is when the shifting norms of the virtual world bleed into real life" (p. 230).

In contrast to Turkle's observation about online behavior is Julian Dibbell's (1993) description of a rape in a role-playing game. The online rape illustrates how the fantasy world of cybersex can stir up passions in the physical flesh existing in the real world. Dibbell (1993) contends: "In this disembodied enactment of life's most body-centered activity is to risk the realization that when it comes to sex, perhaps the body in question is not the physical one at all, but its psychic double, the bodylike self-representation we carry around in our heads" (p. 38). Dibbell goes on to say: "What happens inside a MUD-made world is neither exactly real nor exactly make-believe, but profoundly, compellingly, and emotionally meaningful" (p. 38). On the surface, MUDs appear to be highly stylized games; however, behind the characters are actual people with real emotional responses. In contrast to Turkle's argument that role playing online can be used as a moratorium from real life, this rape in cyberspace shows how people blur the lines between online and real experiences. It exemplifies how the emotional content of online role playing can bleed into the real world. As a result, our virtual roles played in MUDs can influence actual feelings in physical space.

As social laboratories, MUDs can also be used to experiment with social forms that parallel the real world. For example, LambdaMoo, a MUD community started in October 1990 by Pavel Curtis, is currently experimenting with establishing a "virtual" legal system. Mnookin (1996) states: "Just as players may construct themselves in novel and creative ways, they may also imaginatively construct political institutions and social forms." But in online experiences, imagination tends to reflect real life. Curtis (1996) observes: "Social behavior on MUDs is in some ways a direct mirror of behavior in real life, with mechanisms being drawn nearly unchanged from real life" (p. 351). The Lambda legal systems borrows from the U.S. legal system because players assume that freedom of speech and right to privacy in the real world apply to their online experiments. "Often, participants invoke notions of the law based on their (sometimes inaccurate) understanding of law in the real world. For example, nowhere in LambdaLaw is there any explicit codification of either a free speech right or a privacy right, and yet most participants presume that these right exist in the [MUD]" (Mnookin, 1996).

Although legal issues in MUDs parallel real life, this online environment provides an opportunity for participants to engage in debate, experiment with creating laws, and critique behavior on both an individual and social level. As a result, computer-mediated communication has the potential to be a utopian space for creating possible worlds. Mnookin (1996) asserts: "It could provide a space in which participants can remake themselves and their institutions; it could provide a standpoint from which to critique and rethink the institutional structures of the space outside of the [MUD]." Online role-playing games and the virtual communities they create could provide a place for reshaping our understanding of self, politics, and ethics.

COMPUTER-MEDIATED COMMUNICATION AND CHANGING NORMS AND VALUES

In addition to creating a space for examining social behavior, computer-mediated communication alters the ways in which people interact with each other. It challenges us to redefine the relationships between individuals and community, individuals and society, and individual and the law.

One of the most visible ethical issues related to computer use is privacy. "Most legal and ethical systems recognize the right to privacy, the right of the individual to determine what data is collected about them, by whom, and for what purposes" (Huff & Martin, 1995, p. 80). Issues of privacy in computer-mediated communications include: the collection, accuracy, and use of personal information collected in databases; fears about the government's accumulation of personal information; privacy violations by corporate monitoring; and privacy in the relationship to online anonymity.

Collecting information in computer databases is of major concern to the U.S. public. Kling (1996) asserts that "privacy issues have taken on a new form and an new urgency with the advent of computer matching, a technique involving large databases with unrelated purposes that are cross-checked for consistency" (p. 623). Today, many in U.S. society fear that we could become a nation in which the government uses technology to control individuals. George Orwell's (1949) vision of "Big Brother" will become a reality. Although "government agencies are often charged with regulatory and policing activities—social control on a large scale" (Kling, 1996, p. 620)—they could use database information to control other aspects of social life. For example, the government is already checking state automobile registration records against tax records for the purpose of locating individuals who own expensive cars, but report small incomes. Another example is using various government controlled computer systems to track down parents whose child support payments are in arrears.

In addition to concerns about protecting the privacy of database information, individuals are also troubled about privacy and the use of e-mail in corporate settings. Many computer users overestimate their expectations of e-mail privacy. They mistakenly think that e-mail is like a sealed letter or private telephone conversation. In contrast, e-mail messages are stored on corporate computers, and companies can monitor these messages. "For example, Rhonda Hall and Bonita Bourke were fired from their jobs at Nissan Motor Corp. in 1990 when management discovered they were receiving sexually suggestive email messages. Nissan's lawyers argued successfully that the company owned the system and had the right to read anything in it" (Weisband & Reining, 1995, p. 40). Hall and Bourke were fired because of messages that they received; conversely, others have gotten in trouble for information they have helped to distribute.

Currently, the German government is on a crusade to stamp out extremism on the Internet. "Berlin prosecutors are investigating

Angela Marquardt, a 25-year-old deputy leader of Germany's reform communist Party of Democratic Socialism (PDS), to see if she broke the law by putting a 'hyperlink' on her home page to the Radikal magazine" ("Germany clamps down," 1997). A hyperlink is a way to easily access text located on different computer systems. With a click of a button, the connection is made. The electronic link was made from Marquardt's World-Wide Web home page to an article that had been banned from publication in Germany because it had instructions on how to sabotage railway lines. In Germany, it is illegal to teach others how to commit a felony or to support a felony. Although the authors of the article are unidentified, Ms. Marquardt appears to have aided the felony. Like the authors of this article, individuals who want to express a point of view and protect their identity can anonymously distribute messages through the Internet.

Anonymity adds a new ethical dilemma to the discussion about electronic privacy. Computer-mediated human communications introduces new types of identities and social relationships that were previously unimaginable with face-to-face exchanges. Many online service providers allow users to create different identities and use online pseudonyms. To send totally anonymous messages, anonymous computer remailer services are available. "The pseudonymity offered by many information service providers, who maintain records of the real identities of their customers, can be enhanced further to create an almost absolute type of anonymity. This possibility is available through the technical capabilities offered by anonymous remailers" (Lee, 1996). Both the use of pseudonyms on online services and anonymous remailers have raised serious ethical questions about privacy and current laws.

On November 4, 1995, *The Wall Street Journal* ran an article describing a dispute between two America Online (AOL) subscribers. A subscriber called Jenny TRR posted a message on an AOL bulletin board for scuba-diving enthusiasts. "Jenny said that she and her husband had been disappointed by their recent visit to the Carib Inn in the Netherlands Antilles and had moved to another resort" (Johnson, 1995, p. B7). The message described a diving instructor at the resort as being "stoned." The owner of the Carib Inn was incensed and sent several electronic messages demanding a retraction from Jenny TRR. When the retraction did not come, he hired lawyers to file a petition for discovery against AOL to reveal the real name of Jenny TRR. In response, AOL turned over the subscriber's real name, address, credit card and checking account information to attorneys representing the Carib Inn. Johnson (1995) reported:

Critics of the services say subscribers don't expect the services to reveal information about them in civil litigation without a fight. By complying with such requests, some critics add, the services may be compromising the rights of subscribers in an effort to protect themselves.

David Phillips, assistant general counsel for American Online, acknowledges that one of the factors the company considered in weighing the request for information about Jenny TRR was whether it could be sued for defamation. . . .

Mr. Phillips maintains that American Online wasn't legally obligated to protect the subscriber's identity. He adds that the subscriber may have violated America Online's policy against "ad hominem attacks" on individuals. (p. B1)

News about AOL's disclosure of real subscriber's identities sparked a lively debate in online discussion groups. "Some said the request was an invasion of privacy and would have a chilling effect on communication in cyberspace. Others chastised Jenny TRR for posting a defamatory statement" (p. B7). Although subscribers to AOL can use pseudonyms when communicating online, the pseudonyms are connected to a real identity stored in AOL's database. Individuals who want to send anonymous messages and stay anonymous can use an Internet anonymous remailer.

Anonymous remailers strip a message of its address header to make the sender anonymous to the receiver. "This header includes the user name, the domain name, and the time, date, and subject of the post. By sending messages through an anonymous remailer, users can send messages stripped of their original headers and assigned instead random replacement headers" (Lee, 1996). When messages are sent through numerous remailers, the originator of the message can become untraceable; "thus, the remailer acts as a filter that keeps the person receiving the mail from knowing who sent it" (Cavazos & Morin, 1994, p. 16).

There are benefits and disadvantages to sending messages through an anonymous remailer. For instance, whistleblowing is a socially productive use of remailers. "Anonymous remailers permit whistleblowers to expose corruption and dishonesty at far lower risk of being discovered. They also permit persecuted groups to meet online without risk of others discovering their identities and using that information to harass or intimidate individual members" (Rose, 1995, p. 183). Moreover, anonymity can be beneficial because it can shield "individuals from personal retaliation, can encourage speech which otherwise would remain stifled" (Lee, 1996). Members of marginalized social groups can use anonymity to express their point of view without fear of social ostracism.

A disadvantage of remailers is that "people can anonymously transmit all sorts of illegal and injurious materials into public areas:

copyright infringements, obscenity, stolen credit information, lies and slander and so on" (Rose, 1995, p. 183). Anonymous remailers are a way for people to spread hate messages and hide behind a wall of anonymity. Critics of anonymity argue that knowing a speaker's identity is necessary to better evaluate the truthfulness of the assertions. "For example, knowledge of whether a statement describing a drug's causal relationship to birth defects is being made by a disinterested scientist or by a public relations officer of the drug's manufacturer can help consumers to determine the appropriate amount of weight or deference to the given such information" (Lee, 1996).

Proponents of anonymity relate it to U.S. concepts of free speech. They cite a 1960 U.S. Supreme Court decision that upheld the right to conduct some forms of anonymous free speech as support for their argument. In the decision, "the Court invalidated an ordinance requiring all publicity distributed pamphlets to include the name and address of the person who prepared, distributed, or published them" (Cavazos & Morin, 1994, p. 15). The decision was not surprising because Alexander Hamilton, James Madison, and John Jay published the controversial Federalist Papers using the pseudonym "Publius." "The right to express oneself under conditions of anonymity has also been frequently exercised by authors publishing books and articles under pen names" (p. 15).

In contrast to protecting online anonymity, on February 1, 1995, "Finnish police presented Johan (Julf) Helsingius with a warrant demanding he provide them with the true name of the person who [had] been using his well-known anonymity server, anon.penet.fi, to conceal his identity when posting to the Usenet newsgroup alt.religion.scientology" (Barlow, 1995, p. 19). At first, Helsingius refused, but he was told that failure to comply would result in the confiscation of his system with the actual identities of 200,000 people from around the world. Many of these individuals would be considered political criminals by their local standards. "Rather than endanger the lives of the strangers who trusted him, Helsingius complied" (p. 19). Within an hour, the Finnish police gave the name to both the Los Angeles Police Department and the Church of Scientology.

The anonymous user was identified as Dennis Erlich, a former Scientology minister. He had been posting sections of Scientology scriptures and criticizing church practices. Several days after his name was revealed, police officials, officials from the Church of Scientology, and lawyers rang the doorbell at his California home. For seven and a half hours, "they confiscated all magnetic media and deleted from his hard disk any files they found offensive" (p. 20). According to the church, the Scientology scriptures Erlich posted contained private church information or "trade secrets," and Erlich was wrongfully appropriating these for his own use. In the church's complaint, they described the lengths to which they had gone to protect the information Erlich had distributed freely on the Internet. "Had Erlich merely libeled the Church of Scientology or otherwise made statements offensive to it, Helsingius would have been safe and Erlich's anonymity secure" (p. 20). Libel is difficult to prove, but financial damage is a different story. Although this could be considered an unusual case, it illustrates how a group used international legal agencies to silence the voice of a single Internet user.

CYBERRIGHTS: PROTECTING THE RIGHTS OF INDIVIDUALS

Protecting the rights of individuals using computer-mediated communication is a major topic both on- and offline. "Among Internet aficionados, there is a strong libertarian ethic that argues that individuals should be able to 'do what they want, when they want' and that the collective social welfare is advanced by the pursuit of a kind of minimally organized anarchy" (Laudon, 1995, p. 36). The origins of this libertarian ethic can be traced back to "hacker ethics" established in the 1960s. According to Steven Levy (1984), hacker ethics include the following:

1. Access to computers—and anything that might teach you something about the way the world works—should be unlimited and total. Always yield to the Hands-On Imperative!
2. All information should be free.
3. Mistrust authority—promote decentralization.
4. Hackers should be judged by their hacking, not bogus criteria such as degrees, age, race, or position.
5. You can create art and beauty on a computer.
6. Computers can change your life for the better.

Hacker ethics have set the stage for a series of confrontations between individuals, corporations, and government agencies. In The Hacker Crackdown, Bruce Sterling (1992) describes numerous conflicts between hackers and the law: "In 1990 there came a nationwide crackdown on illicit computer hackers, with arrests, criminal charges, one dramatic show trial, several guilty pleas, and huge confiscations of data and equipment all over the United States" (p. xiii). An unprecedented result was the creation, within the "computer community," of the Electronic Frontier Foundation, an organization established to preserve electronic civil liberties. Two notable incidents led to this event—"Operation Sundevil" and the "NuPrometheus League."

Operation Sundevil was a well-publicized clash between legal authorities and hackers. An official press release announcing it was released on May 9, 1990 by the U.S. Attorney's office in Phoenix, AZ. "Eight paragraphs in the press release gave the bare facts: twenty-seven search warrants carried out on May 8, with three arrests, and 150 agents on the prowl in twelve cities across America" (Sterling, 1992, p. 41). The U.S. Secret Service, private telephone security, and state and local law enforcement agencies joined forces to stop hackers from accessing telephone company computer systems. Three hackers—Acid Phreak, Phiber Optik, and Scorpion—were arrested in New York. From the point of view of phone company executives, computer security experts, and law enforcement agents, young hackers are remorseless, malicious invaders of other people's computers. They are a financial strain on the national telecommunications infrastructure and dangerous technoliterate role models for today's youth. Therefore, law enforcement agencies want to crack down on hacker activities.

Looking at the hacker crackdown from the opposite perspective, Dibbell (1996) describes the activities of Phiber Optik as follows:

> For what did his crimes consist of after all? He picked the locks on computers owned by large corporations, and he shared the knowledge of how to do it with his friends (they had given themselves the meaningless name MOD, more for the thrill of sounding like a conspiracy than for the purpose of actually acting like one). In themselves the offenses are trivial, but raised to the level of a social principle, they do spell doom for the locks some people want to put on our cyberspacial future. (p. 136)

Investigating hackers came to the attention of the FBI in June 1989. At that time, several illicit copies of Apple Computer's QuickDraw source code, a closely guarded piece of Apple's intellectual property, had been put into envelopes and mailed to people all over the United States. A group called the "NuPrometheus League" claimed to have committed the crime. When Apple found out, they called the FBI. "The Bureau takes an interest in high-profile intellectual-property theft cases, industrial espionage, and theft of trade secrets" (Sterling, 1992, p. 221). Almost a year after the crime, John Perry Barlow received a visit from a local Wyoming FBI agent because he had been sent one of the illicit disks. Barlow was disturbed when he found himself the object of a two hour interview by Special Agent Richard Baxter, Jr. According to Barlow (1996):

Poor Agent Baxter didn't know a ROM chip from a Vise-grip when he arrived, so much of that time was spent trying to educate him on the nature of the thing which had been stolen. Or whether "stolen" was the right term for what had happened to it.

You know things have rather jumped the groove when potential suspects must explain to law enforcers the nature of their alleged perpetrations. (p. 477)

After the visit from the FBI, Barlow wrote an account of the interview and posted it to the WELL, a San Francisco-based online service. Several days later, Mitch Kapor, the founder of Lotus 1-2-3, stopped in Pinedale, WY for a chat with Barlow. They talked for a couple of hours about Operation Sun Devil, and Kapor decided to get involved. He contacted a civil libertarian lawyer in New York to discuss the case against the hackers and talked to Barlow about setting up the Electronic Frontier Foundation. By June 1990, Kapor and Barlow were making the Foundation a formal organization. The purpose of this organization is to "raise and disburse funds for education, lobbying, and litigation in the areas relating to digital speech and the extension of the Constitution into Cyberspace" (Barlow, 1996, p. 486). The Electronic Frontier Foundation protects the rights of individuals in emerging computer-mediated environments such as the Internet.

PROTECTING THE COMMUNITY

The Internet is described as an antidote to commercial mass media. In contrast to passive, one-directional, and censored information distributed through mass media, the Internet supports interactive mass participation. It enables people to participated in a fully bi-directional uncensored form of communication. Elmer-Dewitt (1995a) contends:

The [Internet] newsgroups are, in their way, the perfect antidote to modern mass media. Rather than catering to the lowest common denominator with programming packaged by a few people in New York, Atlanta and Hollywood and broadcast to the masses in the heartland, the newsgroups allow news, commentary and humor to bubble up from the grass roots. They represent narrowcasting in the extreme: content created by consumers for consumers. While cable-TV executives still dream of hundreds of channels, [the Internet] already has thousands. The network is so fragmented, in fact, that some fear it will ultimately serve to further divide a society already splintered by race, politics and sexual prejudice. That would be an ironic fate for a system designed to enhance communications. (p. 10)

Recently, a movement has started to monitor and censor Internet communication to protect communities from extreme political points of view. "The April 1995 terrorist bombing of the Oklahoma City federal building triggered further calls for Net anarchy to be more closely monitored" (Moore, 1995, p. 181). It was suggested, with no evidence, that the bombers used the Internet to communicate their plans. The Internet was publicized as "fertile ground for anarchist and antiauthoritarian thought, Net political culture also includes heaps of right-wing conspiracy theory, racist patriotism, Waco obsession, weapons fetishism, and bitter, seething resentment against the [U.S.] federal government" (Davis, 1995, p. 28). You can find a conspiracy theory on just about any topic. "Taken individually, many of the posts are just the angry, ignorant, or sad barkings of ordinary men and women. But, collectively they take on the dark obsessive drone of a fever dream" (p. 38). According to Davis (1995), "a host of demons, fetishes, and vengeful archetypes crawl onstage straight from white American's political unconscious" (p. 28). Using information acquired through the Internet, it is feared that terrorists will plant bombs in other communities.

In addition to terrorism, the Internet has been receiving negative press about cyberporn. On July 3, 1995, *Time* magazine ran a cover story called "Cyberporn." The article discussed an academic study, written by a 30-year-old college senior named Marty Rimm, that found 917,410 sexually explicit pictures, short stories, and film clips on the Internet. The story written by Elmer-Dewitt (1995b) sparked a controversy both on- and offline that reached as high as the United States Congress. As soon as the *Time* article hit the newsstands, Rimm's research was criticized by experts on conceptual, logical, and process grounds. Wallace and Mangan (1996) stated: "Within weeks after its publication, the Rimm study had been thoroughly discredited. But the damage had already been done—Senators Grassley and Exon had waved the *Time* article around Congress; Senator Coates had quoted Rimm's phony statistics" (p. 151).

Simultaneously, *Newsweek* ran an article titled "No Place for Kids?" that described tales of sexual predators. It stated: "Until now parents have believed that no physical harm could possibly result when their progeny were huddled safely in the bedroom or den, tapping on the family computer. But then came news of cases like the 13-year-old Kentucky girl found in Los Angeles after supposedly being lured by a grown-up cyberpal" (Levy, 1995, p. 47). Leading the crusade against cyberporn was United States Senator James Exon, who proposed a new Communications Decency Act. The act was signed by President Clinton in February 1996 as part of the Telecommunications Reform Bill. *New York Times* reporter, Peter H. Lewis (1996a) described the Bill as follows:

Lawmakers said the intent of the act was to halt the flow of pornography and other objectionable material on the Internet. . . . The law makes it a felony, punishable by prison terms and large fines, to make indecent or patently offensive materials available on computer systems where children might see them. (p. 1)

On June 12, 1996, federal judges in Philadelphia struck down the Communications Decency Act (CDA). According to Sieger (1996): "The decision represents a landmark victory for individual Internet users, and should preserve the openness and unfettered debate upon which the net was built" (p. 13). He further stated: "The court soundly rejected the arguments offered by the government and the religious right that the Internet should be regulated similar to broadcast mass media" (p. 14). Reversal of the CDA was viewed as a victory for freedom of speech in cyberspace.

However, freedom of speech and cyberporn are not only U.S. issues. "All over the world, a growing number of governments, schools, special interest groups and families are struggling to find acceptable ways of tapping into the riches of the Internet without also hitting the darker veins of the global computer network" (Lewis, 1996b). For example, German officials recently persuaded CompuServe to cut off access to approximately 200 sex-related discussion groups worldwide. "Pressure is intensifying to restrict the flow of pornography, hate speech and other offensive material in electronic form, Internet technologists say that ultimately there is not a completely effective way to block the relatively small number of 'bad bits' out of the torrents of data available to tens of millions of people in more than 150 countries" (p. D1). Internet pornography and hate speech are now global issues. As individual nations begin to censor Internet information, the vision of using the Internet as a global communications medium could come to an abrupt end. Currently, there are conflicting views on whether or not the Internet will culturally tear us apart or bring us together.

CYBERSPACE AND DEMOCRACY

Internet proponents view it as a new tool for community building. Nader (1995) argues that the Internet is a resource for citizens to share ideas. "When hundreds, thousands, or even hundreds of thousands of persons organize themselves in forums to debate important public policy issues, they bring together vast amounts of specialized expertise and information, creating synergies that are more powerful and useful than the most sophisticated database system" (p. 74). Thus, computer networks are viewed as a way to bring people together to renew a sense of democracy. Rheingold (1993) asserts:

> The great power of the idea of electronic democracy is that technical trends in communications technologies can help citizens break the monopoly on their attention that has been enjoyed by the powers behind the broadcast paradigm—the owners of television networks, newspaper syndicates, and publishing conglomerates. (p. 289)

Online advocates hope to see computer-mediated communications revitalize the open and widespread discussion among citizens that feed the roots of democratic societies. Building on the work of Habermas and others, Rheingold (1993) identifies several requirements for authenticity recognized by people who live in a democratic society. These include: "open access, voluntary participation, participation outside institutional roles, the generation of public opinion through assemblies of citizens who engage in rational argument, the freedom to express opinions, and the freedom to discuss matters of the state and criticize the way state power is organized" (p. 284). From this perspective protecting the rights of freedom of speech is essential to online democracy. On- and offline, this appears to be the prevailing social perspective concerning computer-mediated communication. The recent reversal of the Communications Decency Act supports this social trend of protecting freedom of speech over imposing legal restrictions that are designed to protect members of the community.

However, pornography is a good example of how online democracy is faced with the challenge of preserving the rights of individuals while simultaneously protecting innocent groups. Although most people agree that children should not have easy access to sexually explicit material through any medium, the flaw with the Communications Decency Act is that it did not make a distinction between commercial pornography and noncommercial sexual content, including AIDS and sex education information. Consequently, socially valuable sexual information would have been banned from the Internet. By protecting one group, the law was denying others the right to access important information. A technological solution to the problem is for parents to install software programs that would block offensive material based on their own values. This approach places the responsibility for protecting children into the hands of individual parents rather than the larger community. Whether or not, this is an appropriate solution to the problem is still under debate. However, this debate is not only an U.S. issue. Discussions must take place on a global level.

Computer-mediated communications is a global medium that exposes people from a variety of nationalities to different cultural norms. As a result, individual national customs, beliefs, and laws are called into question, and national perspectives become destabilized because this multivocal medium represents diverse social, ethnic, and religious perspectives. To create an orderly online society these desperate points of view must agree on common social norms of behavior. In an attempt to create law and order on the new electronic frontier, people turn to the medium itself to establish a new stability. Much of the discussion about the future of the Internet will take place within the Internet itself.

Ess (1996) argues that Habermasian discourse ethics can be applied as a framework to computer-mediated communications (CMC) to help diverse perspectives reach democratic consensus. He states:

> The discourse ethic, as it circumscribes the form and character of discourse intended to sustain democratic communities, in fact provides powerful theoretical support for current conceptions of democratizing communication via CMC. In particular, the discourse ethic issues in the call for open and equitable communication and the pluralism of currently existing discourse communities. (p. 216)

Thus, Habermasian principles could be applied to online discourse to facilitate understanding between diverse groups.

To resolve difficulties, Habermasian deliberative democracy attempts to find a middle ground between polar positions. Deliberative democracy "reflects a concern that citizens' participation in the demographic process have a rational character—that voting, for example, should not simply aggregate given preferences but rather follow on a process of 'thoughtful interaction and opinion formation' in which citizens become informed of the better arguments and more general interests" (Rehg, 1996, p. ix). Majority rule is not simply a statistical effort to tally votes, but instead "a large social process by which people discuss matters, understand one another, try to persuade each other and modify their views to meet counterarguments" (Sunstein, 1996, p. 29).

The deliberative conception of democracy argues: "Democracy, ideally conceived, is a process by which people do not implement their preferences but consult and deliberate about what values and what options are best" (Sunstein, 1996, p. 29). Habermas views law and democracy as being mutually supportive. Law establishes the preconditions for democracy. It guarantees voting rights, freedom of speech, and political equality, the foundations on which democratic ideals can apprise the suitable content of law. Legitimate law is established through a problem-solving process that "assimilates knowledge in order to program the regulation of conflicts and the pursuit of collective goals" (Habermas, 1996, p. 318).

Ethicists tend to differ on the center of moral authority. "Some argue that moral authority is located in the individual, who through self-analysis and reflection comes to develop a set of rules, or engages in an analysis of self-interest. Others argue that moral authority must be located in larger collectives—the organization, society, or polity" (Laudon, 1995, p. 34). Risk is associated with both of these positions. The former allows individuals to set their own rules, their own ethics, without regarding the larger community; "the latter introduces a potential moral relativism of a different sort: Whatever the group believes is the best becomes the rule" (p. 34). To overcome the risks involved with these different positions, Habermas proposes the concept of a procedural ethic grounded in the principle of universalization.

> For Habermas this is essentially a cognitive task. The mere fact that a particular norm could be accepted by a community as valid does not establish its validity as such. Consequently, it is necessary to turn to the inner logic of moral argumentation to determine the validity or the invalidity of a norm. This assumptions allows Habermas to introduce the principle of universalization. It is precisely through the introduction of the principle of universalization that a rational consensus can be achieved in the context of multitude of opinions which may conflict. The cognitivist principle involved here is that a norm is right when it corresponds to a general or generalizable interest. So conceived, the interest of any individual can be accepted by all those involved. (Rasmussen, 1990, pp. 60-61)

Following the Habermasian ethical procedure, everyone should be given the right to state his or her position and criticize others. Utilizing this framework, individuals with diverse positions could reach agreement. Internet proponents, such as Rheingold and Ess, argue that computer-mediated communication facilitates the process of democratic consensus described by Habermas.

CONCLUSION

To date, many of the legal issues surrounding computer-mediated communication mirror real life. Although people tend to apply principles from the real world, computer-mediated space or cyberspace has the potential to be a utopian space for creating possible worlds. Cyberspace is a place where individuals can experiment with behavioral norms and evaluate the results. As a social space, cyberspace enables individuals to more actively participate in the democratic process. Habermas's concept of deliberative democracy that balances protecting the rights of individuals with maintaining social order could be applied to the formation of new models of democracy developing in computer mediated spaces. Protecting the rights of individuals and creating social order through rational consensus is a goal that would attempt to unite the multitude of opinions currently being expressed online through the Internet. Using this framework, new individual, social, and ethical behavioral norms could begin to emerge. The fragmenting of the postmodern self would then start to reverse as new methods of social interaction bring people together.

REFERENCES

Bakhurst, D., & Sypnowich, C. (1995). *The social self.* London: Sage Publications.

Barlow, J.P. (1995). Property and speech: Who owns what you say in cyberspace? *Communications of the ACM, 38*(12), 19-22.

Barlow, J.P. (1996). Crime and puzzlement. In P. Ludlow (Ed.), *High noon on the electronic frontier* (pp. 459-486). Cambridge, MA: MIT Press.

Bell, T.W. (1995, October). Anonymous speech: Imagine combining free speech with your right to privacy. *Wired*, p. 80.

Bennahum, D. (1994, June). Fly me to the moo: Adventures in textual reality. *Linguafranca*, pp. 1, 22-36.

Bruner, J. (1995). Meaning and self in cultural perspective. In D. Bakhurst & C. Sypnowich (Eds.), *The social self* (pp. 18-29). London: Sage.

Bukatman, S. (1993). *Terminal identity.* Durham, NC: Duke University Press

Cavazos E.A., & Morin G. (1994). *Cyberspace and the law.* Cambridge, MA: MIT Press.

Curtis, P. (1996). MUDding: Social phenomena in text-based virtual realities. In P. Ludlow (Ed.), *High noon on the electronic frontier: Conceptual issues in cyberspace* (pp. 347-373). Cambridge, MA: MIT Press.

Davis, E. (1995, May 2). Barbed wire net: The right wing hunkers down online. *The Village Voice*, p. 28.

Dennett, D.C. (1991). *Consciousness explained.* Boston: Little, Brown.

Dibbell, J. (1996). The prisoner: Phiber Optik goes directly to jail. In P. Ludlow (Ed.), *High noon on the electronic frontier: Conceptual issues in cyberspace* (pp. 133-136). Cambridge, MA: MIT Press.

Dibbell, J. (1993, December 21). Rape in cyberspace: How an evil clown, a Haitian trickster spirit, two wizards, and a cast of dozens turned a database into a society. *The Village Voice*, p. 38. [Also available in P. Ludlow (Ed.). (1996). *High noon on the electronic frontier: Conceptual issues in cyberspace.* Cambridge, MA: MIT Press.]

Elmer-Dewitt, P. (1995a). Welcome to cyberspace. *Time*, pp. 4-9.

Elmer-Dewitt, P. (1995b). On a screen near you: Cyberporn. *Time*, pp. 38-45.

Erikson, E.H. (1963). *Childhood and society.* New York: W.W. Norton. (Original work published 1950)

Ess, C. (1996). *Philosophical perspective on computer-mediated communication.* Albany: State University of New York.

Gardner, H. (1983). *Frames of mind.* New York: Basic Books.

Gaylin, W., & Jennings, B. (1996). *The perversion of autonomy.* New York: The Free Press.

Gergen, K.J. (1996). Technology and the self: From the essential to the sublime. In D. Grodin & T.R. Lindlof (Eds.), *Constructing the self in a mediated world* (pp. 127-140). Thousand Oaks, CA: Sage.

Gergen, K.J. (1991). *The saturated self.* New York: Basic Books.

Germany clamps down on "extremists" in cyberspace. (1997, January 20). *Reuters New Media* [Online].

Giddens, A. (1991). *Modernity and self-identity: Self and society in the late modern age.* Stanford, CA: Stanford University Press.

Grodin, D., & Lindlof, T.R. (1996). *Constructing the self in a mediated world.* Thousand Oaks, CA: Sage

Habermas, J. (1996). *Between facts and norms.* Cambridge, MA: MIT Press.

Haraway, D. (1991). *Simians, cyborgs, and women.* New York: Routledge.

Harré, R. (1989). Language games and the texts of identity. In J. Shotter & K.J. Gergen (Eds.), *Texts of identity* (pp. 20-35). London: Sage.

Huff, C., & Martin, C.D. (1995). Computing consequences: A framework for teaching ethical computing. *Communications of the ACM, 38*(12), 75-84

Johnson, C. (1995, November 24). Anonymity on-line? It depends who's asking. *The Wall Street Journal*, pp. B1, B7.

Kellner, D. (1992). Popular culture and the construction of postmodern identities. In S. Lash & J. Friedman (Eds.), *Modernity & identity* (pp. 141-177). Oxford, UK: Blackwell.

Kling, R. (1996). Information technologies and the shifting balance between privacy and social control. In R. Kling (Ed.), *Computerization and controversy: Value conflicts and social choices* (2nd ed., pp. 614-636). San Diego: Academic Press.

Laudon, K.C. (1995). Ethical concepts and information technology. *Communications of the ACM, 38*(12), 33-39.

Lee, G.B. (1996). Addressing anonymous messages in cyberspace. *Journal of Computer-Mediated Communications, 2*(1).

Levy, S. (1984). *Hackers.* New York: Dell Publishing.

Levy, S. (1995, July 3). No place for kids? *Newsweek,* pp. 47-50.

Lewis, P.H. (1996a). Free speech case: Ruling by panel moves the First Amendment into a new era. *The New York Times,* pp. 1, B10.

Lewis, P.H. (1996b). Limiting a medium without boundaries. *The New York Times,* pp. D1, D4.

Lyotard, J. (1991). *The inhuman.* Stanford, CA: Stanford University Press.

Mead, G. H. (1959). *The philosophy of the present* (A. E. Murphy, Ed.). LaSalle, IL: The Open Court Publishing Company.

Mead, G. H. (1962). *Mind, self, & society* (C. W. Morris, Ed.). Chicago: University of Chicago Press.

Mill, J.S. (1989). *On liberty and other writings.* New York: Cambridge University Press.

Mnookin, J.L. (1996). Virtual(ly) law: The emergence of law in LambdaMoo. *Journal of Computer-Mediated Communications, 2*(1).

Moore, D.W. (1995). *The emperor's virtual clothes.* Chapel Hill, NC: Algonquin Books of Chapel Hill.

Nader, R. (1995, March-April). Citizens and computers. *UNTE Reader,* p. 74.

Orwell, G. (1949). *1984.* New York: Signet.

Poster, M. (1990). *The mode of information.* Chicago: University of Chicago Press.

Poster, M. (1995). *The second media age.* Cambridge, UK: Polity Press.

Rasmussen, D.M. (1990). *Reading Habermas.* Oxford, UK: Basil Blackwell.

Rehg, W. (1996). Translator's introduction. In J. Habermas (Ed.), *Between facts and norms* (pp. ix- xxxvii). Cambridge, MA: MIT Press

Rheingold, H. (1993). *The virtual community.* Reading, MA: Addison-Wesley Publishing.

Rorty, E. (1979). *Philosophy and the mirror of nature.* Princeton: Princeton University Press.

Rose, L. (1995). *Netlaw: Your rights in the online world.* Berkeley: Osborne McGraw-Hill.

Sampson, E.E. (1989). The deconstruction of the self. In J. Shotter & K.J. Gergen (Eds.), *Texts of identity* (pp. 1-19). London: Sage.

Sieger, J. (1996). Communications Decency Act is defeated: Landmark victory for netizens. *Communication of the ACM, 39*(8), 13-15.

Sterling, B. (1992). *The hacker crackdown.* New York: Bantam Books.

Sunstein, C.R. (1996, August 18). Democracy isn't what you think. *The New York Times Book Review,* p. 29.

Turkle, S. (1995). *Life on the screen: Identity in the age of the Internet.* New York: Simon & Shuster.

Van Gelder, L. (1985, October). The strange case of the electronic lover. *Ms.,* pp. 94-95.

Wallace, J., & Mangan, M. (1996). *Sex, laws, and cyberspace.* New York: Henry Holt.

Weisband, S.P., & Reinig, B.A. (1995, December). Managing user perception of email privacy. *Communications of the ACM, 38*(12), 40-47.

19

ETHICAL AND LEGAL ISSUES IN E-MAIL THERAPY

DANIEL EDWARD SHAPIRO AND CHARLES ERIC SCHULMAN

Psychologists and psychiatrists have started using e-mail to conduct therapy. In this chapter the authors explore relevant ethical and legal issues raised by this practice, including the nature of the professional relationship, boundaries of competence, informed consent, treating minors, confidentiality, and the duty to warn and protect. Two services currently operating are used to illustrate and to address client needs and the challenge to create a new ethical standard for e-mail therapy.

Psychologists and psychiatrists have recently started using computers to provide therapy to clients at distant locations. Like populist advice givers (e.g., Ann Landers, Miss Manners), e-mail clinicians offer brief responses to brief questions. Using electronic mail (e-mail) clients send questions (and credit card information) to clinicians who rapidly respond, reportedly between 48 and 72 hours. The questions and answers are brief, approximately a paragraph in length. To illustrate the problems inherent in using the technology in this way we explore two representative services—Shrink-Link and Help-Net. These two services have six psychologists and one psychiatrist each in their employ. In February 1995, Shrink-Link became one of the most popular commercial ventures on the World-Wide Web with over 450 paying users in that month alone (Resnick, 1995). Help-Net came online a number of months later and is very similar in cost and format to Shrink-Link.

A recent telecommunications research survey indicated that up to 40% of households in the United States currently have computers. The same survey found that 8% have online services (Boeck & McLean). Conservative projections indicate that as many as 12% of households will be online by December 1995. These estimates are likely low as they were made before Microsoft successfully bundled a new operating system with an online service. As the sales rate for computers and online memberships accelerate the popularity of e-mail therapists will likely increase.

A BRIEF PRIMER ON E-MAIL

For those readers not acquainted with the Internet and e-mail, we offer the following brief primer. E-mail messages are similar to letters sent by mail. The sender types a message using common computer software and then forwards it from his or her computer by modem. The message is transmitted along phone lines to a communication service such as CompuServe, a university, or an Internet access provider. From there the message is forwarded through a network of linked computers to the receiver. Once in the receivers' "mailbox" he or she may opt to read the message the next time the computer is turned on and the user dials in for messages. One advantage to e-mail is that as long as the senders' and receivers' computers are connected by modem into the Internet, or another communication network, they can be located anywhere (for clearly written sources regarding electronic mail and the other wonders of the Internet, see Gibbs & Smith, 1993, or Glossenbrenner, 1990).

In February 1995, the following electronic advertisement appeared on the World-Wide Web. (The World-Wide Web uses a format known as hypertext that allows the user to interact with a main page of text and graphics that are linked to other pages and information by keywords. For example, in the following advertisement, when a user highlights the words "15-40 years of clinical experience," using a computer mouse or other method, the user is shown a page that lists the names and credentials of the professionals on staff:

Shrink-Link

Cyberlink Consulting Inc. Presents: Shrink Link Shrink-Link helps people develop informed judgments and choices concerning human behavior. Shrink-Link allows direct E-Mail access to a staff of top clinical psychologists and psychiatrists ready to review and comment on almost any important question or conflict in your life. Concerned about your fears? About who you are? Trouble at home or work? Got the blues? Questions about medication? Shrink-Link psychotherapists have been addressing questions such as these in private sessions for years. Whether you need general guidance, are on the verge of a crisis, or are looking for competent peer review, Shrink-Link may be able to help. Panelists also include in their responses useful referral information, when appropriate.

Shrink-Link is not a substitute for face to face counseling, and may not be appropriate for everyone. However, it does focus the attention of a group of highly trained mental health professionals on YOU! The Shrink-Link panel currently includes six psychologists and one psychiatrist, each with 15-20 years of clinical experience. These are the same people who normally charge $100-$200 per 45- or-so minute session!

And through Shrink-Link, you can direct your query to one of eight specialty areas of psychotherapy, such as family issues, drug/alcohol abuse, etc. (The choices are listed on the form page.) Here are a few sample queries (including routings).

The cost for using Shrink-Link is $20 per valid question and response. You can expect to receive a response via E-Mail within 72 hours (often within 24 hours). Sound interesting? Compose a query!

Help-Net, another e-mail therapy service, is remarkably similar. The primary difference is in how questions are distributed to the psychologists or psychiatrists. Although both services allow users to browse the names and credentials of professionals on-staff (Help-Net also provides online photographs of therapists that may be enlarged by clicking on them), Shrink-Link does not allow clients to address queries to specific providers; rather the clients address their question to a specific category, and Shrink-Link routes the query to an appropriate professional. Help-Net allows three methods of question submission. Clients may send their queries directly to a psychologist or psychiatrist they choose, submit questions by an established list of categories, or submit general questions that will be routed by the service to an appropriate provider. As discussed later, this difference does have implications. In June 1995, the president of the American Psychological Association (APA), Robert Resnick, with several board members, asked the Board of Directors of APA to consider the ethics of Internet-facilitated therapy. In July of the same year the APA Ethics Board considered Internet therapy and provided general guidelines directing therapists using telephone, teleconferencing, or Internet services to consider the applicability of the ethical standards applying to therapy. The Ethics Board was general in its response and did not provide guidelines for each treatment modality. This chapter attempts to present the relevant ethical issues and offer guidelines for therapists interested in exploring e-mail-facilitated treatment. Finally, an ethics standard will be presented for this new modality.

EXAMINING A NEW MEDIA AND USE

When considering the ethical issues in any new treatment modality, a helpful starting point is an analysis of the relationship established between the professional and the client.

Professional Relationship

The nature of the professional relationship established by e-mail therapists is important because different relationship structures and modes of treatment have different standards of practice. For example, a media psychologist does not incur the same responsibilities for maintaining records as a clinician treating a patient in traditional face-to-face therapy. A professional conducting a competency evaluation does not offer a client the same provisions for confidentiality as a therapist. Simply put, the structure of the professional relationship dictates the ethical obligations of the treater. To examine the ethical issues and potential dangers assumed by e-mail treaters, we must examine the structure of the relationship first. Professional relationships make service delivery safe and predictable for both the treater and the client. When a psychologist and client enter into a defined professional relationship each has expectations regarding acceptable boundaries and what the costs and benefits of the interaction will be. When traditional therapists establish a professional relationship they abide by, among others, the General Standards (which cover documentation and billing), Therapy Standards (which include informed consent, structuring relationships, and termination), and Privacy and Confidentiality Standards (that mandate maintaining confidentiality and keeping records). Each of these standards are designed to insure safety and predictability for both parties. The therapist following these standards minimizes ambiguity by overtly discussing them early in treatment. Through painful trial and error, psychologists have determined, with few exceptions, that treatment delivery outside of these standards is unviable.

If a professional relationship exists, or should exist, between e-mail psychologists and clients, then the ethical standards applying to treatment could also apply to E-mail clinicians. Does e-mail treatment reach a threshold that establishes a professional relationship? Both the Shrink Link and Help-Net advertisements note that their services are not a substitute for face-to-face counseling. Is this enough to dispel clients' mistaken expectations? Unfortunately, neither advertisement described the nature or limits of the e-mail relationship. There is no mention of confidentiality, billing, informed consent, or what the client can hope to gain from the interaction. Even more troublesome, neither service prohibits repeated communications with the same provider. Thus, it is possible that a client could have an e-mail relationship with an identified therapist over a course of years. This sounds to us like therapy.

We understand how these psychologists arrived at these vague advertisements. A thorough discussion of the limits of the relationship might seriously hamper the persuasive power of the advertisements. The writers of the advertisements clearly took some efforts to overtly state that the service was not psychotherapy, while still implying that the service would be effective for clients. They may believe that they did not need to be specific regarding the limits of the relationship because they were not doing therapy. They might argue that because no professional relationship was offered rational users of the service will not assume that a professional relationship exists. Certainly an argument like this is enhanced for the service, Shrink-Link, that does not allow individuals to select a specific treater. Without knowledge of whom the user is communicating with before getting a response, the user cannot assume that he or she has a professional relationship with any specific individual. The Help-Net service has no such advantage. Because users of the Help-Net service select a particular individual, they may have expectations that they are establishing a relationship with a particular provider.

Regardless of the specific structure used by the service to connect provider to client, the vague state of affairs is inadequate. Because the professionals advertise themselves as psychologists and psychiatrists, and provide no disclaimers indicating that they are practicing something other than psychology or psychiatry, a rational user of the systems could assume that the psychologists and psychiatrists on Help-Net and Cyber-Shrink practice similarly to how these professionals practice everywhere else. The most obvious mistake clients might make are to assume that the communications with the E-mail professionals are confidential, and that, as clients, they will not be abandoned.

Although the advertisements state that the communications are not therapy they do not state what they are. Can the user expect advice? Help? Assistance? Even though the differences between e-mail communication and psychotherapy might appear obvious to most clinicians, it is not so apparent that all laypersons will immediately understand how the structure and benefits of Shrink-Link and Help-Net differ from those experienced in therapy.

So what standard should e-mail clinicians adopt? One approach to evaluating new services is to compare the service to those that are structured similarly. e-mail therapists hoping to avoid encouraging clients to expect a professional relationship might argue that e-mail-facilitated communication is most similar to media psychology. Media psychologists are the only clinicians allowed to practice in any way, under the current ethics code, outside of an established professional relationship. Certainly there are similarities. Like media psychologists the interaction is typically brief and lacks detailed assessment. In both modalities clinicians respond to a specific problem or question from a client who may be geographically distant. The similarities end there.

Ethical standard 3.05 prohibits media psychologists from encouraging patients to infer that a personal relationship has been offered. This is not difficult for media psychologists as any communication is part of a larger broadcast. The rational caller or participant understands that there is an additional, larger purpose to the communication. It is not only to help the patient, but also to educate or entertain an audience. The caller or participant would not be talking to the treater if it were not part of a larger broadcast.

E-mail-facilitated therapeutic communication has no such additional purpose outside of addressing the problem or question posed by the client. A rational client could assume that the treater is establishing a personal relationship with him or her. The owners of Shrink-Link do not prohibit repeat users but have suggested they encourage clients who use the service frequently to seek therapy (Resnick, 1995). Because repeat communications with a paid professional are allowed, the clients of Shrink-Link and Help-Net could infer they have a therapeutic relationship with a trained professional. It is easy to imagine circumstances in which a client who regularly used the service started to develop the same intense feelings and expectations that clients in traditional therapy experience.

If repeat communications were not allowed, queries were worded abstractly rather than personally, and a disclaimer was provided that no professional relationship is offered, Shrink-Link and Help-Net clinicians might be able to ethically argue that a professional relationship was not established. They could argue that instead of therapy they are providing the public with a bridge to the scientific literature. For example, the client might write "What are the symptoms of depression and what should people do about it?" rather than, "I am depressed, please help me Doc."

Although these remedies might address the ethical problems, some legal issues remain. In the past, common law (law created by judges through precedent rather than legislation or statutory law) has imposed liability when individuals, through affirmative acts or misfeasance, harmed another individual. However, with a few important exceptions, the common law has generally not found liability when individuals fail to act to protect another person from harm. The legal term for this nonaction is *nonfeasance.* The rationale for this distinction is that misfeasance creates an extra risk of injury, whereas nonfeasance does not (Prosser & Keeton, 1984). However, according to the common law, when a "special relationship" exists between two people there is a duty to control the other's behavior or to warn third parties of the other's dangerousness (see Restatement (Second) of Torts, 1965). A special relationship exists when one person such as a psychologist takes charge of another, for example, a client. In the past, the courts have recognized specific special relationships such as the following: parent-child, employer-employee, carrier-passenger, innkeeper-guest, landlord-tenant, and those relationships in which a professional is in charge of a dangerous person (see Prosser & Keeton, 1984). Psychologists fit into the latter relationship. Common law, including the Tarasoff court, have found against psychologists when the clinician has known or should have known of the necessity and opportunity for exercising that control (Restatement (Second) of Torts, 1965). In other words, if a psychologist has enough information to recognize a duty to control, he or she must exercise that control. It is possible to imagine a situation in which an e-mail therapist is given enough information to recognize the duty to control.

Assuming a court would find that such a special relationship exists in the e-mail context, the point at which this relationship is established and the duties of that relationship are primarily determined by principles of agency and contract law (*Brinkley v. Farmers Elevator Mutual Insurance Co.*, 1973). Usually, psychologists and clients have an express agreement. The psychologist makes an offer of "advice" via an online advertisement. A client accepts the terms of the contract and pays the fee of $20 per question. The $20 is consideration for the advice given. These events offer acceptance and consideration and legally establish a professional relationship between the e-mail therapist and client (*Committee on Professional Ethics and Grievances v. Johnson*, 1971; *Hunt v. Disciplinary Board*, 1980).

A psychologist may also imply a relationship through his or her actions (McGlothen, 1983). For example, consider the following scenario: A client approaches a psychologist at a party and presents significant evidence of intent and ability to kill a specific victim; the psychologist responds by negligently informing the patient that she is not in danger of acting on her violent impulses and is in no further need of therapy; subsequently, the client kills the victim. In such a case, a court may find that a professional relationship existed (see *Togstad v. Vesley, Otto, Miller & Keefe*, 1980).

In malpractice or breach-of-contract cases the plaintiff has the burden of establishing that a professional relationship existed. For the majority of clients who write in one or even a few questions to Shrink-Link or Help-Net, we suspect that it is unlikely that a court would find that such a relationship exists. But what of the client who slowly escalates the number and detail of questions over time with the same professional, as is not prohibited in either service? Imagine the troubled client who writes a number of questions a week for a few months or even years and comes to depend on the benevolent advice of his e-mail therapist. If something went awry, a plaintiff's attorney would be justified in arguing that this frequency of communication is similar, if not more frequent, than that of most traditional therapies and could illustrate the dependence experienced by the client. A court might very well decide that a professional relationship existed in these circumstances, and that the client was willfully misled into believing he or she could rely on the professional to provide a relationship similar to that experienced in traditional therapy. The possibility of a professional relationship being established moves e-mail treatment closer to other modalities such as telephone therapy. Like clinicians using the telephone, the treater and client may be geographically distant. Telephone treaters are currently held to the same standards as other treaters (American Psychological Association Ethics Committee, 1993). They are obligated to get clients' informed consent prior to treatment, they must discuss confidentiality and fee schedules, and they have the duty to protect clients and potential victims of clients from harm. Unfortunately, as we discuss next, traditional standards may be difficult or impossible for even the most ethical of e-mail clinicians to uphold.

Confidentiality

Neither of the services described earlier mentions confidentiality. Help-Net, however, does suggest that the providers will answer all questions "professionally and privately." This is misleading and troublesome. E-mail is not private, and confidentiality is an impossible standard for e-mail treaters to provide. In fact, contrary to many user's expectations, most experts assume e-mail is not secure or confidential. Glossbrenner (1990), an expert in computer communication, writes "all E-mail messages can be read by people other than their intended recipients, so one must assume that they will be read, even if that isn't actually the case" (p. 12). One journalist called electronic mail a misnomer. He preferred the term *electronic postcard* (Jerome, 1995). Even if "hackers" (individuals who knowingly violate the security of computer networks) did not exist, there would still be serious problems with confidentiality. Many institutions including universities store all information electronically mailed to and from university computer account holders. For example, the University of Florida faculty handbook reads "All electronic mail records are public records and are stored in memory by the Northeast Regional Data Center" (University of Florida, 1993).

The confidentiality of the message is not the only difficulty. Users of both Help-Net and Shrink-Link" e-mail their credit card numbers to pay for the service. American Express recently acknowledged that it stores sorted transaction records and has sold this information to a wide range of organizations (Schwartz, 1992). At first it may seem that few companies would be interested in knowing the names of individuals accessing Help-Net or Shrink-Link. A cursory review of other industries reveals that this is not necessarily the case. In 1991, workers discovered that a Louisiana company had created a massive database that recorded the names of workers who reported injuries while working. Also listed was a detailed history of worker's legal and workingman's compensation histories. The company made the information available for a fee (Lacayo, 1991).

Services such as Shrink-Link and Help-Net may provide hackers with fertile ground. Any hacker with entrepreneurial spirit and organizational skills could use their talents to assemble a list of names of users of Help-Net and Shrink-Link and detailed descriptions of the problems they reported. It is naive to believe that agencies or individuals would not be interested in paying for this information. Insurance companies might be interested in information that would assist them in denying claims, employers might be interested in learning the names of employees or applicants with substance abuse or mental health histories, and spouses might be interested in the secrets of their partners.

These problems must be considered in light of the claims of one of the services examined here, Help-Net, which suggests that privacy is enjoyed by users of their service. We suspect that its advertising claiming "will answer your questions quickly, professionally, and privately" places it at tremendous legal and ethical risk. Imagine an individual who asks a Help-Net clinician to assist her with her great dislike for her boss only to learn that her boss gained access to this information and found reason to fire her! We suspect that courts, ethics committees, and licensure boards would find these circumstances troubling.

Eventually it may be possible to guarantee confidentiality in e-mail-assisted therapeutic communication. Legislation, sophisticated encryption techniques, and enhanced network protection may eventually improve the privacy of electronic mail and billing information. Other countries have taken steps to protect the privacy of their citizens. Britain, for example, treats personal information as property. Britain enacted the Data Protection Act of 1984 to provide protection for individuals from abuse of their personal information contained in various databases. Under this Act, individuals can apply to any corporation keeping a database for all information that pertains to them. In the United States legislation and encryption battles are currently underway (Forester & Morrison, 1995). Unfortunately, there is no guarantee that advocates of privacy will emerge victorious.

Until these issues are resolved, heeding Glossenbrenner's (1990) advice is prudent. For E-mail treaters this means that they must, if they are to remain within the bounds of the ethical standards, warn all users that no E-mail communications are private or confidential. Standard 5.01c also mandates that permission must be secured before electronic recordings of clients are permitted. Although it is not the e-mail clinician that is doing the recording, the professional trying to meet the "spirit" of the standard will also warn users that their communications will very possibly be stored by their network and accessed by others.

In sum, to completely inform a client of the limits of confidentiality the therapist must disclose first, that e-mail systems often store e-mail interactions; second, that individuals other than the intended recipient may have relatively easy access to e-mail; third, that personal computers may store the interactions, and that these may be readable by anyone else with access to the computer; and, finally, as in all therapy cases, the clinician might need to divulge confidential information if he or she perceives that the client is at risk for imminently harming him- or herself or someone else.

Boundaries of Competence

The first and oft-quoted principle of healing is "do no harm." E-mail-facilitated treaters at both Help-Net and Shrink-Link provide professional advice without the benefit of assessment. Such consultation appears to fly in the face of conventional wisdom. Even therapists offering the briefest of treatments maintain some need for assessment. Hoyt, Rosenbaum, and Talmon (1992), who practice single-session therapy, maintain that "collecting useful and essential information" is critical to therapeutic success. Without assessment the potential for misdiagnosing a client's problem or missing dramatic pathology seems unusually high. Most therapists have had the experience of recognizing late in the first session, or even in the fifth, that the patient's problem was not at all what it appeared during the first few moments. The e-mail therapists receive what is on the client's mind for only a few seconds. To most therapy clients the first few seconds of treatment are rarely powerful enough to have any effect, and yet this is precisely what e-mail clinicians offer.

The high potential for misdiagnosis must be considered in light of the client's perceptions of the therapist. Shrink-Link advertises its staff as being "top clinical psychologists and psychiatrists . . . each with 15 to 40 years of clinical experience . . . the same people who normally charge $100-$200 per 45-or-so minute session." Most of Help-Net's staff have similar accolades. The fact that the client could view the therapist as a highly trained and trustworthy professional engaged in a proven modality of treatment, combined with the high probability of misdiagnosing serious problems, is a dangerous and potentially explosive combination. To illustrate the problem, we use one of the example questions and answers provided in the Shrink-Link advertisement.

Question: "I am afraid that I might have a drug addict for a son. The other day, a bag of pills fell out of his backpack as he was heading out the door. I'm not quite sure what kind of pills they are or even if he's taking them, but it's sure scary. Do you think I should confront my son, or would that be showing my hand? Maybe I should, instead, observe his lifestyle and friends a bit closer, without letting him know that I'm on to something. What do you think? Frankly, I have not noticed anything unusual in his behavior at all.

Answer: Closer observation of your son's behavior and friends appears to be warranted. Rather than accusing him of using drugs, which may alienate him, you might, at an appropriate moment, try to engage him in conversation about drug use. Perhaps you may glean something from him regarding his attitudes about drug usage. Being alert to his behavior (e.g.. academic performance, choice of friends, etc.), now that you are aware that he may be using drugs, might give you a different perspective, which will help you determine whether he is a user or not. At this point, you do not seem to have enough evidence for a confrontation, but vigilance is in order!

The therapist appears to respond quite reasonably given the circumstances as presented, and arguably, as well as many clinicians. But the therapist knows very little about the writer's perceptions. Without assessment the therapist has no opportunity to garner more information and must simply take everything the client writes at face value. The parent could be paranoid and delusional, in which case suggesting that "vigilance is in order" would provide little help and be potentially hazardous. It is also possible to imagine that the son is suicidal and has given numerous cues to a parent who is only now just catching on. The parent may be a drug user as well. Without the benefit of querying the parent the therapist responds blindly. Without more information we believe that little helpful advice can be proffered with reliability. The therapist also answers only the question presented and does not address the real needs of this client. We would argue that a thorough professional would provide for the worst case scenario. What if the son is addicted to a drug? The treater offers no advice regarding how to proceed to protect the son or the parent. Another possibility is that the son is dealing drugs. This is not considered in the therapist's response.

Standard 1.04c reads: "In those emerging areas in which generally recognized standards for preparatory training do not yet exist, psychologists nevertheless take reasonable steps to ensure the competence of their work and to protect patients, clients, students, research participants, and others from harm." With no predictable relationship, no assessment, and lightning fast diagnosis and intervention, it seems likely that e-mail clients are not well protected. This in itself does not preclude use of e-mail therapy; rather, it warrants informed consent, like any other experimental treatment. Clients using e-mail therapy should not only be told, as they are in Help-Net and Shrink-Link, that e-mail-facilitated therapeutic communication is not therapy, but also that it is untested and its efficacy may be uncorrelated with the success of traditional therapies. The client needs to know that the information given him or her may be entirely useless and not applicable to the total situation. Without such disclaimers the potential damage to clients is high.

The ethics code does not only protect clients. The code was also established to protect the profession. The ethical code provides minimal rules of conduct that compel psychologists to conduct themselves in ways that will not reflect poorly on the profession. E-mail treatment represents a genuine threat to the profession. Services such as Help-Net and Shrink-Link, if not significantly altered, could result in psychologists being relegated to the status of popular advice columnists. However, in the best-case scenario, e-mail clinicians could serve as models and advertisements for all psychologists. Clients interacting with them could learn that psychologists do not proffer advice without detailed assessments, do not offer unproven treatments without warning and fully informing clients first, and have access to a scientific literature that may be applied with skill to their problem.

Adults: Duty to Warn, Duty to Protect

Imagine a scenario in which a client e-mails the following question to Shrink-Link: "I am so angry I feel I might kill my mother." What are the therapist's obligations? There are a number of issues, not the least of which is the therapist's inability to conduct a reasoned assessment. Although no predictors of violence are impressively accurate, most clinicians consider, among other factors, a past history of violence, means of carrying out the act, substance abuse histories, the patient's appearance or demeanor, and motive in determining the client's potential for dangerousness. E-mail clinicians may not have access to information concerning any of these predictors. Without establishing the patient's history (including medical, psychiatric, or criminal records), motive, and access to victims, the clinician is literally guessing.

The previous scenario illustrates the legal complications that can arise from the combination of the duty to warn or protect and e-mail therapy. In general, psychologists have a duty to protect a client from harm (e.g., suicide) and a duty to warn potential victims of the danger posed by a violent client. Assume that an e-mail client sent the earlier threatening message to a therapist in a different state. The e-mail therapist failed to warn or protect the potential victim, who was later killed. The plaintiff, a family member of both the victim and the killer, decides to sue the therapist after reviewing the E-mail messages exchanged between the therapist and the killer on a home computer. (For the purposes of this chapter we have limited ourselves to e-mail communication contained within the United States. The situation becomes more complicated if the communication is international. It is worth noting, however, that from the standpoint of the capabilities of the Internet it is just as easy to communicate internationally as it is to communicate with a neighbor.)

Which state laws apply in our case depends on where the plaintiff sues; usually where the violent act occurred or where the defendant lives. A savvy plaintiff considers both the benefits of the state law and the convenience or geographical proximity in selecting the state in which to sue. However, the plaintiff must also consider whether the state in which he or she sues has jurisdiction over the defendant therapist. Whether a court has jurisdiction over a defendant e-mail therapist depends on the facts surrounding the e-mail service and the alleged negligence (see Glannon, 1992). The states in which the e-mail service is incorporated will have jurisdiction over a defendant. The states in which the e-mail service does significant business or has a headquarters could also have jurisdiction, depending on the extent of the service's business activities in those states. Furthermore, the state in which the negligent act occurs may also have jurisdiction. Thus, in a case involving individuals located in different states, jurisdiction could depend on where the courts decide Internet communication occurs. Given that an e-mail therapist violates his or her duty to a client, the court would have to decide whether that violation occurred in the therapist's state, the client's state, or both.

It is possible that courts in different jurisdictions will initially make conflicting decisions. For now, the therapist is left in confusion. The message from the client may be received in Florida, where case law in 1991 found the duty to warn "neither reasonable nor workable and is potentially fatal to effective patient-therapist relationships" (*Boynton v. Burglass*, 1991); yet the client may generate the message in Nebraska, where a federal district court found that therapists have a duty to protect even unnamed victims from harm (*Lipari v. Sears Roebuck*, 1980).

Putting aside the question of which state law applies, suppose the therapist decided that the prudent action was to warn a potential victim and to seek to hospitalize the patient. How could he or she act from far away? No states allow practice without valid licensure in that jurisdiction. Although it is conceivable that the therapist might be able to enlist the aid of local professionals, the logistics of such an intervention are nightmarish to contemplate.

This is probably not as important a legal issue as it is an ethical one. In our estimation, it is unlikely that a court would hold an e-mail treater who practiced in a structure similar to Shrink-Link or Help-Net accountable for the death of a client, who was in a different state unless the clinician actively encouraged the act or dissuaded the client from seeking local, more appropriate, help. However, as practiced now, it is conceivable that a court would find that the Shrink-Link and Help-Net advertisements misled clients into believing that they had the attention of skilled professionals who were practicing a proven modality. In fact, both declare that trained professionals will focus their attention on the client. The Help-Net advertisement reads: "While Help-Net employs only experienced therapists, it is not meant as a substitute for therapy. It does, however, focus the attention of a trained professional on your problems and questions." The Shrink-Link advertisement is almost identical. Is this potentially misleading? Although it is the truth that trained professionals do focus their attention on the client, the advertisement does not say that the focus will be incredibly short-lived for most clients, that its effectiveness is not at all related to the effectiveness of therapy, and that without follow-up and assessment the advice provided might be completely inapplicable to the client. A court might rule that the client was misled into believing he or she had the focus of professionals who could help them from far away. With these problems in mind we consider the next ethical problem presented by these services, namely, the need to explicitly describe the nature of any offered psychological services.

DESCRIBING THE NATURE OF RESULTS OF PSYCHOLOGICAL SERVICES

Imagine if a home appraiser with an impeccable reputation advertised that she would focus her attention on a photograph of your house and provide you with a professional response for $20 rather than the $300 charged by competitors who do complete home appraisals. She then glanced at the photograph and provided you with an estimate. Clearly, most people with experience selling or buying a house would recognize the problem with this estimate method. Without knowing the location of the house, or having a chance to evaluate its foundation and workmanship up close, any estimate would be a guess. But some individuals, particularly those without the experience of purchasing or selling a house might not understand this. In fact, those without such experience might be badly misled and make major life decisions based on an incorrect estimate. In sum, they might trust the appraiser and yet receive a badly flawed estimate.

We think this is a reasonable analogy. Many in the public have no concept of what psychologists do. So informing them that e-mail treatment is different from therapy is not enough to protect them from having misleading expectations. Some patients may also be predisposed to investing great faith in a relationship with an E-mail clinician. Patients who are isolated or prone to dependence might empower an impressively credentialed treater and invest great energy in his or her advice. Clearly, prudent e-mail clinicians will be explicit regarding the differences between e-mail therapy and traditional therapy. First, this requires that the therapist explicitly state that the success of e-mail treatment may be uncorrelated with the success of traditional therapies. Second, as presented earlier, the therapist would be wise to discuss confidentiality, the duration of the relationship, and the nature of any records that will be kept.

Unfortunately, we suspect that the therapists themselves running these services may be fairly confused about the benefits and limitations of these relationships. On the one hand, they suggest that the service is not psychotherapy, but then they recommend it for certain groups of clients. Dr. Letwin, a psychologist and part owner of Shrink-Link, was quoted by the *APA Monitor* as saying, "This is definitely not a substitute for face-to face psychotherapy. . . . But in some cases it is terrific when people don't have access to a professional person, like in rural areas" (Sleek, 1995). Letwin seems to be suggesting that for clients who live in remote areas e-mail treatment may be a viable alternative.

To meet the standard mandating that psychologists report the nature of their services to patients they must explain them early. Unlike traditional psychologists who advertise, E-mail treaters do not have the benefit of the first session for explaining the limits of confidentiality, how records will be maintained, and limits of the relationship. The treater has no structure to warn patients about confidentiality, the duration of the relationship, or the experimental nature of the work. Therefore, the e-mail treater must explain these prior to the interaction in the advertisements. This is a new situation. In the past, advertisements have not generally been this explicit. To fully inform clients, advertisements for e-mail therapy must describe in depth the services and nature of the relationship, as well as any factors that might impede clients from wanting to participate.

ETHICAL ISSUES IN E-MAILING

Minors

More and more children are becoming proficient using computers and the Internet. It is common for parents to joke that they do not understand what to do with their computer because their child has not taught them yet. Currently, any child with Internet access and a credit card can ask these providers questions. It is unclear how e-mail providers would respond. Healthcare professionals generally do not treat minors without the consent of their parents. This trend may be changing however. For example, recent Supreme Court rulings on abortion have changed the legal obligations of healthcare professionals and, as a result, in some circumstances, it is now legal to treat a child older than 12 without a parent's consent. In fact, few healthcare providers have been sued successfully for providing children with needed treatment. Although the legality of offering a child professional psychological advice without the consent of a parent is clear (it is usually not legal), how the courts would respond is more hazy. Still, the conservative approach is to ask parents before providing any psychological service to a minor.

Assume that a careful e-mail clinician has asked, and received assent, from a parent to correspond with a child. As with adults, the treater should make clear to the child that the e-mail is not confidential. In addition to providing the child with the same warnings given to adults (e.g., that e-mail systems often store e-mail interactions, that hackers may have relatively easy access to e-mail, and that the clinician would be obligated to act if he or she perceived that the child was at risk for imminently harming him- or herself or someone else), the treater should also remind the child that if any interactions between the child and therapist are stored, parents will have legal rights to those records.

What if a custodial parent discovered this correspondence and wrote to the treater asking for detailed descriptions of the e-mail interactions? In this circumstance the e-mail treater would be legally obligated to provide the parent with relevant summaries of stored information. This is not an obscure possibility. Many parents, when reviewing credit card charges, may have a reaction and seek to find out what their children are spending money on. With these factors in mind the prudent treater would warn minors in advertisements that e-mail correspondences may be accessed by parents.

More complicated issues are raised by situations in which a clinician suspects that a child is being abused or neglected. Although all jurisdictions mandate reporting of child abuse, the specifics vary considerably. To treat minors using e-mail, the clinician would have to be quite expert regarding the laws of the jurisdiction in which the child lives. There are two decisions that must be made when a child reports abuse to a psychologist. First, the clinician must decide if abuse or neglect is occurring or is likely to occur. In many situations this will not be difficult as the circumstances might obviously meet criteria for abuse or neglect in any jurisdiction. In some circumstances, however, this decision cannot be made without understanding how abuse and neglect are defined in the given jurisdiction. For example, some states have specific lists of circumstances that meet the requirements for reportable conditions. Other states do not define abuse or neglect at all. The important distinction is the standard required for reporting. In some circumstances the psychologist is only required to report when there is an immediate and substantial risk of sexual abuse or physical or mental injury to a minor, whereas other states require reports when there is even a slight suspicion of child abuse or neglect (Clearinghouse on Child Abuse and Neglect, 1986). Clearly, the conservative approach is to report whenever abuse is suspected. But in states in which the therapist is required to report his or her own name, and does not have the benefit of assessing the validity of the report, this can become troublesome.

The clinician also needs to know where reports should be directed in the jurisdiction where the child resides. In 30 jurisdictions reports are made to child protective agencies, in 9 the reports are to law enforcement, and in 25 the clinicians have a choice. With adequate time, most clinicians should be able to use telephone information services to find relevant numbers. A more difficult problem is preparing children for the likely consequences from such a report. Without understanding the typical responses of child protective services or law enforcement in a given jurisdiction, the clinician will be unable to prepare the child or answer even basic questions: Will the police be coming to my house? Will I be taken away from my family? How soon will all of this happen? Where will I go if I cannot live with my parent? What if I do not want to press charges? Preparing a child psychologically for the process of leaving a home or other consequences may also be difficult or impossible for an e-mail treater. Although meeting the clinical, ethical, and legal challenge of reporting abuse and neglect is feasible, we are not confident that most psychologists will adequately prepare themselves in advance to make timely reports in each of the 55 jurisdictions in the United States. We say this in light of research indicating that mental healthcare professionals including psychologists are notoriously unfamiliar with reporting requirements and consequences of reporting in their own jurisdictions (Muehleman & Kimmons, 1981).

A PROPOSED NEW ETHICAL STANDARD

In July 1995, the APA Ethics Board provided a general statement that described the ethics code applicable to therapists using telephone, teleconferencing, and Internet services. In our opinion, although this document offers valuable general guidelines, it suffers from a lack of specificity. The Internet offers a number of different modalities of communication. Each one will require examination on its own merits and potential threats to ethical conduct. To protect clients and the profession we offer the following to apply specifically to e-mail treatment:

Psychologists offering e-mail-facilitated therapeutic communication encourage clients to ask general questions that do not refer to a specific individual. Psychologists advertising such services include in advertisements all information necessary for clients to understand (a) the modality is experimental and its usefulness may be unrelated to the success of traditional therapies, (b) the communication is not confidential, (c) no therapist-client professional relationship exists, (d) repeat communications with the same professional are discouraged and (e) records of the interaction may be stored with no report of such storage available to the client. Psychologists using e-mail to communicate with new clients encourage clients to seek more traditional therapies. Psychologists do not transmit confidential information, including payment information such as credit card data, by e-mail without using encryption programs considered the standard.

Although this standard was written to apply to e-mail treatment specifically, it contains principles that can be applied in developing ethics standards for future modalities. These principles are the following: Psychologists should make every effort to (a) provide all information necessary to achieve informed consent with the client, especially when using new structures to deliver services; (b) prevent detrimental reliance on advice given via any modality, and (c) insure the greatest level of privacy practical.

CONCLUSION

The duty to warn and the boundaries of competence sections of this chapter both point out that lack of assessment is a major stumbling block for e-mail as a mode of service delivery. In light of the limitations of e-mail therapy, it is worth considering what current or future technologies might provide solutions to these limitations. Sophisticated videoconferencing and computerized access to encrypted medical and psychiatric records might allow therapists to better assess a remote client's condition.

It is interesting to note that individuals who grow up with computers will likely have very different views of how to use new technologies than those who came of age prior to the computer age. Those in the older generations generally view face-to-face communication as a prerequisite for trust and trust a prerequisite for effective therapy. Younger generations may rely as heavily on computer-facilitated communication and conferencing. Interestingly, this concept or paradigm will likely change as society adjusts to new technological possibilities. Thus the next question is not whether this paradigm will change with the advent of new technologies, but rather how fast it will change and in what direction (see Kuhn, 1970).

To psychologists we recommend caution and critical evaluation of all new technologies used to deliver services. Throughout history new technologies have been excitedly embraced long before careful introspection and evaluation revealed problems that should have been noticed earlier (see Mander, 1991). It is our hope that psychologists will not be among those leading the way to blindly embrace new technologies during the upcoming explosion of new communication modalities.

REFERENCES

American Psychological Association Ethics Committee. (1995, July). *Telephone, teleconferencing, and Internet services.* Washington, DC: American Psychological Association.

Boeck, S., & McLean, E. A. (1995, July 11). U.S. homes getting wired. *USA Today*, p. 1B.

Boynton v. Blurglass, 590 So. 2d 466 (Fla. Dist. Ct. App. 1991).

Brinkley v Farmers Elevator Mutual Insurance Co., 485 F2d 1283 (CA10. 1973). Committee on Professional Ethics and Grievances v. Johnson, 447 F2d169 (CA3 1971).

Clearinghouse on Child Abuse and Neglect Information (1986). Washington, DC: U.S. Department of Health and Human Services, National Center for Child Abuse and Neglect.

Committee on Professional Ethics and Grievances v. Johnson, 447 F2d 169 (CA3 1971).

Forester, T., & Morrison, P. (1995). *Computer ethics: Cautionary tales and ethical dilemmas in computing.* Cambridge MA: MIT Press.

Gibbs, M., & Smith, R. (1993). *Navigating the internet.* Carmel, IN: Prentice Hall.

Glannon, J. (1992). *Civil procedure.* Boston MA: Little, Brown.

Glossenbrenner, A. (1990). *The complete handbook of personal computer communications: The bible of the online world.* New York: St. Martin's Press.

Hunt v. Disciplinary Board 381 So.2d 52 (Ala. 1980).

Hoyt, M.F., Rosenbaum, R., & Talmon, M. (1992). Planned single-session psychotherapy. In S. H. Budman, M.F. Hoyt, & S. Friedman (Eds.), *The first session in brief therapy* (pp. 59-86). New York: Guilford Press.

Jerome, M. (1995, July 2). Big brother wants easy access to your E-mail. *Boston Globe*, p. A20.

Kuhn, T. (1970). *The structure of scientific revolutions.* Chicago: University of Chicago Press.

Lacayo, R. (1991, November 11). Nowhere to hide. *Time*, pp. 40-43.

Lipari v Sears Roebuck 497 F. Supp. 185 (D. Neb. 1980).

Mander, J. (1991). *In the absence of the sacred: The failure of technology and the survival of the Indian nations.* San Francisco: Sierra Club Books.

McGlothen 99 Wah.2d 515. (1983).

Muehleman, J.T., & Kimmons, C. (1981). Psychologists' views on child abuse reporting, confidentiality, life, and the law: An exploratory study. *Professional Psychology, 12,* 631-638.

Prosser, W. L., & Keeton, W. P. (1984). *Law of torts* (5th ed.). St. Paul, MN: West Publishing.

Resnick, R. (1995, March 27). Shrink-Link & beyond. *The Miami Herald* [Online Column].

Restatement (Second) of Torts. (1965). American Law Institute. St. Paul, MN: West Publishing.

Schwartz, E. I. (1992, June 8). The rush to keep mum. *Business Week*, p. 33.

Sleek, S. (1995, November). Online therapy services raise ethical questions. *APA Monitor*, p. 9.

Togstad v. Vesley, Otto, Miller & Keefe, 291 NW2d 686 (Minn 1980).

University of Florida Office of Academic Affairs. (1993). *University of Florida faculty handbook.* Gainesville: University of Florida.

Author Index

CASE INDEX

Jones v. Wilkinson, 193, *202*
Joseph Burstyn, Inc. v. Wilson, 174, 177*n*, *178*

K

Katz v. United States, 88, *93*, 242*n*, *249*, 338, *345*
Kingsley International Picture Corp. v. Board of Regents, 173, *179*
Konigsberg v. State Bar of California, 175*n*, *179*

L

Ladue v. Gilleo, 175*n*, *179*
Layne v. Tribune Co., 77, *93*
Lipari v. Sears Roebuck, 412, *418*
Lovell v. Griffin, 175*n*, *180*

M

MAI System Corp. v. Peak Computer, 219, *225*
Marsh v. Alabama, 83, *93*, 341*n*, *346*
Martin v. Struthers, 175*n*, *180*
Martin Luther King Jr. Center for Social Change, Inc. v. American Heritage Products, 273, *285*
Mazer v. Stein, 209, *225*
McIntyre v. Ohio Elections Commission, 263, *266*, 338, 344*n*, *346*
Medphone Corp. v. DeNigris, 310, *322*
Miami Herald Publishing Co. v. Tornillo, 78, *94*
Miller v. California, 137, *150*, 185, *202*, 315, *322*
Mutual Film Corp. v. Industrial Commission of Ohio, 172, 177*n*, *180*

N

National Bank of Boston v. Bellotti, 177*n*, *180*

Near v. Minnesota, 314, *322*
New York Times Co. v. Sullivan, 176*n*, *180*, 315, *322*
New York Times Co. v. U.S., 314, *322*
New York v. Ferber, 139, 140, *150*, 165*n*, *166*, 173, 176*n*, *180*, 315, *322*

O

O'Connor v. Ortega, 332, *346*

P

Pacific & Southern Co. v. Duncan, 216, *225*, 244*n*, *249*
Paramount Communications v. Gibraltar Casualty Co., 307, *322*
Paris Adult Theatre I v. Slaton, 143, 144, *150*
Playboy Enterprises, Inc. v. Frena, 221, *225*, 233, 243*n*, *249*
Posadas de Puerto Rico Associates v. Tourism Company of Puerto Rico, 356, *369*
Princeton University Press v. Michigan Document Services, 216, 221, *225*
Pruneyard Shopping Center v. Robins, 341*n*, *346*

Q

Quill Corp. v. North Dakota, 241, *249*

R

R.A.V. v. City of St. Paul, 176*n*, *180*
Red Lion Broadcasting Co., Inc. et al. v. Federal Communications Commission et al., 43, *49*, 190, *202*
Robinson v. Random House, 255, *266*
Rosemont Enterprises v. Random House, Inc., 273, *285*
Roth v. U.S., 138, *150*, 176*n*, 315, *323*

SUBJECT INDEX